Indiana

PROGRAM AUTHORS

Dr. Candy Dawson Boyd
Professor, School of Education
Director of Reading Programs
St. Mary's College
Moraga, California

Dr. Geneva Gay
Professor of Education
University of Washington
Seattle, Washington

Rita Geiger
Director of Social Studies and
Foreign Languages
Norman Public Schools
Norman, Oklahoma

Dr. James B. Kracht
Associate Dean for Undergraduate
Programs and Teacher Education
College of Education
Texas A&M University
College Station, Texas

Dr. Valerie Ooka Pang
Professor of Teacher Education
San Diego State University
San Diego, California

Dr. C. Frederick Risinger
Director, Professional Development
and Social Studies Education
Indiana University
Bloomington, Indiana

Sara Miranda Sanchez
Elementary and Early Childhood
Curriculum Coordinator
Albuquerque Public Schools
Albuquerque, New Mexico

CONTRIBUTING AUTHORS

Dr. Carol Berkin
Professor of History
Baruch College and the Graduate
  Center
The City University of New York
New York, New York

Lee A. Chase
Staff Development Specialist
Chesterfield County Public Schools
Chesterfield County, Virginia

Dr. Jim Cummins
Professor of Curriculum
Ontario Institute for Studies in
  Education
University of Toronto
Toronto, Canada

Dr. Allen D. Glenn
Professor and Dean Emeritus
Curriculum and Instruction
College of Education
University of Washington
Seattle, Washington

Dr. Carole L. Hahn
Professor, Educational Studies
Emory University
Atlanta, Georgia

Dr. M. Gail Hickey
Professor of Education
Indiana University-Purdue
  University
Fort Wayne, Indiana

Dr. Bonnie Meszaros
Associate Director
Center for Economic Education and
  Entrepreneurship
University of Delaware
Newark, Delaware

Editorial Offices: Glenview, Illinois • Parsippany, New Jersey • New York, New York
Sales Offices: Parsippany, New Jersey • Duluth, Georgia • Glenview, Illinois •
  Coppell, Texas • Ontario, California

www.sfsocialstudies.com

ISBN: 0-328-01789-2

Contents

Social Studies Handbook

"I am much pleased with this country. Nothing can exceed its beauty and fertility."

—William Henry Harrison, describing central Indiana, 1801

Unit 1 The Land Called Indiana

Chapter 1 • The Geography of Indiana   8

Unit 2 Exploration and Conquest in Indiana

"Great things have been effected [done] by a few men well conducted . . ."

— letter from George Rogers Clark before his march on Vincennes, 1779

Unit 2 Continued

Unit 3 The Great State of Indiana

"We the Representatives of the people of the Territory of Indiana . . . do mutually agree with each other to form ourselves into a free and Independent state."

— Preamble of the 1816 Indiana State Constitution

Unit 3 Continued

Unit 4 A Divided Country

"Bear in mind that . . . with you . . . is the question: Shall the Union and shall the liberties of this country be preserved . . . ?"

—President-elect Abraham Lincoln, to a crowd in Indiana, February, 1861.

vii

Unit 5 Indiana Grows

"In regard to population, wealth, progress, enterprise, commerce, manufactures, agriculture, intelligence, the State of Indiana . . . is in all senses, a First Rate State."

—A historian writing in 1876, cited in *Indiana, An Interpretation* by John Bartlow Martin

Unit 6 Into the Twenty-first Century

"To know America, you have to take a good, long look at the Wabash River."

—from *The Wabash* by William E. Wilson

Reference Guide

★BIOGRAPHY★

Charts, Graphs, Diagrams, Tables, Time Lines

Let the Discovery Begin

Your world can turn upside down on a roller coaster—like this one at Six Flags Magic Mountain that has six loops and rolls. Many people experience thrills and chills every year on hundreds of roller coasters in the United States.

Make an exciting discovery of your own: Find a cool coaster in your state. The Legend is a favorite at Holiday World in Indiana. This wooden coaster is 11 stories high, and riders twist and turn at 65 miles an hour through four tunnels and a double loop. Let's go!

Building Citizenship Skills

There are six ways to show good citizenship: through respect, fairness, caring, responsibility, courage, and honesty. In your textbook, you will learn about people who used these ways to help their community, state, and country.

Respect
Treat others as you would want to be treated. Welcome differences among people.

Fairness
Take turns and follow the rules. Listen to what other people have to say.

Caring
Think about what someone else needs.

Responsibility
Do what you are supposed to do and think before you act.

Courage
Do what is right even when the task is hard.

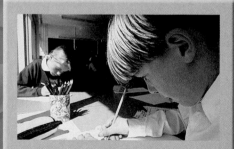

Honesty
Tell the truth and do what you say you will do.

★ Citizenship in Action ★

Good citizens make careful decisions. They solve problems in a logical way. How will these students handle each situation as good citizens?

Decision Making

The students are choosing a pet for their classroom. The following steps will help them make a decision.

1 **Tell what decision you need to make.**

2 **Gather information.**

3 **List your choices.**

4 **Tell what might happen with each choice.**

5 **Act according to your decision.**

Problem Solving

Sometimes students argue at recess over whose turn it is to have a ball. The fourth-graders can use the following steps to help them solve the problem.

1 **Name the problem.**

2 **Find out more about the problem.**

3 **List ways to solve the problem.**

4 **Talk about the best way to solve the problem.**

5 **Solve the problem.**

6 **Then figure out how well the problem was solved.**

Building Geography Skills

Five Themes of Geography

Geography is the study of Earth. This study can be divided into five themes that help you understand why the earth has such a wide variety of places. Each theme reveals something different about a spot, as the following example of Hoosier National Forest shows.

Location

Where can something be found?
Hoosier National Forest is located at about 38.30°N, 86.40°W.

Place

How is this area different from others?
Hoosier National Forest has rolling hills, rivers, lakes, and beautiful scenery.

Human/Environment Interaction

How have people changed this place?
People built dams as a way to control floods.

Movement

How has movement changed the region? American Indians, European explorers, and African Americans left a rich history as they passed through.

Region

What is special about Hoosier National Forest's region?
The forest is in an area of Indiana that is very hilly.

Building Geography Skills
Map and Globe Skills Review

What Does a Globe Show?

This is an image of Earth. It lets you clearly see some of Earth's large landforms (continents) and bodies of water (oceans).

The image below shows Earth as it actually is.

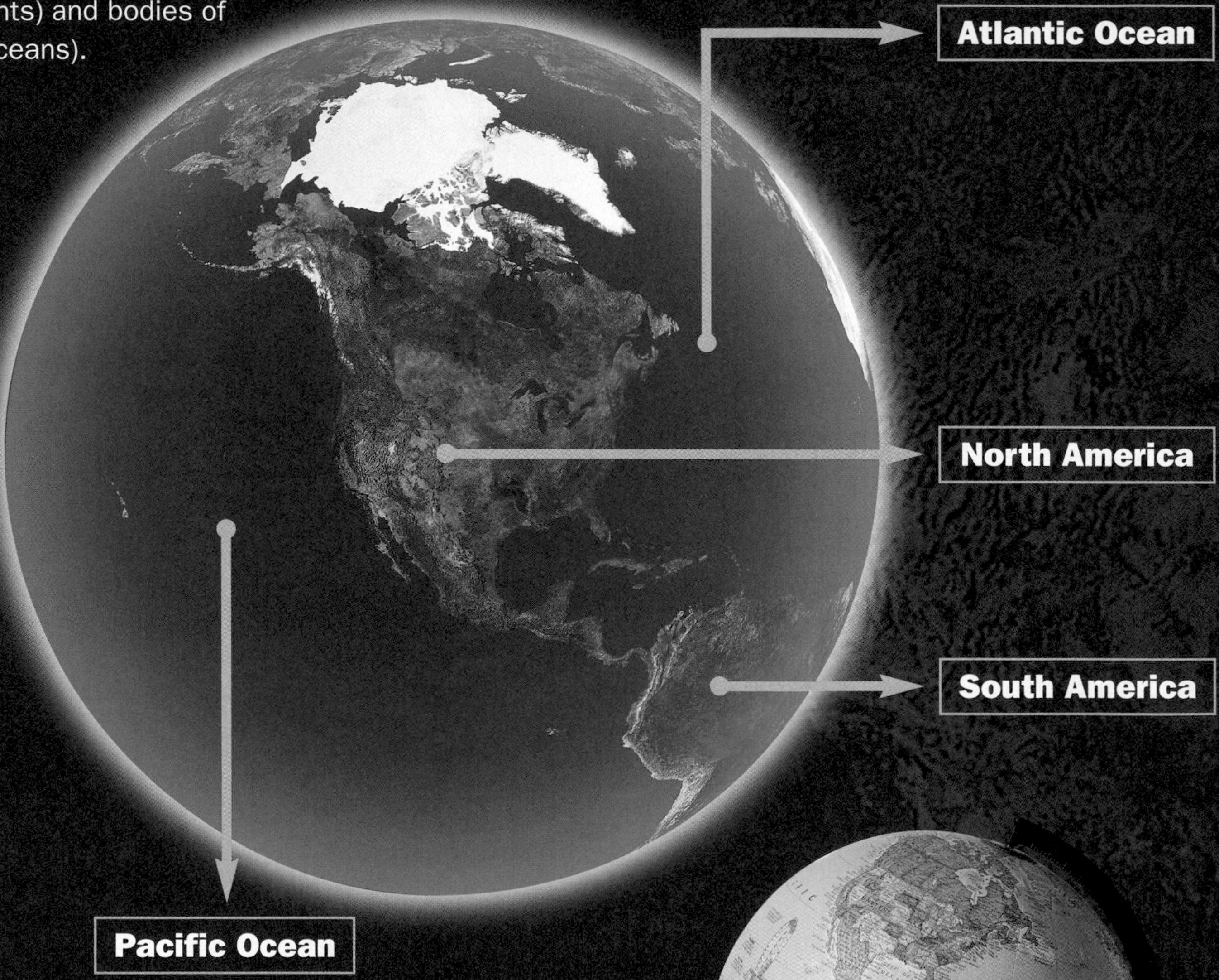

Atlantic Ocean
North America
South America
Pacific Ocean

At the right is a **globe,** a small copy of Earth you can hold in your hands. It has drawings of Earth's seven continents and four oceans. Can you name the continents and oceans not shown here?

Also, a globe shows the two imaginary lines that divide Earth into halves—the **equator** and the **prime meridian.**

NORTH
ATLANTIC
OCEAN

Hemispheres: Northern and Southern

Like any kind of a ball, you can see only half of Earth and a globe at a time. Half views of Earth have names—**hemispheres**—and the illustration at left below shows Earth separated into these views at the equator line. The **Northern Hemisphere** is the half north of the equator, which circles Earth halfway between the poles. However, there is only one way to see the Northern Hemisphere all at once. You have to turn a globe until you are looking down directly at the North Pole. The picture below shows that view. What are the only continents not found, at least in part, in the Northern Hemisphere?

The **Southern Hemisphere** is the half of Earth south of the equator. The picture below turns the globe until you are looking down directly at the South Pole. You see all of the Southern Hemisphere. Which hemisphere—northern or southern—contains more land?

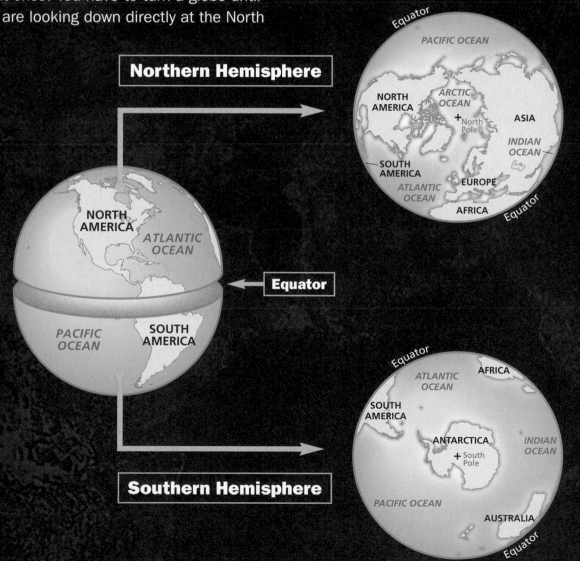

Northern Hemisphere

Equator

Southern Hemisphere

Building Geography Skills
Map and Globe Skills Review

Hemispheres: Western and Eastern

Earth has two other hemispheres. They are formed by dividing Earth into halves a different way, along the prime meridian. The prime meridian is an imaginary line that runs from the North Pole to the South Pole. It passes through Greenwich, England, an area of London. The **Eastern Hemisphere** is the half east of the prime meridian. The prime meridian passes through which continents?

The **Western Hemisphere** is the half of Earth west of the prime meridian. Which two continents are found entirely within this hemisphere? Which of the four oceans is not found in this hemisphere? In which two hemispheres is the United States found?

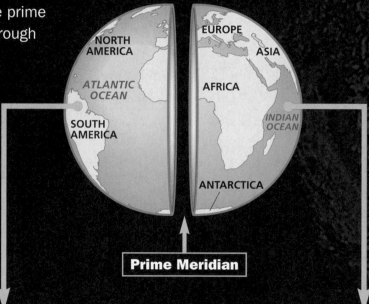

Prime Meridian

Western Hemisphere

Eastern Hemisphere

Understand Latitude and Longitude

Mapmakers created a system for noting the exact location of places on Earth. The system uses two sets of imaginary circles crossing Earth. They are numbered in units called **degrees.**

Lines of **latitude** are the set of circles that go east and west. The Equator is 0 degrees (0°) latitude. From there, the parallel circles go north and south. They get smaller and smaller until they end in dots at the North Pole (90°N) and the South Pole (90°S). The globe below at the left is tilted to show latitude lines 15° apart up to the North Pole. Most of the United States falls between which degrees of latitude?

Lines of **longitude** go north and south. They are all the same size. The Prime Meridian is 0° longitude. However, from there, the degrees fan out between the North and South poles. They are not parallel and go east and west for 180°, not just 90°. The globe below at the right shows longitude lines 15° apart. They meet at 180° on the other side of Earth directly behind the Prime Meridian. Most of Africa falls between which degrees of longitude?

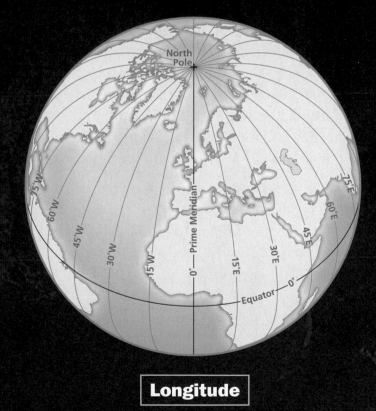

Longitude

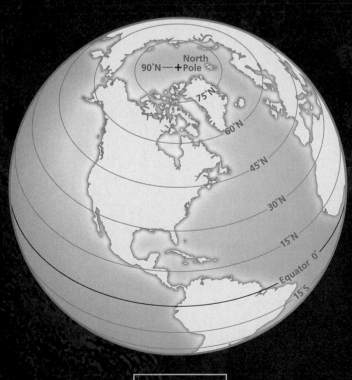

Latitude

Use Map Features to Help Read Maps

A **title** tells what a map is about. What is the title of the map to the right?

A **political map** shows the location of cities, states, and countries. A **physical map** adds landforms and water such as mountains and rivers. What kind of map is on this page?

A **compass rose** is a pointer that shows the four major directions, or **cardinal directions.** On the compass roses in this textbook, **north** is straight up and is marked with an N. **East** is to the right, **south** is straight down, and **west** is to the left. This compass rose also shows **intermediate directions,** which are pointers halfway between cardinal directions. Intermediate directions are **northeast, southeast, southwest,** and **northwest.** What cities are northeast of Indianapolis?

Many maps have **symbols** in a **key** or legend. A symbol is a mark, a drawing, or a color that stands for something else. What mark below shows cities with more than 500,000 people?

Some maps have a **locator,** a small globe or map found in a corner. It shows where the main map is located within a larger area of Earth. Describe what you see in the locator.

Indiana: Largest Cities

Key to Population
- ● Between 500,000 and 900,000
- ○ Between 100,000 and 500,000
- • Between 50,000 and 100,000

Use Scale

A **scale** will help you figure out how far it is in real miles or kilometers from one point on a map to another. It can be found in a nearly empty spot to make it easier to read. Starting at 0, a scale marks off tens, hundreds, or even thousands of miles. The measurement chosen depends on the size of the area shown.

One way to use the scale is to hold the edge of a scrap of paper under the scale and copy the scale onto it. Then you can place your copy directly on the map and measure the distance between two points. Use the scale on the map below to help you find out about how far it is in miles from Spring Mill Village to the Lanier Mansion. Then find out how far it is in miles from the Lincoln Boyhood National Memorial to the T. C. Steele State Historic Site.

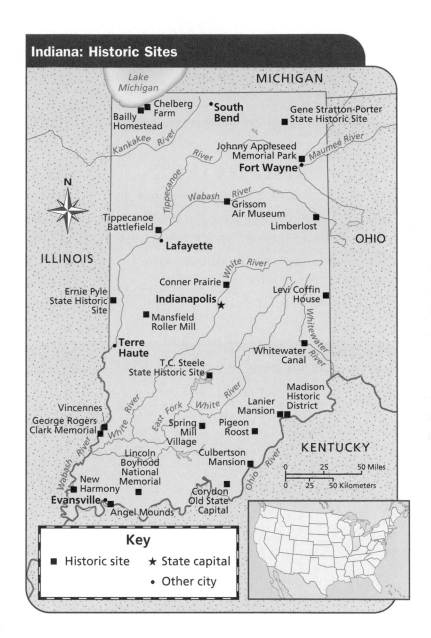

Indiana: Historic Sites

Building Geography Skills
Map and Globe Skills Review

Use a Grid

A city map shows the streets of a city. It might also show some points of interest to visitors or natural features such as rivers and lakes. What natural features do you see on the map of downtown Vincennes below? Point to and name a street.

This map also has a **grid.** A grid is a system of rows of imaginary squares on the map. The rows of squares are numbered and lettered along the edges of the map. You can find places where rows of numbers and letters cross. All you need is an index.

An **index** is an alphabetical listing of places you are likely to be searching for. The number-letter combination attached to each then tells you where the two rows cross. In this square, you can find the place you are looking for.

Suppose you want to find where Gregg Park is. Look for "Gregg Park" in the Index. You'll see that it is located in B5. Find the "B" row on the map and move your finger to where the "5" row crosses it. Now find the Knox County Public Library the same way.

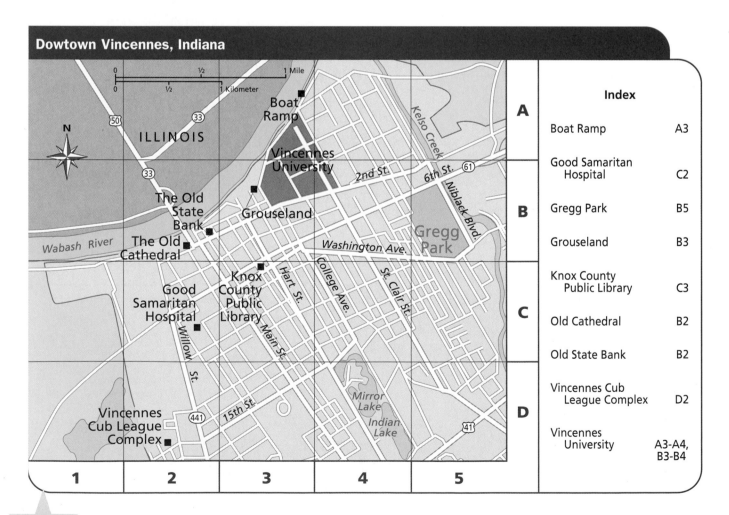

Dowtown Vincennes, Indiana

Index	
Boat Ramp	A3
Good Samaritan Hospital	C2
Gregg Park	B5
Grouseland	B3
Knox County Public Library	C3
Old Cathedral	B2
Old State Bank	B2
Vincennes Cub League Complex	D2
Vincennes University	A3-A4, B3-B4

Use Latitude and Longitude for Exact Location

Lines of latitude and longitude act similarly to city-map grid rows. Think of latitude as the east-west rows of letters on the grid map on the opposite page. Think of longitude as the north-south rows of numbers. The point where latitude and longitude cross is an exact location. If a city or place is found where latitude and longitude lines cross, the city or place takes those two numbers as its exact location.

Look at the map of Indiana below. The exact location of Muscatatuck National Wildlife Refuge is near 39°N, 86°W. The Lincoln Boyhood National Memorial is almost at 38°N, 87°W. What is near 38°N, 88°W?

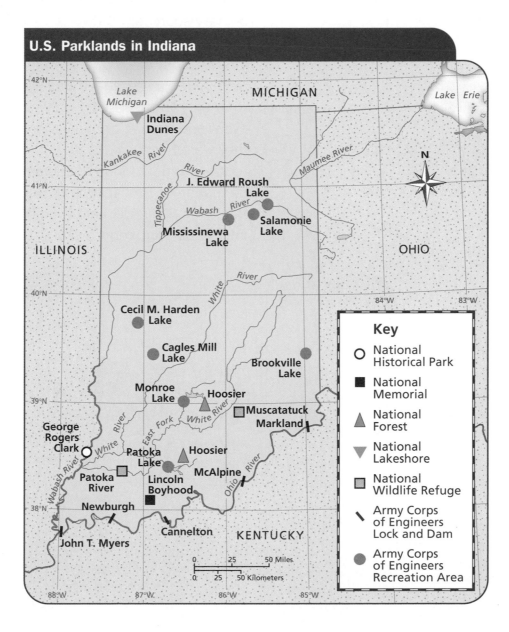

U.S. Parklands in Indiana

When you need to find information for a report or a project, you can use three main resources:

Technology Resources

Print Resources

Community Resources

The information you find can be from either primary or secondary sources. **Primary sources** are documents that were written by people who were at an event and saw it or who lived at that time. Journals, diaries, letters, and photographs are all primary sources. When you write an entry in your journal, you are creating a primary source. Items from an event such as a program or a store receipt are also primary sources.

Secondary sources are descriptions of an event written by people who have researched the event. These people tell what they learned from reading about the event and looking at primary sources, but they were not there.

Look for both kinds of sources when you do research. This section of Building Research Skills will help you find information and report what you have found.

Technology Resources

There are many kinds of technology resources that you can use when you look for information. You can use the Internet, CD-ROMs, software such as databases, television programs, and radio programs.

The Internet is a system of linked computers that can store information for others to find and use. The World Wide Web, which is part of the Internet, has a great deal of information.

It is important to know who put the information on the Web. Check your information by finding at least three reliable sources that give similar information.

On the computer, you can mark the sites you want to look at again. Click BOOKMARKS at the top of your screen and choose ADD BOOKMARK.

Search Engines

Before you turn on your computer, you need to plan your research. If you want to do research on the Wabash River, write down some words that you can use to search the World Wide Web. The name of the river would be a good search term. The name of a town through which it passes might also be a good search term. If you have not used the Internet before, you might want to ask a librarian, teacher, or parent for help.

Search by Subject To find the search engines, click on SEARCH or NET SEARCH at the top of your screen. Type one of your subject words into the search engine field. Then click SEARCH or GO.

If you can't find what you need, try a different search engine. It might be connected to a different site with more information.

Search by Address World Wide Web sites have Uniform Resource Locators, or URLs. A URL is like an address. If you already know the address of a site that might have the information you need, type it in the LOCATION/GO TO box in the upper left corner of the screen. Here is an example of a URL: *www.sfsocialstudies.com*

Print Resources

There are many reference tools that you can use to find information. A reference tool is any source of information.

Books are reference tools. Libraries often have reference shelves with books such as atlases and almanacs, as well as dictionaries and encyclopedias. Usually, reference materials in a library cannot be checked out, but you can use them to look up information while you are at the library.

Encyclopedia

An encyclopedia is a collection of articles, listed alphabetically, on various topics. When you need information quickly, an encyclopedia is a good choice. Electronic encyclopedias, available on the Internet or CD-ROM, have sound and video clips in addition to words.

Dictionary

A dictionary is a collection of words, their spellings, their meanings, and their pronunciations. Words in a dictionary are arranged in alphabetical order. If you find a word you don't understand, you can look it up in a dictionary. Many dictionaries also include abbreviations, names, and information about well-known people and places.

Atlas

An atlas is a collection of maps. Some atlases have one particular kind of map. Others have a variety of maps showing elevation, crops, population, natural resources, languages spoken, or historical developments. Teachers and librarians can help you find the type of atlas that would be best for your search.

Almanac

An almanac is a book or computer resource that lists many facts about a variety of topics. Almanacs are usually organized in sections by topic. Much information is given in charts, tables, and lists. Almanacs are usually updated every year, so they have the latest statistics on populations, sports records, political events, weather, and other interesting topics.

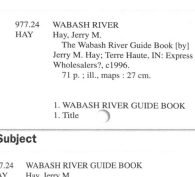

```
977.24   WABASH RIVER
HAY      Hay, Jerry M.
            The Wabash River Guide Book [by]
         Jerry M. Hay; Terre Haute, IN: Express
         Wholesalers?, c1996.
            71 p. ; ill., maps : 27 cm.


            1. WABASH RIVER GUIDE BOOK
            1. Title
```
Subject

```
977.24   WABASH RIVER GUIDE BOOK
HAY      Hay, Jerry M.
            The Wabash River Guide Book [by]
         Jerry M. Hay; Terre Haute, IN: Express
         Wholesalers?, c1996.
            71 p. ; ill., maps : 27 cm.


            1. WABASH RIVER GUIDE BOOK
            1. Title
```
Title

```
977.24   Hay, Jerry M.
HAY         The Wabash River Guide Book [by]
         Jerry M. Hay; Terre Haute, IN: Express
         Wholesalers?, c1996.
            71 p. ; ill., maps : 27 cm.


            1. WABASH RIVER GUIDE BOOK
            1. Title
```
Author

Nonfiction Books

A nonfiction book is a book on a particular topic that was researched and written by someone who knows about that topic. Nonfiction books can be a valuable reference tool.

In a library, all nonfiction books are numbered and placed in order on the shelves. Books on the same subject are grouped together. Whether your library has a computer catalog or a card catalog, you can search for a book by title, subject, or author.

Once you find information on a book that looks interesting, look for the call number of the book. That number will guide you to the area of the library where you will find the book. A librarian can help you.

Periodicals

A periodical, such as a newspaper or a magazine, is published on a regular basis, usually daily, weekly, or monthly. Most libraries have a special periodical section. Many magazines and newspapers also have their own Web sites where you can read all or part of the publication on-line.

Libraries have guides that list magazine articles by subject. The *Children's Magazine Guide* and the *Readers' Guide to Periodical Literature* are the most frequently used guides. These guides list information by title, subject, and author. Each entry in the guide lists the title of the article or story, the author, the name and date of the magazine, and the page number on which the article appears. If your library has the magazine, you can find it and read the article.

Community Resources

In addition to the Internet and reference tools, the people in your community are good sources of information. If you are studying the birds at Hoosier National Forest, you can talk to people at government agencies, such as the Hoosier National Forest Supervisor's Office. Or try a local college, university, or a nearby natural history museum for information. Perhaps you know someone who has visited the park often for many years. You might want to interview that person for more information.

Interviews

An interview is a good way to find out what people in your community know. This means asking them questions about the topic you are studying. Follow these steps:

Plan ahead

- List the people you want to interview.
- Call or write to ask if you can interview them. Let the person know who you are and why you need information.
- Agree on a time and place for the interview.
- Find out about the topic that you want to discuss.
- Write down questions that you want to ask at the interview.

Ask/Listen/Record

- Ask questions clearly.
- Listen carefully. Be polite. Do not interrupt.
- Write notes so that you will remember what was said. Write down the person's actual words. If possible, use a tape recorder to help you remember.

Wrap-up

- Thank the person when you are finished with the interview.
- Send a thank-you note.

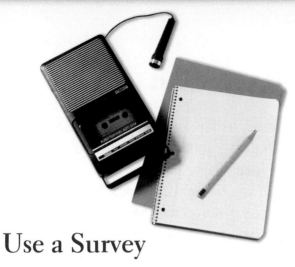

Use a Survey

Another way to find information in your community is to conduct a survey. A survey is a list of questions that you ask people, recording everyone's answers. This gives you an idea about what the people in your community know, think, or feel about a subject. You can use yes/no questions or short-answer questions. To record the things you find out, you will want to make a tally sheet with a column for each question. If you were doing research about a river that is near your town, your survey sheet might look this this:

The following steps will help you plan a survey:

- Write down a list of questions.
- Where do you want to conduct the survey? How many people do you want to ask?
- Use a tally sheet when conducting the survey so that you can record people's answers.
- After the survey, look through the responses and write what you found out.

Write for Information

Another way to get information from people or organizations in your community is to e-mail or write a letter asking for information. Use these steps:

- Plan what you want to say before you write.
- Be neat and careful about spelling and punctuation.
- Tell who you are and why you are writing.
- Thank the person.

Our River

	How long have you lived in our community?	How often do you visit the river?	How has the river changed since you have been coming here?	What do you like about the river?
Person 1	30 years	Not very often— I haven't been there for years.	It seems dirtier. I hear that there are fewer fish because it's so polluted.	It's peaceful there.
Person 2	Two years	Every day	There used to be more ducks and a few geese. Now there are more geese.	I like fishing. I throw everything back, but it's relaxing to fish.

Writing a Research Report

Prewrite

- Decide on a topic for your report. Your teacher may tell you what kind of report to research and write and how long it should be.
- Write down questions that you want to find out about the topic.
- Use different sources to find information and answer your questions. Be sure to write down all your sources. This list of sources is called a bibliography.
- Take notes from your sources.
- Review the notes you have taken from all your sources.
- Write down the main ideas that you want to write about. Two or three ideas are enough for most reports.
- Make an outline, listing each main idea and some details about each main idea.

Write a First Draft

- Using your outline, write what you have learned, using sentences and paragraphs. Each paragraph should be about a new idea.
- When you use exact words from your sources, write down the source from which you got the information. This list will become part of your bibliography.

Revise

- Read over your rough draft. Does it make sense? Do you need more information about any main idea?
- Change any sentences or paragraphs that do not make sense. Add anything that will make your ideas clear.
- Check your quotations to make sure they are accurate.

Edit

- Proofread your report. Correct any errors in spelling, grammar, capitalization, sentence structure, and punctuation.

Publish

- Add pictures, maps, or other graphics that will help make your report interesting.
- Write or type a final copy as neatly as possible.

The Land Called
Indiana

What is special about this land we call Indiana?

"I am much pleased with this country. Nothing can exceed its beauty and fertility."

—William Henry Harrison, describing central Indiana, 1801

Theodore Clement Steele painted *The Oaks of Vernon* in 1887.

Meet the People

John Chapman
1774–1845
Birthplace: Leominster, Massachusetts
Planter, preacher
- Began walking through Ohio, Illinois, and Indiana around 1800, selling and planting apple seeds and creating apple orchards
- One of his largest orchards is in Fort Wayne, Indiana
- Became known as "Johnny Appleseed"

Theodore C. Steele
1847–1926
Birthplace: Spencer, Indiana
Artist
- Started painting at age five; won awards by the time he was fourteen
- Studied painting in Germany for five years
- Leader of a group of landscape painters who started an artists' colony in Brown County

Paul Dresser
1858–1906
Birthplace: Terre Haute, Indiana
Composer
- Gained fame as a popular songwriter in the 1890s
- Wrote "On the Banks of the Wabash, Far Away" in 1899
- Indiana adopted "On the Banks of the Wabash, Far Away" as the state song in 1913

Juliet Strauss
1863–1918
Birthplace: Rockville, Indiana
Journalist
- Wrote column called "Ideas of a Plain Country Woman" for *Ladies' Home Journal*
- Among the first to call for forest land to be conserved in Indiana
- Helped make Turkey Run area a state park

1775	1800	1825	1850	1875

1774 • John Chapman 1845

1847 • Theodore C. Steele

1858 • Paul Dresser

1863 • Juliet Strauss

1869

For more information, go online to *Meet the People* at **www.sfsocialstudies.com**.

Richard Lieber

1869–1944

Birthplace: St. Johann-Saarbrüecken, Germany

Businessman, journalist, conservationist

- Appointed director of Indiana State Department of Conservation in 1919
- Organized the state park system of Indiana
- Helped save Turkey Run forest from being cut down for lumber

Bess Sheehan

1882–1968

Birthplace: Jackson County, Michigan

Teacher, author, activist

- Called the "Lady of the Dunes"
- Served as chairperson for the State Federated Women's Club Dunes Park Committee
- Led movement to make the Indiana Dunes a state and national park

Virgil Ivan (Gus) Grissom

1926–1967

Birthplace: Mitchell, Indiana

Astronaut

- Second American astronaut to travel into space, July 1961
- Became first man to make two trips into space
- Killed in 1967 during a fire in a space capsule

Curtis Stevens

b. 1968

Birthplace: Michigan City, Indiana

Geographer

- Studied how African Americans settled in Indiana along Underground Railroad routes
- Former geography professor at Valparaiso University
- Worked with inner-city youth in Michigan City

1900 | 1925 | 1950 | 1975 | 2000

1926
1906
1918
• Richard Lieber 1944
1882 • Bess Sheehan 1968
1926 • Virgil Ivan (Gus) Grissom 1967
b. 1968 • Curtis Stevens

5

The Land of Indiana

Main Idea and Details

- The main idea is the most important idea in a paragraph or longer passage.
- The details support and give more information about the main idea.

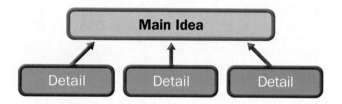

- Recognizing the main idea of a paragraph or passage will help you understand what you are reading.
- The main idea of a paragraph may be directly stated in the topic sentence. If it is not, you need to use the supporting details to identify the main idea.

Read the following paragraph. The **main idea** and the **details** have been highlighted.

In Chapter 1, you will read about the land called Indiana. Indiana is an interesting and exciting place to live. You can visit state parks and covered bridges. You can watch cars race at the Indianapolis Motor Speedway. You can even fish in lakes that are fourteen thousand years old.

An Interesting and Varied Land

How would you describe Indiana to someone who has never been here? You might say that Indiana is a varied land. It has flat plains, hills, and valleys. It has lakes and rivers, forests and beaches.

Indiana has three main natural regions: the Great Lakes Plain region, the Tipton Till Plain region, and the Southern Hills and Lowlands region. Each region is interesting. The Great Lakes Plain region is full of lakes and ponds. The Tipton Till Plain region has flat land and rich soil. The Southern Hills and Lowlands region has springs and caves.

Indiana is rich in fuels such as coal and natural gas. Farmers grow corn and soybeans in its fertile soil. Red fox, deer, and coyotes are found in the state. Its many lakes, ponds, and rivers are sources of water. They are also places to enjoy nature.

Indiana's forests are one of its most valuable resources. Forests once covered much of the state. Many were cut down to make way for farmland or industry. Today the forests that are left help keep the soil from eroding. They also provide homes for wild animals.

Use the reading strategy of identifying the main idea and details to answer these questions.

1 Which sentence states the main idea of the passage?

2 Identify a detail that supports the following main idea: *Indiana is a land of many natural resources.*

3 What is the main idea of the last paragraph?

Lesson 1

Indiana
Indiana is called the "Crossroads of America."

1

Lesson 2

Indiana Dunes National Lakeshore
Hoosiers know the importance of preserving the state's many resources.

2

Lesson 3

Hoosier National Forest
Indiana is a land of natural wonders.

3

NORTH AMERICA

Great Lakes

Indiana Dunes National Lakeshore

INDIANA

UNITED STATES

Hoosier National Forest

PACIFIC OCEAN

ATLANTIC OCEAN

Gulf of Mexico

Why We Remember

We all know that our state is in the central United States. But who can really describe the land, the people, and the spirit of Indiana? We Hoosiers—people who come from Indiana—are very proud of our state. We like to share Indiana with others. Artists paint its landscapes. Musicians and writers celebrate the state in songs and poems. Business and government leaders promote Indiana's products and resources. You might already know a lot about our state. Soon you will know even more!

INDIANA

PREVIEW

Focus on the Main Idea
Indiana is located in the Western Hemisphere on the continent of North America.

PLACES

Indiana
Lake Michigan
Great Lakes Plain
Tipton Till Plain
Southern Hills and Lowlands
Lake Wawasee
Chain O' Lakes State Park

PEOPLE

Gus Grissom
Paul Dresser

VOCABULARY

hemisphere
equator
prime meridian
continent
glacier
landform
waterway

EVENTS

Ice Age
Feast of the Hunter's Moon
Madison Regatta
Sugar Creek Canoe Race

A Bird's-Eye View of Indiana

You Are There
The countdown begins. Your heart pounds with excitement. You're going to be the first student to fly into space and orbit Earth. For 90 minutes, you'll be circling 125 miles above Earth's surface. In school you learned about fellow Hoosier Gus Grissom. In 1961, he became the second American to fly into space. His journey in the *Liberty Bell 7* space capsule lasted just 15 minutes and 37 seconds.

As you prepare for takeoff, you think of your home state. Your job on this trip is to observe Indiana from space. The countdown ends, and you are on your way.

Main Idea and Details
As you read, look for main ideas and details on each page.

▶ From space, Earth's round shape
is clearly visible.

The View from Above

You watch land and winding rivers grow smaller as your spaceship climbs higher. Before you know it, you are high above Earth, looking down on the planet as **Gus Grissom** may have many years ago. From here you notice that Earth is round like the globe in your classroom. In order to make our globe easier to study, we divide it into halves. We call these halves of the globe **hemispheres.**

We use the equator to divide Earth into northern and southern hemispheres. The **equator** is an imaginary line that circles Earth midway between the North and South Poles. Places to the south of the equator are in the Southern Hemisphere. Places to the north are in the Northern Hemisphere. **Indiana** is in the Northern Hemisphere.

To divide the globe into eastern and western halves, we use an imaginary line that extends from the North Pole to the South Pole. We call this line the **prime meridian.** It passes through Greenwich, England. Places east of Greenwich are in the Eastern Hemisphere. Places west of Greenwich, such as Indiana, are in the Western Hemisphere.

REVIEW In which hemispheres is Indiana located? ⟳ **Main Idea and Details**

North America and the World

Looking down from space, the next thing that you notice is how much water you can see. Water, in the form of oceans, lakes, and rivers, covers about seventy percent of Earth's surface. You can also see large areas of land. We call these areas **continents.** There are seven continents: Africa, Antarctica, Asia, Australia, Europe, North America, and South America.

North America is made up of several countries, including Canada, Mexico, and the United States. The United States is made up of fifty states, and one of them is Indiana. A Hoosier writer has described his state as "not Out West or Way Down East or Up North or South in Dixie. Rather, it's smack in the middle of America." Indiana's state motto, "Crossroads of America," describes its central location along roads, rivers, and train lines. Today more major highways pass through Indiana than through any other state.

REVIEW On what continent is Indiana located? ↪ **Main Idea and Details**

The Seven Continents

MAP SKILL

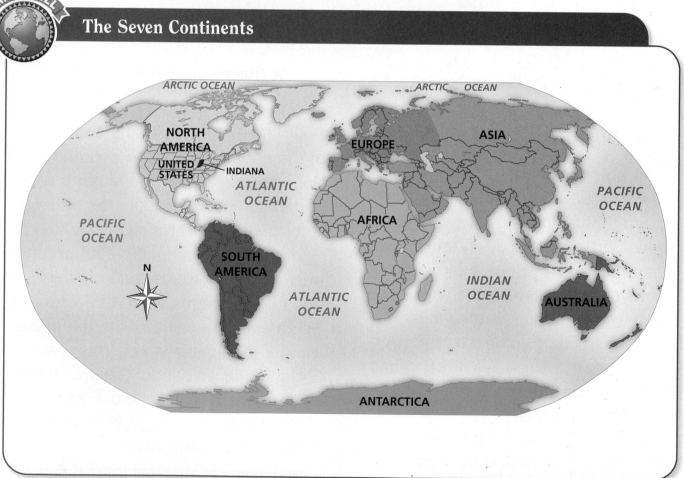

ARCTIC OCEAN

ARCTIC OCEAN

NORTH AMERICA

UNITED STATES

INDIANA

ATLANTIC OCEAN

EUROPE

ASIA

PACIFIC OCEAN

PACIFIC OCEAN

AFRICA

N

SOUTH AMERICA

ATLANTIC OCEAN

INDIAN OCEAN

AUSTRALIA

ANTARCTICA

▶ Within the continent of North America, the United States is highlighted in green.

MAP SKILL Location *Describe the location of Indiana within the United States.*

Sizing Up Indiana

Look at the map. You can see that Indiana is shaped almost like a boot. The state is nearly 180 miles wide at its greatest width. It is about 285 miles long at its greatest length. It has an area of 36,420 square miles. Indiana is the thirty-eighth largest state. The largest state, Alaska, is about 590,000 square miles. It would take more than sixteen Indianas to fill Alaska.

Indiana has neighbors on all four sides. **Lake Michigan** and the state of Michigan border Indiana on the north. Ohio borders Indiana on the east. Kentucky borders us on the south, and Illinois borders us on the west.

As you will read later, Indiana was once part of a large area called the Northwest Territory. This was later divided into two parts: the Northwest Territory and the Indiana Territory. How people formed these territories and made them into states is part of our exciting history.

REVIEW What states border Indiana? ⟳ **Main Idea and Details**

Indiana Today

▶ The shaded areas on the map indicate hills and valleys.

MAP SKILL Understand Map Symbols *Which city is located where three rivers meet?*

THE PEOPLE OF

INDIANA

WELCOME YOU

Map Adventure

Touring Indiana

Indiana has many towns, cities, and areas with claims to fame. Read the description of each place. Then follow these steps:

1. Draw the shape of Indiana on a sheet of paper.
2. Label your hometown or the nearest big town.
3. Starting from your home, plan a trip to three places.
4. Write **1** next to the first place you wish to visit, **2** next to the second place, and **3** next to the third place. Draw arrows showing the route you will take.

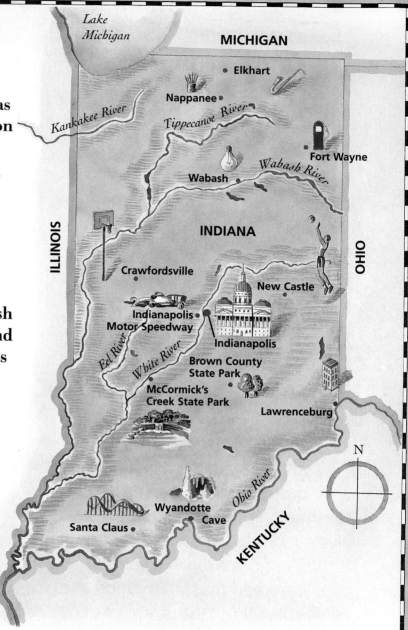

Cities/Towns

Crawfordsville: Birthplace of Indiana basketball

Elkhart: Band instrument capital of the world

Fort Wayne: Home of the first gas pump

Indianapolis: State capital

Lawrenceburg: First "sky scraper" in Indiana

Nappanee: Largest collection of miniature buildings made out of toothpicks and craft sticks

New Castle: Home of Indiana Basketball Hall of Fame

Santa Claus: Home of first amusement park in nation, Holiday World

Wabash: First public lights powered by electricity

Features

Brown County State Park: Largest state park in Indiana

Indianapolis Motor Speedway: Home of the Indy 500

McCormick's Creek State Park: Oldest state park in Indiana

Wyandotte Cave: Contains interesting natural formations such as stalagmites and stalactites

Hills, Valleys, Lakes, and Plains

As you fly over Antarctica, you see only ice. Long ago, ice and snow covered Indiana too. We call this period the **Ice Age.** During the Ice Age, huge masses of ice called **glaciers** moved south from the north. Glaciers covered many parts of North America.

For almost 400,000 years, glaciers covered the northern two-thirds of Indiana. As the glaciers drifted, they changed the natural features of the land. They flattened land and cut the peaks off hills. The glacial activity created three great landform regions in Indiana. A **landform** is a natural feature on the surface of Earth. Hills, valleys, lakes, and plains are types of landforms.

▶ Glaciers are still found in many parts of the world. This one is in Argentina.

North of Indiana, the glaciers also dug huge holes. These holes became lakes and ponds. Five of them became the Great Lakes. Now we call the northern region of Indiana closest to Lake Michigan the **Great Lakes Plain.**

MAP SKILL

Indiana's Regions

Key

☐ Great Lakes Plain	★ State capital
☐ Tipton Till Plain	• Other cities
☐ Southern Hills and Lowlands	

▶ Indiana is divided into three main natural regions, as shown.

MAP SKILL Use a Map Key *Which region contains Indiana's capital city?*

In the middle of the state, the glaciers left large amounts of till. Till is the soil and rock that gets trapped in glaciers. This region of the state is called the **Tipton Till Plain** because of the till that covers much of the land.

The lower one-third of the state is different from the rest of the state because it has many hills and valleys. It was not as affected by glaciers as areas to the north. We call this region the **Southern Hills and Lowlands.**

REVIEW How did glaciers change the landscape of Indiana?
🔄 **Main Idea and Details**

15

▶ Today canal boats like this one are popular tourist attractions.

Indiana's Waterways

Indiana's waterways have helped make our state the "Crossroads of America." **Waterways** include lakes, rivers, and streams. Early settlements and small towns grew up around lakes and rivers. Before train travel, people built canals to link rivers. These canals made transportation of goods and people much easier. At first, canal boats were pulled by horses or mules. Then boats with steam engines took over. These boats could move more easily, even against the current.

Lake Michigan gives Indiana its identity as a Great Lakes state. The forty-one miles of shoreline on Lake Michigan form part of our northern border. It is a major location for industry. The lake also links Indiana to Canada and to the Atlantic Ocean.

Glaciers carved about four hundred lakes into the northern region of Indiana. The state's largest lake is **Lake Wawasee.** It has eighteen miles of shoreline. Its name comes from an American Indian chief whose nickname was "Old Flat Belly."

The Wabash River is probably Indiana's most famous waterway. In 1897, composer **Paul Dresser** published "On the Banks of the Wabash, Far Away." It is now the state song of Indiana. The Wabash flows across northern and central Indiana.

Literature and Social Studies

In 1919, Indianapolis journalist William Herschell wrote "Ain't God Good to Indiana?" This poem reflects the pride that Hoosiers feel when we look at our farms, our businesses, and our land. Below is the first stanza of the poem.

Ain't God good to Indiana?
Folks, a feller never knows
Just how close he is to Eden
[a beautiful place]
Till, sometime, he ups an' goes
Seekin' fairer, greener pastures
Than he has right here at home,
Where there's sunshine in th'
*   clover*
An' there's honey in th' comb;
Where the ripples on th' river
Kinda chuckles as they flow—
Ain't God good to Indiana?
Ain't He, fellers? Ain't He,
*   though?*

Then it turns and flows south to Terre Haute and on to the Ohio River. As it flows toward the Ohio River, the Wabash forms part of the border between Indiana and Illinois. Finally, it joins the Ohio River, which is the border between Indiana and Kentucky.

Our waterways can be a place for fun too. People enjoy boating and canoeing. Lakes and rivers are also the settings for fairs, such as the **Feast of the Hunter's Moon** in Tippecanoe County. Hoosiers also hold races on waterways. These include the **Madison Regatta** on the Ohio River and the **Sugar Creek Canoe Race** in Crawfordsville.

REVIEW What are some of Indiana's important waterways? ◉ **Main Idea and Details**

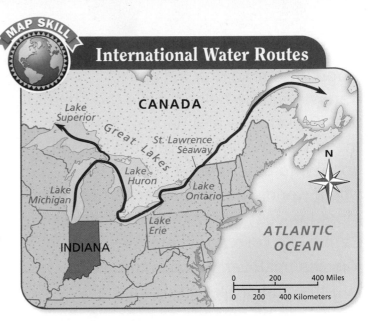

International Water Routes

▶ Through Lake Michigan, ships from Indiana can reach Canada and the Atlantic Ocean.

MAP SKILL Understand Intermediate Directions *In what direction do ships travel from Lake Erie through the St. Lawrence Seaway?*

Chain O' Lakes State Park

Then and Now

At **Chain O' Lakes State Park,** you can canoe and fish in the lakes that give this park its name. You can choose from eight lakes connected by small streams—in a chain. These lakes are special. They are called kettle lakes and are about 14,000 years old!

▶ Chain O' Lakes is a peaceful spot for these people fishing and canoeing (*above*). The Nature Center (*left*) used to be a school.

17

Links to the World

You have read how Indiana's waterways have helped make the state the "Crossroads of America." Some of these waterways, however, link Indiana not just to other states but to the whole world. The Ohio River carries more low-cost freight than the Panama Canal. The Ohio flows into the Mississippi River, which in turn flows into the Gulf of Mexico. From there goods can be shipped all over the world. Southwind Maritime Center, near the town of Mount Vernon, is Indiana's largest port on the Ohio River.

Portage, about ten miles east of Gary, on the shores of Lake Michigan, is Indiana's largest port city. It connects Indiana to the world by way of the St. Lawrence Seaway. From this port, enormous ships, called freighters, carry Indiana steel

▶ **Ships such as these carry goods through the Great Lakes, the St. Lawrence Seaway, and out to sea.**

and other products to markets around the world.

REVIEW Which sentence expresses the main idea of this section?
⟳ **Main Idea and Details**

Summarize the Lesson

- **Indiana is located in the Northern and Western Hemispheres, on the North American continent, in the United States of America.**

- **Four states border Indiana.**

- **Indiana has a variety of landforms and waterways.**

LESSON 1 ⟩ REVIEW

Check Facts and Main Ideas

1. ⟳ **Main Idea and Details** Use a sheet of paper. Write details to support the following main idea.

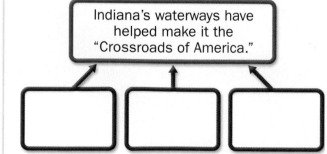

Indiana's waterways have helped make it the "Crossroads of America."

2. Where on Earth and in the United States is Indiana located?

3. What helped shape the three different natural regions of Indiana?

4. What types of landforms are found in Indiana?

5. **Critical Thinking:** *Analyze Information* Why does Indiana's location make it the "Crossroads of America"?

Link to ⛓ Science

Find a Glacier Use the Internet, reference books, and other resources to find out where glaciers still exist. How do these glaciers benefit Earth, and how can they change it?

Virgil I. "Gus" Grissom 1926–1967

In 1961, Gus Grissom became the second American to fly into space. In 1965, he became the first to do it twice. Gus Grissom just loved to fly. He was only six years old when he took his first plane ride with his father.

As a boy, Grissom had a strong sense of adventure. He loved to explore the area around his home in Mitchell. After college, he joined the Air Force. He flew jets in the Korean War. He taught pilots how to fly.

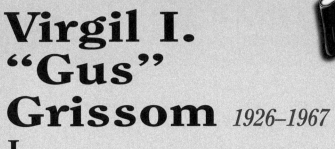

BIOFACT

Gus Grissom was too short to make his high school basketball team. Later his height worked in his favor. Early space capsules were too small for anyone taller than 5' 11".

Grissom also tested planes for the military. In 1959, the U.S. government chose Grissom to become an astronaut. Later he wrote,

"If my country decided that I was one of the better qualified people for this new mission, then I was proud and happy to help out. I guess there was also a spirit of pioneering and adventure involved in the decision."

Grissom flew two successful missions into space. In 1967, a fire killed Grissom and two other astronauts at Cape Canaveral, Florida. They had been preparing for a moon flight.

Learn from Biographies

Why do you think Gus Grissom felt that being an astronaut was like being a pioneer?

For more information, go online to *Meet the People* at **www.sfsocialstudies.com.**

Map and Globe Skills

Use an Elevation Map

What? **Elevation** (el-uh-VAY-shun) is the height of the land above sea level. Elevation is usually measured in feet or meters. At sea level, the elevation is zero feet or zero meters.

An **elevation map** shows the height of land areas. The elevation map on page 21 will help you understand the geography of Indiana.

The map uses different colors to show how the elevation changes from one part of Indiana to another. Four different levels of elevation are indicated by the key on the map on page 21.

Why? An elevation map tells you how high above sea level the land in an area is. It can also show the courses of rivers. If you know that rivers flow from higher elevations to lower ones, you can use an elevation map to follow a river's course.

How? To use an elevation map, first scan the map. Then read the map key. Finally, compare the information in the key with the features shown on the map.

Look at the map on page 21. Notice how the colors change as your eye moves across the map.

On the map, the key shows elevations as blocks of color. To see if any part of Indiana is below sea level, first find the color for 0 feet/meters elevation on the map key. You can see that purple is used to show areas that are below sea level. Now look to see if there are any areas of purple on the map of Indiana. You will see that no part of Indiana is below sea level.

Now find the Wabash River on the map. Trace the Wabash River from its highest point to its lowest point. Remember that water flows from a higher elevation to a lower elevation.

▶ **The Wabash River's elevation decreases as it flows through Indiana.**

Indiana's Elevation

Key

Feet	Meters	
980	300	★ State capital
650	200	• Other cities
0	0	▲ Highest point in Indiana
Below Sea Level		▽ Lowest point in Indiana

The area where the Wabash crosses from Ohio into Indiana is in light green. On the map key, this represents an elevation of more than 650 feet. This means that the Wabash enters Indiana at between 650 and 980 feet above sea level. Now trace its path as it flows south to the Ohio River. You will notice that the colors on the map change from light green to dark green. This means that the river is flowing through areas of lower and lower elevation until it reaches the Ohio River.

Think and Apply

1 What is the elevation of the yellow areas of Indiana?

2 What is the elevation of Indianapolis?

3 What is the elevation of the place where the Wabash meets the Patoka?

For more information, go online to the *Atlas* at **www.sfsocialstudies.com**.

Glaciation

During the Ice Age, glaciers covered the area of the world that later became the state of Indiana. Deep ice also covered many other parts of the world. Glaciers are thought to have shaped the landscape of Indiana and the world. Glaciers still exist in the world's high mountain ranges. Over the last 2 million years, glacier buildup has happened each time a cold glacial period follows a warmer interglacial period. Today, Earth is thought to be in an interglacial period of glacier melting. When a glacier melts, it leaves bouldery gravel mounds. The gravel heaps are known as the terminal moraine of the glacier.

Pacific Ocean   *Pack-ice*

Satellite Snowscape
This satellite photo of Alaska's coast shows how ocean water freezes into pack ice.

Continental Ice Sheet
Most of Greenland and Antarctica are covered with ice sheets thousands of feet thick. The ice thins near the ocean. Near the northwest Greenland coast, valley glaciers cut through surrounding mountains. The glacial ice pushes and carries rocks along its path.

Ice sheet

Terminal moraine

Valley glacier

Crevasse (kreh VAS), a deep crack

From Snow to Ice

Snow is made of fluffy flakes that trap air in the new snow layer. As new snow melts in the day and refreezes at night, it gets more compact. This mature snow is called *névé* (nay vay). It soon packs into hard ice.

Freshly fallen snow

New snow

Névé

Glacier ice

Air squeezed out

Impermeable ice (ice that fluids cannot pass through)

Creating Fjords

When Ice Age glaciers melted, seas rose and flooded valleys carved by glaciers in mountainous coasts. In Norway, these deep inlets are called fjords (FEE ords). Fjords also cut into the New Zealand, Antarctic, and Canadian coasts.

Bedrock

Glacier ice

Plucked boulder

Meltwater seeps into cracks.

Plucked Rock

Glaciers "pluck" rocks and carry them in the moving ice. Water seeps into cracks in rock formations, freezes, and lifts fragments off the valley floor into the ice as it passes.

Boulder clay cemented with lime

Scratch marks made by rock fragments trapped in glacier

Glacial fragments in rock

Glacier Grater

Rock fragments trapped in the flowing glacier polish the floor of the glacial valley. The smooth stone face (left) shows glacial scratches. Glaciers carry loads of boulders, stones, fragments and rock powder. When a glacier melts, it dumps this material in great heaps, which harden into boulder clay (right).

Limestone rock from Switzerland

Chalky boulder clay

Indiana Dunes National Lakeshore

Preserving Indiana

You Are There
You launch a boat onto the Grand Calumet River. You plan to explore the river as it flows into Lake Michigan.

At first you drift past a beautiful landscape. But soon all you see are factories! The river water doesn't look very clean. Signs warn you not to eat any fish that you might catch. You don't see many birds or other signs of wildlife.

Later you learn that before people knew the kind of damage dumping waste could cause, some of these industries dumped waste into the river. Now people and industries are working hard to clean it up. They want to make this river a good place for fish and other wildlife—and for people too.

Main Idea and Details
As you read, look for main ideas and details that tell you about the natural resources of Indiana.

Our Hidden Treasures

A **natural resource** is a material found in nature that people can use. People use natural resources for food, protection, comfort, and recreation. Indiana has many natural resources. They include water, trees, soil, and minerals. We divide our natural resources into two categories: renewable and nonrenewable. Renewable resources can be replaced as we use them—as long as we act responsibly. Trees are one example. But nonrenewable resources cannot be replaced. The process that created them took millions of years. Natural gas, coal, oil, and limestone are examples of nonrenewable resources.

For example, Indiana has used up much of its natural gas. In the 1880s, people discovered natural gas in an area they named the "Gas Belt." It stretched from central Indiana south to the Ohio River. Soon the area became the world's largest producing field of natural gas. Industries used the cheap and plentiful fuel. They built many factories there. Then, in 1898, most of the gas ran out. Today Indiana must import some natural gas.

REVIEW What is a natural resource? Give two examples of natural resources that cannot be renewed.

↻ **Main Idea and Details**

▶ **Strahl Lake in Brown County is a resource that is protected as part of a state park.**

Mineral Resources

Scientists believe that about 300 million years ago, the land that is now southern Indiana was a shallow ocean bed. When fish and other creatures died, they drifted to the ocean floor. Over time these animal remains built up and formed a thick, smooth rock called limestone. Today limestone is an important resource, mined from quarries near Bedford and Bloomington. Quarries are pits from which stone is cut or blasted. Many famous buildings are built from Indiana limestone. They include the Empire State Building in New York City and the Pentagon near Washington, D.C. The Pentagon, damaged in the September 11, 2001, terrorist attacks, was repaired using Indiana limestone.

Coal, another mineral resource, comes from plants that lived millions of years ago. Over time pressure and heat caused the remains of dead plants to harden into this important natural resource. Today people in southwestern Indiana mine coal. This coal provides the main source of heat and electricity in the state.

▶ The steel-making process calls for iron to be heated to extremely high temperatures.

Limestone and coal are two of the resources needed to make steel. Steel is a strong, flexible metal produced when wastes are burned off from iron. Steel making became a big industry here in the early 1900s. Indiana had both coal and limestone. Iron ore, the third main resource used in steel, was shipped here from Wisconsin and Minnesota. Today Indiana produces more steel than any other state. People use this steel to make everything from cars to cooking pots and even the frames of huge skyscrapers.

REVIEW What nonrenewable resources are used in making steel?
◉ **Main Idea and Details**

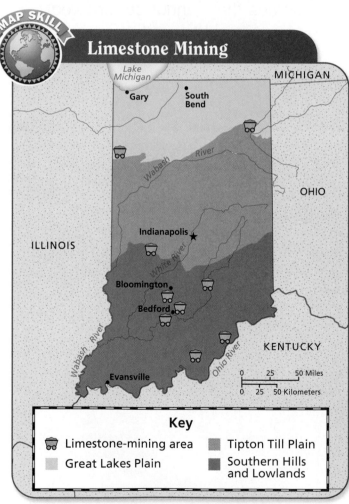

MAP SKILL

Limestone Mining

Lake Michigan

MICHIGAN

Gary

South Bend

Wabash River

OHIO

Indianapolis ★

White River

ILLINOIS

Bloomington

Bedford

Wabash River

KENTUCKY

Ohio River

Evansville

0   25   50 Miles

0   25   50 Kilometers

Key

🛒 Limestone-mining area

Great Lakes Plain

Tipton Till Plain

Southern Hills and Lowlands

▶ Limestone mining is a major industry.

MAP SKILL Use a Product Map *Which of Indiana's regions contains the most limestone mines?*

Forest Resources

With the proper care, renewable resources can be reused, reproduced, or replaced. Forests, soil, and water are examples of renewable resources. If we use these resources carefully, they will be available to people in the future.

Forests are one of nature's most valuable resources. They provide shelter for wild animals. They help keep soil in place. They also help Earth store water for use during dry times. Forests help clean our air. They provide wood for building and fuel. Trees supply the pulp we use to make paper. Parts of trees are also used to make plastics and medicines.

A hundred and fifty years ago, forests covered much of Indiana.

As people cleared land for farming and cut trees for lumber and fuel, most of these forests disappeared. Now forests cover only one-fifth of the state. But they are still a valuable resource for Indiana. Today people plant small trees to replace the trees they cut down. They are following the example of **John Chapman.** He is the real person behind the legend of Johnny Appleseed. Chapman knew the value of trees. He walked from Pennsylvania to Indiana. Along the way he planted apple seeds and created orchards. One of his largest orchards is near Fort Wayne.

REVIEW Why did so many trees disappear from Indiana?
Cause and Effect

▶ **This apple orchard shows another way trees help people: by providing food.**

► People can take steps to help prevent soil erosion along riverbanks.

The Soil

Soil is another of Indiana's precious natural resources. Farmers rely on Indiana's rich soil to help their crops grow. Soil, like a forest, can be renewed. But we must also take care of it.

When Indiana lost its forests, it also lost some important protection for its soil. Trees help prevent soil erosion. **Erosion** happens when water or wind wears away soil or stone. Beneath the topsoil, or top layer of soil, is a layer called subsoil. It is hard to grow crops in subsoil. We can keep our rich topsoil from eroding by growing plants and grass. Their roots and leaves provide nutrients and help hold the soil in place.

► Roots hold soil in place.

REVIEW What causes soil erosion?
Cause and Effect

Water Resources

Water is our most important natural resource. We could not live without it. We need it for drinking, for washing, and for cooking. We use it to put out fires and to help plants and crops grow. We use it for transportation and to make electricity. We even use water to have fun. How could we go swimming, fishing, or boating without it?

Fortunately, Indiana has many lakes, rivers, and streams. It also has many underground sources of water. Rain and melting snow keep these sources of water full.

But our waterways face many threats. In areas where all the trees have been cut, rainwater does not sink into the ground quickly. It just flows over the surface. This water carries soil and other materials from the ground. When it flows into a river, the soil and materials can pollute the river water. To **pollute** means to make something unclean. People and industries can also pollute water by allowing waste to enter our waterways. Drinking polluted water can make us sick. Fish cannot live in it. The good news is that water is a renewable resource. Rain and snow refill our water supply. We can work to clean polluted water and protect it from further pollution.

REVIEW What causes water to become polluted? **Cause and Effect**

Protecting Our Resources

Conservation means protecting natural resources by using them wisely. You practice conservation when you turn off lights or when you pick up trash from a park. You also practice conservation when you recycle cans, bottles, or old newspapers. Recycling allows us to use these things more than once, although not always in the same way.

Many United States citizens became interested in conservation about 150 years ago. They realized that human activities were destroying forests. Soon their concern spread to other natural resources. People worked alone and in groups to stop the careless use of our land and resources. Indiana's history is filled with citizens who helped protect our environment.

REVIEW How can people help conserve Indiana's natural resources?
⊙ **Main Idea and Details**

▶ Grasses hold some of the dunes at Indiana Dunes National Lakeshore in place. Other dunes have no plants and can shift locations.

29

Hoosiers: Indiana's Greatest Resource

If you have grown up in Indiana, you have probably heard the word *Hoosier* since you were little. But just where did this word come from anyway? The answer is that there is no answer—at least not a good one. There are lots of explanations, though. Among them:

- When a visitor to a pioneer cabin knocked on the door, the settler would say, "Who's yere?"

- Early Indiana rivermen were so tough that when they fought with other people, they shut them up, or hushed them. They became known as "hushers" and, eventually, "Hoosiers."

- A canal contractor named Sam Hoosier liked to hire Indiana workers. They were called "Hoosier's men" and, later, just Hoosiers.

- James Whitcomb Riley, "The Hoosier Poet," offered this joking explanation: The early settlers were rowdy and they often had fights. It was common for one of them to bite off an opponent's ear. The next day someone would find an ear on the floor and ask, "Whose ear?"

- Jacob Piatt Dunn, Jr., a historian, points out that the word *hoozer* comes from England, where it refers to anything large, such as a hill. It was often used to describe people who lived in the hills of southern Indiana, the part of the state settled first.

Do you know of another explanation? If not, use your imagination and what you know about Indiana to make one up.

Hoosiers Who Cared

In 1915, **Bess Sheehan** of Gary learned that the owners of steel mills wanted to build factories on the dunes of Lake Michigan. Dunes are hills made of sand and formed by the wind. Sheehan and other local women worked for years to save the dunes. Finally in 1925, Indiana created the **Indiana Dunes State Park.** But the fight was not over. Industries continued to take over other areas of the lakeshore. Then in 1966, the **Indiana Dunes National Lakeshore** was created. This gave the dunes added protection.

In the early 1900s, timber companies bought many Indiana forests to cut down the trees and sell the wood. Cutting down trees and not replacing them can harm the environment. But the timber companies did not worry about replacing the trees. Before long Hoosiers saw their forests disappearing.

In 1915, a magazine writer named **Juliet Strauss** wanted to protect a forest area called Turkey Run. She wrote to Governor Samuel Ralston and asked him to help. The governor asked Strauss to join a committee to protect the forest. In 1916, the committee bought the forest from the timber company.

At about the same time, **Richard Lieber** was trying to convince Indiana's officials that creating state parks was a good way to protect land

MAP SKILL

Indiana's State Parks

State parks can be found throughout Indiana.

MAP SKILL Use a Map *Describe the location of Turkey Run State Park.*

and natural resources. Like Strauss, Lieber wanted to protect forests and land from industry. He also wanted Hoosiers to learn about their history. In 1916, Lieber helped create **McCormick's Creek State Park** southwest of Indianapolis. It became Indiana's first state park. The second was the forest Juliet Strauss helped buy: **Turkey Run State Park.** Today we have more than twenty state parks.

REVIEW Which of Indiana's state parks was the first? **Sequence**

What Can You Do?

You don't have to be a Juliet Strauss or a Richard Lieber to help conserve our resources. Here are some things everybody can do:

1. Don't waste water.
2. Turn off lights when you're not using them.
3. Buy recycled and recyclable products.
4. Reuse and recycle.
5. Fix things instead of throwing them away.
6. Use your bike, skates, or feet!

REVIEW If you follow the suggestions above, what do you have in common with Juliet Strauss and Richard Lieber?

Compare and Contrast

▶ People can help save resources by recycling goods rather than throwing them away.

Summarize the Lesson

- **Natural resources are materials found in nature that people use.**
- **Nonrenewable resources, such as many fuels and minerals, cannot be replaced.**
- **Renewable resources, such as trees and water, can be replaced.**
- **Hoosiers have a history of working to protect and preserve the natural resources of their state.**

LESSON 2   REVIEW

Check Facts and Main Ideas

1. 🔄 **Main Idea and Details** Use a sheet of paper. Write details to support the following main idea.

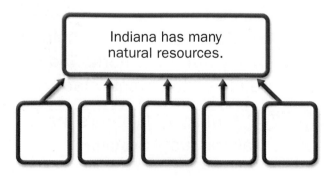

Indiana has many natural resources.

2. Identify Indiana's major renewable and nonrenewable resources.
3. Why are some of Indiana's natural resources gone or in danger of disappearing?
4. What are some causes of water pollution?
5. **Critical Thinking: *Draw Conclusions*** How can you help protect our natural resources?

Link to —◯◯— Writing

Write an Article Write an article for your school newspaper that will persuade your fellow students to help clean up a local park or playground.

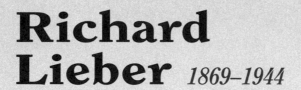

Richard Lieber *1869–1944*

Richard Lieber was born in Germany. In 1891, when he was twenty-two years old, he moved to Indiana. He held many jobs, but he was really interested in protecting nature. Lieber began a career in conservation. In 1919, he was appointed the first director of the Indiana State Department of Conservation. At one time, Lieber visited a friend in Brown County, Indiana. The area's great beauty amazed him. During this visit, he said he "heard the call to . . . build our Indiana State Parks."

Before Richard Lieber died in 1944, he selected a favorite spot in Turkey Run State Park where he wanted to be buried.

BIOFACT

Lieber worked with Juliet Strauss to help save Turkey Run forest. He wanted it to be part of a statewide park system. He hoped that the parks would encourage Indiana's citizens to protect their state's natural resources. He also felt that state parks would help the people of Indiana. He thought that

". . . the chief purpose of State Parks is to refresh and strengthen and renew tired people, and fit them for the common round of daily life."

Learn from Biographies

Why did Richard Lieber think that visiting a park would make people's lives better?

For more information, go online to *Meet the People* at **www.sfsocialstudies.com**.

Taking Action

What is one way to show respect for the environment? Use a talent you have to protect a natural resource from destruction! Read about how Juliet Strauss used her talent for writing to start a campaign to save a forest in Indiana.

▶ **Juliet Strauss**
1863–1918

As a child, Juliet Strauss played in the forest near her home in Rockville. The woods were known as Turkey Run.

In 1915, Strauss heard that a timber company might buy Turkey Run. She didn't want to see the forest cut down. By then she was writing articles for magazines. She decided to use her writing skills to help save the forest. Governor Sam Ralston agreed to help.

A committee was set up to raise money to buy the forest. The land was to be sold in May 1916. At the auction, Strauss's committee and the timber company both bid on the land. The price rose higher and higher. Finally, the timber company raised the bid by another $100. Strauss's committee could not go higher. The forest was sold to the timber company. Strauss was heartbroken at the loss of the forest. "I am sick of soul," she told a friend.

BUILDING CITIZENSHIP
Caring
Respect
Responsibility
Fairness
Honesty
Courage

She went on to say,

> *"Who would have dreamed that a few men's dollars could step in and destroy all this, the most beautiful spot in all Indiana, one that all the money in the world could not restore once it is gone."*

Strauss refused to give up. She raised more money and tried to convince the timber company to sell the land. Finally, in November 1916, the Hoosier Veneer Company agreed to sell the forest to Strauss and her committee for a $10,000 profit. Turkey Run soon became Indiana's second state park.

Juliet Strauss's respect for nature saved a precious resource. She wanted future generations to be able to enjoy and learn from nature, just as she and her family had done.

Respect in Action

Research the story of a person or a group of people who are trying to protect one of Earth's natural resources. How are these people showing respect for nature through their actions?

Hoosier
National
Forest

Natural Indiana

PREVIEW

Focus on the Main Idea
Many kinds of plants and animals live in Indiana.

PLACES

Pinhook Bog
Hoosier National Forest

VOCABULARY

climate
temperate
precipitation
habitat

You Are There

You wake up on a bright, cold January morning. Today your family has planned a hike in Hoosier National Forest. As you pull on your heavy winter clothes, you think of the steamy days of summer. You remember playing in the hot July sun. Now the warmth of summer seems very far away. You wonder if all of Indiana is cold today, or if the weather is different in another part of the state.

Finally, everyone is ready to go. You remember to bring along a book that lists animal tracks. You'll use it to identify tracks you find in the snow. You want to learn about the creatures that walk the Indiana woods in the wintertime.

Main Idea and Details
As you read, notice how each section focuses on one main idea.

Taking Indiana's Temperature

Climate and weather are different. Weather changes from day to day. **Climate** is the pattern of weather in a region over a long period. It is the kind of weather an area has year after year.

Indiana has a **temperate** climate. That is, our weather changes with the four seasons, but it is usually not extremely hot or extremely cold. Indiana's distance from the equator is one reason for our temperate climate. Places close to the equator are usually warmest throughout the year because the sun shines strongest there. Places far from the equator, like the poles, are coldest. That's why Indiana has a warmer climate than many places to the north and a cooler climate than places to the south. We have warm, humid summers and chilly winters. Southern Indiana is slightly warmer than northern Indiana.

Precipitation, which includes rain, sleet, and snow, is also a part of the climate. The southern part of Indiana gets the most rain each year. The northern region, especially around Lake Michigan, gets more snow. The average snowfall for

▶ Snow is common in the Indiana winter.

Rainfall Amounts

All areas of Indiana receive at least three feet of rain each year, on average.

MAP SKILL Use a Climate Map *How much annual rainfall does South Bend receive, on average?*

Key

Inches	Centimeters	
More than 44	More than 112	★ State capital
40–44	102–112	• Other cities
36–40	91–102	
Less than 36	Less than 91	

Indiana is 20 inches a year. But the northern border often gets more than 100 inches a year!

Lake Michigan affects the climate of northwest Indiana. In the fall, the lake's water remains warm from the summer. This warms the air above the lake and keeps temperatures mild. But in the spring, the water stays cold from the winter. This cools the air and keeps the temperature lower.

REVIEW What kind of climate does Indiana have? ↻ **Main Idea and Details**

▶ Wildflowers, hardy dune grasses, and Pitcher plants can all be found growing in Indiana.

Plants in Indiana

You've probably noticed the colorful wildflowers that grow along many roads in our state. Most of these flowers are common plants, such as goldenrod, clover, and violets. You can find many of these plants growing all over North America.

But not all of Indiana's plants and flowers are common. Our state holds a few surprises. Pitcher plants, sundews, and bladderworts grow in **Pinhook Bog** near Lake Michigan. These plants may look harmless, but to some creatures they are not. Fortunately, we don't need to worry. These plants catch only insects.

The dunes in northern Indiana are home to many unusual plants living side by side. Mosses usually found in the Arctic grow in the dunes. So do orchids usually found in tropical areas. Wetlands loosestrife grows in the dunes. As its name suggests, it usually grows in damp areas. On the other hand, desert cactus grows here too. The dunes provide a home to many rare plants and ferns.

The dunes' environment continues to change. As plants find homes there, they change the environment. For example, they make shade where there used to be sun. Other shade-loving plants then find homes in the newly shaded areas.

REVIEW Name some unusual plants that grow in Indiana. ↻ **Main Idea and Details**

From Flowers to Corn

Indiana has two kinds of vegetation—natural and cultivated. Many of our wildflowers, trees, grasses, vines, and bushes are examples of natural vegetation. They grow naturally, without help from people. Natural vegetation is very important. It helps prevent soil erosion. It can add nutrients, or nourishing ingredients, to the soil. The nutrients help plants grow. Natural vegetation also provides wildlife with food and shelter.

Other plants that grow in Indiana are cultivated. Cultivated vegetation is planted and cared for by people to help it grow. Corn is our most important cultivated crop. People have been growing corn here since prehistoric times.

We grow most of our corn in northwest and central Indiana. People all over the country eat Indiana corn when they snack on popcorn or eat corn cereal for breakfast. Cornstarch and corn syrup are ingredients in many foods. Farmers also feed corn to their hogs, cattle, and chickens.

During the 1920s, many farmers decided to grow soybeans. At first, people mainly used the crop to feed animals. Then during World War II, people started using soybean oil to replace products they could not get because of the war. Today, soybeans are Indiana's second most valuable crop. Wheat follows in third place.

REVIEW What is the difference between natural vegetation and cultivated vegetation?
Compare and Contrast

▶ Thousands of Indiana acres are cultivated to grow corn.

Wild Indiana

If you walk very quietly through **Hoosier National Forest,** you'll probably spot some of Indiana's wild animals. You might glimpse a deer or coyote. A red fox might run by. You can often see hawks flying overhead. If you look carefully, you might see a beaver or a skunk. Once these animals moved freely. Now protected areas, such as state and national parks, provide safe homes for them.

Years ago, other large mammals, such as black bears and elk, lived in Indiana. But they slowly disappeared. People hunted these animals. Also, when people cleared land for farming and housing, they destroyed the animals' habitats. A **habitat** is a place where an animal naturally lives and grows.

Now other animals are close to disappearing from the state. We rarely see bobcats or badgers here. Indiana bats are getting harder to find. The number of river otters living in Indiana is low.

If you travel through Indiana's lake regions, you can see many interesting birds and waterfowl. You might see a great blue heron standing near the dunes. You might find black ducks nesting. Our state bird is the cardinal, but horned owls, wild turkeys, and bluebirds also call Indiana home. Bald eagles live in Indiana, but there are few of them living here—or anywhere in the United States. Some Hoosiers are working to help the eagle population grow.

REVIEW Why are some wild animals in danger of disappearing from Indiana? **Cause and Effect**

▶ **Water pollution has become a serious danger to river otters.**

From Hogs to Ostriches

Take a tour of Indiana's farms. The animals you'll find may surprise you. Some farmers raise ostriches for their meat, eggs, and feathers. Others raise llamas for their fleece. Most farmers, however, raise hogs, beef and dairy cattle, sheep, chickens, turkeys, and ducks. Indiana is the top duck producer in the United States. Our duck farms supply almost one-third of the nation's ducks.

▶ Today there are about three people for every two hogs in Indiana.

Hogs are our most common farm animal—and one of Indiana's most valuable products. People used to allow their hogs to wander freely. The hogs ate whatever they could find. Then farmers began fencing them in and feeding them corn. By 1860, there were two hogs for every person in Indiana. In 1980, Indiana still had a hog population equal in number to its human population.

REVIEW Compare the habitats of one wild animal and one farm animal. **Compare and Contrast**

Summarize the Lesson

- Indiana has a temperate climate.
- Indiana has many natural and cultivated plants.
- Indiana has many wild animals and farm animals.

LESSON 3 · REVIEW

Check Facts and Main Idea

1. **Main Idea and Details** Use a sheet of paper. Write details to support the following main idea.

   > Indiana has a temperate climate.

   [ ] [ ] [ ]

2. Why is natural vegetation important?
3. Why did black bears and elk disappear from Indiana?
4. Name two kinds of animals that live in Indiana, and explain their importance to the state.
5. **Critical Thinking: *Analyze Information*** Why is cultivated vegetation important to Indiana?

Link to ⌘ Science

Learn About Animals Learn about an endangered or threatened animal that lives in Indiana. Draw or find a picture of that animal. Use the picture to describe the animal. Explain why it is endangered.

Chapter Summary

Main Idea and Details

On a sheet of paper, write details to support the main idea.

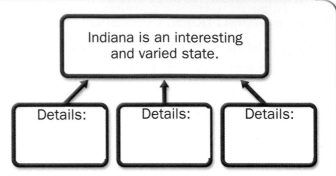

Indiana is an interesting and varied state.

Details:

Details:

Details:

Vocabulary

Match each word with the correct definition or description.

1. hemisphere (p. 11)

2. equator (p. 11)

3. glacier (p. 15)

4. natural resource (p. 25)

5. pollute (p. 28)

6. climate (p. 37)

7. temperate (p. 37)

8. habitat (p. 40)

a. a moving mass of ice

b. a half of the globe

c. established pattern of weather

d. not extreme

e. imaginary line around Earth halfway between the two poles

f. an animal's natural home

g. useful material found in nature

h. to make unclean

People and Places

Write a sentence about each of the following people and places. You may use two or more in a single sentence.

1. Gus Grissom (p. 11)

2. Lake Michigan (p. 13)

3. John Chapman (p. 27)

4. Juliet Strauss (p. 31)

5. Richard Lieber (p. 31)

6. Turkey Run State Park (p. 31)

7. Pinhook Bog (p. 38)

8. Hoosier National Forest (p. 40)

Internet Activity

To get help with vocabulary, people, and terms, select the dictionary or encyclopedia from *Social Studies Library* at **www.sfsocialstudies.com**.

Facts and Main Ideas

1. In which two hemispheres is the state of Indiana located?

2. What are two renewable resources found in Indiana?

3. What are two major crops grown in Indiana?

4. What did Richard Lieber do for the people of Indiana?

5. **Main Idea** Why is Indiana known as the "Crossroads of America"?

6. **Main Idea** Why is conservation of resources important?

7. **Main Idea** What are some unusual plants and animals found in Indiana?

8. **Critical Thinking:** *Make Inferences* Why does Indiana have such a varied landscape?

Write About Geography

1. **Write a letter** to a pen pal who has never visited Indiana. Describe some landforms and waterways to your friend.

2. **Write a poem** about all the things you find interesting or beautiful about your state. Then make a list of words describing these things. Use your lists to write a poem about Indiana.

3. **Write an advertisement** asking people to help protect the endangered animals of the state. Make a poster using drawings, slogans, or quotations from famous people to draw attention to your message.

Apply Skills

Use Elevation Maps

Look at the elevation map below. Then answer the questions.

1. How do you know that the map below is an elevation map?

2. What two features of the map help you see the different heights of places in Indiana?

3. What conclusion can you make about the physical geography of Indiana from looking at an elevation map?

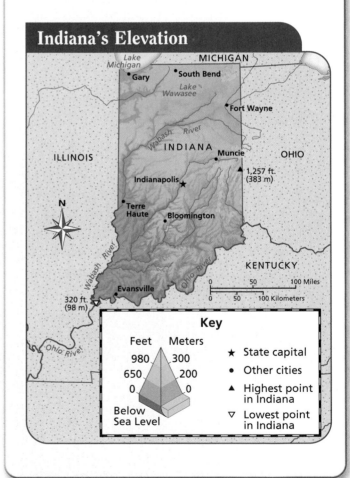

Indiana's Elevation

43

CHAPTER 2

The Natural Regions of Indiana

Lesson 1

Southern Hills and Lowlands

This region includes some of Indiana's most beautiful and varied scenery.

1

Lesson 2

Tipton Till Plain

This region has some of Indiana's most fertile farmland.

2

Lesson 3

Great Lakes Plain

In this region, you can find huge sand dunes as well as industrial areas.

3

3

2

1

NORTH
AMERICA

GREAT LAKES
PLAIN REGION

TIPTON TILL
PLAIN
REGION

UNITED STATES

SOUTHERN
HILLS AND
LOWLANDS
REGION

PACIFIC OCEAN

ATLANTIC
OCEAN

Gulf of Mexico

Why We Remember

Indiana is made up of three very different regions. Each has its own special qualities. This land has shaped the lives of all who have lived here. Where they lived influenced how they lived. Early residents settled near the Ohio River to be near transportation. Farmers discovered the rich soil of central Indiana and stayed to raise crops. Later, workers headed north to industries on Lake Michigan's shore. You may know what makes your region special. Now you will learn about the other regions.

Bloomington

Evansville

Southern Hills and Lowlands

PREVIEW

Focus on the Main Idea
The Southern Hills and
Lowlands region is located
in southern Indiana.

PLACES
Southern Hills and Lowlands
Wabash Lowland
Wyandotte Cave
Evansville
Bloomington
Jug Rock

PEOPLE
Theodore Clement Steele

VOCABULARY
silt
knob
hub
landmark
shale

You Are There

Wow! Our state is a really cool place. Now it's time to see it up close. You're going on a tour of Indiana. Grab your camera and pack your bags!

The tour starts with a visit to a limestone quarry. As you put on your hard hat and goggles, you hear blasts of explosives and the roar of machinery. Clouds of limestone dust rise into the air. You walk past huge piles of stone. The quarry guide explains that this stone will become part of a skyscraper in Asia. You think of other famous buildings made from Indiana limestone. You can hardly wait for the rest of the tour.

Summarize As you read, look for details to help you create a description that summarizes the Southern Hills and Lowlands region.

The Bounty of the Land

You already know that a landform is a natural feature on the surface of Earth. Hills, plains, and valleys are some examples of landforms. You also know that there are three main landform regions in Indiana. These are the Great Lakes Plain in the north; the Tipton Till Plain in central Indiana; and the **Southern Hills and Lowlands** in the southern part of the state. Within these major regions you can also find many variations. These landforms are what give Indiana its unique character.

The Southern Hills and Lowlands region borders the Ohio River to the south. The western part of the region borders the Wabash River. The region changes a great deal from west to east.

The Southern Hills and Lowlands region is made up of rounded hills, some forests, limestone caves, and rich, fertile lowlands. Part of the Southern Hills and Lowlands region—Brown County—has long inspired artists with its natural beauty. You will read more about some of these artists later in this book.

▶ This region of Indiana has inspired many great artists.

MAP SKILL

Southern Hills and Lowlands

▶ The borders of this region are largely created by rivers.

MAP SKILL Understand Borders *Which state borders Indiana to the south?*

REVIEW What landforms can be found in the Southern Hills and Lowlands region? ⟳ Main Idea and Details

A Land of Contrasts

The part of this region near the Wabash River is sometimes called the **Wabash Lowland.** This area of southwestern Indiana has the most fertile soil in the region. That's because silt from the Wabash River has been carried there. **Silt** is soil carried and then left behind by streams and rivers. Silt makes the soil good for farming. People sometimes call the southwest corner of the Wabash Lowland "the Pocket." It is famous for the melons grown there. Other natural resources in the area include coal and petroleum. The state's lowest point is here, at only 320 feet (98 meters) above sea level.

The area to the east of the Wabash Lowland is hilly, with sharp ridges, caves, and waterfalls. Glaciers did not flatten it, and limestone is found here. It is sometimes called the Caves and Limestone area. A "limestone belt" runs from Bloomington to the Ohio River. Towns like Bedford opened limestone quarries more than a hundred years ago.

Over time water has worn huge underground holes in the limestone, forming caves. **Wyandotte Cave,** near Leavenworth, has five levels and twenty-five miles of passages. Historians believe that people lived here in prehistoric times.

Farther east is an interesting area. A series of cone-shaped hills runs

▶ Knobs—cone-shaped hills—characterize parts of this region.

north and south through it. These hills are called **knobs.** Artists have come to this area for a long time because of its natural beauty. **Theodore Clement Steele** is a famous Indiana landscape artist. In the early twentieth century, he helped start an artists' colony in Brown County.

For the most part glaciers did not affect the Southern Hills and Lowlands. However, a glacier did move into the southeastern part of the Southern Hills and Lowlands region about 100,000 years ago. When it melted, the water formed streams. Over time, these streams eroded deep valleys in the soil leading to the Ohio River.

Some dairy farmers make their living in this area. There are also pockets of natural gas found in this corner of the state. It is sometimes called the Ancient Glacier area.

REVIEW Why is the soil in the Wabash Lowland more fertile than the soil in other areas of the Southern Hills and Lowlands region? **Cause and Effect**

▶ Indiana Memorial Union, or IMU, is a center of activity at Indiana University in Bloomington.

Major Cities

From 1853 until the 1860s, the city of **Evansville** was the southern landing point of the Wabash and Erie Canal. This canal connected Lake Erie to the Ohio River. The city is still a **hub,** or center, for business. From the mid-1800s until the 1930s, Evansville was famous for manufacturing furniture. Local forests supplied oak, cherry, walnut, and other fine hardwoods. By 1930, however, forests had been cut down. Supplies of hardwood dropped. During World War II, it was hard to get materials to make furniture. After the war, competition from furniture made in North Carolina hurt Evansville factories.

By the 1950s, many young workers joined local automobile, appliance, and plastics factories. They saw a better future in these modern industries.

Today Evansville is known as "Plastics Valley" because of the many plastics companies there. Medicines, aluminum, and food products are also made in Evansville. The city also has two universities, a museum, and a zoo.

Bloomington was founded in 1818. In 1820, Indiana University was established in the city. Today Bloomington has limestone quarries and factories that make refrigerators and electronic equipment. The city is also home to the famous Lilly Library.

REVIEW What are two major cities in the Southern Hills and Lowlands region? ⟳ **Main Idea and Details**

Natural Landmarks

A **landmark** is an object that you can notice easily on the land. It helps identify a place. Some landmarks, such as mountains, are made by nature. Other landmarks, such as buildings and bridges, are made by people.

Jug Rock in Martin County is a famous natural landmark. This huge sandstone pillar is located northwest of Shoals. It stands 60 feet high and is 15 feet wide. To the east, the Knobs form another natural landmark. These cone-shaped hills are made of shale. **Shale** is a type of rock. It is made of clay that once formed the bottom of the sea that covered this part of Indiana.

▶ Jug Rock was formed by powerful forces of nature.

REVIEW What is the difference between a landmark such as a building and a landmark such as the Knobs? **Compare and Contrast**

Summarize the Lesson

• **The Southern Hills and Lowlands region contains a variety of landforms, including rich farmland, rocky ridges, limestone caves, knobs, and deep valleys.**

• **Evansville and Bloomington are two major cities in this region.**

• **Jug Rock and the Knobs are two natural landmarks in this region.**

LESSON 1   REVIEW

Check Facts and Main Ideas

1. **Summarize** Use a sheet of paper. Write details to support the following main idea.

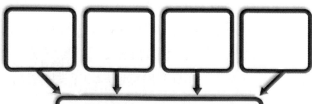

The Southern Hills and Lowlands is a region that changes from west to east.

2. Where in Indiana is the Southern Hills and Lowlands region located?

3. What are some important industries in Evansville and Bloomington?

4. Describe the Southern Hills and Lowlands region of Indiana, including natural landmarks.

5. **Critical Thinking:** *Analyze Information* Why is Jug Rock considered a landmark?

Link to ∞ Science

Use a Library or the Internet Discover how the caves in the Southern Hills and Lowlands were formed. Draw a picture that shows what you have learned.

Theodore Clement Steele *1847–1926*

When Theodore Clement Steele was five years old, a sign painter gave him some paints to use. By the time he was fourteen, his paintings were winning awards.

By 1870, Steele was supporting himself by painting portraits, or pictures of people. Later he also started painting landscapes, or scenes from nature.

In the early 1900s, artists began to gather each summer in Brown County. They found the natural beauty of the area perfect for landscape painting. In 1907, Steele and his wife moved there. Other artists followed. Steele encouraged young artists to paint pictures of the region. Steele's paintings celebrate nature. During a lecture, he told his audience:

> *"[T]here is offered to us, for our delight, this ever changing miracle of nature if we have eyes to see."*

Today painters, potters, and weavers carry on the tradition of celebrating Indiana's beauty.

BIOFACT

Steele and his wife built a house on top of a Brown County hill in 1907. They named it "The House of Singing Winds."

Learn from Biographies

What do you think Theodore Clement Steele found so interesting about painting landscapes?

For more information, go online to *Meet the People* at **www.sfsocialstudies.com**.

Tipton Till Plain

PREVIEW

Focus on the Main Idea
The rich, fertile soil of the Tipton Till Plain region is ideal for farming.

PLACES
Tipton Till Plain
Indianapolis
Muncie

VOCABULARY
market
moraine

You Are There
You've explored many interesting sites in the Southern Hills and Lowlands region. Now you head north into the Tipton Till Plain.

You start your tour in the western part of the region. Parke County is the home of Indiana's famous covered bridges. You really want to explore all thirty-three of these beautiful bridges. In Turkey Run State Park, you travel across the longest single-lane covered bridge in the world. Then you explore Leatherwood Station bridge. The bridges are beautiful, but there is a lot more to learn about the Tipton Till Plain. Let's start the rest of the tour.

Main Idea and Details As you read, pay attention to details that can help you visualize the Tipton Till Plain region.

A Rich and Fertile Land

The first thing you notice about the **Tipton Till Plain** region is how the landscape has changed. In the Southern Hills and Lowlands region, you saw hills, ridges, and valleys. Now you see farms, swaying fields of corn and soybeans, and flat, flat land. In the distance you spot long, low hills. They look like waves on a calm sea.

Even though the region is flat, the highest point in Indiana is in the Tipton Till Plain! In Wayne County near the Ohio border, a hilltop reaches 1,257 feet above sea level.

Because this region is so flat, water does not drain from the land easily. Hundreds of years ago, this region was mostly swampland and forests. People moving into the area discovered how rich and fertile the soil was and decided to use the land for farming. They drained the swamps and cleared the forests to build farms.

The soil here is the most fertile in the state because of the till that glaciers left behind. This glacial soil is a mix of gravel and clay. It is the best mix for growing crops. The agriculture belt of the Tipton Till Plain region is

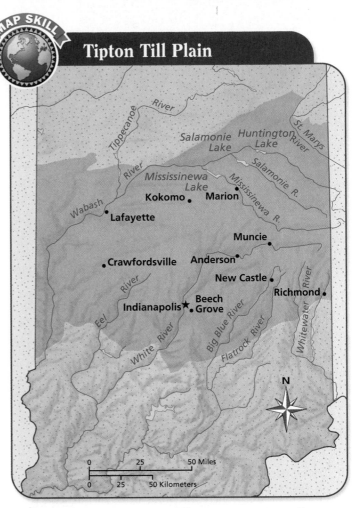

MAP SKILL Tipton Till Plain

▶ Glaciers once covered the area we now call the Tipton Till Plain.

MAP SKILL Use a Landform Map *What differences do you see between the Southern Hills and Lowlands and the Tipton Till Plain?*

dotted with large farms, fields of crops, and pens of hogs and cattle.

Indiana ranks fifth in the nation in corn production. Most of Indiana's corn is grown in this central region. Farmers here also grow soybeans, wheat, and hay. They raise hogs, cattle, and chickens. Milk and eggs are also important products of the region.

REVIEW What are the main differences between the Southern Hills and Lowlands region and the Tipton Till Plain region? **Compare and Contrast**

Major Cities

Indianapolis was founded in 1821 to be the capital of Indiana. The site of the city was chosen because of its central location. Still, it was an unusual place to locate a capital city. Unlike most major cities of the nineteenth century, Indianapolis was not near a waterway that could be used for steamboat travel. Some people even nicknamed the city "India-no-place." However, the city did grow, and the expansion of roads and railroads during the 1800s helped Indianapolis grow even larger.

Indianapolis attracted industries in the late nineteenth century because of its nearby source of natural gas. One of these industries was the automobile industry. This industry helped inspire one of Indiana's best-known events. In 1911, the Indianapolis Motor Speedway held its first 500-mile race around a 2.5-mile track. A locally made car won the race. The tradition of the annual Memorial Day Indianapolis 500 was born. Today the "Indy 500" draws drivers from all over the world, as well as more than 300,000 spectators.

In the center of Indianapolis is Monument Circle. Completed in 1901, the Soldiers' and Sailors' Monument is a famous Indianapolis landmark. It honors Hoosiers who fought in the Civil War, as well as in other wars.

Tourists who visit Indianapolis often head for its famous Children's Museum. Founded in 1925, it is the largest hands-on children's museum in the world. After visiting the museum, tourists might go to the Indianapolis Zoo. Visitors can ride camels, watch dolphins play, and see how reptiles live in the desert.

▶ **The winner at the Indy 500 is given a traditional bottle of milk at the finish line.**

▶ **Indianapolis** (*above*). In Muncie (*right*) children visit the Minnetrista Cultural Center.

Indianapolis is a hub for road, air, and train travel. The city is an important grain market. A **market** is a place where products are bought and sold. Indianapolis is a center for banks and other firms that manage money for people and businesses. The city is also an industrial center. Telephones, prescription drugs, and machinery are all manufactured here. Indianapolis is home to many colleges and universities as well.

A second city in the Tipton Till Plain region is **Muncie,** Indiana's eighth largest city. It was named for the Munsee clan of the Lenape people, who once lived in this area. Muncie is on the White River, about sixty miles northeast of Indianapolis.

Muncie became an industrial center in the late 1800s when natural gas was discovered. Industries such as the Ball brothers' glass-making factory moved to Muncie to use the natural gas. The natural gas was soon used up, but many industries stayed.

Muncie is proud of its Minnetrista Cultural Center and its Children's Museum. The Minnetrista Cultural Center shows local art and teaches about local history. The Muncie Children's Museum invites visitors to "taste, see, hear, touch, and feel" exhibits. Muncie is also home to Ball State University.

REVIEW What are the two main cities in the Tipton Till Plain region? Which city is the capital of Indiana?
↻ **Main Idea and Details**

A Flat Landscape

Someone once said that in the Tipton Till Plain region, you "may ride upon the railroad train for hours without seeing a greater elevation than a haystack or a pile of saw dust." The region has few natural landmarks because glaciers flattened the landscape here thousands of years ago. But this flatness gives the region its special character and beauty.

As the glaciers that flattened this land moved through, they left till deposits of varying heights. We call these landforms **moraines.** From a distance, they look like waves. Moraines are the only landforms that occasionally break up the flat appearance of the Tipton Till Plain. This type of formation is also known as till plain, giving the region its name.

At the far end of a glacier, the till deposit—and the moraine—is higher. These moraines are known as end moraines. As a glacier retreats, it leaves low moraines known as ground moraines. After a glacier has retreated for some time, it may pause and leave a recessional moraine.

▶ As a glacier melts, it retreats, or moves back, and leaves till deposits.

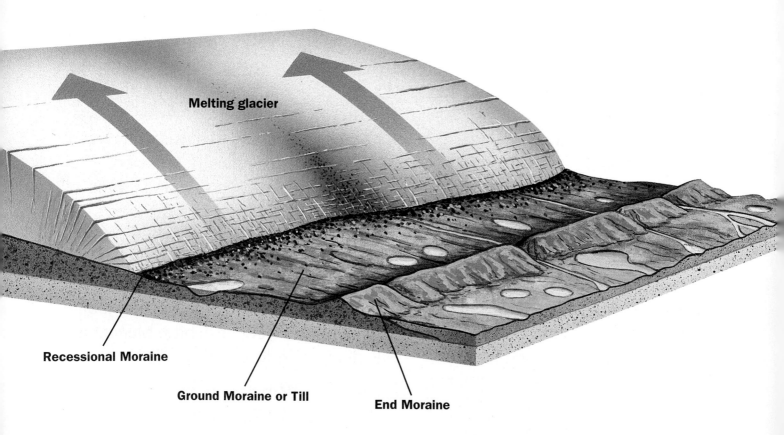

Melting glacier

Recessional Moraine

Ground Moraine or Till

End Moraine

▶ Moraines create a wavy appearance on Indiana's landscape.

You can find the highest moraines of this region near Crawfordsville. You can also find moraines near Wabash, in the eastern part of the region.

REVIEW Why is the landscape of the Tipton Till Plain region so flat? Cause and Effect

Summarize the Lesson

• The Tipton Till Plain region is made up of flat land with low, rolling hills.

• Two major cities in this region are Indianapolis and Muncie.

• The region has moraines that occasionally rise above the plain.

LESSON 2 REVIEW

Check Facts and Main Idea

1. 🔄 **Main Idea and Details** Use a sheet of paper. Write details to support the following main idea.

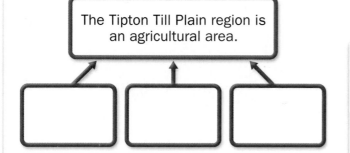

The Tipton Till Plain region is an agricultural area.

2. What happened to the forests that used to cover this region?

3. How did moraines form?

4. What attracts tourists to Indianapolis?

5. **Critical Thinking:** *Make Inferences* Why did many industries stay in Muncie even after the natural gas was used up?

Link to 🔗 Mathematics

Figure It Out Figure out how many times a car would have to go around the 2.5-mile track at the Indianapolis Motor Speedway in order to complete the Indianapolis 500 race.

Indianapolis and Madrid
Cities of Rails & Roads

A freight train loaded with electronic equipment pulls out of Indianapolis. At the same time, a high-speed passenger train pulls into the Spanish capital of Madrid. These cities are on two different continents and in two different time zones. Indianapolis is almost two-hundred years old, Madrid is centuries old. Yet they have much in common. Indianapolis is at the "Crossroads of America." Madrid is near the center of the Iberian Peninsula. Unlike many big cities, neither is located on a major waterway. So roads and railroads have been important to their growth.

▲ Cars stream into busy downtown Indianapolis.

▶ Trains bring goods to and from Indiana factories and farms.

casa de cultura

ayuntamiento

correos
telégrafos

guardia civil

biblioteca municipal

◀ Beautiful Plaza de la
Independencia in central
Madrid is busy with traffic.
Madrid sometimes has
traffic jams at 4 A.M.!

▶ High speed trains like this one provide
an alternative to driving the crowded
roads around Madrid.

LESSON 3

•Gary

Great Lakes Plain

PREVIEW

Focus on the Main Idea
The Great Lakes Plain region is largely an industrial area.

PLACES

Great Lakes Plain
Calumet
Gary
South Bend
Fort Wayne

PEOPLE

Curtis Stevens
Studebaker brothers

VOCABULARY

pipeline

You Are There
You're on the last leg of your Indiana tour now. It's time to explore the Great Lakes Plain region. Northwestern Indiana seems more crowded than most of the other areas you have visited. There are more factories and mills than in other parts of the state.

As you take pictures of the cities and towns, you think what an amazing photo journal you will have to show everyone back home! "Hmmm . . . What should I call my photo journal?" you ask yourself. But there's no time to think of that now. In the distance you see something that you just have to photograph!

Sequence As you read, note the sequence of events that helped shape the features of this region.

60

A Land of Variety

Like the Tipton Till Plain, the **Great Lakes Plain** is mostly flat. However, the hundreds of lakes and ponds in this region make it different from its neighbor to the south.

The area called the **Calumet** is located along Lake Michigan. It has more people than any other area of similar size in Indiana except the city of Indianapolis.

The Calumet did not always have lots of residents. But in 1889, the Standard Oil company came to this largely unsettled area. It laid **pipelines**—long systems of pipes for moving gas, water, or oil—from Ohio to the shores of Lake Michigan. There it built a refinery—a kind of factory for turning oil into useful products.

Other companies soon followed. Lake Michigan provided transportation and access to resources for making steel. Today this area is one of the world's great industrial centers. It has oil refineries, steel mills, and other kinds of factories.

MAP SKILL Great Lakes Plain

The area near Lake Michigan has become a center for industry.

MAP SKILL Region *How does the Great Lakes Region differ from the Tipton Till Plain?*

The Great Lakes Plain is not all industrial. The Indiana Dunes area east of the Calumet is home to the National Lakeshore and to Indiana Dunes State Park. Hundreds of lakes, including Lake Wawasee, Indiana's largest, give the Lake Country its name. Today farmers here raise soybeans, corn, chickens, and beef cattle.

REVIEW Why do so many people live in the Calumet area? **Cause and Effect**

Before the days of refrigeration, companies "harvested" ice from the lakes of the Lake Country, as shown here.

Major Cities

Gary is the state's fourth largest city. In 1905, the U.S. Steel company bought nine thousand acres of land in northwestern Indiana. Most of it was swamp and sand dunes. The company wanted to build a steel mill and a town for its workers. Huge dunes were leveled. Grass wouldn't grow in the sandy soil, so the company shipped in tons of topsoil. By 1909, the steel mill was running and Gary was a busy town.

During World War I (1914–1918) and World War II (1939–1945), Gary's African American population increased greatly. Many came to work in the mills and factories. In 1967, the people of Gary elected Richard G. Hatcher as one of the first African American mayors of a major city.

Another leader from the Calumet region is **Curtis Stevens.** A geographer studying the routes of African American settlement in Indiana, Stevens has also worked with the Boys' and Girls' Club in his hometown of Michigan City.

South Bend, in north central Indiana, is named for its location on a bend of the St. Joseph River. The city is perhaps most famous as the home of the University of Notre Dame and its "Fighting Irish" sports teams.

The **Studebaker brothers** opened a blacksmith and wagon shop in South Bend in 1852. The Union Army used Studebaker wagons during the Civil War. Pioneers used their wagons to go west. When automobiles were invented, the Studebaker brothers began making the bodies for cars. Their company continued to make cars until 1963.

Fort Wayne, on the border of the Tipton Till Plain, is Indiana's second largest city. It has been an industrial center since the Erie and Wabash Canal was built in the 1830s. Today it is a center for manufacturing and higher education. It is also the home of the Lincoln Museum.

REVIEW Who built Gary and why?
◑ **Main Idea and Details**

▶ Studebaker cars from Indiana traveled the nation's roads for much of the 1900s.

► **The dunes of Indiana are a beautiful landmark.**

Sand Dunes

The sand dunes on the shores of Lake Michigan are famous landmarks in northern Indiana. Along with hills of sand, this area also includes sandy beaches, swamps, grassy hills, and forests. Plants and grasses cover some sand dunes. These are called dead, or stabilized, dunes because they do not move. There are also live, or traveling, dunes. Wind and water cause these dunes to shift and travel. They remain bare. Plants cannot grow on them because they move too much.

Mount Baldy is a very tall dune that is always shifting and, therefore, remains bald. The highest dune, Mount Tom, is dead. It reaches 190 feet and covers 100 acres of land. Tourists visit it to see the many trees and plants that grow there.

REVIEW Why do Indiana's sand dunes attract many visitors? **Draw Conclusions**

Summarize the Lesson

• **The Great Lakes Plain region includes the Calumet, the Indiana Dunes area, and the Lake Country.**

• **Three major cities in this region are Gary, South Bend, and Fort Wayne.**

• **The Indiana Dunes are a natural landmark in this region.**

LESSON 3   REVIEW

Check Facts and Main Ideas

1. Sequence Use a sheet of paper. Write the sequence of events in the development of the Calumet area.

> Few people lived in the Calumet.
> ↓
>
> ↓
>
> ↓
>

2. What makes the Great Lakes Plain different from other natural regions of Indiana?

3. What are some of the different areas within the Great Lakes Plain region?

4. Describe the Great Lakes Plain region, including its major cities.

5. Critical Thinking: *Compare and Contrast* What are the two types of Indiana sand dunes, and how are they alike and different?

Link to ⚭ Art

Draw a Picture Illustrate the way you picture one of the places described in this lesson. Be sure to include specific details.

Make Generalizations

What? A **generalization** is a broad statement or rule that applies to many examples. Clue words such as *all, most, many, some, sometimes, usually, seldom, few,* and *generally* often tell you that a generalization is being made.

Here is an example of a generalization: *Most pizzas have cheese on them*.

Readers can make generalizations based on main ideas, details, and their own knowledge as they read.

A generalization can be valid or faulty. A valid generalization is supported by facts and examples. A faulty generalization is not supported by facts and examples.

Three Regions of Indiana

Areas	Features	Resources	Industries
Great Lakes Plain	lakes and ponds; industrial lands; on the shores of Lake Michigan; flat, swampy land; heavily populated; Indiana Dunes	corn, soybeans, chickens, cattle	farming, steel mills, oil refineries, recycling plants, cement plants
Tipton Till Plain	flat, level land; moraines; covered bridges; rich, fertile soil; farmland; large cities; manufacturing	corn, soybeans, wheat, hay, hogs, cattle, eggs, milk	farming, automotive factories, transportation, electronics industries, machine industries
Southern Hills and Lowlands	hills, valleys, lowlands, forests; hidden caves; some fertile soil near Wabash River; border is Ohio River	limestone, natural gas, coal, petroleum, corn, melons, forests	farming, mining, plastics manufacturing, transportation, electronics industries

Regions of Indiana

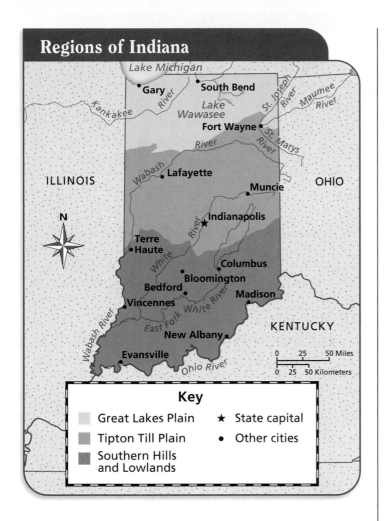

Key

- ▢ Great Lakes Plain
- ▩ Tipton Till Plain
- ▨ Southern Hills and Lowlands
- ★ State capital
- • Other cities

Why? In this chapter, you read about the three regions of Indiana. One way to understand the facts in the lesson is to make generalizations about them. Making generalizations helps you see similarities between ideas and facts that may appear unrelated at first.

How? To make a generalization, you gather and compare information about a topic. Then you bring this information together to make a general statement.

In some cases, you add your own knowledge to the information.

Suppose you wanted to make a generalization about the three regions of Indiana. First, read the table on page 64 and look at the map on this page to review and gather information about these three regions. In what ways are they similar? In what ways are they different? When you find similarities, you have the beginnings of a generalization. Before you make your generalization, be sure that you have enough facts or examples to support it. Otherwise your generalization may be faulty.

Think and Apply

1. What industry is shared by all three regions of Indiana? Give your response in the form of a generalization.

2. What generalization can you make about the major resources of all three regions?

3. Tell whether the following generalization is valid or faulty: *All three regions are about the same shape and size.* Explain your answer.

Chapter Summary

 Main Idea and Details

On a sheet of paper, list important main ideas and details about the three natural regions of Indiana.

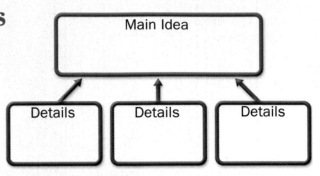

Vocabulary

On a sheet of paper, use each vocabulary word in a sentence. Give clues about the meaning of the vocabulary word in the sentence.

1. **silt** (p. 48)

2. **knob** (p. 48)

3. **hub** (p. 49)

4. **landmark** (p. 50)

5. **shale** (p. 50)

6. **market** (p. 55)

7. **moraine** (p. 56)

8. **pipeline** (p. 61)

Facts and Main Ideas

1. Why is the Tipton Till Plain region ideal for farming?

2. Name two important resources that come from the Southern Hills and Lowlands region.

3. In what region of Indiana is the Calumet area located?

4. What is the capital city of Indiana? In which region is it located?

5. **Main Idea** Describe the Southern Hills and Lowlands region.

6. **Main Idea** What are some of the attractions found in Indianapolis?

7. **Main Idea** Why do more people live in the Great Lakes Plain region than in the other regions of the state?

8. **Critical Thinking:** *Compare and Contrast* How is the Southern Hills and Lowlands region different from the Tipton Till Plain region?

Write About Geography

1. **Write a description** of the area in Indiana in which you live. Describe the natural features, interesting landmarks, and major resources and industries in your area.

2. **Write slogans** that sum up the best qualities of the three regions of Indiana. Create one brief slogan for each region.

3. **Write a paragraph** for the Indiana tourist bureau's Web site in which you persuade people to vacation in the Southern Hills and Lowlands region of Indiana.

People and Places

Match the people and places to the correct definition.

1. **Wabash Lowland** (p. 48)
2. **Theodore Clement Steele** (p. 48)
3. **Tipton Till Plain** (p. 53)
4. **Great Lakes Plain** (p. 61)
5. **Curtis Stevens** (p. 62)
6. **Studebaker brothers** (p. 62)

a. area with many lakes and ponds

b. wagon and car makers

c. area in southwest Indiana

d. geographer

e. landscape artist

f. area where soil is very fertile

Apply Skills

Make Generalizations

Look at the chart below. Answer the questions.

Four Areas of the Southern Hills and Lowlands Region			
Areas	**Features**	**Major Products**	**Industries**
Wabash Lowland	fertile soil, lowlands	melons, corn, coal, petroleum	farming, plastics, mining
Caves and Limestone	rugged hills and valleys, caves, waterfalls	limestone	mining
Knobs	forests, hills, valleys	forest products	tourism
Ancient Glacier	valleys	natural gas, dairy products	farming, gas

1. How can you use the information in this chart to make a generalization?

2. What features do the Caves and Limestone and the Knobs share?

3. Finish this generalization: Some areas of Indiana are known for their _____.

Internet Activity

To get help with vocabulary, people, and terms, select the dictionary or encyclopedia from *Social Studies Library* at **www.sfsocialstudies.com**.

Johnny Appleseed

A Tall Tale Retold by Steven Kellogg

The story that follows begins with Johnny Appleseed's journey westward.

During the next few years, John continued to move westward. Whenever he ran out of apple seeds, he hiked to the eastern cider presses to replenish his supply. Before long, John's plantings were spread across the state of Ohio.

Meanwhile, pioneer families were arriving in search of homesites and farmland. John had located his orchards on the routes he thought they'd be traveling. As he had hoped, the settlers were eager to buy his young trees. John went out of his way to lend a helping hand to his new neighbors. Often he would give his trees away. People affectionately called him Johnny Appleseed, and he began using that name.

He particularly enjoyed entertaining children with tales of his wilderness adventures and stories from the Bible.

In 1812 the British incited the Indians to join them in another war against the Americans. The settlers feared that Ohio would be invaded from Lake Erie.

It grieved Johnny that his friends were fighting each other. But when he saw the smoke of burning cabins, he ran through the night, shouting a warning at every door.

After the war, people urged Johnny to build a house and settle down. He replied that he lived like a king in his wilderness home, and he returned to the forest he loved.

During his long absences, folks enjoyed sharing their recollections of Johnny. They retold his stories and sometimes they even exaggerated them a bit.

Some recalled Johnny sleeping in a treetop hammock and chatting with the birds.

Others remembered that a rattlesnake had attacked his foot. Fortunately, Johnny's feet were as tough as elephant's hide, so the fangs didn't penetrate.

It was said that Johnny had once tended a wounded wolf and then kept him for a pet.

An old hunter swore he'd seen Johnny frolicking with a bear family.

The storytellers outdid each other with tall tales about his feats of survival in the untamed wilderness.

As the years passed, Ohio became too crowded for Johnny. He moved to the wilds of Indiana, where he continued to clear land for his orchards.

UNIT 1

Review

Test Talk

Look for key words in the question.

Main Ideas and Vocabulary

Read the passage below and use it to answer the questions that follow.

Indiana is located in the Western and Northern Hemispheres, on the continent of North America. It has a variety of landforms and waterways.

Indiana's renewable resources include forests, fertile soil, and water. Its nonrenewable resources include limestone, coal, petroleum, and natural gas. Hoosiers have a history of protecting their environment and their resources.

Indiana's climate is temperate. It usually has chilly winters and warm, humid summers.

Major Indiana crops include corn, soybeans, and wheat. Many kinds of wild animals can be found in the state. Farm animals in Indiana include hogs, cattle, and ducks.

Indiana has three natural regions. The Southern Hills and Lowlands region is made up of valleys, hills, caves, and lowlands. Evansville and Bloomington are two cities in this region.

The Tipton Till Plain region is flat with some low hills called moraines. The soil is fertile and ideal for farming. Indianapolis and Muncie are here.

The Great Lakes Plain region is mostly flat with hundreds of small lakes and ponds created by glaciers. Parts of this region are heavily industrialized. Gary, South Bend, and Fort Wayne are located in this region. The Indiana Dunes are a major landmark.

1 In this passage, landforms means
A objects made by people that are easily noticed on the land.
B rainstorms.
C floating islands of ice.
D natural features on Earth's surface.

2 According to this passage, which of these is an important Indiana resource?
A gold
B spices
C limestone
D coffee

3 Moraines are
A caves.
B storms.
C low hills.
D glaciers.

4 Where are the Indiana Dunes?
A Southern Hills and Lowlands
B Great Lakes Plain
C Wabash Lowlands
D Tipton Till Plain

Places and Vocabulary

Match each place and vocabulary word to its definition.

1. **continent** (p. 12)
2. **erosion** (p. 28)
3. **conservation** (p. 29)
4. **precipitation** (p. 37)
5. **Jug Rock** (p. 50)
6. **Gary** (p. 62)

   a. wearing away by wind or water
   b. the protection of natural resources
   c. industrial city along Lake Michigan
   d. large area of land
   e. Southern Hills and Lowlands landmark
   f. rain, sleet, and snow

Write and Share

Make a Booklet Divide into six groups, one for each lesson in Unit 1. Each student in a group should choose a different topic from the lesson to write about. Everyone in a group should write a one-page essay on his or her topic and illustrate the information. Then combine the group's information with information from other groups. Make a class booklet called "What's So Special About Indiana?" Donate the booklet to the school library.

Apply Skills

Use an Elevation Map to Describe a Journey
Study the elevation map of Indiana on page 21. Choose one city in each natural region to visit. Trace the route as you describe the elevation changes you would pass through as you drove from one city to the next.

Read on Your Own

Look for these books in the library.

UNIT 1 Project

Eye on Our Region

Take visitors on a video tour of your region of Indiana. Show what's great about it.

1 **Form** a group. Choose an interesting topic about your region of Indiana.

2 **Make** a map of your region.

3 **Make** a list of facts about your topic. Draw pictures that illustrate your facts. Write a sentence or two to describe each picture.

4 **Put** your group's pictures together. Put them in the sequence in which you will show them. Use your map as an introduction. This is your video tour to share with the class.

Internet Activity

Learn more about Indiana. Go to **www.sfsocialstudies.com/activities** and select your grade and unit.

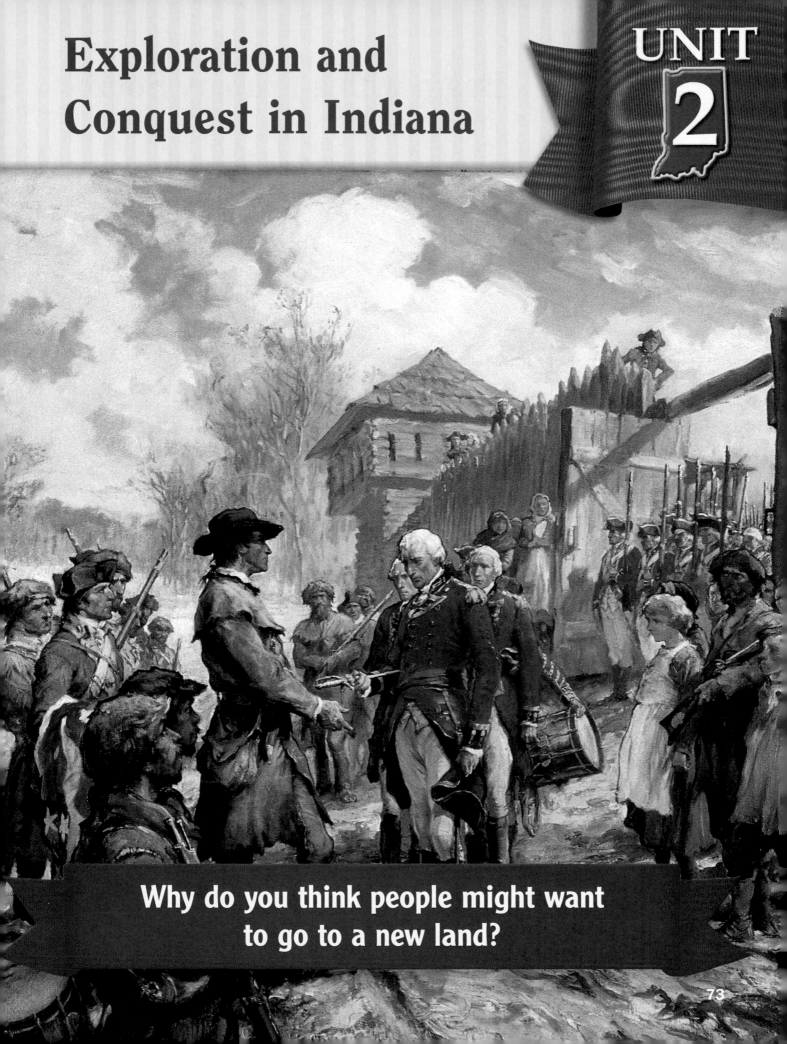

Exploration and Conquest in Indiana

UNIT

2

Why do you think people might want
to go to a new land?

1400   **1500**   **1600**

1400–1600
Mississippian people
disappear from
Indiana.

"Great things have been effected [done] by a few men well conducted...."

—letter from George Rogers Clark before his march on Vincennes, 1779

Frederick Yohn painted the British surrender in the *Fall of Fort Sackville.*

1700

1800

1679
First Europeans known to visit Indiana

1680s
New groups of American Indians begin to move into Indiana.

1754
French and Indian War begins.

1775
American Revolution begins.

1779
George Rogers Clark retakes Fort Sackville for the Americans.

Meet the People

Father Louis Hennepin

1626–c. 1701
Birthplace: Ath, Belgium
Missionary, explorer

- Traveled with La Salle as he explored the Illinois and Mississippi Rivers
- Captured by the Sioux and rescued by a French *voyageur*
- Wrote book about his adventures in North America

La Salle

1643–1687
Birthplace: Rouen, France
Explorer

- First European known to have visited present-day Indiana
- Met with American Indians in Indiana to express peace and friendship
- Claimed Mississippi River and surrounding land for France

Pontiac

c. 1720–1769
Birthplace: near present-day Detroit, Michigan
Ottawa chief

- Rebelled against British rule in the Great Lakes region
- Organized thousands of American Indians for an attack against the British
- Signed peace treaty with British to end rebellion

Françoise Outelas

1730–1801
Birthplace: near Kaskaskia
Businesswoman, homemaker

- Married to Drouet de Richerville
- Widowed young and raised three children
- Probably ran family business after her husband's death

```
1620        1640        1660        1680        1700        1720
```

1626 • Father Louis Hennepin   c.1701

1643 • La Salle   1687

Unknown

For more information, go online to *Meet the People* at **www.sfsocialstudies.com**.

Henry Hamilton

c. 1734–1796

Birthplace: Dublin, Ireland

British Army officer

- Commanded British troops at Fort Detroit during American Revolution
- Urged American Indians to attack settlers in Kentucky
- Lost Fort Sackville to American troops led by George Rogers Clark

La Demoiselle

Unknown–1752

Birthplace: possibly Kekionga

Piankashaw chief

- Began trading with British instead of French
- Started trading center at Pickawillany for trade with the British
- Killed during battle with French forces

George Rogers Clark

1752–1818

Birthplace: near Charlottesville, Virginia

Surveyor, frontiersman, military leader

- Led campaign against British in Ohio Valley
- Captured Fort Sackville from the British
- Victory considered one of the most significant events in Indiana's history

1740	1760	1780	1800	1820

La Demoiselle 1752

c. 1720 • Pontiac 1769

1730 • Francoise Outelas 1801

c. 1734 • Henry Hamilton 1796

1752 • George Rogers Clark 1818

Exploration and Conquest in Indiana

 Target Skill

Compare and Contrast

To **compare** is to tell how two or more things are alike. To **contrast** is to tell how two or more things are different.

Alike

Different

Compare: how things are alike → Contrast: how things are different

- Clue words such as *like, as,* and *also* often show comparisons.

- Clue words such as *unlike, different,* or *but* often show contrasts.

- Writers do not always use clue words. Readers may have to make comparisons and contrasts themselves.

Read the following paragraph. The sentences that include **comparisons** and **contrasts** have been highlighted.

In Unit 1, you read about the natural regions of Indiana. The Great Lakes Plain region is very flat. The Tipton Till Plain region is also very flat. The Tipton Till Plain region and the Southern Hills and Lowlands region are different from each other. The Tipton Till Plain has rich soil that is good for farming. The Southern Hills and Lowlands region has hills, forests, and valleys. It is not as good for farming.

Who Came to Indiana Long Ago?

The first people who came to the land now called Indiana lived thousands of years ago during the Ice Age. They were hunters. They hunted large animals such as giant bison. They moved from place to place, following the herds of animals.

When the Ice Age ended, some of the large animals died out. The people had to live in a different way. They now hunted smaller forest animals. The people ate fish and gathered nuts and berries from the forests. These foods became a more important part of the people's diet than they were in the past.

Eventually, the people learned to grow their own food. They still hunted, but they no longer had to follow the herds of animals. They settled into villages. They traded with other groups. They made pottery and decorated it. Later, the people lived in larger towns that were surrounded by small farming villages. They grew corn and stored it for use during the winter.

Use the reading strategy of comparing and contrasting to answer these questions.

1 In what ways were the lives of the people of Indiana during the Ice Age and after the Ice Age alike?

2 In what ways were the lives of the people of Indiana during and after the Ice Age different?

3 What clue words in the passage help you notice comparisons and contrasts?

Lesson 1

Bering Land Bridge
Hunters from Asia may have followed mammoths and other large animals into North America.

1

Lesson 2

**1680
Kekionga**
New groups of American Indians arrive in Indiana.

2

ASIA

Bering Land
Bridge

Bering Strait

NORTH
AMERICA

Kekionga

PACIFIC
OCEAN

ATLANTIC
OCEAN

SOUTH
AMERICA

Why We Remember

Today we think of ourselves as Hoosiers. But what did the first people who lived here call themselves? We will never know. These people lived some thirteen thousand years ago and did not leave written records. Objects they left behind tell about how they lived. But there is still a lot we don't know. We know more about the people who lived here three hundred years ago. Europeans who came here then wrote about what they saw. From their writings, we can learn about life in Indiana in the 1700s.

LESSON 1

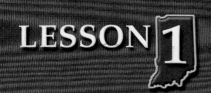

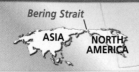

Bering Strait
ASIA
NORTH AMERICA

Humans Arrive

PREVIEW

Focus on the Main Idea
The first people to live in what is now Indiana were hunters.

PLACES
Bering Strait
Bering Land Bridge
Mounds State Park
Angel Mounds

VOCABULARY
migrate
archaeologist
prehistoric
artifact
adapt
mound
culture
government
cultural group

You Are There It is still dark out, but it is time to get up. You and the others must find the herd of bison you spotted the other day. Your families are almost out of meat, and the nuts, roots, and berries gathered by the women will not last.

You join the men and follow the trail left by the bison. Soon you catch up with them. You grip your spear and walk quietly toward the huge animals.

That evening, the group feasts. Everyone eats as much meat as they can. The rest will be dried. The women will clean the hides and make clothing from them. The animals' bones will make good tools.

Courtesy of Lubbock Lake Landmark, Museum of Texas Tech University, Lubbock, TX.

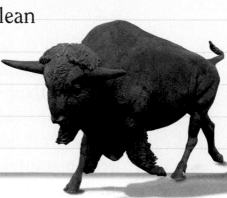

Compare and Contrast (Target Skill) Look for ways in which the lives of the earliest people were different from your own.

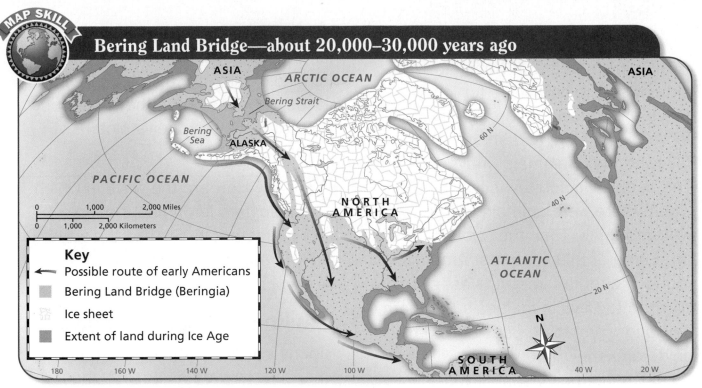

MAP SKILL
Bering Land Bridge—about 20,000–30,000 years ago

Key
← Possible route of early Americans
◾ Bering Land Bridge (Beringia)
◾ Ice sheet
◾ Extent of land during Ice Age

▶ The earliest Americans may have followed these routes.

MAP SKILL Movement *According to this map, where did the earliest Americans' routes start?*

People Arrive

Many scientists think that the first people to live in North America probably came from Asia. There are other ideas about where they came from. For example, some groups believe that people have always been here and did not come from far away. But many scientists believe that they came during the last Ice Age—20,000 to 30,000 years ago. This was a period when ice and snow covered much of North America.

Today the **Bering Strait** is a waterway. It separates Asia and North America. You can see it on the map. During the Ice Age, some seas froze, and the water level of the strait dropped. The land underneath was exposed. This land formed a bridge connecting the continents of Asia and North America. Herds of animals, such as giant bison, moved onto the bridge to graze on grass growing there. Many scientists believe that as animals moved across the land bridge, people followed them.

The first people to cross the **Bering Land Bridge** stayed in the north. Gradually, however, their descendants— their children, grandchildren, and so on—moved south. These early Americans migrated. To **migrate** means to move from place to place. They moved throughout North and South America. Today we usually call their descendants American Indians.

REVIEW What was the area around the Bering Strait like during the last Ice Age? What is it like today?
🔄 Compare and Contrast

83

People on the Move

The early settlers of North America did not stay in one place for long. Since they depended on wild animals for food, clothing, and shelter, they followed these animals' movements. The people would stay for a while where there were animals to hunt and water to drink. Then they would move on. Some of these earliest Americans found shelter in caves. Caves, such as Wyandotte Cave in Indiana's Southern Lowlands, protected people from the cold, rain, snow, and wind.

Finding out how people lived thousands of years ago is a hard job. An **archaeologist** is a scientist who studies the lives and cultures of people from the past. Some archaeologists study prehistoric people. **Prehistoric** times are the times before writing was used in a given area. Archaeologists look for clues that tell them when and how early people lived. Many of these clues are found underground. Scientists dig carefully in places where they think these people might have lived. They look for pottery, weapons, and other objects. An object made by human beings is called an **artifact.** Archaeologists may also look for burial places or bones. Then they use these clues to piece together a picture of life long ago.

REVIEW How are the ways in which archaeologists learn about people from prehistoric times like the ways you find out about a new topic?
➲ **Compare and Contrast**

Earliest People of Indiana

Many scientists think that the first Americans arrived in Indiana about 13,000 years ago. These people were hunters and gatherers. They gathered nuts, berries, and other foods. They probably ate fish and shellfish from the rivers. They lived in small groups and moved often to follow the animals they hunted. The hunters used spears with sharp points that they made from chipped stone.

▶ Woolly mammoths were a food source for people.

They used them to kill deer, elk, and larger animals such as giant bison, mammoths, and mastodons.

Around 8000 B.C.E., the Ice Age ended. As the climate grew warmer, large animals such as the giant bison and mammoth died out. Trees and plants grew. The people had to **adapt**, or change their ways, to suit the new environment.

People living after the Ice Age were still hunters and gatherers. However, they began to stay in one place for longer periods of time. They set up a main camp with smaller camps nearby for hunting and gathering food. Their population grew. Small groups settled throughout Indiana—many along the Ohio, Wabash, and White Rivers. They used tools to fish. Mussels—a kind of shellfish—were probably a main part of their diet. Archaeologists have uncovered huge mounds of mussel shells in southwestern Indiana along these rivers. As the environment changed, so did the animals the people relied on for food. Now they began to hunt smaller animals. As a result, their hunting tools changed too.

REVIEW What characteristics do the people living during and after the Ice Age share? How do these two groups differ? ↺ **Compare and Contrast**

▶ **Mounds at Mounds State Park**

The Woodland Indians

Around 1000 B.C.E., American Indians in the Indiana area learned how to grow their own food. Now they didn't have to rely only on hunting, fishing, and gathering for all their food. They did not have to follow herds of animals. They did not have to depend on river mussels.

The first Indiana farmers grew corn, squash, and sunflowers—native plants they learned how to grow as crops. Their diet improved and became more varied. Today we call these people Woodland Indians.

Growing their own food changed the way people lived. Farming also took less time than hunting for food. This left the Woodland Indians with more time for other activities. They began making pottery to store food. Their pottery was thick and heavy. They learned how to bake it in a fire to harden it. They decorated the pottery by pressing cords into the clay before it was fired, or baked.

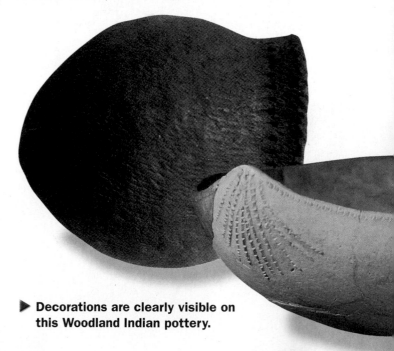

▶ **Decorations are clearly visible on this Woodland Indian pottery.**

Farming also allowed the Woodland Indians to settle permanently in one place. They built log tombs for their dead. These tombs were burned and then covered with earth. The result was a **mound,** or pile of earth. In fact, the Woodland Indians are sometimes called "Mound Builders." Some of their mounds were about 70 feet high. In **Mounds State Park,** near Anderson, there are ten of these mounds. The largest is 6 feet high and 360 feet across.

Woodland Indians may have had a trading system that covered much of North America. In some of their burial mounds, scientists have found things that came from areas far away from Indiana. They have found grizzly bear teeth from the Rocky Mountains. They have also found shells from the Gulf of Mexico and copper from the upper Great Lakes region. The Woodland Indians may have traded their pottery for these things.

REVIEW How were the lives of the Woodland Indians similar to and different from the lives of earlier peoples? ⟳ **Compare and Contrast**

© A. Goodall/Glenn A. Black Laboratory of Archaeology / Indiana University

MAP SKILL

Mounds in Indiana

Lake Michigan

MICHIGAN

•Gary   •South Bend

Kankakee River   Maumee River

Fort Wayne

Wabash River

ILLINOIS

Muncie   OHIO

■ Mounds State Park

N

Indianapolis ★

•Terre Haute

White River   East Fork White River

0   25   50 Miles
0   25   50 Kilometers

Ohio River

•Evansville ■   **Key**
Angel Mounds   — Mound site
State Historic Site   KENTUCKY

▶ **American Indians built mounds throughout Indiana.**

MAP SKILL Place *Describe how the area around what is now Evansville must have looked at the time of the Woodland Indians.*

The Mississippian People

About a thousand years ago, a new group of American Indians settled along the Ohio River in southwest Indiana. They are called the Mississippians. Their way of living, or **culture,** was similar to that of other people living along the Mississippi River. They were different from peoples who came before them, though. The Mississippians lived in towns, some with several thousand people. They had a **government** —a system for making rules and decisions. And they had an organized religion. The Mississippian people formed a **cultural group,** or a group of people who share a common language, religion, and customs.

Around Mississippian towns were smaller farming villages. Although the people still hunted for meat, they were farmers. They grew corn, squash, melons, beans, and tobacco. They also made tools from stone, bones, and shells. Like the Woodland Indians, the Mississippians traded with other groups.

The Mississippians were also mound builders. They built their mounds as

▶ **Mississippian mounds were platforms for important buildings.**

platforms for important buildings. The buildings were usually rectangular. The walls were made of wooden stakes and twigs covered with mud. The homes of powerful people were closer to the center of the village.

The largest Mississippian town in Indiana was located at **Angel Mounds,** near where Evansville is today. The town existed between 1050 and 1400. It had a population of about one thousand people. It was a center for trade, politics, and religion. In the town center, there was a 44-foot-high mound. The building on top was probably the town's most important building. It may have been the chief's home. Other buildings sat on smaller mounds.

▶ **Mississippian people built buildings like this one.**

There was an open plaza near the town center. A thick wall of wooden stakes around the town kept out animals and attackers.

What happened to the town at Angel Mounds and to Indiana's Mississippian people? This is one of history's mysteries. Sometime during the 1400s, the town was abandoned. Archaeologists can only guess why. Maybe the local wood supply ran out. Maybe the soil was no longer good for growing crops. There may have been trouble among the town's leaders. Archaeologists know only that all the Mississippians had disappeared from Indiana before the first Europeans arrived in the 1600s.

REVIEW Both the Woodland people and the Mississippian people built mounds. How were these mounds different? ⮌ **Compare and Contrast**

Summarize the Lesson

- **20,000–30,000 years ago** The first people arrived in North America.
- **13,000 years ago** The first people arrived in Indiana.
- **3,000 years ago** People in Indiana began growing their own food.
- **400–600 years ago** Mississippian people disappeared from Indiana.

LESSON 1 REVIEW

Check Facts and Main Ideas

1. ⮌ **Compare and Contrast** On a sheet of paper, contrast the lives of people in Indiana during the Ice Age with the lives of people in Indiana one thousand years ago.

Ice Age	1,000 Years Ago
moved from place to place	settled in villages

2. How do many scientists think the first people probably came to North America?
3. Why did people follow herds of animals?
4. How did early Americans change over time?
5. **Critical Thinking: *Analyze Information*** Why did growing their own food allow people to stay in one place for longer periods of time?

Link to 🔗 Science

Other Theories A theory is an idea that is supported by many pieces of information. That people came to the Americas over a land bridge is a theory. However, some scientists think that people came to the Americas by different routes. New discoveries are being made at sites in North and South America. Research this topic. Find out what other theories are being developed.

Recognize Fact and Opinion

What? A **fact** is a statement that can be proven to be true. For example, if you say that Ohio is east of Indiana, you can prove your statement by looking at a map. An **opinion** is how a person thinks or feels about something. Opinions cannot be proven. Words such as *think, believe, feel, best,* and *worst* sometimes signal that a statement is an opinion.

Opinions on a thing or idea may vary from person to person. Your opinion may depend on your own experience and on what you have learned from other people. For example, the two postcards on this page show places in Indiana. That is a fact. Which place do you think is more beautiful? The answer to that question is an opinion.

Why? Facts and opinions are often mixed together. Television, magazines, and Web sites often combine fact and opinion. In order to understand what you are reading or hearing, you need to be able to tell the difference between a fact and an opinion.

Indianapolis, Indiana

Lake Michigan

MI

Gary •South Bend

Kankakee River

Fort Wayne •

N

River

Wabash River

OHIO

INDIANA

Area of Inset

ILLINOIS

★Indianapolis

Terre Haute •

White River

0   25   50 Miles
0   25   50 Kilometers

• Bloomington

KENTUCKY

Ohio River

0   5 Miles
0   5 Kilometers

• Evansville

Indianapolis

■ Indianapolis Motor Speedway

White River

Key
★ State capital
• Other cities

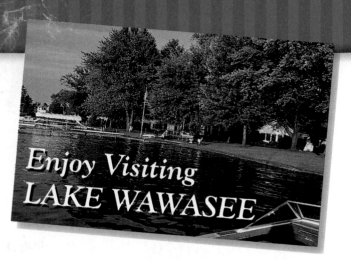

Enjoy Visiting
LAKE WAWASEE

How? To decide whether a statement is a fact or an opinion, you need to ask yourself if you can prove the statement. Look for proof in resources such as an encyclopedia, a dictionary, an atlas, a textbook, or an almanac. If you can find proof in these sources that the statement is true, then it is a fact.

Look at the postcard of Lake Wawasee. Think about the following statement: "Lake Wawasee is the best place to vacation in Indiana." Is this statement a fact or an opinion? Can you find proof of this statement in a resource mentioned earlier? No, you can't. It is an opinion.

Now think about this statement: "Lake Wawasee is the largest lake in Indiana." Can you find proof of this statement? Yes, you can because it is a fact.

Think and Apply

Use the map to help you decide which of the following are facts and which are opinions. After each statement, write **O** for opinion or **F** for fact.

1. The Indianapolis Motor Speedway is located near Indianapolis.

2. Indianapolis is the nicest city in the state of Indiana.

3. To reach Evansville, travel south and west from Indianapolis.

91

Kekionga

1400   1500   1600   1700

1400–1600
Mississippian people disappear from Indiana.

1680s
New groups of American Indians begin to move into Indiana area.

PREVIEW

Focus on the Main Idea
After 1680, new groups of American Indians migrated to and settled in what is now Indiana.

PLACES
Kekionga

VOCABULARY
clan
band
confederacy
colonist
wigwam
longhouse
sachem

TERMS
Iroquois Confederacy

New Groups

You Are There The spring sun is hot as you bend over to plant squash seeds. This new land that your family has moved to is good for farming. Many other people have moved into the area too.

You can hardly wait for the day's work to end. During the winter, you live in a hunting camp with your family. When spring comes, all the families move back to the village. You can see your friends and tell stories about your winter adventures. Some people might even come to visit for a few days and share their stories.

© Detroit Institute of Arts

Compare and Contrast Think about how the lives of the American Indian groups you read about are alike and different.

The People of Indiana in the 1600s

Beginning around 1680, new American Indian groups began to settle in what would one day be Indiana. The Miami were the largest of these. This group included the Miami and their relatives, the Wea (WEE ah) and the Piankashaw (pee AHNGK ah shah). Members of the Miami group spread out over much of the area, as you can see on the map at the right.

The Potawatomi (paht uh WHAT uh mee) were the other large and important group in the area at this time. They settled in the northern area and along Lake Michigan. Other groups, such as the Shawnee, also settled here. The Lenape migrated to Indiana and settled near the White River.

A group called the Kickapoo settled in what would become western Indiana. They made their home along the Wabash in the fertile Tipton Till Plain.

REVIEW What were the two largest American Indian groups in Indiana after 1680? **Main Idea and Details**

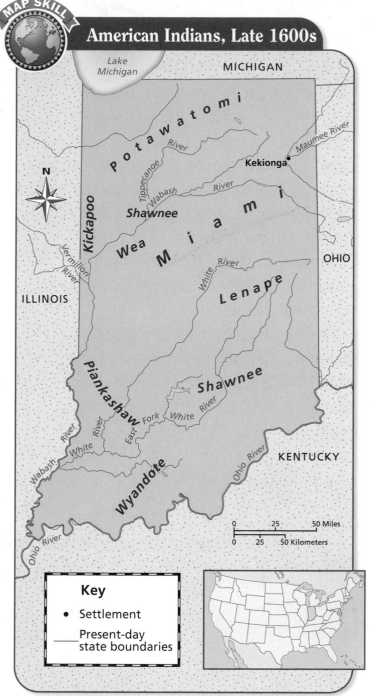

MAP SKILL

American Indians, Late 1600s

Key
- Settlement
— Present-day state boundaries

▶ American Indian groups settled in various parts of what would later become Indiana.

MAP SKILL Location *In what part of Indiana did the Potawatomi live?*

▶ Containers and a pipe made by American Indians

93

Why They Came to Indiana

New groups of American Indians migrated to Indiana during the late 1600s and early 1700s. They came from different areas of North America. Some came to establish farms. Others came because they had been forced from their homelands. They were pushed from their homes by more powerful American Indian groups and later by Europeans.

The two most powerful groups in Indiana migrated from the north and west. The Potawatomi came to northern Indiana from what is now Wisconsin and Michigan. The Miami and their **clan** members, or related groups, came from the areas that are now Wisconsin, Illinois, and Iowa. Bands of Miami families settled throughout Indiana. A **band** is a small group. They were hunters and farmers. Indiana's thick forests, rich soil, and plentiful water provided all they needed to live.

Other groups settled in Indiana because they had been forced from their homelands—some by the **Iroquois Confederacy**. A **confederacy** is a group of people or smaller groups joined together for a common purpose. The Iroquois Confederacy was made up of several groups. They shared a similar culture and language. The Iroquois lived in what is now Pennsylvania, New York, and parts of Canada.

The Iroquois were warriors. For men, respect was earned on the battlefield.

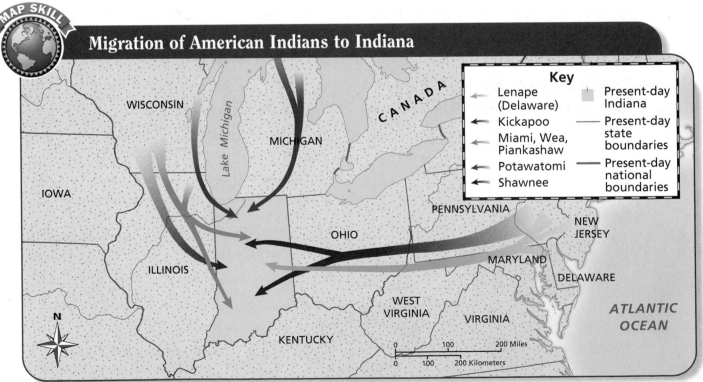

Migration of American Indians to Indiana

Key

- Lenape (Delaware)
- Kickapoo
- Miami, Wea, Piankashaw
- Potawatomi
- Shawnee
- Present-day Indiana
- Present-day state boundaries
- Present-day national boundaries

WISCONSIN • MICHIGAN • CANADA • IOWA • Lake Michigan • PENNSYLVANIA • OHIO • NEW JERSEY • ILLINOIS • MARYLAND • DELAWARE • WEST VIRGINIA • VIRGINIA • ATLANTIC OCEAN • KENTUCKY

N

0 100 200 Miles
0 100 200 Kilometers

▶ American Indians migrated to what we now call Indiana for a variety of reasons.

MAP SKILL Trace Movement on Maps *From which present-day states did American Indians migrate to Indiana?*

Other smaller, less powerful American Indian groups could not stand up to the Iroquois. Eventually, the Iroquois helped drive the Shawnee, the Lenape, and the Kickapoo from their homelands.

REVIEW Why did new groups of American Indians come to the Indiana area during the 1600s? **Cause and Effect**

A New Threat from Europe

The Iroquois were not alone in forcing less powerful nations off their land. European colonists also did this. A **colonist** is a person who settles a new country but is still ruled by his or her home country. European colonists took over lands that American Indians had lived on for centuries. Sometimes the colonists forced them off the land. Other times they bought the land from American Indians, who then moved west.

The Lenape originally lived along the Atlantic Ocean, from what is now the state of Delaware to Long Island in New York. Their friendliness to the early colonists in the area did not spare them from trouble with the Europeans. By 1690, the Lenape had been forced off their own land by European colonists and onto Iroquois land. To escape the Iroquois, the Lenape began moving west. Some of them eventually reached Indiana. Some stayed, while others kept moving farther west.

The Shawnee were driven off their land in what is now Ohio, West

► Iroquois warriors drove other groups from their lands.

Virginia, and Pennsylvania by the Iroquois. Some migrated to Indiana's northern region, near the Maumee River. About fifty years later, most Shawnee left and moved west too.

The Kickapoo were fierce warriors who lived in what is now Ohio, Michigan, and Wisconsin. Sometimes their battles took them as far as what is now Alabama, New York, and Mexico. In the 1640s, the Kickapoo fought the Iroquois. The Iroquois forced them south into what is now Illinois and western Indiana. The Kickapoo did not stay in Indiana for long, however. They fought Europeans moving onto their land and lost. They migrated south and west. Most went to what is now Kansas, Oklahoma, and Texas.

REVIEW Why did the Shawnee, Lenape, and Kickapoo migrate to the land we call Indiana? **Summarize**

FACT FILE

American Indian Names and Languages

You have learned where the American Indians settled in the land that became Indiana. Now look at the chart below to learn more about their names. Most of the peoples were known by several different names, each with a special meaning.

American Indians					
Most Common Name	Comes From	Meaning	Other Traditional Names	Meaning	Language
Miami	Algonquian name *Oumani*	"people of the peninsula"	Twightwee, Beaver People	"the call of the crane"	Algonquian
Potawatomi	Algonquian word *potawatimink*	"people of the place of fire" and "keepers of the sacred fire"	Nishanabek or Anishinabe	"people"	Algonquian
Kickapoo	Algonquian word *Kiwegapawa*	"he stands about" or "he moves about"	Auyax, Hecahpo, Higabu, Ikadu, Tekapu		Algonquian
Delaware	named this by Europeans	named for the area in which they lived	Lenape	"original people," "true men," or "grandfathers"	Algonquian
Shawnee	Algonquian word *shawun*	"southerner"	Shawano, Ani-Sawanugi		Algonquian

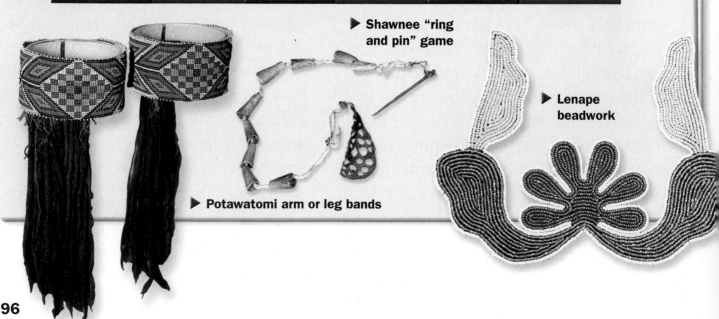

▶ Shawnee "ring and pin" game

▶ Lenape beadwork

▶ Potawatomi arm or leg bands

96

American Indian Life

The American Indian groups who lived in the Indiana area during the 1600s and 1700s had many things in common. They shared a language called Algonquian, or Algonkian. They were farmers and hunters. The men hunted and trapped animals and taught the boys how to do the same. The women and girls planted and harvested the crops. They gathered nuts, berries, and other foods such as seeds to eat during the long winters. They sewed clothing from the skins of animals.

Many American Indians lived in villages during the summer. Large families, including grandparents, aunts, uncles, parents, and children, often lived together. The Miami home was called a wigwam. A **wigwam** was a round house built from young, flexible trees. The trees were cut, then stood upright in a circle of holes and tied together at the top. The sides were then covered with bark or mats that could be rolled up and down. Potawatomi homes were usually large and rectangular.

After the harvest, villages divided into small family groups. Each group moved into different hunting camps for the winter. Villages did this because each area could provide only enough hunting for a small group.

Respecting the land was an important part of Potawatomi and Miami culture. They used its natural resources, but only what they needed. They also shared a love of telling stories, drumming, and dancing.

REVIEW How was life different in the winter and summer? ↻ **Compare and Contrast**

▶ Wigwam

Miami and Potawatomi Communities

Many American Indian villages also had larger community buildings that were used for meetings and ceremonies.

Each Miami village had a council with an elected chief. During times of war, a war chief was elected. This chief had to be brave and know how to prepare for war.

Each Potawatomi village was independent. No single leader spoke for the whole group. But during a war, one war chief was often in charge of several villages.

Both the Miami and Potawatomi were religious. The Miami believed in one powerful god served by several lesser gods. They also believed in another life that began after death. The Potawatomi had special groups that performed ceremonies when the village was threatened by outsiders or illness.

The main Miami settlement in Indiana was at **Kekionga** (kek ee AHNG guh), on the Maumee River. This area is now downtown Fort Wayne. Representatives from Miami villages gathered there for meetings.

The Miami traded with other villages and with early French traders. The French got furs from the Miami and gave them pots and beads in return.

REVIEW Who was the leader of the Potawatomi group? **Main Idea and Details**

Lenape, Shawnee, and Kickapoo Life

The Lenape, Shawnee, and Kickapoo in Indiana were farmers and hunters. Like the Miami and the Potawatomi, they lived in villages during the summer and in camps in winter.

The Lenape lived in large family groups in **longhouses.** These large, rectangular houses were built of trees and covered with bark. Each longhouse had a **sachem** (SAY chem), or chief, who was also a member of the village council. This council governed the community. The oldest woman of the family chose or dismissed the sachem.

The Shawnee title of *chief* was usually passed down from father to son. But special Shawnee war chiefs were chosen for their bravery and war skills. The Shawnee celebrated the planting and harvest seasons with ceremonies and dances.

While the Kickapoo had much in common with their neighbors, they

▶ **A longhouse had places to sleep and store things.**

98

had some differences too. They were among the first American Indians in the area to hunt with horses. They learned how to use horses for hunting from American Indians on the plains to the west. Horses were brought to America by Europeans.

The Kickapoo fought very hard to keep their culture from being changed by Europeans. They rarely allowed traders into their villages.

REVIEW How was the sachem chosen for a Lenape longhouse? How did a person become the chief of a Shawnee village? ⟳ **Compare and Contrast**

Summarize the Lesson

- New groups of American Indians moved into the land we now call Indiana after 1680.
- Some American Indians migrated to this area looking for good farmland and hunting grounds. Others came because they had been forced off their land by the Iroquois or by Europeans.
- The various American Indian groups in this area shared ways of life.

LESSON 2   REVIEW

Check Facts and Main Ideas

1. ⟳ **Compare and Contrast** On a sheet of paper, fill in the ways in which the Miami and Lenape were alike and different.

Alike	Different
Both hunters and farmers	The Miami
	The Lenape

2. Name the largest and most powerful American Indian groups in the Indiana area after 1680.

3. Where did these major groups live before migrating to Indiana?

4. What did the Miami and the Potawatomi have in common?

5. **Critical Thinking:** *Cause and Effect* Why did the Miami and other American Indians migrate to the Indiana area?

Link to 🔗 **Art**

A Day in the Life of a Miami Village Draw a picture of daily life in a Miami village. Include wigwams, people working and playing, and other details you choose.

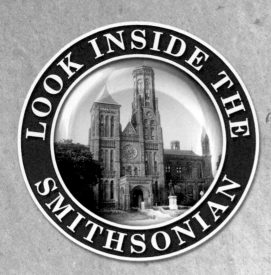

LOOK INSIDE THE SMITHSONIAN

American Indian Artifacts

By the time Europeans began exploring the Americas, North America had been home to many different groups of American Indians for thousands of years. The artifacts on this page represent some of the work of American Indians from areas throughout North America.

Pawnee War Bonnet
The war bonnet is a symbol of honor and achievement for the American Indians who lived on North America's Great Plains. This war bonnet is made of the much-prized tail-feathers of the golden eagle.

Beaded Pouch
This pouch may have been used for carrying small items of food or other goods on a journey. Either the Seminole, from Florida, or the Creek, from Oklahoma, made this pouch.

Alibamu Ornaments
This set of silver ornaments was made to be worn as a breastplate or necklace. It is from the Alibamu, or Alabama, Indians. Today, the Alabama are part of the Alabama-Coushatta of Texas.

Lakota Cradleboard
Lakota parents wrapped their babies in blankets and placed them in cradleboards such as this one. Worn on a parent's back, the cradleboard was a way to carry a baby and to allow the baby to see the world from a grown-up's point of view.

Child's Shirt
This shirt of animal hide, beads, and wool was part of the clothing of an Absaroke (Crow) child. The Absaroke are Plains Indians who once lived throughout the northern Great Plains.

Comanche Parfleche Case
Parfleche is a sturdy type of rawhide used to make shields and carrying cases. This parfleche case may have been used to store feathers, religious items, or other possessions.

Navajo Blanket
The Navajo live in the Southwestern region of the United States. Some Navajo are expert weavers. They spin and weave the wool of their sheep into patterned blankets.

Artifacts are from the Smithsonian Institution.

1000 B.C.E.   500 B.C.E.

1000 B.C.E.
Woodland Indians
in Indiana grew
their own food.

Chapter Summary

Target Skill

Compare and Contrast

On a sheet of paper, fill in the ways in which the Miami and Mississippian people were alike and different.

Alike

Both hunters and farmers

Different

Miami:

Mississippian:

Places and Terms

List three important facts about each of the following places and terms.

1. **Bering Strait** (p. 83)
2. **Bering Land Bridge** (p. 83)
3. **Mounds State Park** (p. 87)
4. **Angel Mounds** (p. 88)
5. **Iroquois Confederacy** (p. 94)
6. **Kekionga** (p. 98)

Vocabulary

Complete each sentence with the correct word from the box.

migrate (p. 83)	**band** (p. 94)
adapt (p. 85)	**wigwam** (p. 97)
culture (p. 88)	

1. The Miami used young trees to build a _____.

2. The Mississippian way of life, or _____, was very different from that of the people who came before them.

3. People have to _____ to new conditions in order to survive.

4. American Indians often traveled in _____, or small groups of families.

5. Groups of American Indians had to _____ into Indiana from the east.

Facts and Main Ideas

1 How do many scientists think people came from Asia to North America thousands of years ago?

2 How did the end of the Ice Age affect the people living then?

3 What two American Indian groups built mounds?

4 **Time Line** How much time passed between the arrival of the Mississippian people in the Indiana area and their complete disappearance?

5 **Main Idea** What did the American Indians who settled in the Indiana area after 1680 have in common?

6 **Main Idea** In what two ways did American Indians change over time?

7 **Main Idea** Why did new groups of American Indians start moving into the Indiana area after 1680?

8 **Critical Thinking:** *Make Inferences* Why do you think the various American Indian groups in the Indiana area had so many ways of life in common?

Write About History

1 **Write a paragraph** about a Kickapoo girl or boy who is learning how to farm or hunt.

2 **Write a set of instructions** that tell how to build a wigwam. Be sure to tell what kinds of trees to use.

3 **Write an essay** describing which group of American Indians you would most like to have lived with in Indiana. Explain.

Apply Skills

Identify Fact and Opinion

Use the map on page 91 to help you decide whether the following statements are fact or opinion.

1 The Ohio River flows near Evansville.

2 Bloomington is in the most beautiful part of Indiana.

3 South Bend and Gary are both in northern Indiana.

Internet Activity

To get help with vocabulary, people, and terms, select the dictionary or encyclopedia from *Social Studies Library* at **www.sfsocialstudies.com**.

Lesson 1

1608
New France
France establishes New France in North America.

1

Lesson 2

1763
Fort Detroit
Chief Pontiac rebels against the British in what is today the state of Michigan.

2

Lesson 3

1779
Vincennes
George Rogers Clark marches on the British Fort Sackville.

3

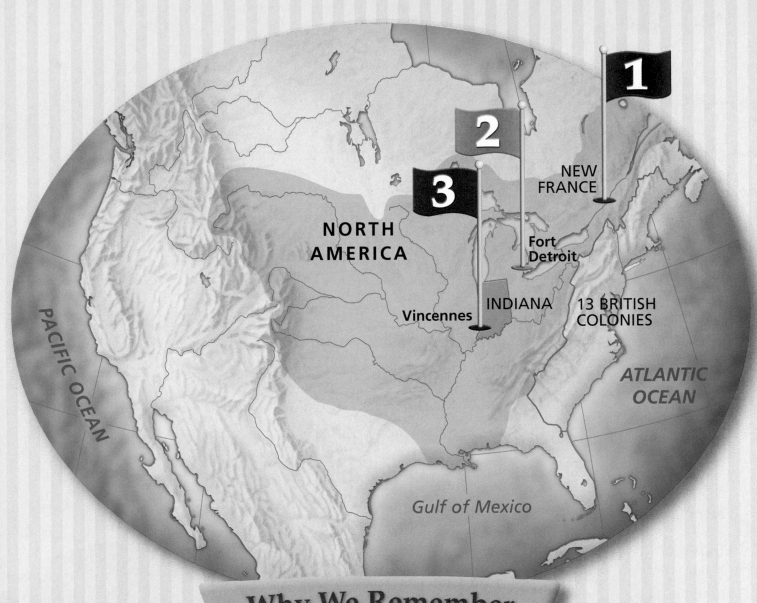

Why We Remember

About four hundred years ago, Europeans began arriving in North America. French explorers and missionaries were among the first. The British set up colonies. They were looking for a better life, as well as riches. Soon Britain and France went to war over who would control the land. The British won, but peace did not last. In 1775, the colonies rebelled against Britain. American Indians fought the takeover of their lands as well. Before long, the war reached the territory that is now Indiana.

NEW FRANCE

| 1660 | 1680 | 1700 | 1720 |

1673
Marquette and Jolliet explore the Mississippi.

1682
La Salle claims Mississippi River and its valley for France.

1704–1732
France builds forts along Wabash and Maumee Rivers.

PREVIEW

Focus on the Main Idea
The first Europeans to arrive in Indiana were French traders who lived peacefully among the American Indians.

PLACES
New France
Fort Ouiatenon
Fort Miami
Fort Vincennes

PEOPLE
Father Jacques Marquette
Louis Jolliet
René-Robert Cavelier, Sieur de La Salle
Father Louis Hennepin

VOCABULARY
colony
voyageur
stockade

The French

You Are There
You and your family live in New France. Your father is a French fur trader, called a *voyageur* (vwah yah ZHUR). He was born in Europe and came to New France hoping to become rich.

Today you and your mother are going to visit her family. They live in a small village several miles away. Together you decide what gifts to take. You choose beads and toys for your cousins. Your mother takes spices and metal cooking pots for your aunts.

You can't wait to get to the village and play with your cousins!

Summarize As you read the lesson, note information you can use to create a summary of the French in North America in the 1600s.

106

▶ A French artist depicted the French arrival in the St. Lawrence River area.

Europeans in North America

During the 1500s and 1600s, Europeans began arriving in North America. Many of them were English, French, Spanish, and Dutch. They left their homes for many reasons. Some were explorers looking for a new trade route to Asia through North America. Others had heard tales of great wealth to be found on the continent. Some left their homes looking for religious freedom.

Early in the 1500s, the Spanish arrived in the southern part of North America. They claimed the area they named Florida for Spain in 1513. They also claimed the land we now call Mexico. Soon the Spanish had claimed more large areas in southern North America. Look at the map on page 108 to see the land claimed by Spain during the 1500s and 1600s.

The English and French were not far behind the Spanish in claiming land in North America. In 1607, the English established their first settlement in Jamestown, Virginia. In 1620, the Pilgrims arrived to settle the Plymouth Colony in Massachusetts.

In 1609, Henry Hudson sailed up the river that would come to have his name. He was an Englishman, but he was sailing for the Dutch. The Dutch claimed lands that are now New York and New Jersey. At about the same time, French people were settling around the St. Lawrence River in what is now Canada. They called this area **New France.** Later, they started to explore south of the Great Lakes.

REVIEW Compare the reasons some Europeans came to North America in the 1600s. ⟳ **Compare and Contrast**

The French in North America

By 1608, many French people had settled in Canada, in what is now Quebec. You can see on the map that they claimed large areas around the St. Lawrence River. They set up colonies there. A **colony** is an area claimed, settled, and governed by another country. The French colonists called their land New France. French explorers, missionaries, and traders set off to explore the Great Lakes, the Mississippi River, and as far south as the Gulf of Mexico.

French traders met different groups of American Indians on their travels, including those in Indiana. The traders, called **voyageurs**, soon made deals with American Indians. They brought them European goods. These included cloth, jewelry, tools, weapons, spices, salt, blankets, metal cooking pots, dishes, candles, and tea. In return, the Potawatomi, Miami, and other American Indian groups provided the French with valuable furs.

The fur trade at this time was very important. In Europe, fur was in great demand. Men and women both wore clothing trimmed with fur. Beaver fur was especially valuable. Felt hats were the latest style. Felt made from beaver fur lasted for years. The best skins were those that American Indians had treated in a special way. They slept on the skins for a year. By that time, the outer coat of coarse,

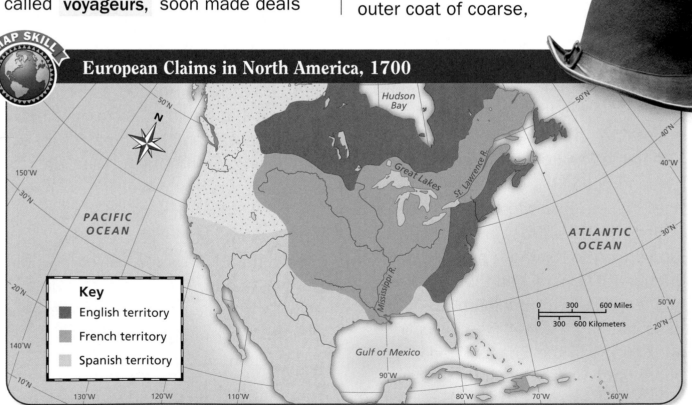

MAP SKILL

European Claims in North America, 1700

Hudson Bay

PACIFIC OCEAN

Great Lakes

St. Lawrence R.

ATLANTIC OCEAN

Mississippi R.

Key

■ English territory

■ French territory

□ Spanish territory

Gulf of Mexico

0   300   600 Miles
0   300   600 Kilometers

▶ The French, English, and Spanish all claimed large areas in North America in the 1600s.

MAP SKILL Understand Cardinal Directions *Which European country claimed land both north and east of the French?*

▶ **American Indians make a deal with a fur trader.**

reddish hairs had worn off. Underneath was the valuable soft, gray coat of fur.

Trade with the French changed the lives of the American Indians in a number of ways. Many American Indians came to rely on the goods they got from the French. In order to have furs to trade, men began hunting animals for their fur instead of their meat. Animals that had once been a source of food started to disappear as more and more were killed for their skins. Some people had to leave their homes in order to find new sources of meat. Various groups fought as they competed for trading areas.

For hundreds of years, only the chiefs and councilors held power over the people of various groups. Now, the French had power too, because they had goods that American Indians wanted. This upset relationships within and between groups.

Although trading became important to many American Indians, most remained farmers. They still relied on the crops they grew for their food and on the grain they stored to support them through the long, cold winters.

The French brought two other things that would change American Indian life forever. Catholic missionaries tried to change the American Indians' religions. The French also carried European diseases, such as smallpox and measles. American Indians had never been exposed to these diseases which killed many people. As their populations shrank, American Indians found it harder to defend their lands and their way of life.

REVIEW How did the way American Indians hunted change after they began trading with Europeans?
↻ **Compare and Contrast**

The French in Indiana

Once the French had settled in the St. Lawrence Valley in what is now Canada, they became curious about the lands around them. **Father Jacques Marquette** arrived in North America in 1666. He visited the western Great Lakes. Then he met **Louis Jolliet,** another French explorer. In 1673, Marquette joined Jolliet to explore the Mississippi River. They wanted to find out whether the great river flowed into the Gulf of Mexico or into the Pacific Ocean. The men and their crew reached the Mississippi from Lake Michigan a month later. They traveled south on the Mississippi. They never reached the Gulf of Mexico, but they decided that the Mississippi must flow into it. Then they began their journey back to New France. Some people think that Marquette may have been the first European to set foot in the land we now call Indiana. Unfortunately, most records of the journey were lost, and Father Marquette died on his way back to New France.

Several years later, another Frenchman was inspired by the tale of Marquette and Jolliet's journey. **René-Robert Cavelier** (kah vul YAY), **Sieur** (syur) **de La Salle,** had arrived in New France in 1666. He dreamed of claiming an empire for France. In 1679, he left New France to explore the Mississippi River and to claim land for France. La Salle and his men traveled along the Great Lakes to the southern end of Lake Michigan.

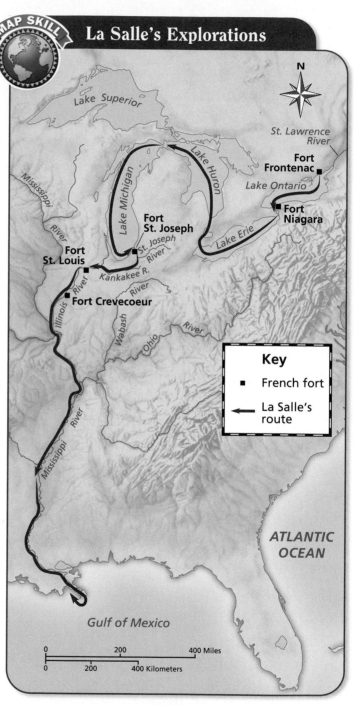

La Salle's Explorations

MAP SKILL

Key
- ■ French fort
- ← La Salle's route

▶ La Salle set off to explore the Mississippi River area in 1679.

MAP SKILL Trace Movement on Maps
On which bodies of water did La Salle travel?

Although Marquette may have visited the land we now call Indiana, La Salle was the first European known to have done so. Of this land, La Salle wrote, "Those lands surpass all others in everything." He wanted to find land for French settlement.

He also wanted to set up a trading pact with American Indians in the area. In 1681, he met with the chiefs of the Miami and the Illinois. They met at the south bend of the St. Joseph River, where South Bend is now located. La Salle promised peace to these chiefs. The meeting took place under a large oak tree called the Council Oak. This tree stood in South Bend for another 310 years. It survived until 1991, when it was finally struck down by a storm. Hennepin's record of this journey is the first known written history of the region.

▶ La Salle (*above*) and Hennepin explored much of the Midwest.

From this point, they followed the St. Joseph River and carried their canoes over land to the Kankakee River. They then paddled down the Illinois River to the Mississippi River.

In February 1680, three men left the larger group in order to explore the Illinois River. One of the men, **Father Louis Hennepin,** kept a diary of the journey and later published it. It told of their daily lives and of the things they learned on the journey.

La Salle and the remaining men reached the Gulf of Mexico. In April 1682, La Salle claimed the Mississippi River and its huge valley for France. He named the area Louisiana in honor of Louis XIV, King of France.

REVIEW Place the following events in the order that they happened. *Sequence*

1. Father Hennepin left the main group to explore the Illinois River.
2. Father Marquette and Louis Jolliet explored the Mississippi River.
3. La Salle claimed the Mississippi River and its valley for France.

French Forts

The French soon realized the value of the lands along the Wabash and Maumee Rivers. Furs were the greatest source of wealth in New France. The French wanted to keep the British from the fur trade. They also wanted to protect their water route between the Great Lakes and the Mississippi River from the British. In order to do this, the French built three forts between 1704 and 1732.

Fort Ouiatenon (wee AHT uh nahn) was near present-day Lafayette, in the middle of Wea land. The French hoped this fort would strengthen ties with the Wea and the Miami. At Kekionga, the traditional meeting place of the Miami, the French built Fort St. Philippe. Later it was rebuilt as **Fort Miami.** Then the French built **Fort Vincennes** on the lower Wabash. High fences called **stockades** protected these forts from attack.

REVIEW Why did the French decide to build forts? **Cause and Effect**

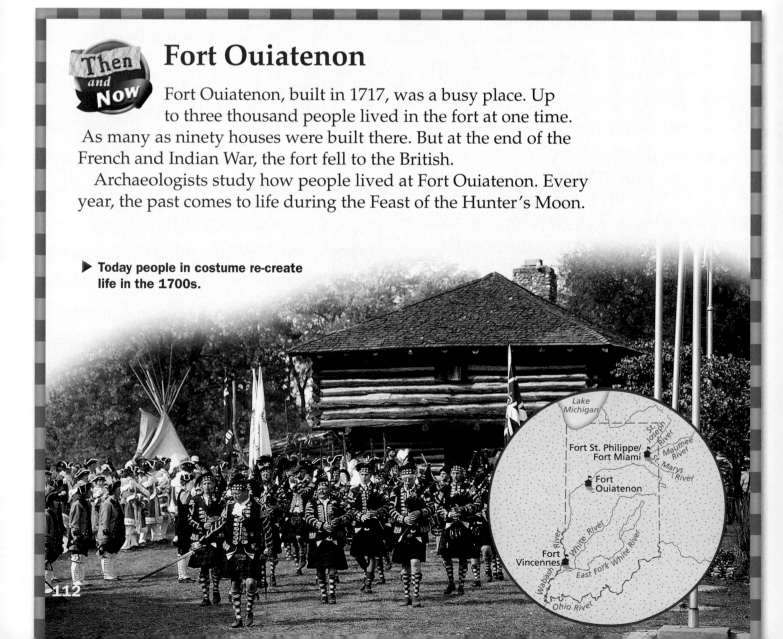

Fort Ouiatenon

Fort Ouiatenon, built in 1717, was a busy place. Up to three thousand people lived in the fort at one time. As many as ninety houses were built there. But at the end of the French and Indian War, the fort fell to the British.

Archaeologists study how people lived at Fort Ouiatenon. Every year, the past comes to life during the Feast of the Hunter's Moon.

▶ Today people in costume re-create life in the 1700s.

Map Adventure

Exploring Indiana and the Mississippi

You have been invited to travel with La Salle as he sets out from New France to explore the Mississippi River.

1. You have just traveled up across Lake Huron. Look at the route planned on your map. Which Great Lake will you travel on next?

2. Next, you need to reach the St. Joseph River. In which direction should you travel on Lake Michigan?

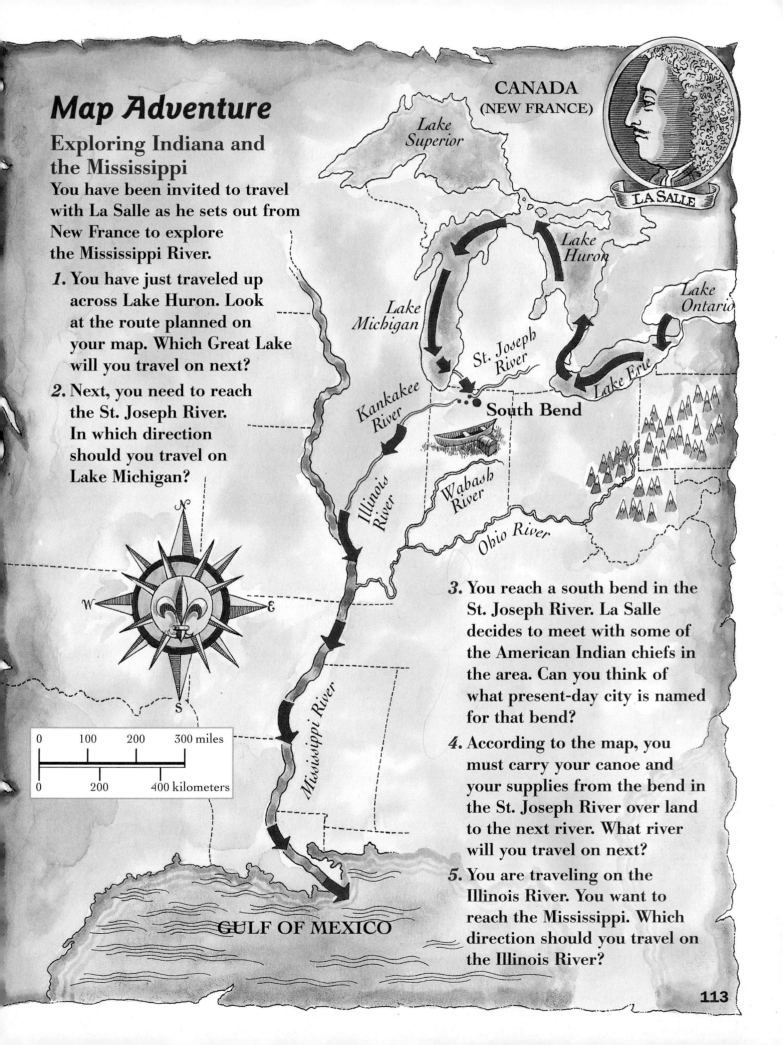

CANADA (NEW FRANCE)

LA SALLE

Lake Superior

Lake Huron

Lake Michigan

Lake Ontario

Lake Erie

St. Joseph River

Kankakee River

South Bend

Wabash River

Illinois River

Ohio River

Mississippi River

GULF OF MEXICO

0 100 200 300 miles

0 200 400 kilometers

3. You reach a south bend in the St. Joseph River. La Salle decides to meet with some of the American Indian chiefs in the area. Can you think of what present-day city is named for that bend?

4. According to the map, you must carry your canoe and your supplies from the bend in the St. Joseph River over land to the next river. What river will you travel on next?

5. You are traveling on the Illinois River. You want to reach the Mississippi. Which direction should you travel on the Illinois River?

113

The French and the American Indians

French traders and hunters in Indiana lived in peace with the American Indians. Many Frenchmen adopted their ways. Some married American Indian women. The French did not try to force the American Indians off their land. The fur trade was important to France, so they remained friendly.

The British also wanted to trade with American Indians for furs. This made them rivals of the French. During the mid-1700s, American Indians found themselves caught between the two powerful European countries as both fought to control American Indian lands. Because their relationship was good, most American Indians sided with the French.

REVIEW How did the French treat the American Indians? **Main Idea and Details**

Summarize the Lesson

- **1600s** Europeans claimed land in North America and set up colonies.
- **1673–1682** French explorers traveled the Mississippi River and claimed land for France.
- **1704–1732** French built three forts along the Wabash and Maumee.

LESSON 1   REVIEW

Check Facts and Main Ideas

1. Summarize On a sheet of paper, write down information to support the summary given.

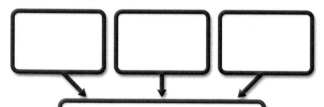

The French had a big impact on the American Indians in North America.

2. Which European countries sent colonists to North America?

3. What different things did Europeans hope to find in North America?

4. Why did the French set up forts along the Wabash and Maumee Rivers?

5. Critical Thinking: *Draw Conclusions* How did European goods change the daily lives of American Indians?

Link to ──∞── Art

Trading Poster Make a poster to illustrate the goods the French and American Indians traded with each other. When possible, use different items to represent each kind of trade item. For example, use beads to represent jewelry.

René-Robert Cavelier, Sieur de La Salle *1643–1687*

La Salle was born in Rouen, France. While studying to be a priest, he found himself longing for a life of adventure. At twenty-two, he sailed for New France. La Salle knew it would be easier to make friends with the American Indians if he could speak their languages. So he learned eight different ones.

The governor of New France called La Salle

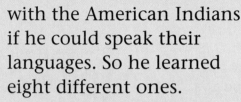

BIOFACT

The Seneca taught La Salle how to survive a long march on foot with only a small bag of grain and the animals he could catch.

"... a man of intelligence and ability, more capable than anybody else I know here to accomplish every kind of enterprise and discovery. ..."

La Salle explored the land that would become Indiana and Illinois. In 1682, he claimed the Mississippi River and its valley for France. Two years later, La Salle set out to enter the Mississippi from the Gulf of Mexico. But the expedition was a disaster. When the ships reached the Gulf of Mexico, La Salle could not find the entrance to the Mississippi. The group wound up in present-day Texas, where a few of his men mutinied and killed him.

Learn from Biographies

How did La Salle's ability to speak so many languages help him?

For more information, go online to *Meet the People* at **www.sfsocialstudies.com.**

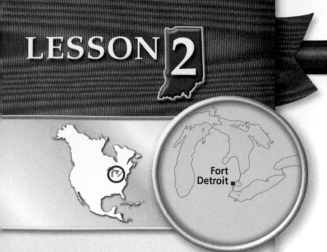

LESSON 2

1600   1700   1800

1607
English settle at Jamestown.

1747
Miami settle Pickawillany.

1754–1763
French and British fight the French and Indian War.

1763
French and British sign the Peace of Paris.

Fort Detroit

PREVIEW

Focus on the Main Idea
Both the French and the British wanted to control the land and resources of Indiana and the area around it.

PLACES
Roanoke Island
Jamestown
Pickawillany
Fort Detroit

PEOPLE
Chief La Demoiselle
Pontiac

VOCABULARY
ally
rebellion
proclamation

EVENTS
French and Indian War

The British

You Are There
You're busy making barrels in your father's shop. You have to pay attention and do a careful job. These barrels will carry food and supplies across the ocean to North America.

It seems that everyone in London is talking about the voyage. A hundred people will be sailing next month. No one really knows what they will find. They must be very brave. You can't even imagine leaving England!

Now you hear your father talking to the sailors who have just come into the shop. You can make out words like "gold" and "treasure." But your father pokes his head in when he hears your hammer stop and tells you to get back to work.

Compare and Contrast As you read, contrast how the British and the French treated the American Indians.

The English in North America

During much of the 1500s, the English watched as their rival Spain grew wealthy from its North American colonies. But by the late 1500s, England had decided to set up its own permanent colonies in North America. Colonies would provide resources for England—and opportunities for English people. Sir Walter Raleigh organized one of the first attempts. In 1585, he sent English settlers to **Roanoke Island** off the coast of present-day North Carolina. This settlement lasted only a year. In 1587, English settlers tried to form another colony on Roanoke Island under Governor John White. After arriving at the island, White had to sail back to England for supplies. When he returned in 1590, the colony had disappeared. No one has ever discovered what happened to the settlers.

In 1607, England finally settled its first successful, permanent colony. It was located in **Jamestown,** in present-day Virginia. Some of those who left their homes in England sailed for the new colony hoping to find quick wealth. Others wanted to claim land for England in order to limit Spain's power in North America. Some saw a chance to own large areas of land and be more independent.

The Jamestown colony was followed by other English colonies on the East Coast of America. But the English did not stop there. As you will read, they were exploring and trading with American Indians in the Indiana area by the 1700s.

REVIEW How were the Roanoke Island and Jamestown colonies alike? How were they different? ↩ **Compare and Contrast**

▶ **John White found only a tree carving at Roanoke Island.**

The British in Indiana

The French generally treated the American Indians as equal partners, showing respect for their traditions. The English—who became part of Great Britain in 1707—were different. They showed little respect for American Indian traditions. Their goal was to claim land.

The British knew that one great source of wealth in North America was furs. By the 1740s, British traders had moved west. They wanted to trade with the American Indians in the Indiana area who had, so far, only traded with the French. Of course, the French did not want this to happen.

But the French had problems because of a war in Europe. They had trouble getting the goods they needed to trade for furs. British traders, on the other hand, could get goods quickly because British ships were not involved in a war. Their goods were often cheaper and of better quality.

These goods tempted many American Indians. In 1747, a Piankashaw chief named **Chief La Demoiselle** (duh mwa ZEL) left Kekionga and set up a new village called **Pickawillany** (pik ah WIL ah nee). It was in what is now Ohio, closer to the British traders. Other Miami followed. Soon, Pickawillany rivaled Kekionga as a trading center. The American Indians at Pickawillany signed a treaty of trade and friendship with the British.

This treaty was a threat to the French. It weakened their control of the fur trade and threatened their trade route between Canada and Louisiana.

REVIEW Why did some American Indians prefer to trade with the British? **Main Idea and Details**

MAP SKILL

French Trade Routes

Key
- British
- Spanish
- French
- ← French trade route

Hudson Bay

Disputed

Great Lakes

St. Lawrence River

Kekionga

Wabash River

Pickawillany

Ohio R.

Disputed

Mississippi River

ATLANTIC OCEAN

Gulf of Mexico

PACIFIC OCEAN

0   500   1,000 Miles

0   500   1,000 Kilometers

▶ Trade between American Indians and British at Pickawillany threatened the French.

MAP SKILL Observe Change Through Maps
Why would it be easier to trade with the British from Pickawillany than from Kekionga?

The French and Indian War

The British continued to trade with the Miami at Pickawillany. The French saw their control of the fur trade slipping away. Finally, they took action against the British and Miami. The French destroyed Pickawillany. They killed Chief La Demoiselle and at least one British trader. The Miami were forced to return to their old villages.

The French won the battle, but they were losing control in the Ohio River Valley. They tried to strengthen their hold by building new forts along the Ohio River. In 1754, war broke out between the French and British. The **French and Indian War** lasted for nine years.

At first, it seemed as if France would win the war. Many American Indian groups, such as the Potawatomi, fought on the French side. For the first four years, these allies won many victories. An **ally** is a partner or supporter. But the war turned against the French and their American Indian allies by the end of 1757. France was running out of

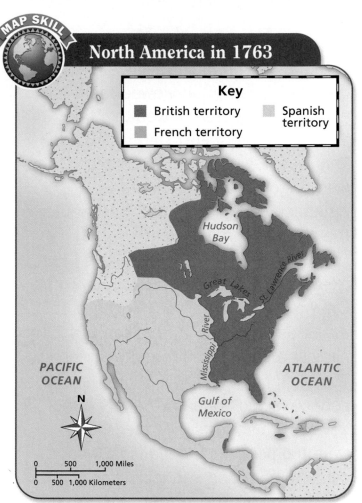

North America in 1763

Key

■ British territory

■ French territory

■ Spanish territory

Hudson Bay

Great Lakes

St. Lawrence River

Mississippi River

PACIFIC OCEAN

N

ATLANTIC OCEAN

Gulf of Mexico

0   500   1,000 Miles

0   500 1,000 Kilometers

▶ European land claims in North America changed after the French and Indian War.

MAP SKILL Observe Change Through Maps
Which European country lost the most land as a result of the French and Indian War?

money and supplies. The British had plenty of both.

The British won the war in 1763. Both sides signed a treaty called the Peace of Paris. France lost most of its claims in North America—all of Canada and all lands east of the Mississippi. The map above shows European claims in North America after the French and Indian War.

REVIEW List events leading up to the French and Indian War in order. Sequence

▶ A battle scene from the French and Indian War

Pontiac's War

The American Indians' lives had changed. The British viewed them mainly as a source of wealth. The British captured **Fort Detroit** in 1760. This was in what is now Michigan. They wanted to build settlements on American Indian land, and they wanted the American Indians out.

American Indians resented this treatment. **Pontiac** (PAHN tee ak), an Ottawa chief, led a **rebellion** against the British in 1763. A rebellion is a fight against a government or other authority. The Miami, Potawatomi, Shawnee, and Lenape joined Pontiac. They captured several British forts. But the British were too powerful. Pontiac lost what came to be called Pontiac's War.

Now, the British wanted peace and the American Indians' goodwill. They issued a **proclamation**—an official announcement. The Proclamation of 1763 closed land west of the Appalachian Mountains to British settlers. But settlers ignored this law. By the 1770s, many had crossed the Appalachians and forced American Indians out.

REVIEW Why did American Indians resent the British? **Main Idea and Details**

Summarize the Lesson

- **1607** English settled Jamestown.
- **1747** Miami settled Pickawillany.
- **1754–1763** French and Indian War
- **1763** Peace of Paris
- **1763** Pontiac's War began

LESSON 2 REVIEW

Check Facts and Main Ideas

1. ⟳ **Compare and Contrast** On a sheet of paper, contrast how the French and the British treated American Indians.

French	British
gave gifts to American Indians	

2. What were English colonists hoping to find in North America?

3. Why did some American Indians prefer to trade with the British?

4. What was one cause of the French and Indian War?

5. **Critical Thinking:** *Draw Conclusions* Why did Pontiac lead a war against the British?

Link to 🔗 Writing

Write a Paragraph Work in a small group. In your library, look for more information about how the British tried to colonize lands west of the Appalachians. Then, with your group, write a paragraph explaining the British point of view about their land claims in the West. Why did they think they had the right to claim the land? Why didn't they want the American Indians to stay on the land?

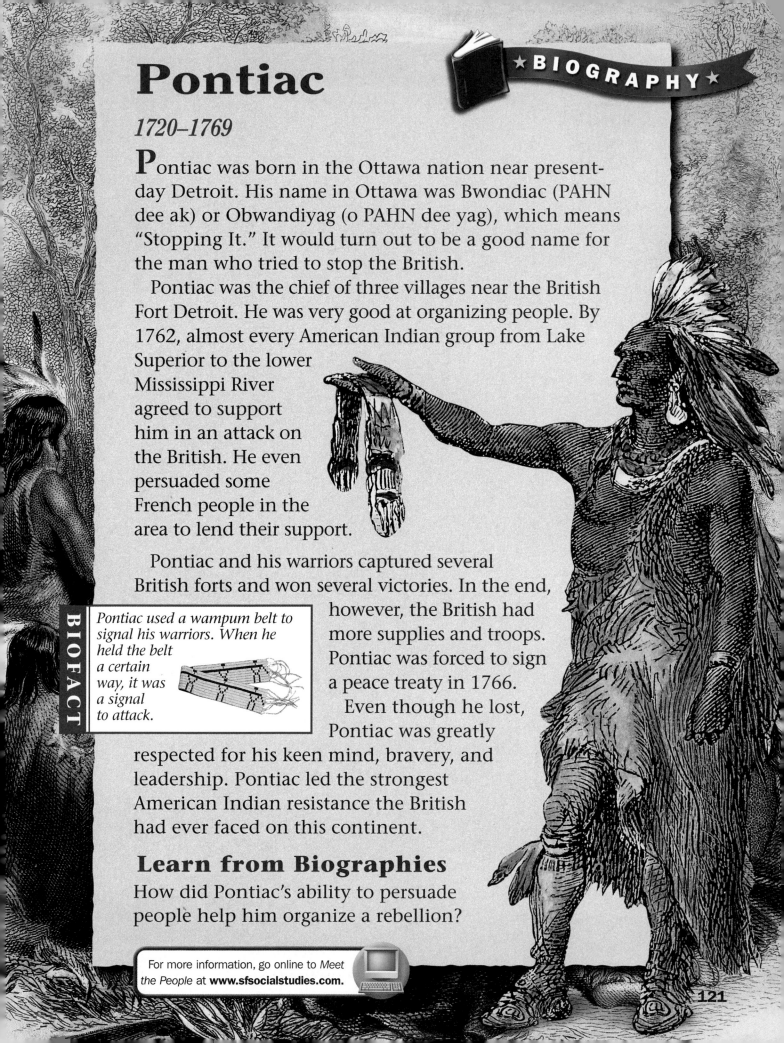

Pontiac

1720–1769

Pontiac was born in the Ottawa nation near present-day Detroit. His name in Ottawa was Bwondiac (PAHN dee ak) or Obwandiyag (o PAHN dee yag), which means "Stopping It." It would turn out to be a good name for the man who tried to stop the British.

Pontiac was the chief of three villages near the British Fort Detroit. He was very good at organizing people. By 1762, almost every American Indian group from Lake Superior to the lower Mississippi River agreed to support him in an attack on the British. He even persuaded some French people in the area to lend their support.

Pontiac and his warriors captured several British forts and won several victories. In the end, however, the British had more supplies and troops. Pontiac was forced to sign a peace treaty in 1766.

Even though he lost, Pontiac was greatly respected for his keen mind, bravery, and leadership. Pontiac led the strongest American Indian resistance the British had ever faced on this continent.

BIOFACT
Pontiac used a wampum belt to signal his warriors. When he held the belt a certain way, it was a signal to attack.

Learn from Biographies
How did Pontiac's ability to persuade people help him organize a rebellion?

For more information, go online to *Meet the People* at **www.sfsocialstudies.com**.

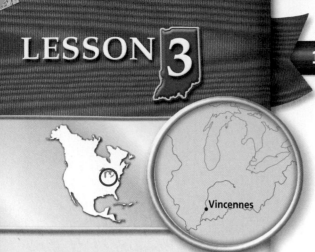
1770   1780

1773
Boston
Tea Party

1776
Declaration of
Independence
is signed.

1779
George Rogers
Clark takes Fort
Sackville for the
second time.

1781
Cornwallis
surrenders
at Yorktown.

Vincennes

The American Revolution

You Are There It is really unfair! Imagine the British army telling you that you have to house and feed the soldiers in your own homes!

Those soldiers have your mother working from morning till night. "Make me a cup of tea, please, Mistress Squires," says one of them.

At least he is polite. The other British soldier is rude. He leaves his things all over the house. And he always takes the biggest helping at supper.

Everyone is tired of how the British treat the colonists. Some say there will be a war. You hope not. But it certainly would be nice to have your house to yourselves again.

Sequence As you read, note the sequence of events in North America after 1763.

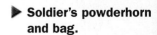

▶ Soldier's powderhorn and bag.

Revolution in the Colonies

Before 1763, the British let their colonies in North America take care of themselves. People living in the colonies had a great deal of control over their government and their lives. However, the French and Indian War had been expensive. Great Britain now owed a lot of money. The British wanted the colonists to help pay these costs. They began taxing the colonists to raise money to pay their debts. Great Britain passed the Stamp Act—a tax on legal papers, licenses, and newspapers. The British also passed the Quartering Act. This law said that the colonists had to let British soldiers stay in their homes. They also had to provide them with food and other supplies. This saved the British government a lot of money. It also showed the colonists who was in charge.

Many colonists thought these new laws were unfair. They didn't want British soldiers living in their houses. They were already angry that land in the West had been closed to settlers. Now they had to pay high taxes too. They had to pay even though they did not have any representatives in the British government. Many colonists were beginning to feel that Great Britain had gone too far.

The colonies began to protest against the new taxes. Their protests worked. By 1770, Great Britain had

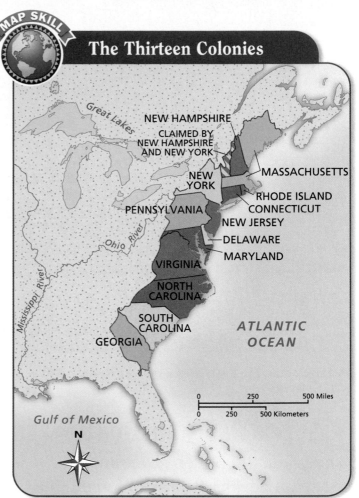

MAP SKILL The Thirteen Colonies

► **By 1770, many colonists wanted independence from Britain.**

MAP SKILL Use a Map *Name the thirteen colonies.*

repealed, or canceled, the most unpopular taxes. But the colonists no longer trusted their British rulers. Most colonists didn't want a break with Great Britain. They wanted to be loyal to Great Britain and the king, but they wanted more rights. Other colonists wanted to break all ties with Great Britain. They wanted independence.

REVIEW How did Great Britain's attitude toward the colonies in North America change after 1763?
 Compare and Contrast

▶ **The Boston Tea Party was a protest against British policies.**

A Tea Party in Boston

In 1773, the British government passed a new law. This law forced the colonists to buy tea only from Britain. Then the British put a tax on tea. Some colonists were furious! A group of Boston citizens took action. Some dressed as American Indians and sneaked onto the British ships in Boston Harbor. They threw 342 boxes of British tea into the water. This event became known as the **Boston Tea Party.** The British government reacted quickly. It closed Boston's port and outlawed meetings. It sent more troops to the city. A British military commander became governor of Massachusetts. More and more colonists began to believe that the colonies should be independent from Great Britain.

The first battles of the American Revolution were fought at **Lexington** and **Concord,** Massachusetts, in April of 1775. In July 1776, the Continental Congress, a meeting of colonial leaders, met in Philadelphia, Pennsylvania. On July 4, they signed the **Declaration of Independence,** written largely by Thomas Jefferson. It said that the American colonies were "free and independent states." The signers of the Declaration knew that they had to unite all thirteen colonies if they were to succeed. John Adams was a representative to the Continental Congress. He wrote that uniting the colonies was "a singular example in the history of mankind. Thirteen clocks were made to strike together."

REVIEW Why do you think some colonists chose to dump British tea into Boston Harbor? **Draw Conclusions**

The Revolution in Indiana

The American Revolution began in the East in 1775. For several years, it had little effect on the West, including Indiana. The Proclamation of 1763 had closed Western lands to settlers. But some people made their way to what is now Kentucky. Most of them came from Virginia and North Carolina.

After the French and Indian War, the British abandoned their forts in Indiana. They took little interest

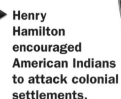

▶ Henry Hamilton encouraged American Indians to attack colonial settlements.

in their lands there. However, as the American Revolution raged, both the British and the colonists realized that the American Indians in the West could be valuable allies. When war finally reached the West, it was a battle for control of the land and of the American Indians.

The British established a base at Fort Detroit under the command of Lieutenant Governor **Henry Hamilton**. Hamilton met with the Miami and Potawatomi, dressed in American Indian clothing. He sang their war song and gave them food, weapons, and supplies. Then he urged them to attack colonial settlements in the Kentucky area. He told them that if the colonists won the war, they would take all the American Indians' land. His tactics worked. The Miami and Potawatomi began attacking colonial settlements. Hamilton became one of the most hated figures of the war for many colonists.

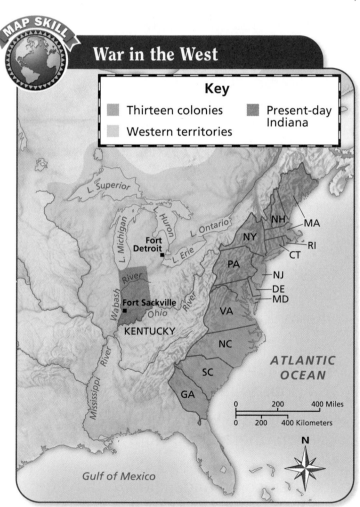

MAP SKILL

War in the West

Key
- ▨ Thirteen colonies
- ▨ Western territories
- ▨ Present-day Indiana

L. Superior
L. Michigan
L. Huron
L. Ontario
L. Erie
Fort Detroit
Wabash River
Ohio River
Fort Sackville
KENTUCKY
PA
NY
NH
MA
RI
CT
NJ
DE
MD
VA
NC
SC
GA
Mississippi River
ATLANTIC OCEAN
Gulf of Mexico

0   200   400 Miles
0   200   400 Kilometers

N

▶ As the American Revolution raged, Great Britain battled for control of the West.

MAP SKILL Measure Distance *How far was Fort Detroit from Fort Sackville?*

REVIEW Why did American Indians attack settlements in Kentucky?
Cause and Effect

The Colonists Take Control

The colonists knew that the British were behind the American Indian attacks. **George Rogers Clark,** a young Kentucky man, had a plan. He would lead a volunteer force and capture the old French forts along the Wabash and the Mississippi. They would then use the forts to stop the attacks. Next, this volunteer force would march to Fort Detroit and capture British headquarters.

Clark was able to get only 175 men. In May 1778, Clark's men traveled down the Ohio River, then marched across the land. They reached **Kaskaskia** on the Mississippi River and were able to take the fort with no fighting. The villagers swore loyalty to Clark.

▶ **General Clark at Kaskaskia**

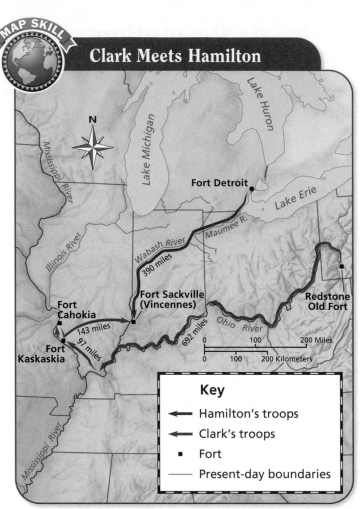

MAP SKILL **Clark Meets Hamilton**

Key
- ← Hamilton's troops
- ← Clark's troops
- ■ Fort
- — Present-day boundaries

▶ George Rogers Clark set off to capture British forts in the West.

MAP SKILL Use a Map Key *Did Clark's troops ever reach Fort Detroit? Explain.*

Their next target was **Cahokia,** about sixty miles north. Once again, the villagers welcomed Clark's men, who took the fort with no problems. From there, Clark sent one of his captains to **Vincennes,** in Indiana. The British had built **Fort Sackville** there and then abandoned it. The villagers there also swore loyalty to Clark.

British commander Henry Hamilton was stunned. He set off for the Wabash region with his troops. As he marched, he added hundreds more.

Hamilton's forces reached Vincennes in December of 1778. They were able to overwhelm the soldiers protecting Fort Sackville. The soldiers **deserted**, or abandoned, the fort. Clark's captain had to **surrender.** He had no choice but to give up.

Hamilton was not expecting a counterattack during the winter. He let many of his troops go home. When Clark heard of the British success at Fort Sackville, he knew that his only chance was a surprise attack.

On February 9, 1779, Clark and about 175 men started their march to Vincennes. Conditions were awful. Melting snow and ice and cold rain caused rivers to flood. The men walked 180 miles, some of the time through waist-high icy water. By the end of the march, their food was almost gone. The men were exhausted. They reached Vincennes on February 23. Clark gave the villagers a choice. They could stay in their homes and out of his way. Or, if they wished to remain loyal to the British, they could retreat into the fort. They stayed in their homes.

Clark's surprise attack succeeded. The local Piankashaw supported Clark's troops. Clark forced Hamilton to surrender, then sent him to prison in Williamsburg, Virginia. Clark had recaptured Fort Sackville.

Hamilton had used American Indians to try to clear the West of American colonists. Now Clark's victory helped make settlement possible for American colonists.

REVIEW Why did George Rogers Clark plan a surprise attack on Fort Sackville? **Main Idea and Details**

Literature and Social Studies

Joseph Bowman was a captain in George Rogers Clark's force. He wrote these diary entries in late February, just before Clark's troops reached Fort Sackville.

22d. *Colonel Clark encourages his men, which gave them great spirits. Marched on in the waters. Those that were weak and famished from so much fatigue went in the canoes. . . .*

23d. *Set off to cross the plain called Horse-shoe Plain, about four miles long, all covered with water breast high. Here we expected some of our brave men must certainly perish. . . . [W]e plunged into it with courage, Colonel Clark being first, taking care to have the boats try to take those that were weak and numbed with cold into them. Never were men so animated with the thought of avenging the wrongs done to their back settlements as this small army was.*

The War Ends

While Clark and his men fought for control of the West, war was also raging from Canada to South Carolina. The fighting that began in 1775 continued until 1781. General George Washington led the main force of the Continental Army, the army of the

► George Washington led the Continental Army in the struggle for independence.

colonies. They suffered many defeats. But the colonists believed in their cause, so they kept fighting. In October 1781, with the help of the French navy, Washington and his men defeated the army of Lord Cornwallis at Yorktown, Virginia. Though the two sides did not sign a treaty until 1783, the victory at Yorktown signaled the war's end.

REVIEW Compare the experiences of Clark's troops and Washington's troops. ⟲ **Compare and Contrast**

Summarize the Lesson

- **1773** Boston Tea Party took place.
- **1776** Declaration of Independence was signed.
- **1779** Clark retook Fort Sackville.
- **1781** Cornwallis surrendered at Yorktown.

LESSON 3   REVIEW

Check Facts and Main Ideas

1. Sequence On a sheet of paper, write the sequence of events in the conflict between the British and the colonists after 1763.

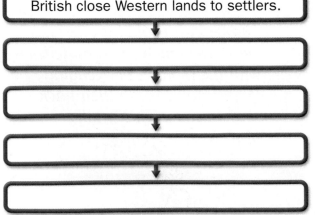

British close Western lands to settlers.

2. How did Great Britain's treatment of the colonies change after 1763?

3. How did George Rogers Clark and his troops lose, then regain, Fort Sackville?

4. Whom did both the British and the colonists want to control in the West during the American Revolution?

5. Critical Thinking: *Draw Conclusions* Why do you think the villagers of Vincennes switched loyalties between the British and the colonists?

Link to ⚭ Writing

Write a Letter You are a young American living in Kentucky in 1778. Write a letter explaining how you feel about George Rogers Clark and his attempt to capture the French forts.

Françoise Outelas *1730–1801*

Françoise Outelas lived in the fort town of Kaskaskia with her parents. In 1756, she married Drouet de Richerville and moved to Vincennes. Her husband was a successful businessman. He was much older than his wife. Historians describe her as a strong woman who looked after herself, her affairs, and her children very well. She helped her husband with his business. She may have even carried on his business after his death.

Madame de Richerville's husband died while their three children were still very young. She was left to bring them up alone in the frontier town. Her children grew up to be successful. Within her lifetime, the Richerville name became one of the most important in the entire area.

Madame de Richerville lived to be seventy-one years old. Church records noted that she had died "after a very edifying old age."

BIOFACT *A great nephew of Madame de Richerville was chief of the Miami from 1813 until 1841. Miami chiefs wore a type of turban.*

Learn from Biographies

Very little has been written about the women who lived in what is now Indiana during the 1600s and 1700s. What kinds of sources do you think historians use to find out how women such as Françoise Outelas lived?

For more information, go online to *Meet the People* at **www.sfsocialstudies.com**.

HERE AND THERE

Indiana and Virginia

The American Revolution

The American Revolution was fought in many places. In the Indiana Territory, George Rogers Clark and his troops captured Fort Sackville at Vincennes in 1778, and then again in 1779. This helped the Americans win the West.

In Virginia the war went on for another two years. The British Commander, Lord Cornwallis, marched his troops to Yorktown in July 1781. They were soon trapped between the Americans on land and the French fleet at sea. Their one hope was that the British fleet, sailing toward Yorktown, could rescue them. But the French fleet kept them out. By October 19, Cornwallis had little choice but to surrender.

Fort Sackville (*left*) and Yorktown (*below*) were both important victories for the Americans.

INDIANA

Vincennes

VIRGINIA

Yorktown   ATLANTIC OCEAN

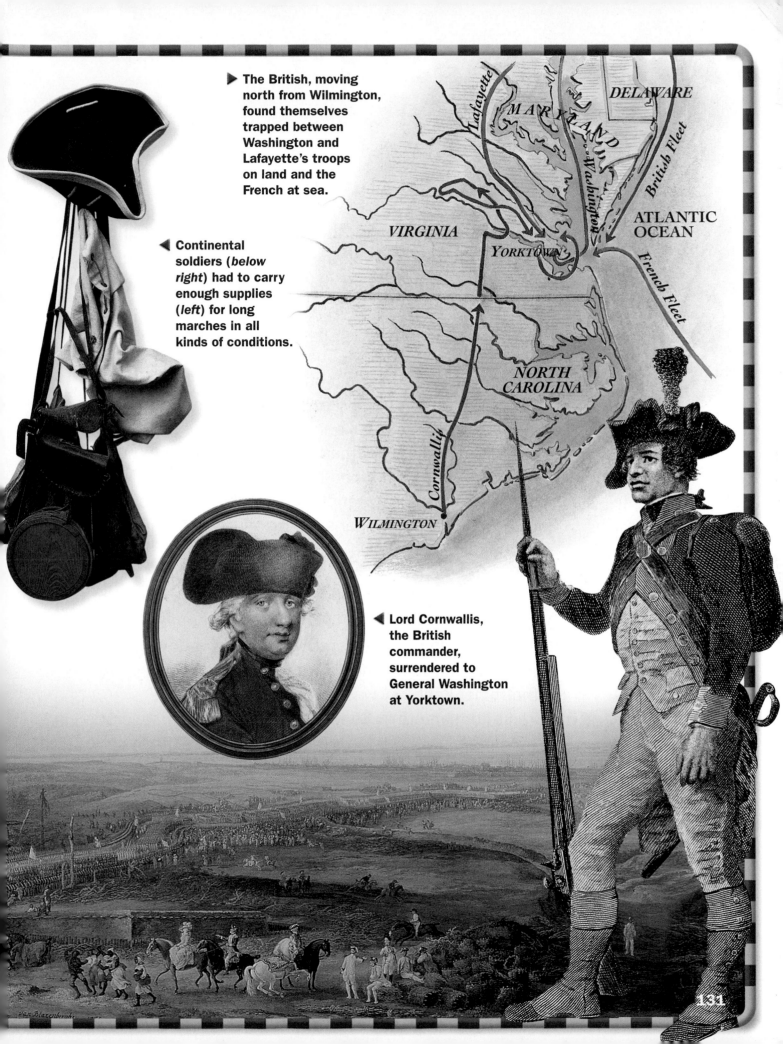

▶ The British, moving north from Wilmington, found themselves trapped between Washington and Lafayette's troops on land and the French at sea.

◀ Continental soldiers (*below right*) had to carry enough supplies (*left*) for long marches in all kinds of conditions.

DELAWARE

MARYLAND

Lafayette

Washington

VIRGINIA

YORKTOWN

ATLANTIC OCEAN

British Fleet

French Fleet

NORTH CAROLINA

Cornwallis

WILMINGTON

◀ Lord Cornwallis, the British commander, surrendered to General Washington at Yorktown.

131

Against the Odds

Sometimes people risk their lives for what they think is right. George Rogers Clark faced overwhelming odds when he set out to fight the British in the West.

George Rogers Clark was born on November 19, 1752. His family lived in a cabin on the banks of a river near what is now Charlottesville, Virginia. When he was five, his family moved to a plantation in southwest Virginia.

As a boy, George learned to plant crops and to hunt and trap. He also learned how to read and write. Most important, George's grandfather taught him to be a surveyor. *To survey* means to "measure and mark land." Settlers could not claim land until it had been surveyed.

The British had passed a law against settling land west of the Appalachian Mountains. But George Rogers Clark longed to travel west. At nineteen, he set off on a surveying trip to the West. Over the next four years, he claimed land in Kentucky for himself and his family. At that time, Kentucky was part of Virginia.

Life for settlers in Kentucky was becoming dangerous. A British official was encouraging American Indians to attack the settlers. George Rogers Clark spoke before the colonial government in Williamsburg, Virginia. He asked the government to help the settlers protect their land.

▶ **Surveyors used chains to make their measurements. These chains were used in Indiana in the early 1800s.**

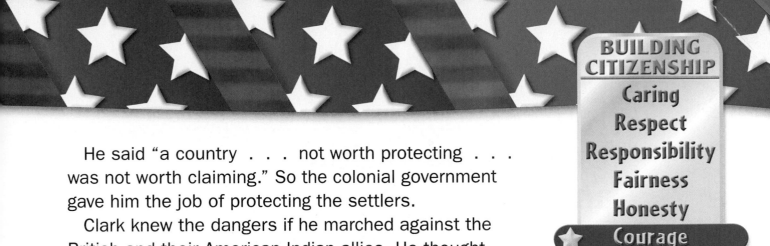

BUILDING CITIZENSHIP
Caring
Respect
Responsibility
Fairness
Honesty
★ Courage

He said "a country . . . not worth protecting . . . was not worth claiming." So the colonial government gave him the job of protecting the settlers.

Clark knew the dangers if he marched against the British and their American Indian allies. He thought also of the personal sacrifices ahead.

When Clark marched against the British with fewer than two hundred men, it showed his enormous courage. Arriving at Fort Sackville in February 1779, he knew the chances of success were poor. In the spring, the British would get more troops, making an attack more difficult. Clark thought that possible victory made the attack necessary. He believed that

> "[O]ur cause is just and . . .
> our country will be grateful. . . ."

Clark's victory at Fort Sackville helped the United States claim land in the West after the American Revolution. When Clark died in 1818, he was called "the mighty oak of the forest" and the "father of the western country."

Courage in Action

Research the story of a young person or a group of people who are working for a cause they believe in. For example, the people below volunteer their time to Habitat for Humanity. They show their courage by doing difficult tasks so that families that need homes get them.

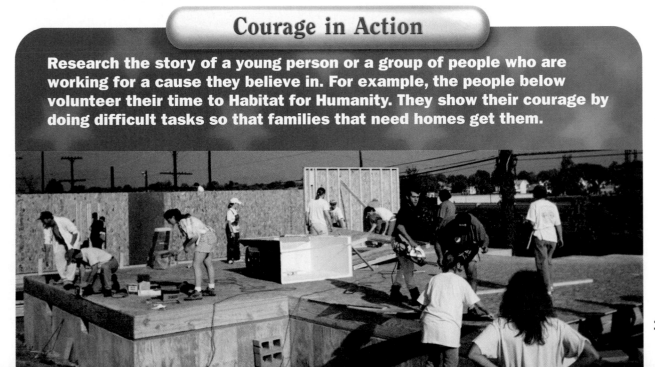

Map and Globe Skills

Understand Latitude and Longitude

What? Latitude and longitude are lines that mapmakers draw on maps or globes. Each latitude and longitude line is numbered. The lines give an "address," or location, to cities, towns, and other places on Earth.

Look at the globes below. The lines that extend from east to west on the left-hand globe are called lines of **latitude.** We also call them **parallels.** The equator is a parallel that lies halfway between the North and South Poles. It is numbered 0°. Parallels north of the equator are labeled *N*. Lines to the south are labeled *S*.

Lines of **longitude,** shown on the right-hand globe, extend from the North Pole to the South Pole. We also call these lines **meridians.** The **prime meridian,** like the equator, is numbered 0°. Lines west of the prime meridian are labeled *W.* Lines to the east are labeled *E.*

Notice that the lines also have numbers and this symbol: °. This symbol stands for the word *degree*. A **degree** is a unit of measure. On these globes, the lines of latitude and lines of longitude are 20° apart.

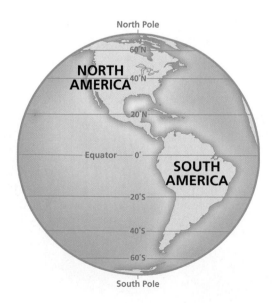

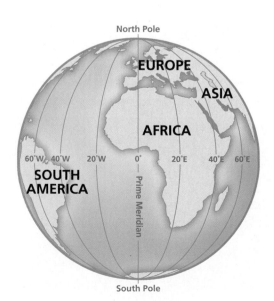

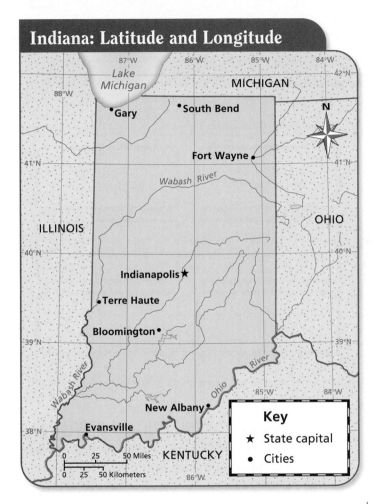

Indiana: Latitude and Longitude

Lake Michigan

MICHIGAN

87°W 86°W 85°W 84°W 42°N

88°W

•Gary •South Bend

N

Fort Wayne•

41°N 41°N

Wabash River

ILLINOIS

OHIO

40°N 40°N

Indianapolis ★

•Terre Haute

Bloomington•

39°N 39°N

Wabash River

Ohio River

85°W 84°W

New Albany•

38°N

Evansville•

86°W

KENTUCKY

0 25 50 Miles
0 25 50 Kilometers

Key
★ State capital
• Cities

How? Look again at the globes on page 134. You see that lines of latitude and longitude together make a grid. A grid is a network of horizontal and vertical lines. Study the grid on the map of Indiana. Now identify the latitude and longitude of Fort Wayne. Find the line of latitude closest to this city. Write down the number. Then find the line of longitude closest to Fort Wayne. Write down that number. Be sure to include direction labels for both latitude and longitude.

Think and Apply

1. How many degrees apart are the lines of latitude and of longitude on the map of Indiana?

2. Which line of latitude is closest to Evansville? Which line of longitude is closest?

3. Which two cities shown on the map of Indiana are closest to the equator?

For more information, go online to the *Atlas* at **www.sfsocialstudies.com**.

Why? Lines of latitude and longitude help you find the exact location of a place, such as a city or a mountain. This is important to people such as ship captains. Suppose you were far out on the ocean in a boat. How would you know where you were? Knowing your latitude and longitude would tell you. You could use this information to plan where you needed to go.

1600				1750	

1607
English established colony at Jamestown.

1608
French settled in Canada.

1673–1682
French explored Mississippi River and area.

1754–1763
French and Indian War was fought.

Chapter Summary

Compare and Contrast

On a sheet of paper, compare the travels of Marquette and Jolliet to the voyage of La Salle.

Marquette/Jolliet	La Salle
explored the Mississippi	explored the Mississippi

Vocabulary

Use each of the following words in a sentence that explains its meaning.

1 colony (p. 108)

2 voyageur (p. 108)

3 stockade (p. 112)

4 ally (p. 119)

5 rebellion (p. 120)

6 proclamation (p. 120)

7 repeal (p. 123)

8 desert (p. 127)

9 surrender (p. 127)

People and Events

Match each person with the correct description.

1 Chief La Demoiselle (p. 118)

2 Pontiac (p. 120)

3 Henry Hamilton (p. 125)

4 George Rogers Clark (p. 126)

a. led rebellion against the British

b. settled village of Pickawillany

c. captured Fort Sackville for Americans

d. urged American Indians to attack settlers in Kentucky

1760	1770	1780

1773 Boston Tea Party took place.

1775 First battles of American Revolution were fought.

1776 Declaration of Independence was signed.

1779 George Rogers Clark took Fort Sackville.

1781 Cornwallis surrendered at Yorktown.

Facts and Main Ideas

- Why was the fur trade so important to Europeans in North America?

- Why did Chief La Demoiselle settle a new village at Pickawillany?

- Why was George Rogers Clark able to retake Fort Sackville after losing it?

4. **Time Line** How many years passed between the time Clark took Fort Sackville and Cornwallis's surrender?

- **Main Idea** What was the main purpose of French settlement in North America?

6. **Main Idea** Why did the French and British fight the French and Indian War?

- **Main Idea** What did the American colonists want to gain from the Revolution against the British?

8. **Critical Thinking:** *Draw Conclusions* Why did the French build forts along the Wabash and the Maumee Rivers?

Write About History

- **Write a letter** to a friend as a member of George Rogers Clark's force. Describe your experiences.

- **Write a comparison** of what you think life was like for American Indians both before and after they started trading with the French.

- **Write an essay** explaining why American Indians should or should not be trading with the British during the 1740s.

Apply Skills

Understand Latitude and Longitude

Look at the map and answer the questions.

1. Which city is the farthest north—Gary, Fort Wayne, or Indianapolis?

2. Which two cities are closest to 39°N latitude and 87°W longitude?

3. South Bend is nearest what latitude? What longitude?

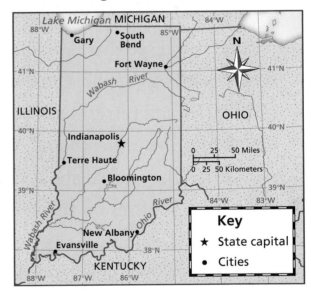

Internet Activity

To get help with vocabulary, people, and terms, select the dictionary or encyclopedia, from *Social Studies Library* at **www.sfsocialstudies.com**.

End with a Story

Even before the American Revolution reached Indiana, young people in the East were learning what it meant to be at war. In December of 1776, ten-year-old Ellen Toliver overhears her grandfather and her mother as they place a secret message inside a loaf of bread. The message is for General George Washington. Grandfather's plan for delivering the message is ruined when he sprains his ankle. Who can deliver the message without causing suspicion? Could the timid Ellen find the courage to be a hero?

Toliver's Secret

by Esther Wood Brady

Ellen could see that Grandfather was very serious about the need to send his message. She, too, had been worried about all the news of lost battles and retreats, especially since Ezra [her brother] was with that army. She remembered how joyous everyone had been last July when they heard about the Declaration of Independence. There had been bonfires on the village green and singing and dancing in the streets. And then the British army came to New York and there had been three months of defeat.

"If you understand how important it is to take the message, Ellen, I'll tell you how it can be done. And then you are to decide."

Ellen listened and didn't say a word.

"You walk down to the docks near the Market-house and get on a farmer's boat—or an oysterman's. They come over early every morning and they go back to Elizabeth-town at eleven o'clock. Elizabeth-town is a very small town. When you get off the boat, you'll find the Jolly Fox Tavern without any trouble. My good friend Mr. Shannon runs the tavern, and you give the loaf of bread to him. That's all there is for you to do, Ellen. The Shannons will welcome you and take good care of you."

Sailing across the bay didn't seem so hard. It was finding a boat here in New York and asking a stranger for a ride that worried her.

"How could I find the right boat to take me?" she asked. She didn't intend to go, but she thought she'd ask anyway.

"The docks are right near Front Street where we walked on Sunday afternoon. The farmers and the oystermen tie up their boats near the Market-house. They are friendly people and they often take passengers back to Elizabeth-town since the ferryboat stopped running. I'll give you money to pay."

"And how would I get home again—if I should decide to go?" she said in a very low voice.

"Oh, the Shannons will put you on a boat early in the morning. You'll be back here by ten o'clock."

"Does Mr. Shannon take the bread to General Washington?" she asked.

"No, he takes it to a courier who will ride part of the way. Then he'll give it to another courier who will ride through the night with it. And finally a third man will carry it to the General in Pennsylvania."

Review

Main Ideas and Vocabulary

TEST PREP

Read the passage below and use it to answer the questions that follow.

Scientists think that thousands of years ago, people arrived in North America. These hunters eventually learned to grow their own food and settled in villages.

Some descendants of these people came to the land we now call Indiana. Later, new groups arrived. The Miami and Potawatomi cultural groups were the largest and most powerful.

During the 1600s, Europeans arrived. France claimed land in Canada. England settled colonies along the Atlantic.

French explorers traveled down the Mississippi. French traders lived among the American Indians, whose lives were changed forever.

The French and the British both wanted to control trade, land, and the people. They fought the French and Indian War in the mid-1700s. France lost. American Indians were unhappy under the British. The Ottawa chief Pontiac led a rebellion, but lost to the stronger British army.

The British raised money by taxing the colonies. The colonists rebelled. The American Revolution began in 1775 and reached Indiana several years later. Henry Hamilton, a British commander, urged American Indians to attack settlers. The settlers, led by George Rogers Clark, fought back, capturing three forts. The colonists won their independence.

1 What led some early Americans to settle in one place?
   A learning to hunt bison
   B developing their own culture
   C learning to fish
   D learning to grow their own food

2 In this passage, cultural group means people who
   A move.
   B live in the same village.
   C share language, religion, and customs.
   D hunt food.

3 The French and British fought over
   A control of the land, trade, and people in the West.
   B taxes.
   C Spanish land in Florida.
   D problems between colonists and American Indians.

4 In this passage, colonists means people who
   A win freedom.
   B settle a new country.
   C support the government.
   D sign a peace treaty.

Vocabulary

Match each word to its definition.

1. **archaeologist** (p. 84)

2. **prehistoric** (p. 84)

3. **artifact** (p. 84)

4. **clan** (p. 94)

5. **longhouse** (p. 98)

6. **sachem** (p. 98)

7. **voyageur** (p. 108)

8. **stockade** (p. 112)

9. **proclamation** (p. 120)

10. **desert** (p. 127)

a. official announcement

b. high fence

c. rectangular house made of trees and bark

d. Lenape chief

e. French fur trader

f. object made by humans

g. leave or abandon

h. times before written histories

i. scientist who studies the lives and cultures of people from the past

j. related groups

Write and Share

Present a Documentary Your class has been asked to produce a TV documentary about the people of Indiana from prehistoric times to the 1600s. Break into three groups. Each group should do one of these tasks: **1.** Write a brief script about the people. **2.** Write a description of important events. **3.** Create visuals—pictures, drawings, posters, charts. Then come back together to perform your documentary.

Read on Your Own

Look for these books in the library.

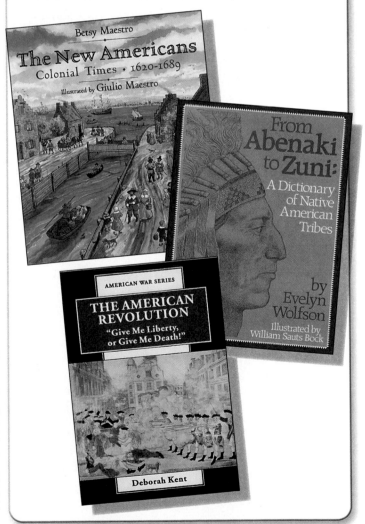

Apply Skills

Use Latitude and Longitude to Locate Cities Look at a globe or an atlas. Choose three cities in the Western Hemisphere. Write the names of the cities on one sheet of paper. On a second sheet, write the degrees of latitude and longitude closest to each city. Exchange the second sheet with a partner. Identify the cities closest to the "addresses" your partner has listed.

On the Spot

Life was often challenging for America's early settlers, as well as for American Indian groups who had lived in Indiana for hundreds of years. Make a documentary about their experiences.

1 Form a group and choose American Indians or early European settlers who settled in Indiana.

2 Write sentences about their experiences and observations. Include a variety of topics.

3 Make a diorama or model to show the environment and settlements. Include where they lived, other buildings, and the physical setting.

4 Present your documentary. Show the diorama or model to the class.

Internet Activity

Learn more about the early history of Indiana. Go to **www.sfsocialstudies.com/activities** and select your grade and unit.

The Great State of
Indiana

What makes an area a good place to live?

UNIT 3

Begin with a Primary Source

1780

1800

1787
Northwest
Ordinance
is passed.

1811
William Henry Harrison
defeats Shawnee at
Battle of Tippecanoe.

"We the Representatives of the people of the Territory of Indiana . . . do mutually agree with each other to form ourselves into a free and Independent state."

—Preamble of the 1816 Indiana State Constitution

This 1855 engraving by an unknown artist shows Robert Owen's utopian community, New Harmony.

1820

1840

1812
Americans defeat British and American Indian allies in War of 1812.

1816
Indiana becomes a state.

1825
Robert Owen buys New Harmony.

1836
Legislature passes Internal Improvements Act.

Meet the People

Anthony Wayne
1745–1796
Birthplace: near Paoli, Pennsylvania
Soldier
- Fought bravely in the American Revolution
- Served in Georgia House of Representatives
- Defeated American Indians at Battle of Fallen Timbers

Little Turtle
c. 1752–1812
Birthplace: near Fort Wayne, Indiana
Miami leader
- Defeated Americans in 1790s
- Defeated at Fallen Timbers
- Signed the Treaty of Greenville

Tecumseh
1768–1813
Birthplace: near Springfield, Ohio
Shawnee leader
- United American Indians to fight against white settlement
- Fought on British side in the War of 1812
- Killed at the Battle of the Thames

Robert Owen
1771–1858
Birthplace: Newtown, Wales
Factory owner, reformer
- Worked to improve society
- Started several cooperative villages in Great Britain
- Founded New Harmony, Indiana, as a utopian community

1740   1760   1780   1800

1745 • Anthony Wayne   1796

c. 1752 • Little Turtle   1812

1768 • Tecumseh   1813

1771 • Robert Owen

1773 • Frances Slocum

1788 • Sally Bush Lincoln

For more information, go online to *Meet the People* at **www.sfsocialstudies.com**.

Frances Slocum

1773–1847

Birthplace: Warwick, Rhode Island

- Captured at the age of five by the Lenape
- Settled in a Miami village in Indiana as the wife of a chief
- Refused to leave her village and her children when relatives located her

Sally Bush Lincoln

1788–1869

Birthplace: Hardin County, Kentucky

- A widow, married Tom Lincoln after his wife's death
- Helped raise Abraham and Sarah Lincoln in addition to her own three children
- Encouraged Abe's learning and believed he would grow up to be a great man

Caleb Mills

1806–1879

Birthplace: Dunbarton, New Hampshire

Teacher

- Started school that became Wabash College
- Worked to start a public school system in Indiana
- Became first State Superintendent of Public Instruction

Abraham Lincoln

1809–1865

Birthplace: Hardin County, Kentucky

Lawyer, politician

- Moved to Indiana in 1816 as a young boy
- President of the United States, 1861 to 1865
- Led the nation during the Civil War

1820	1840	1860	1880

1858

1847

1869

1806 • Caleb Mills   1879

1809 • Abraham Lincoln   1865

The Great State of Indiana

Sequence

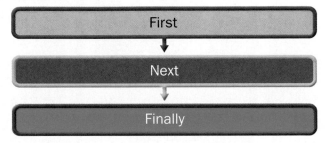

- *Sequence* means the order in which things happen.
- Clue words such as *first, next, then, after,* and *finally* show sequence.
- Dates and times of day also show sequence.
- Sometimes events are told out of order. Verb tenses or clue words can help you figure out sequence.

Read the following paragraph. Words that show sequence have been highlighted.

After the American Revolution, the territory of Indiana was part of the nation's western lands. Then Congress made it part of the Northwest Territory. When Ohio became a state, what is now Indiana was part of the Indiana Territory. As soon as five thousand free, adult men lived in Indiana, they elected a legislature. Finally, when sixty thousand free people lived in Indiana, it became a state. The year was 1816.

Changes in Indiana

The land we call Indiana changed in many ways from the end of the American Revolution to the 1850s. Right after the Revolution, the land had few European settlers. Then Congress passed the Northwest Ordinance. This law set up a government, protected civil liberties, and outlawed slavery. After the law was passed, settlers began to arrive.

American Indians had been in the land of Indiana long before the new settlers. Soon conflict began between the groups. American Indians tried to hold on to their homelands. At first, they defeated the United States troops in several battles. But at the Battle of Fallen Timbers in 1794, the Battle of Tippecanoe in 1811, and the Battle of the Thames in 1813, the larger United States forces defeated the American Indians.

While some of these battles were taking place, the population of Indiana continued to grow. Soon Indiana was on the way to becoming a state. In 1816, with a population of sixty thousand free settlers, the new state of Indiana was welcomed into the Union.

All these new residents needed transportation. Canals and railroads were built. Soon, Indiana was no longer the "frontier." Indiana in the 1850s barely looked like the Indiana Territory of the 1790s.

Use the reading strategy of sequence to answer these questions.

1 What words tell you when the population of Indiana began to grow?

2 In the conflict between American Indians and the United States troops, which group was successful at first?

3 What else was happening in Indiana during the conflict between American Indians and the United States?

CHAPTER 5

The Americans

Lesson 1

1785
Clarksville
New laws set up the Northwest Territory.

1

Lesson 2

1780s–1813
Northwest Territory
American Indian groups sign treaties giving up control of large amounts of land.

2

Locating Time and Place

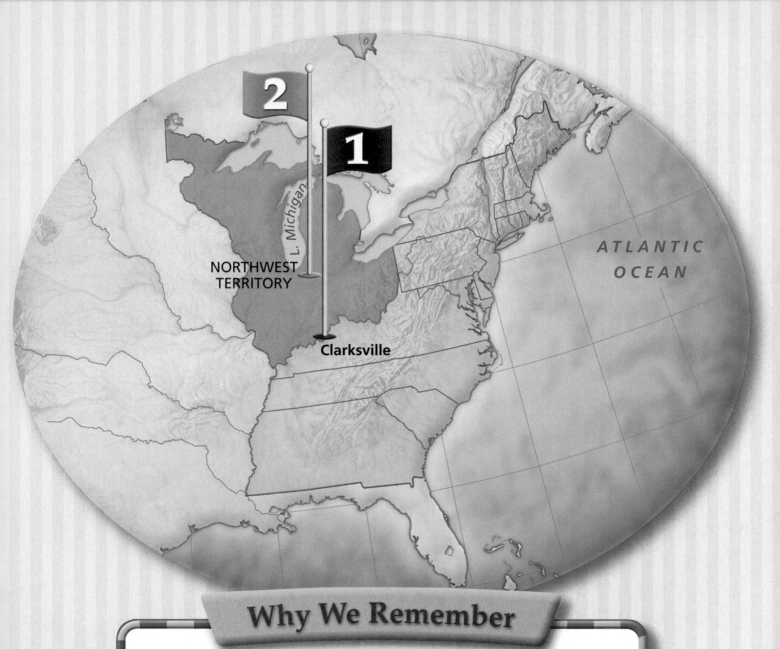

Why We Remember

Today Indiana is one of fifty states. But after the American Revolution, Virginia claimed this land that we call home. American Indian groups—who had lived here all along—claimed the land too. As new settlers poured into the territory, one question became very important: Who owned the land? That question would not be an easy one to answer. The conflict over Indiana's future would shape the state we know today.

LESSON 1

1780　　1785　　1790　　1795　　1800

1784
Virginia gives
up claims to
western lands.

1787
Congress passes
Northwest Ordinance.

Clarksville

PREVIEW

Focus on the Main Idea
The United States government
made laws for western lands.

PLACES
Clarksville
Northwest Territory

VOCABULARY
cede
ordinance
township

TERMS
Northwest Ordinance of 1787

Laws of the Land

You Are There — From a corner of the cabin, you listen to your parents. They are talking about leaving Virginia for land in the west. "The land there is rich," your father says. "We could farm much more land than we now have. After all, the land is owned by Virginia. George Rogers Clark himself saw to that!"

"There's no law out there," your mother replies. "And there's no real government. We could claim some land, but it wouldn't be a legal claim. I don't want to move until I know the land will be ours—that no one could take it away."

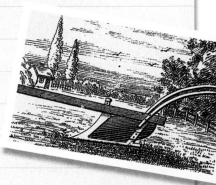

 Sequence As you read, look for words that show sequence, or the order in which events happened.

▶ Farmers in the 1700s and 1800s used plows like this one to break new soil.

▶ This antique map shows that states such as Virginia held vast claims to lands west of the original thirteen states.

Virginia's Claims

Who owned the lands west of the Appalachians, the mountains that extend along the East Coast of the United States? Several of the original thirteen states claimed that land. Virginia had large land claims in the West. It had sent George Rogers Clark to hold the western lands for the United States during the Revolution. His brave actions strengthened Virginia's claims.

The states with no land claims feared that the states with western lands would become rich and powerful. Meanwhile, they would be poor and weak.

Fortunately, states such as Virginia saw the wisdom of ceding their claims to the national government. To **cede** is to give up. This allowed all the states to work together toward the goal of building a nation. Congress promised that new states would be set up as the lands were settled.

In 1784, Virginia gave up its claims to western lands. In return, it asked that Congress honor a promise made to Clark and the men who fought with him in 1778 and 1779. Congress gave the men land across the Ohio River from Louisville, Kentucky. The town of **Clarksville** was founded there in 1784.

REVIEW When did George Rogers Clark and his men receive land in Indiana? ⟳ **Sequence**

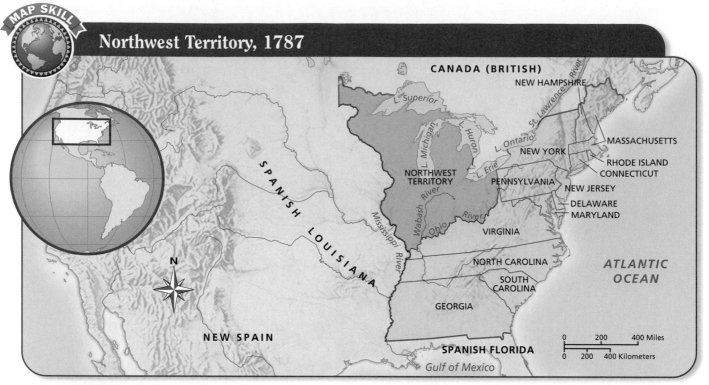

CANADA (BRITISH)

NEW HAMPSHIRE

L. Superior

L. Michigan

L. Huron

L. Ontario

St. Lawrence River

MASSACHUSETTS

NEW YORK

RHODE ISLAND
CONNECTICUT

NORTHWEST
TERRITORY

L. Erie

PENNSYLVANIA

NEW JERSEY

DELAWARE

MARYLAND

Wabash River

Ohio River

VIRGINIA

SPANISH LOUISIANA

Mississippi River

NORTH CAROLINA

ATLANTIC
OCEAN

SOUTH
CAROLINA

GEORGIA

N

NEW SPAIN

SPANISH FLORIDA

Gulf of Mexico

0   200   400 Miles
0   200   400 Kilometers

▶ After independence, the United States faced the question of how to settle its vast Northwest Territory.

MAP SKILL Use a Historical Map *How did the Northwest Territory compare in size to the existing thirteen states?*

The Northwest Ordinance

Thomas Jefferson called the western lands "an Empire of Liberty." But before this empire could grow, the nation needed to agree on rules about how to use it. Many settlers wanted to move west. They needed a government for the territory, however. They also needed rules for dividing the land so it could be bought and sold.

In the 1780s, Congress passed several ordinances to solve these problems. An **ordinance** is a law.

Congress approved the Land Ordinance in 1785. This divided the land into a grid, or series of rectangles. The basic unit of land was a **township.** Each township was divided into thirty-six sections, each covering 640 acres—a square mile. Sections could be divided into smaller parts for sale.

▶ Land in many western states was divided into grids, or rectangles, as shown in this modern photograph.

The **Northwest Ordinance of 1787** set up rules for creating states from the **Northwest Territory.** Another important part of the Northwest Ordinance was its bill of rights. It guaranteed the civil rights of American settlers. It promised freedom of religion, the right to a trial by jury, and other basic rights. These later became part of the Bill of Rights of the United States Constitution. The Northwest Ordinance also outlawed slavery. It called for one section of each township to be used for the support of public education. Finally, the law said,

"The utmost good faith shall always be observed to the Indians."

In the next lesson, you will learn what actually happened to the American Indians of the Northwest Territory.

REVIEW List in order the steps Congress followed to divide the land of the Northwest Territory.
➲ Sequence

Summarize the Lesson

- **1784** Virginia gave up its claims to western lands.
- **1785** Congress approved the Land Ordinance.
- **1787** Congress passed the Northwest Ordinance, guaranteeing civil rights for settlers in the Northwest Territory.

▶ **First page of the printed Northwest Ordinance.**

LESSON 1   REVIEW

Check Facts and Main Ideas

1. ➲ **Sequence** On a sheet of paper, write one event from the lesson and its date in each box. Put the boxes in order.

```
┌────────────────────────┐
│                        │
└────────────────────────┘
           │
           ▼
┌────────────────────────┐
│                        │
└────────────────────────┘
           │
           ▼
┌────────────────────────┐
│                        │
└────────────────────────┘
```

2. Where was the Northwest Territory?
3. How did the western lands cause conflict among the states?

4. What were the most important things the Northwest Ordinance did?
5. **Critical Thinking:** *Point of View* Why did people want a guarantee of their civil rights before they moved to the Northwest Territory?

Link to ⚭ Mathematics

Make a Grid Cut a large square out of a piece of paper. Fold the square in half. What shape is the folded paper? Measure its sides. Fold the paper in half again. What shape is the folded paper now?

155

Chart and Graph Skills

Compare Line Graphs and Bar Graphs

What? A graph is a special kind of picture. It shows and compares information. Two common kinds are line graphs and bar graphs.

- A **line graph** often shows how something has changed over time. For example, the line graph here shows how the population of Indiana changed from 1800 to 1850.
- A **bar graph** often compares things by showing their sizes or their numbers.

▶ Growing families have meant a growing population in Indiana.

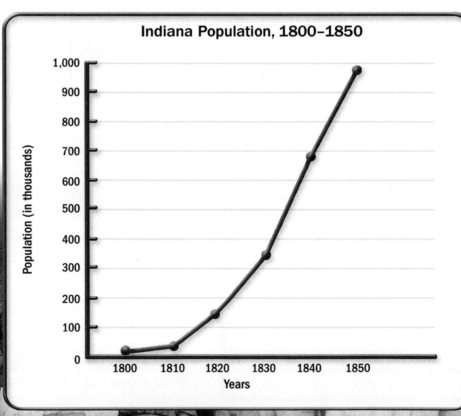

Indiana Population, 1800–1850

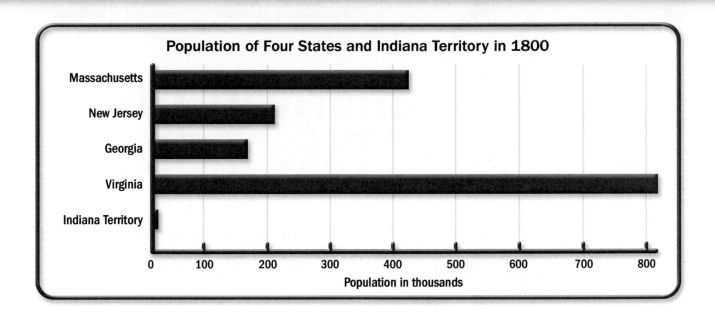

Population of Four States and Indiana Territory in 1800

Massachusetts
New Jersey
Georgia
Virginia
Indiana Territory

0   100   200   300   400   500   600   700   800

Population in thousands

Why? Graphs help you understand and show information at a glance. Understanding the purpose of a graph helps you use it correctly. Choose the correct graph for the kind of information you want to learn or show.

How? Start with the title. It tells what the graph is about. What is the title of the graph on page 156? What is the title on page 157?

Now look at the parts of each graph. On the bar graph, notice that the states are labeled on the left side of the graph. On the bottom, numbers stand for thousands of people. Which state shown had the largest population in 1800?

Where are years shown on the line graph? Did the population of Indiana grow slowly or quickly in the years shown?

Think and Apply

1 Would you choose a bar graph or a line graph to show changes in your height each year since your birth?

2 Suppose you wanted to show the number of workers in several industries in Indiana. What kind of graph would better show that information?

3 Look at the line graph. In which ten-year period did Indiana's population grow the fastest? How did you find your answer?

1780 1790 1800 1810 1820

1794	1795	1811	1813
Battle of Fallen Timbers	Treaty of Greenville	Battle of Tippecanoe	Battle of the Thames

NORTHWEST TERRITORY

Prophet's Town

American Indians Take a Stand

You Are There

You and your two brothers are scared. There is a lot of noise and everything seems very confused. The men are getting ready for battle again. Someone said that the great Little Turtle himself will be leading the fight.

It does not seem fair. Your family has lived in this area for only a short time, but there has been a lot of fighting. Your father says that all anyone wants to do is get back to farming and trading. You want to live peacefully with your neighbors. It may not be possible. Too many people want to control the land. When will this ever end?

▶ **Chief Little Turtle was a brilliant American Indian leader in the late 1700s.**

Sequence As you read, make a list of battles between American forces and American Indians, noting their dates and results.

Frontier Conflicts

The new nation of the United States faced many problems. One was the conflict between some of its settlers and certain American Indian groups.

The American Indians of the Northwest Territory had claims to the land. They had been living on this land for a long time. The British still held some forts in the territory, even though they had lost the American Revolution. The British encouraged American Indians to raid new American settlements. Both groups thought this would stop settlers from entering the territory. The United States government sent troops to stop these attacks.

In 1790, General Josiah Harmer led troops against the Miami. The Miami lived along the Maumee River. Harmer's troops were ambushed near the village of **Miamitown.** Led by **Chief Little Turtle,** the American Indian force included Miami, Lenape, Shawnee, Wyandot, and other groups.

▶ New settlers had to clear the land of trees before planting crops.

© Central Photo Archive / Brooklyn Museum of Art

General Harmer's soldiers fled in disgrace. The American Indians had shown that they could be strong opponents. They had won this round of the conflict.

REVIEW Why did American Indians attack U.S. settlements in the Northwest Territory? **Cause and Effect**

▶ **The Battle of Fallen Timbers was a terrible defeat for the American Indians.**

Little Turtle

Little Turtle was a Miami chief. His Miami name was Michikinqua. People respected his intelligence and his bravery. In August 1791, another U.S. force attacked a large Miami village on the Wabash River. The soldiers burned the village and two hundred acres of corn. They killed eleven warriors. They also took forty women and children as hostages. Afterward, American Indian leaders from several groups in the area met. They chose Little Turtle as their leader.

In September 1791, Major General Arthur St. Clair led troops into Miami territory. On November 4, Little Turtle surprised St. Clair's force. The American Indians killed or wounded about 920 soldiers. The rest of St. Clair's men fled.

President George Washington became very angry. Little Turtle and his troops had made the U.S. army look bad. Many had lost their lives.

President Washington made General **Anthony Wayne** the new head of the army in the Northwest Territory. Wayne had fought bravely in the American Revolution. In fact, Wayne had earned the nickname "Mad Anthony" because he was so daring in battle.

REVIEW What happened after St. Clair and his men were defeated?
◑ **Sequence**

Fallen Timbers

General Wayne spent two years training his army. In 1794, he marched north from Fort Greenville to the Maumee River. There he built Fort Defiance.

In August, he led about one thousand men south from Fort Defiance. They came to a place where a tornado had pulled up many trees. About two thousand American Indians under Shawnee leader **Blue Jacket** were waiting.

They came from many groups, including the Miami, Shawnee, Lenape, Ottawa, and Huron. Some Wea, Potawatomi, and Kickapoo may have been there as well. Wayne knew that American Indian warriors usually fasted, or stopped eating for a time, before battles. He let it be known that he would attack on August 17. But instead, he waited. He knew that the warriors would be weak with hunger. Finally, on the morning of August 20, 1794, Wayne attacked. The **Battle of Fallen Timbers** lasted less than two hours. Its results lasted much longer. The American Indians were defeated.

After his victory, Wayne built **Fort Wayne** at the head of the Maumee River. Then he headed for Fort Greenville. Over one thousand American Indian leaders came to

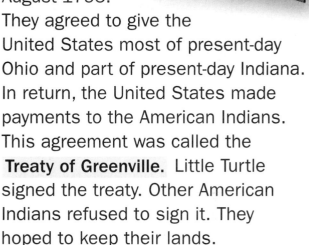

▶ Signatures from some of the American Indian chiefs and warriors who signed the Treaty of Greenville

Greenville in August 1795. They agreed to give the United States most of present-day Ohio and part of present-day Indiana. In return, the United States made payments to the American Indians. This agreement was called the **Treaty of Greenville.** Little Turtle signed the treaty. Other American Indians refused to sign it. They hoped to keep their lands.

REVIEW Why was Wayne able to defeat the American Indians at Fallen Timbers? **Cause and Effect**

▶ The Treaty of Greenville gave the United States control of a huge chunk of American Indian land in Ohio and Indiana. Some American Indian leaders refused to sign it.

Tecumseh and Tenskwatawa

In 1800, Congress divided the Northwest Territory. Part of it became the **Indiana Territory.** This territory included most of the **Northwest Territory** except Ohio. Congress made **William Henry Harrison,** who had fought at Fallen Timbers, its governor. The capital was at Vincennes.

One of Harrison's goals was to take more land from the American Indians. He used tricks and threats. He got the Lenape, Potawatomi, Wea, Miami, and other groups to give up land. By 1809, American Indians had been forced to cede the southern third of present-day Indiana and most of Illinois. Many

▶ Tecumseh (*left*) and Tenskwatawa (*below*) commanded a wide following.

American Indians did not want to surrender, or give up, this land. Shawnee leader **Tecumseh** did not believe anyone had the right to sell land. He said,

> *"Sell a country! Why not sell the air, the clouds and the great sea, as well as the earth?"*

In 1808, Tecumseh and his brother **Tenskwatawa,** called "the Prophet," started a settlement called **Prophet's Town** on the Tippecanoe River in Indiana. People from different tribes came to live there together. Tenskwatawa urged them to return to their own traditions. He told them to stop wearing white people's clothing. He urged them not to eat white people's foods. He even told them not to use guns.

Tecumseh wanted to unite all American Indians to fight against the United States. He organized several peoples into a confederacy, or a group united for a common cause.

▶ Prophet's Town was at the heart of Tecumseh's confederacy of American Indian groups.

Governor Harrison met several times with Tecumseh. He wanted the leader to stop fighting. Tecumseh said, "You have taken our lands from us and I do not see how we can remain at peace with you if you continue to do so." Harrison decided to destroy Prophet's Town.

On November 7, 1811, Harrison marched close to Prophet's Town. He knew Tecumseh was away. Tecumseh had warned his brother not to fight without him. But Tenskwatawa attacked Harrison's forces anyway.

The **Battle of Tippecanoe** followed. The Prophet led about 650 men against Harrison's force of 1,200. Included among Harrison's men was **John Tipton,** who would later hold several important posts in Indiana. After hours of fierce fighting, the American Indians retreated. Harrison waited for a second attack, but it never came. Instead, Tenskwatawa and his followers left Prophet's Town. Harrison's men burned it.

Harrison became famous as the hero of Tippecanoe. It helped him become President of the United States years later, in 1840. John Tyler was his running mate. Their supporters shouted the slogan "Tippecanoe and Tyler, Too!"

Tecumseh continued to fight. But his confederacy had been weakened.

REVIEW What events led to the Battle of Tippecanoe? ● Sequence

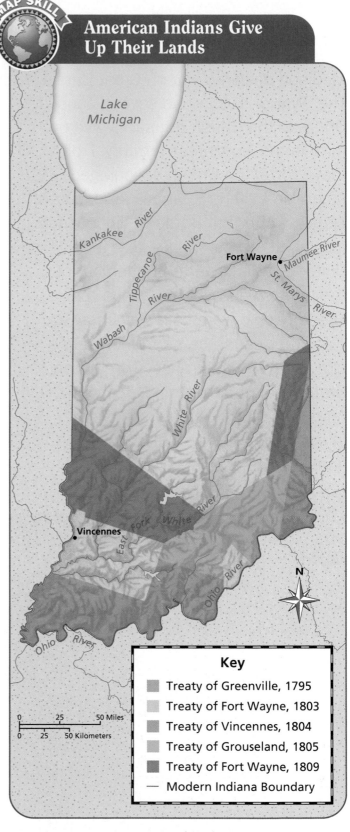

American Indians Give Up Their Lands

MAP SKILL

Key
- ◼ Treaty of Greenville, 1795
- ◻ Treaty of Fort Wayne, 1803
- ◼ Treaty of Vincennes, 1804
- ◻ Treaty of Grouseland, 1805
- ◼ Treaty of Fort Wayne, 1809
- — Modern Indiana Boundary

▶ Little by little, treaties with American Indians gave the United States control of Indiana.

MAP SKILL Location *What portion of Indiana was the first to come under control of the United States?*

The War of 1812

On June 18, 1812, President James Madison declared war on Great Britain. The **War of 1812** had several causes. One was the British refusal to give up forts in the Northwest Territory. From these forts, the British encouraged American Indians to attack American settlers. After the Battle of Tippecanoe, many settlers demanded that the United States drive the British out of the territory and out of Canada too. These people were called **war hawks.**

Another cause came from Britain's ongoing war with France. The United States claimed that the British seized American ships trading with France. In addition, British soldiers boarded American ships. They kidnapped

▶ This picture is called *The Death of Tecumseh at the Battle of the Thames, 5 October 1813.*

American sailors and forced them to serve in the British Navy.

At first, the Americans seemed to be losing. The British captured Detroit.

MAP SKILL

Key Battles in the War of 1812

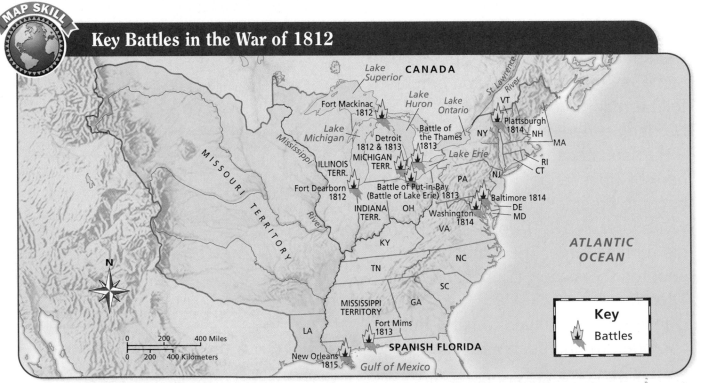

▶ Many key battles of the War of 1812 took place in the land of the Northwest Territory.

MAP SKILL Understand Map Symbols *On this map, how many battles are shown taking place in the land of the old Northwest Territory?*

A group of Potawatomi took over Fort Dearborn. American Indian raiding parties traveled deep into southern Indiana.

Then William Henry Harrison became commander of the army in the Northwest Territories. His army burned American Indian villages, fields, and crops. Harrison even attacked groups that were neutral. **Neutral** means not taking sides. By the summer of 1813, the American Indians of the Indiana Territory had been defeated.

The final blow came at the **Battle of the Thames** on October 15, 1813. Harrison had captured Detroit and marched into Canada. At the Thames River, he met a combined American Indian and British force. During the battle, Tecumseh, who was fighting for the British, was killed.

In other parts of the country and at sea, the Americans fought well. However, the British were able to attack the shores of Chesapeake Bay and burn the President's house in Washington, D.C.

REVIEW What were the main causes of the War of 1812? **Cause and Effect**

"The Star-Spangled Banner"

Francis Scott Key wrote these words during the War of 1812. They show the pride Americans had in their new nation.

....

*Oh, say can you see, by the
    dawn's early light,
What so proudly we hailed at
    the twilight's last gleaming,
Whose broad stripes and
    bright stars through the
    perilous fight,
O'er the ramparts we
    watch'd, were so gallantly
    streaming?
And the rocket's red glare, the
    bombs bursting in air,
Gave proof through the night
    that our flag was still
    there.
Oh, say, does that star-
    spangled banner yet wave
O'er the land of the free and
    the home of the brave?*

Peace

In time, the Americans fought the British to a standstill. A peace treaty ended the war in 1814. The treaty had some important results. American Indians no longer fought settlers in the Northwest. Many American Indian groups moved further west. Others were forced to move to reservations. These were pieces of land set aside for them. Even the Miami, who had tried hard to

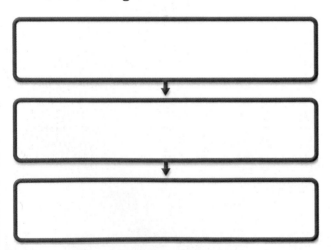

▶ This document—the Treaty of Ghent—brought an end to the War of 1812.

remain neutral, had their homes and fields destroyed.

Though not a clear victory, the war's outcome gave Americans new pride in their country. The nation had become a first-rate naval power. Now, along with the rest of the country, Indiana was ready to grow.

REVIEW What was the result of the War of 1812 for American Indians?
Cause and Effect

Summarize the Lesson

- **1790** Little Turtle defeated General Harmer
- **1794** Battle of Fallen Timbers
- **1795** Treaty of Greenville
- **1811** Battle of Tippecanoe
- **1813** Battle of the Thames

LESSON 2   REVIEW

Check Facts and Main Ideas

1. ↻ Sequence On a sheet of paper, list in order three events that led up to American Indians leaving Indiana.

```
┌─────────────────────────────┐
│                             │
│                             │
└─────────────────────────────┘
             │
             ▼
┌─────────────────────────────┐
│                             │
│                             │
└─────────────────────────────┘
             │
             ▼
┌─────────────────────────────┐
│                             │
│                             │
└─────────────────────────────┘
```

2. What happened at the Battle of Fallen Timbers?

3. What message did Tenskwatawa bring to American Indians?

4. Explain the outcomes of the Battle of Fallen Timbers and the Battle of the Thames.

5. **Critical Thinking:** *Draw Conclusions* Why did Tecumseh want to bring many American Indian groups into a confederacy?

Link to ∞ Writing

Prepare an Interview Write three questions that you would like to ask Little Turtle, Tecumseh, or William Henry Harrison. Then write the answers that you think that leader might have given.

Tecumseh

1768–1813

Tecumseh was born in a Shawnee village near what is now Springfield, Ohio. White settlers killed his father. His mother taught him that the coming of white people meant that American Indians would lose their land. He grew up to become famous as a brilliant general, a great speaker, and a political genius.

Tecumseh began to fight battles at the age of fourteen. He fought on the British side in the American Revolution. He fought at the Battle of Fallen Timbers in 1794. He refused to sign the Treaty of Greenville. Instead, he worked to unite the many groups of American Indians. He wanted them to work together to stop white settlers from taking their land. He also wanted them to be proud of their heritage. He said,

> **"Here is a chance . . . such as will never occur again—for us Indians of North America to form ourselves into one great combination."**

Tecumseh was killed in 1813, fighting for the British in the War of 1812. After his death, attempts by American Indians to stop white settlement in the Northwest Territory ended.

BIOFACT

This compass in a brass case was presented to Tecumseh in August of 1812.

To Tecumseh from "Brock" Aug 1812.

Learn from Biographies

Why do you think Tecumseh chose to fight on the British side in the American Revolution?

For more information, go online to *Meet the People* at **www.sfsocialstudies.com.**

CHAPTER REVIEW 5

1780	1785	1790

1784 Virginia gave up claims to western lands.

1787 Congress passed the Northwest Ordinance.

1790 Miami defeated General Harmer's troops.

1794 Wayne defeated American Indians in the Battle of Fallen Timbers.

Chapter Summary

 Sequence

Make a chart like this one on a sheet of paper. Fill in the events in the order they happened.

- Tecumseh is killed at the Battle of the Thames.
- Tecumseh tries to unite American Indians to stop settlers.
- Harrison destroys Prophet's Town.

Vocabulary

Complete each sentence with the correct word.

cede (p. 153)   war hawks (p. 164)
ordinance (p. 154)   neutral (p. 165)
townships (p. 154)

1. Virginia decided to ____, or give up, its claims to western lands.

2. Countries or groups that do not take sides are called _____.

3. The Northwest ____ of 1787 was a law passed by Congress.

4. People who pushed for the War of 1812 were called _____.

5. The western lands were broken up into large divisions called _____.

People and Events

Write a sentence explaining why each of the following people or events was important in the history of the Northwest Territory and Indiana Territory. You may use two or more in a single sentence.

1. **Chief Little Turtle** (p. 159)

2. **Anthony Wayne** (p. 160)

3. **Battle of Fallen Timbers** (p. 161)

4. **Treaty of Greenville** (p. 161)

5. **Tecumseh** (p. 162)

6. **William Henry Harrison** (p. 162)

7. **Battle of Tippecanoe** (p. 163)

8. **John Tipton** (p. 163)

9. **Battle of the Thames** (p. 165)

1795	1800	1805	1810	1815

1795
Many American Indian groups signed the Treaty of Greenville.

1811
Harrison destroyed Prophet's Town at the Battle of Tippecanoe.

1813
Tecumseh was killed at the Battle of the Thames.

Facts and Main Ideas

1. How did Tecumseh's idea of land ownership differ from William Henry Harrison's?

2. What happened at the Battle of Fallen Timbers?

3. **Time Line** How many years passed between the Miami victory over General Harmer and the death of Tecumseh at the Battle of the Thames?

4. **Main Idea** Why did Congress pass the Northwest Ordinance, and how did it protect settlers?

5. **Main Idea** How did the outcome of the War of 1812 affect the future of the Indiana Territory?

6. **Critical Thinking: *Analyze Information*** Why might the idea of Prophet's Town have appealed to American Indians in the early 1800s?

Write About History

1. **Write a journal entry** as an American settler thinking about moving to the Northwest Territory in the late 1700s. What attracts you to the territory? What problems do you think you might face there?

2. **Write a conversation** between Tecumseh and William Henry Harrison about the future of American Indian lands.

3. **Write a "What If" story** describing what might have happened if Virginia and other large states had refused to give up their claims to the Northwest Territory.

Apply Skills

Compare Line Graphs and Bar Graphs

Use the graphs on pages 156–157 to answer the following questions.

1. Which graph shows how the population of Indiana changed between 1800 and 1850?

2. Which state or territory had the greatest population in 1800?

3. During which ten-year period between the years 1800 and 1850 did Indiana's population grow by the greatest number of people?

Internet Activity

To get help with vocabulary, people, and terms, select the dictionary or encyclopedia from *Social Studies Library* at **www.sfsocialstudies.com.**

CHAPTER 6

Indiana Gains Statehood

Lesson 1

1816
Corydon
Indiana joins the Union.

1

Lesson 2

1824
Indianapolis
Indiana grows quickly.

2

Lesson 3

1826
New Harmony
Different types of people become Hoosiers.

3

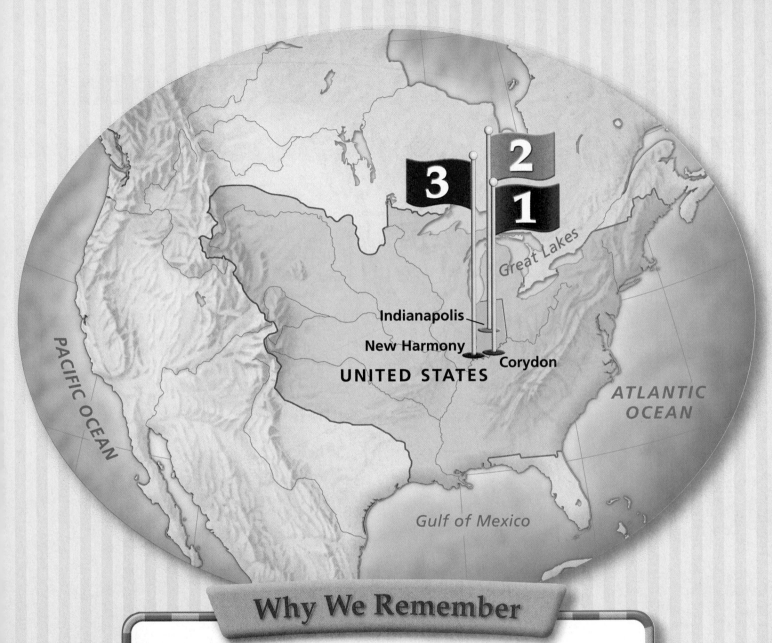

Why We Remember

After becoming the nineteenth state, Indiana grew quickly. People from other states—and from many countries—chose to make their homes here. Strong pioneers turned forests into farms. Others tried to create perfect communities and to improve the lives of their fellow Hoosiers. At the same time, American Indians were forced to give up their homes in the state. These early Hoosiers and these events put their mark on the state—a mark that is still seen today.

Corydon

| 1810 | 1815 | 1820 | 1825 | 1830 |

1810
Capital is moved to Corydon.

1816
A constitution is written; Indiana becomes a state.

PREVIEW

Focus on the Main Idea
In 1816, Indiana became the nineteenth state in the Union.

PLACES
Corydon

PEOPLE
Jonathan Jennings

VOCABULARY
legislative branch
executive branch
judicial branch

TERMS
Enabling Act
Constitutional Convention

The Nineteenth State

You Are There Nothing much ever happens here in the small town of Corydon. But now a group of men have come here to write a constitution for Indiana. They started working inside the stone capitol building. But the weather has turned hot. So the delegates decided to work outside under the shade of a large elm tree. They seem to be working hard. You know that they'll make a good plan for the government of the new state.

Sequence As you read, look for the steps on Indiana's path to statehood.

▶ The great Constitutional Elm shaded delegates to the first constitutional convention.

OLD CONSTITUTIO

© Indiana Picture Collection/ Indiana State Library

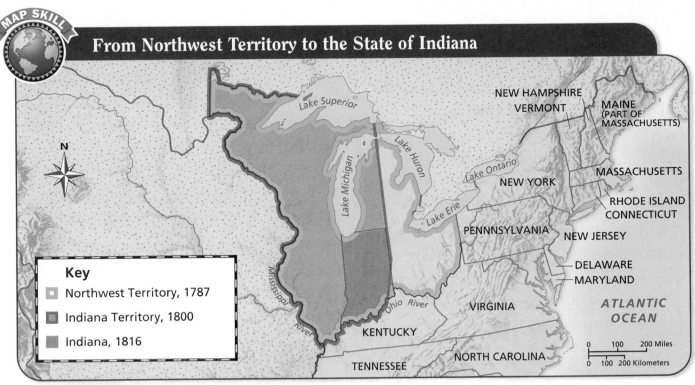

NEW HAMPSHIRE
VERMONT
MAINE (PART OF MASSACHUSETTS)

Lake Superior

Lake Michigan

Lake Huron

Lake Ontario

NEW YORK

MASSACHUSETTS

RHODE ISLAND
CONNECTICUT

Lake Erie

PENNNSYLVANIA

NEW JERSEY

N

DELAWARE
MARYLAND

Key

☐ Northwest Territory, 1787

▨ Indiana Territory, 1800

▨ Indiana, 1816

Mississippi River

Ohio River

VIRGINIA

ATLANTIC OCEAN

KENTUCKY

0   100   200 Miles

0 100 200 Kilometers

TENNESSEE

NORTH CAROLINA

▶ First the Indiana Territory and then the State of Indiana were carved from the Northwest Territory.

MAP SKILL Observe Change Through Maps *How does "Indiana" change over time?*

Steps Toward Statehood

By 1809, the Northwest Territory had been divided several times. First, Ohio became a state. Next, the Michigan Territory split from the Indiana Territory in 1805. Then, in 1809, the Illinois Territory was created. New borders of the Indiana Territory were set. Now the territory was on the road to statehood.

In 1810, the legislature moved its capital from Vincennes to **Corydon.** The Indiana Territory kept growing. By 1815, its population had climbed to more than sixty-three thousand free people. To become a state, it needed to have at least sixty thousand.

In January 1816, **Jonathan Jennings** went from Indiana to Washington, D.C., to represent the territory. He asked Congress to pass an **Enabling Act.** This law would enable, or allow, Indiana to become a state. Congress passed the law that April.

Next, representatives from different parts of Indiana came to Corydon. They met to write a constitution. This **Constitutional Convention** lasted only eighteen days.

These representatives had come to live in Indiana from many places. They came from nine states. Four came from Ireland, one from Switzerland, and one from Germany. They selected Jennings to lead the convention.

REVIEW List the steps involved in Indiana's becoming a state.
↻ **Sequence**

Our First Constitution

The representatives wrote a constitution for Indiana. They decided that the government should have three parts: the legislative, executive, and judicial branches. The federal government had been set up the same way. The **legislative branch** makes laws. The **executive branch** carries out these laws. The **judicial branch** decides questions about these laws.

The constitution promised that the state would protect the basic rights of the people. These include freedom of religion and freedom of speech.

Recall that slavery was not allowed in the Northwest Territory. Some delegates thought Indiana should allow it. The final constitution, however, outlawed slavery.

The new constitution went into effect on June 29, 1816. On December 11, President James Madison signed the papers making Indiana the nineteenth state. Jonathan Jennings became its first governor.

▶ **In its day, the State House at Corydon was an impressive building.**

© Indiana State Library / Indiana State Library

REVIEW How was Indiana's constitution like the United States Constitution? Compare and Contrast

Summarize the Lesson

- **1810** The capital was moved from Vincennes to Corydon.
- **1815** Indiana Territory's population was sixty-three thousand.
- **1816** The constitution was written and Indiana became a state.

LESSON 1 REVIEW

Check Facts and Main Ideas

1. ⟳ Sequence Draw the chart below on a sheet of paper. Write three events that led to Indiana becoming a state. Following the correct sequence, write one event in each box.

[ ]
↓
[ ]
↓
[ ]

2. In what year did Indiana become a state?
3. What final decision about slavery was written in Indiana's constitution?
4. What were the most important parts of Indiana's Constitution of 1816?
5. **Critical Thinking:** *Analyze* Why do you think people wanted Indiana to become a state?

Link to ∞ Art

Draw a Cartoon Draw a cartoon map showing the eighteen states of the Union in 1816 welcoming Indiana as the newest state. Label each state.

Frances Slocum *1773–1847*

Five-year-old Frances Slocum lived with her family in the Wyoming Valley of Pennsylvania, near Wilkes-Barre. One November day in 1778, three Lenape men kidnapped her. Her brothers searched but could not find her. Slocum ended up in a Miami village in Indiana. A couple who lived there adopted her. Later, she married a Miami chief named Shepoconah (shee PA co nah) and had many children. She took the Miami name Maconaquah (mah co NAH kwah).

In 1837, her brothers Joseph and Isaac Slocum heard about a woman who could be their sister living among American Indians near Logansport. Isaac Slocum visited Maconaquah and was able to identify her! The Slocums wanted Maconaquah to return to their home. She chose not to. She said she was an old woman and happy with her American Indian family.

In 1840, the Miami were forced to give up their lands along the Wabash. Maconaquah's brothers asked Congress to allow her to remain in her Indiana home. Congress granted land to her children. The family was able to stay in Indiana.

BIOFACT

Maconaquah said that her name meant "little bear woman."

Learn from Biographies

To be loyal means to be faithful. Describe examples of loyalty in the story of Frances Slocum.

For more information, go online to *Meet the People* at **www.sfsocialstudies.com**.

1810 1815 1820 1825 1830

1816
Abraham Lincoln
arrives in Indiana.

1818
The New
Purchase opens
central Indiana
for settlement.

1825
Indianapolis
becomes new
capital.

•Indianapolis

PREVIEW

Focus on the Main Idea
Once Indiana became a state,
it changed in many ways.

PLACES
St. Mary's, Ohio
Indianapolis
Vevay

PEOPLE
Abraham Lincoln

VOCABULARY
immigrate

TERMS
Treaty of St. Mary's
New Purchase

Moving North

You Are There
You're headed for the new governor's house in Indianapolis. You're carrying the laundry your mother has just finished washing and ironing. This is the first time she has sent you to deliver the laundry by yourself. You run through the busy streets. You watch out for horses, carts, and wagons. The streets are crowded. About a thousand people live in Indianapolis now. New buildings seem to appear overnight. When you reach the market, you know you are almost there. After you deliver the laundry, you buy an apple at the market.

© Indiana State Library/Indiana State Library

▶ **An early building in Indianapolis**

Sequence As you read, think about the changes that took place in Indiana after the New Purchase.

The New Purchase

In 1818, the Miami were forced to give up most of the land they still held in Indiana. These lands covered the central third of the state. Except for a few reservations, American Indians now held no lands south of the Wabash River. Governor Jonathan Jennings traveled to **St. Mary's, Ohio,** to accept the Miami surrender. The Americans called this agreement the **Treaty of St. Mary's.** It was also called the **New Purchase.** In return for land, the United States government gave the Miami individual grants of land, $15,000 a year, 160 bushels of salt a year, two mills, and some tools.

Some American Indian groups, including the Lenape, left Indiana. Other groups stayed but lost land. In return, the government paid them a yearly fee. The American Indians were forced to change the way they lived. For example, they could now hunt only in certain areas.

The New Purchase and other treaties allowed settlers to buy land in central and northern Indiana. As a result, the General Assembly—Indiana's legislature, or law-making body—decided to move the capital to a central location. Alexander Ralston designed a city to be built in the exact center of the state. The new city, called **Indianapolis,** was laid out in 1821.

Mary Catherine Anderson was a child when her uncle, the state treasurer, helped move the state records and treasury to Indianapolis. She described entering the new capital:

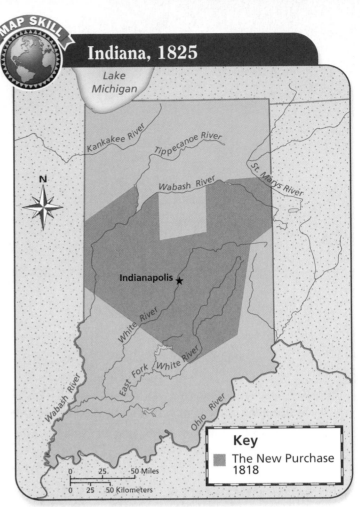

Indiana, 1825

Lake Michigan

Kankakee River

Tippecanoe River

St. Marys River

Wabash River

N

Indianapolis ★

White River

Wabash River

East Fork White River

Ohio River

Key

The New Purchase 1818

0   25   50 Miles
0   25   50 Kilometers

▶ The New Purchase greatly expanded the area open for American settlement.

MAP SKILL Understand Borders and Capitals
What does it mean that Indianapolis was located in about the center of the state?

"So we went into the seat of government with fine, large strong horses strung with bells, all ringing."

REVIEW Why did the General Assembly move the capital to Indianapolis? **Cause and Effect**

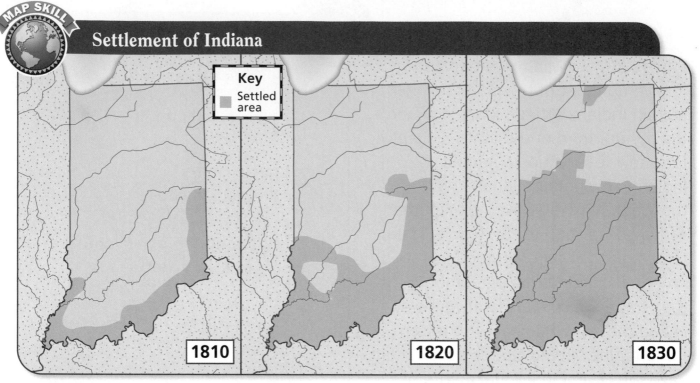

Key
Settled area

1810

1820

1830

▶ Settlement of Indiana was moving steadily northward in the early 1800s.

MAP SKILL Movement *How do you think the movement of American settlement affected the movement of American Indian populations?*

New Settlers Move In

By 1850, almost half of the newcomers to Indiana from other parts of the United States came from the South. The Lincolns were one such family. In 1816, they moved from Kentucky to Indiana. **Abraham Lincoln,** who became our sixteenth President, was only seven at the time. You'll read more about Lincoln later.

Many people immigrated to Indiana from foreign countries. To **immigrate** means to come to a new country from one's homeland. Immigrants came from many different countries.

Between 1816 and 1860, many people came to Indiana from Ireland. Many immigrants came from Switzerland too. The earliest Swiss settlement was at **Vevay.** It was founded by J. J. Dufour and his family. Dufour was sure that he could grow grapes in Indiana. He was right. Soon many Swiss families had vineyards in Vevay. In 1814, Vevay became part of a new county—Switzerland County.

Some German immigrants came directly from Germany. But one group of German-speaking people came to Indiana from Pennsylvania. They were Amish. Members of this religious group believe in living very simply. They work together in farming communities.

▶ Today the Amish continue to live as they did nearly two hundred years ago.

Amish people who came to Indiana settled mainly in Elkhart, Marshall, and LaGrange counties.

REVIEW Compare and contrast the different groups of people who settled in Indiana between 1816 and 1860. Compare and Contrast

The End of the Frontier

The new state grew quickly. By 1830, Indiana's population was 343,000. Parts of central Indiana grew by as much as six hundred percent. By 1850, Indiana had a population of about 988,500.

Newcomers settled in Indiana in stages. (The United States government defined *settled* as having at least two people per square mile.) First, newcomers settled in the southern part of the state. Then settlers moved into the central part after the New Purchase in 1818. The northern third was the last part of the state to be settled.

REVIEW Describe the sequence of settlement in Indiana. Sequence

FACT FILE

Who Were the Early Hoosiers?

Immigrants from Selected Foreign Countries Living in Indiana in 1850

source: 1850 census

Population Change in Indiana, 1800–1840			
Years	Beginning Population	End Population	Percent Increase
1800–1810	5,641	24,520	335%
1810–1820	24,520	147,178	500%
1820–1830	147,178	343,031	133%
1830–1840	343,031	685,866	100%

Where Hoosiers Came From in the United States

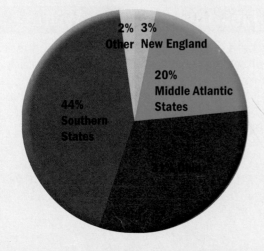

2% Other
3% New England
20% Middle Atlantic States
44% Southern States

© Courtesy Frances Eagleston/Hancock County Historical Society, Inc.

179

Getting Settled

New settlers cleared trees and started large, productive farms. They built towns with stores and churches. The first towns grew near rivers because boats provided the best method of transportation. These river towns included New Albany, Terre Haute, and Evansville. As the central and northern parts of the state were settled, towns such as Paoli and Lafayette grew. Logansport, Fort Wayne, and South Bend grew in the 1820s and 1830s.

Indiana was no longer a frontier land. Indiana was brimming with settlers and ready to move forward with roads, factories, and cities.

REVIEW How did settlers change the land in Indiana? **Main Idea and Details**

Summarize the Lesson

- **1816** Abraham Lincoln moved to Indiana.
- **1818** The Treaty of St. Mary's (New Purchase) opened central Indiana for settlement.
- **1825** Indianapolis became the state capital.

▶ **The growth of towns marked the end of Indiana's frontier.**

© "Courtesy, The Lilly Library, Indiana University, Bloomington, Indiana"/The Lilly Library

---

LESSON 2   REVIEW

Check Facts and Main Ideas

1. ⟳ Sequence Draw the chart below on a sheet of paper. Write three important events from the lesson. Put one event in each box in the correct order.

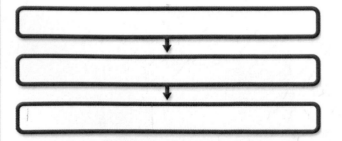

2. What city was built as the new capital of Indiana?

3. How did central Indiana come to be open for settlement by newcomers?

4. Where did the new settlers to Indiana come from?

5. **Critical Thinking:** *Summarize* What changes marked the closing of the frontier era in Indiana?

Link to 🔗 Writing

Write a letter from J. J. Dufour to a cousin in Switzerland. Describe Indiana, particularly your town, Vevay. Invite a cousin to come live there. Tell him or her why it would be a good thing to do. You may need to do some research to learn more about Vevay.

Abraham Lincoln

1809–1865

In 1816, Tom Lincoln moved his family from Kentucky to Indiana. Lincoln's son, Abraham, was just seven years old. The Lincolns lived in a cabin near Little Pigeon Creek in southwest Indiana for fourteen years. Then the family moved to Illinois. Abraham Lincoln later wrote of his home in frontier Indiana:

> *"We reached our new home about the time the state came into the Union. It was a wild region, with many bears and other wild animals. There I grew up."*

BIOFACT

Once Lincoln's ax slipped and nearly cut off his thumb. He had a scar on his hand for the rest of his life.

Abraham Lincoln never forgot the many hours he spent clearing land in Indiana. Someone gave him an ax when he was very young. He almost always carried it with him. It was useful for many frontier tasks, such as cutting trees and splitting logs.

Learn from Biographies

In 1860, Abraham Lincoln became President of the United States. What do you think he learned on the Indiana frontier that helped him in this job?

 For more information, go online to *Meet the People* at **www.sfsocialstudies.com**.

Raising a President

Abraham Lincoln's stepmother, Sarah (Sally) Bush Lincoln, helped young Abe become a great man. Many people think he became the greatest President the United States ever had.

Sally Bush and Tom Lincoln were neighbors in Kentucky. Lincoln married Nancy Hanks. Bush married David Johnston. The Lincolns had two children, Sarah and Abraham. The Johnstons had three.

In 1816, the Lincolns moved to Indiana. Two years later Nancy Hanks Lincoln died. Abraham was nine years old.

Life was hard for a single parent on the frontier. Tom Lincoln did not have the time or the skills to clean, make clothes, and cook good food. The family cabin was filthy, and the children's clothes were like rags.

In 1819, Tom Lincoln went back to Kentucky. There he learned that Sally Bush Johnston's husband had died. Lincoln asked Sally Bush Johnston to marry him. She accepted. When Tom Lincoln returned home, he introduced the new Mrs. Lincoln to his children with these words:

► **Lincoln Boyhood National Memorial**

"Here's your new mammy."

Sally Bush Lincoln worked hard to be a good mother to Abraham, Sarah, and her own children. She made life better for the Lincolns right away. She had brought furniture, pillows, and kitchen things from Kentucky. The cabin soon looked like a home.

BUILDING CITIZENSHIP
Caring
Respect
Responsibility
Fairness
Honesty
Courage

With a large family living in a one-room cabin, Sally Bush Lincoln had plenty of work. She kept the cabin clean. She was always busy sewing and mending clothes for the family. Most important for young Abe, she showed that she loved him.

Abe loved to read. Although his stepmother had no education herself, she knew that reading was important. She encouraged Abe and gave him peace and quiet so he could study. Abe kept notebooks for arithmetic, quotations, and ideas. He read them over and over. Sally Bush Lincoln didn't mind. She said that Abraham was going to be a great man someday.

In 1830, the Lincoln family moved to Illinois. Abe knew he did not want to be a farmer. He tried a number of different jobs. Then he became active in government. After a while, he was very successful. He served in Congress and then was elected President of the United States in 1860. When Lincoln left Illinois for Washington, D.C., he made a special trip to say good-by to his loving stepmother.

Caring in Action

Link to Current Events Research the story of a person or group working with young children today. What does the person do? How does he or she feel about caring for children?

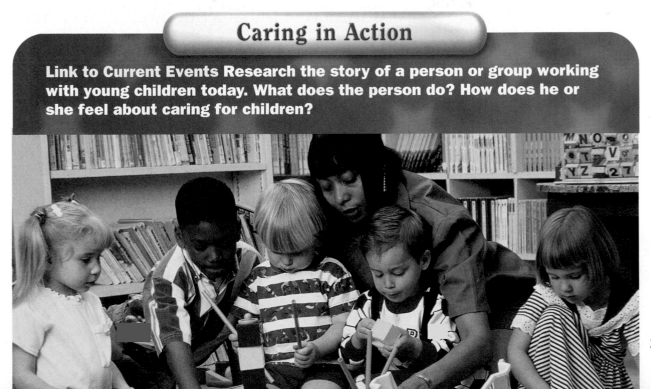

1810   1820   1830   1840   1850

1814
George Rapp
starts Harmonie.

1824
Robert Owen buys
New Harmony.

1838
Potawatomi march
the Trail of Death.

New Harmony

PREVIEW

Focus on the Main Idea
In the early 1800s, various groups in Indiana had many different experiences.

PLACES
New Harmony

PEOPLE
Menominee
George Rapp
Robert Owen

VOCABULARY
enforce
fugitive slave
utopia

TERMS
Trail of Death

The Hoosiers

You Are There
You feel lucky that your family lives in Indiana. Papa is a blacksmith. Sometimes you help him in his shop.

A lot of different people have been coming to Indiana because it is such a good place to live. Some of your friends' families came to Indiana with French traders many years ago. Others have arrived since Indiana became a state. You are proud because the 1816 Constitution of Indiana outlawed slavery. You think that it is only fair for everyone to be free. Of course, there are still things that aren't fair. For example, African Americans aren't able to vote or go to school. You wonder if there will ever be a time when all people are treated the same.

Main Idea and Details As you read, find details about the events of the early 1800s that brought new Hoosiers to the state.

The African American Experience

In the early 1800s, Indiana looked like a good place to settle for many people. As you have read, Hoosiers came from many states and nations. Some came from Africa.

Africans may have first come to what is now Indiana with French traders. Later, people from other states brought enslaved African Americans into the territory. But before Indiana became a state, few African Americans lived here. In 1810, only 630 African Americans lived in Indiana. Of these, 237 were enslaved.

As you know, the 1816 Constitution of Indiana outlawed slavery. Still, for several years, some people remained enslaved. In some places, laws against slavery were not **enforced,** or carried out. Some African Americans who arrived in Indiana before 1860 had been born free. Others had gained freedom from slavery and then moved to Indiana. A third group included people called **fugitive slaves.** They had escaped from slavery and come to the free state of Indiana. Fugitive slaves lived in constant danger. If caught, they could be sent back south into slavery.

African Americans in Indiana held many kinds of jobs. Some owned or worked on farms. In towns, some held jobs as laborers or servants. Many were skilled workers, such as barbers, carpenters, and blacksmiths.

Although African Americans in Indiana were free, the law did not treat them equally. They could not become citizens. They could not vote. Their children could not attend public schools. Many African Americans worked hard to gain more rights.

▶ Slaveowners paid large rewards for the return of fugitive slaves.

$150 REWARD

RANAWAY from the subscriber, on the night of the 2d instant, a negro man, who calls himself *Henry May,* about 22 years old, 5 feet 6 or 8 inches high, ordinary color, rather chunky built, bushy head, and has it divided mostly on one side, and keeps it very nicely combed; has been raised in the house, and is a first rate dining-room servant, and was in a tavern in Louisville for 18 months. I expect he is now in Louisville trying to make his escape to a free state, (in all probability to Cincinnati, Ohio.) Perhaps he may try to get employment on a steamboat. He is a good cook, and is handy in any capacity as a house servant. Had on when he left, a dark cassinett contee, and dark striped cassinett pantaloons, new—he had other clothing. I will give **$50** reward if taken in Louisvill; **100** dollars if taken out of this State, and delivered to me, or secured in any jail so that I can get him one hundred miles from Louisville in this State, and **150** dollars if taken out again. *Bardstown, Ky., September 3d, 1838.* WILLIAM BURKE.

REVIEW How was life as a free African American in Indiana different from life as a fugitive slave? How was it similar?

Compare and Contrast

▶ **American Indians on horseback**

© Courtesy of the Tippecanoe County Historical Association, Lafayette, Indiana / Tippecanoe County Historical Association

American Indians in the Growing State

As you know, treaties and laws took away most of the American Indian land in southern and central Indiana. By 1840, the government had also taken away American Indian land in the northern part of the state.

Some American Indian groups were removed—forced to leave—to make room for new settlers. After the New Purchase, the Lenape were removed to Mississippi. A United States law forced the Potawatomi to leave Indiana. Their leader, **Menominee,** protested. He said:

> *"I have not sold my lands. I will not sell them. I have not signed any treaty, and will not sign any."*

Menominee's words did not stop the removal of his people. Soldiers led eight hundred Potawatomi on a march to their new homeland in Kansas in 1838. The march was terribly difficult. Forty-two Potawatomi—most of them children—died along the way. For this reason, the march is known as the **Trail of Death.**

The Miami stayed in Indiana until 1840. Then many of them were also removed to new lands in Kansas. However, about one hundred Miami returned to Indiana. They asked the legislature to let them stay. About half were allowed to remain in Indiana. In 1850, about 250 Miami lived scattered throughout the state.

REVIEW Why were American Indians removed from their land in Indiana? **Cause and Effect**

186

Searching for Utopia

Most newcomers to Indiana dreamed of a new life. Some dreamed of creating a **utopia.** This is a perfect society where government and laws work to make everyone happy.

George Rapp led a group of followers from Germany to Pennsylvania. In 1814, they moved to Indiana. These people were called Harmonists. They shared religious beliefs and valued hard work. The Harmonists built a community called Harmonie near the Wabash River. The community prospered. However, in 1824, they decided to sell their land and return to Pennsylvania.

They sold it to a mill owner from Scotland named **Robert Owen.** He renamed the community **New Harmony.**

Owen wanted to create a utopia too. Many writers, scientists, and thinkers came to New Harmony. However, the community never lived up to Owen's ideal. Residents quarreled often, and many lacked useful skills, such as farming, building, or cooking. In 1827, a disappointed Owen gave up and returned to Scotland.

REVIEW Compare the experiences of the Harmonists and the followers of Robert Owen in Indiana.
Compare and Contrast

Summarize the Lesson

— **1814** George Rapp started Harmonie.

— **1824** Robert Owen established New Harmony.

— **1838** The Potawatomi were forced to follow the Trail of Death.

LESSON 3 REVIEW

Check Facts and Main Ideas

1. Main Idea and Details On a sheet of paper, write three details to support the main idea given.

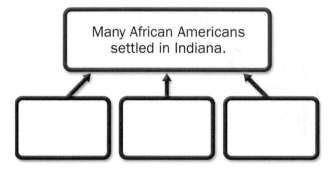

Many African Americans settled in Indiana.

2. What is meant by *fugitive slaves,* and why were they in danger?

3. Describe the utopias of George Rapp and Robert Owen.

4. What was the Trail of Death?

5. Critical Thinking: *Draw Conclusions* Why did New Harmony fail as an ideal community?

Link to Music

Pioneer Songs Find a song that has to do with some part of pioneer life. (It doesn't have to be about Indiana.) Present the song to your class. Discuss the topics it talks about. Use the library or the Internet for your research.

187

Research and Writing Skills

Take Notes and Write Outlines

What? Taking **notes** means writing down the main ideas about a topic you are learning about. Later you can read your notes to review the most important ideas.

An **outline** is a plan that shows information in an orderly way. Outlining helps you review the main topics you have studied.

Notes and outlines are study tools. They can help you remember what you hear in class and read in books.

Why? Taking notes and outlining help you to study faster and better. When you prepare for a test, for example, you can study your notes or your outline. You do not need to reread all the pages in your book.

How? After you read a lesson, think about the main idea. Write it on note paper. Do not copy sentences from the book. Use your own words. Then add details that you think are important.

Indiana Gains Statehood

I. The Nineteenth State
   A. Steps Toward Statehood
   B. Our First Constitution

II. Moving North
   A. The New Purchase
   B. New Settlers Move In
   C. The End of the Frontier
   D. Getting Settled

III. The Hoosiers
   A. The African American Experience
   B. American Indians in the Growing State
   C. Searching for Utopia

Use abbreviations. Make up your own, if necessary. For example, you might write *IN* for Indiana or *NH* for New Harmony. Your notes are your own. Use what works for you!

One quick way to take notes is to use a web. Write the main idea in the center. Then add details in smaller circles around it. The web on this page shows details about William Henry Harrison, an important Hoosier—the main idea.

Outlines follow a standard form. The outline on page 188 is of Chapter 6. The chapter title is at the top. The titles of the lessons are main headings. The headings in each lesson are written under the main headings. Notice that different kinds of numbering and lettering are used in the outline. Use Roman numerals for the main headings. Use capital letters for the next level.

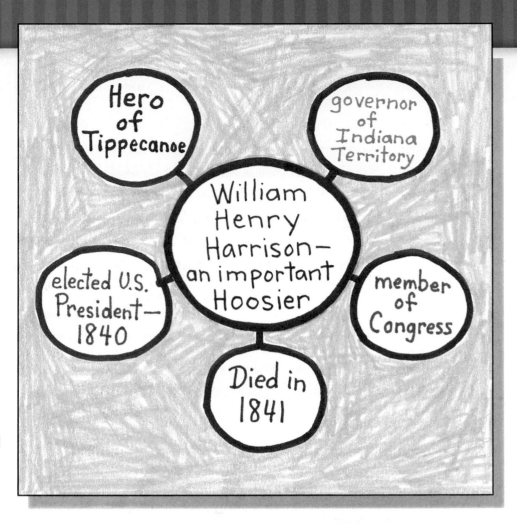

Think and Apply

2 How do you know which idea in the web is the main idea?

2 What is an outline?

3 How can you identify the main topics in the outline shown on page 188?

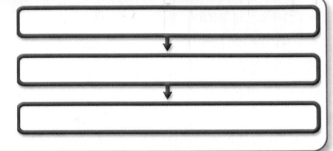

1810   1815   1820

1814
George Rapp
started Harmonie.

1816
Indiana became a state.
Abraham Lincoln came
to Indiana.

1818
The New
Purchase

Chapter Summary

Target Skill

Sequence

Draw the chart on a sheet of paper. In each box, write a sentence that describes one stage in the settlement of Indiana. Make sure the stages are in order.

Vocabulary

Match each word with the correct definition or description.

1. **legislative branch** (p. 174)

2. **executive branch** (p. 174)

3. **judicial branch** (p. 174)

4. **immigrate** (p. 178)

5. **enforce** (p. 185)

6. **fugitive slave** (p. 185)

7. **utopia** (p. 187)

a. to carry out

b. to move to a new country

c. branch of government that carries out laws

d. a perfect community

e. branch of government that makes laws

f. enslaved person who has run away

g. branch of government that decides questions about laws

People and Terms

Write a sentence explaining why each of the following people or terms was important in Indiana. You may use two or more in a single sentence.

1. **Jonathan Jennings** (p. 173)

2. **Enabling Act** (p. 173)

3. **Constitutional Convention** (p. 173)

4. **Treaty of St. Mary's** (p. 177)

5. **New Purchase** (p. 177)

6. **Abraham Lincoln** (p. 178)

7. **Menominee** (p. 186)

8. **Trail of Death** (p. 186)

9. **George Rapp** (p. 187)

10. **Robert Owen** (p. 187)

1825	1830	1835	1840

1824
New Harmony was started by Robert Owen.

1825
Indianapolis became capital.

1838
Potawatomi were forced onto Trail of Death to Kansas.

Facts and Main Ideas

1. How did central and northern Indiana become open for settlement?

2. Why did the legislature choose the location of Indianapolis for its capital?

3. Where did newcomers to Indiana come from in the frontier years?

4. **Time Line** How many years passed between the New Purchase and the Trail of Death?

5. **Main Idea** List the major steps required for Indiana to become a state.

6. **Main Idea** What did the Treaty of St. Mary's give the Miami?

7. **Main Idea** How did life change for American Indians in Indiana in the early 1800s?

8. **Critical Thinking: *Draw Conclusions*** Why did New Harmony fail as a utopian community?

Write About History

1. **Write a short skit** that takes place in frontier Indiana. Do research so you can include details about how frontier Hoosiers lived and worked.

2. **Write a news report** about the Trail of Death. Include information that tells who, what, when, where, and why.

3. **Write a poem** about your pride in being a Hoosier. It may be serious or humorous.

Apply Skills

Notes and Outlines

Copy the web below. Add details from Lesson 3 of this chapter to give more information about the topic in the center of the web.

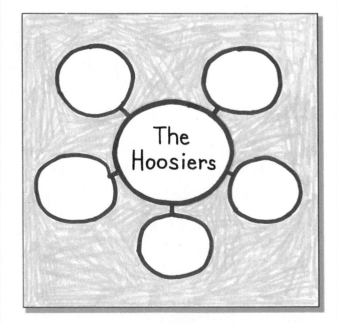

The Hoosiers

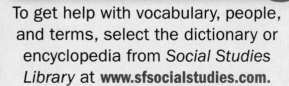

Internet Activity

To get help with vocabulary, people, and terms, select the dictionary or encyclopedia from *Social Studies Library* at **www.sfsocialstudies.com**.

CHAPTER 7

Growth and Change

Lesson 1

1836
Madison
New ways of traveling change the state.

1

Lesson 2

1846
Bloomington
Support for public schools grows.

2

Lesson 3

1850
Indianapolis
Most Hoosiers are still farmers, but towns and cities are growing.

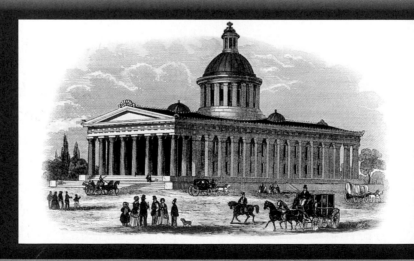

3

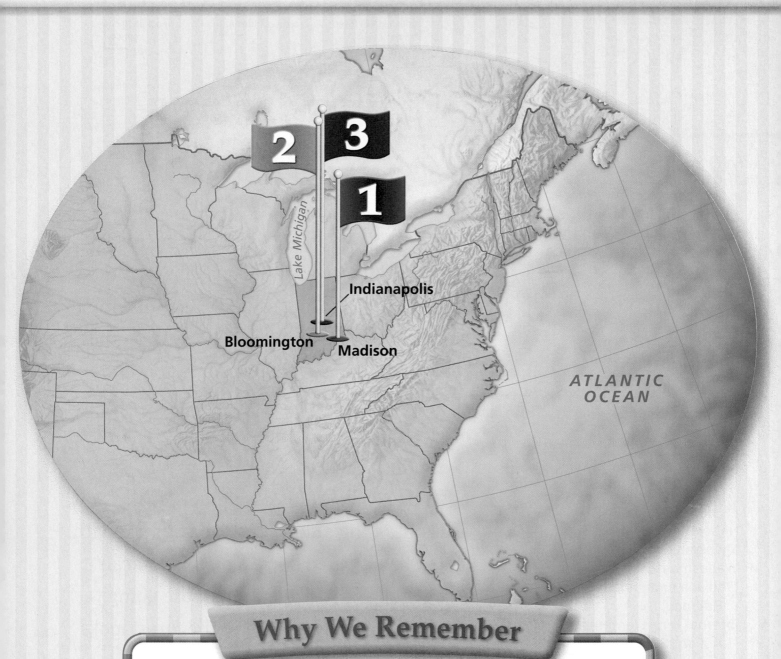

Lake Michigan

2

3

1

Indianapolis

Bloomington

Madison

ATLANTIC OCEAN

Why We Remember

Do you know our state motto? It is *Crossroads of America*. A crossroads is where roads meet. In fact, Indiana had few roads in the early 1800s. But as the United States expanded across the continent, Indiana's location near the center made it a busy place. By the 1850s, it not only had many good roads, it had miles and miles of canals and railroads too. Indiana had become an important transportation center—a true crossroads of the nation.

Madison

1810   1820   1830   1840   1850

1811
First steamboat
sails on Ohio River.

1834
National Road
crosses Indiana.

1847
First railroad
line in Indiana
opens.

PREVIEW

Focus on the Main Idea
Indiana built new ways to
travel and to transport goods.

PLACES

Madison
Lafayette
New Albany

VOCABULARY

manufacture
trade
canal
demand

TERMS

National Road
Michigan Road
Wabash and Erie Canal
Madison and Indianapolis
   Railroad
Internal Improvements
   Act of 1836

New Ways to Travel

You Are There
You are following the road
toward Indianapolis in the
spring of 1839. But you aren't
going anywhere right now. The mud on the
road holds like glue! Your poor horse
struggles to pull his hooves out of the sticky,
black stuff. He only sinks deeper.

You're afraid to dismount. You might not
be able to walk in this deep mud. Finally, you
slide out of the saddle. With all your strength,
you pull your tired horse along. If you can
just get off the road, you think, the going
will be easier. The ground in the forest looks
fairly dry.

 Sequence As you
read, look for the
ways in which travel
improved in Indiana
over time.

▶ Muddy roads made
travel difficult.

The Need for Roads

On the whole, Indiana pioneers were very successful. They managed to feed themselves, keep warm and dry, and take care of their families. Many grew enough food so that they had extra to sell. With the cash from the sale of corn and hogs, families could afford to buy manufactured products. To **manufacture** means to make in a factory. For example, pioneers might buy cloth and tools.

Before farmers could sell their hogs, corn, and other products, they had to get them to market—a place where buyers and sellers exchange goods and services. This exchange of goods and services is called **trade.** People who manufactured goods needed to get them to their Indiana customers too.

▶ **Hoosiers used specialized craft such as this flatboat to transport goods by river.**

In the early 1800s, this was not easy. Indiana had few roads. Roads that existed were just paths, and they were often muddy. Most Hoosiers carried their goods by water. Boats moved along the Wabash and Ohio Rivers. They headed down the Mississippi River to New Orleans, Louisiana. From there the goods could be shipped to other parts of the world.

People used two main kinds of boats on the rivers. Flatboats, as the name suggests, had flat bottoms. They carried products downstream only. Keelboats could go downstream or upstream. They were lighter than flatboats. Their hull was a different shape. The crew used poles and ropes to push and pull them along.

REVIEW Why did farmers need a good system of transportation?
Summarize

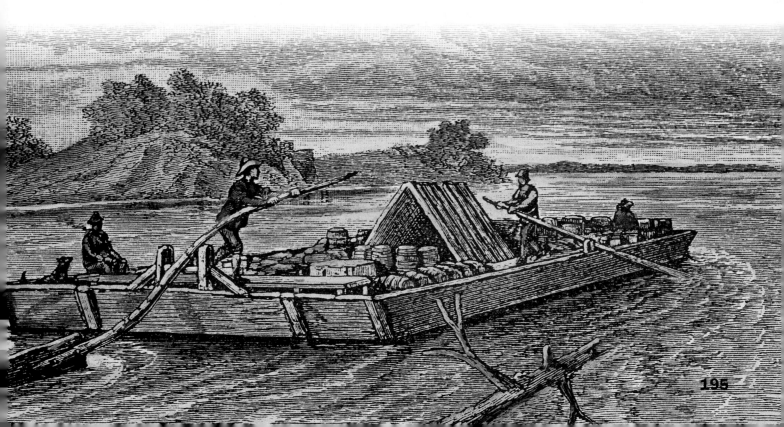

Roads and Canals

In 1811, the United States government began work on the **National Road.** This road would link Maryland on the Atlantic Coast to the Mississippi River. The road was completed through Indiana in 1834. Today, U.S. 40 follows much of its route. Next, the state of Indiana built the **Michigan Road.** When it was finished in 1836, it connected **Madison,** on the Ohio River, to Lake Michigan. Even these big roads were not like the roads we have today. They were really just cleared paths.

Traveling by steamboat—a boat powered by a steam engine—was much more comfortable than traveling by road. Plus, steamboats could carry more freight faster and more cheaply than other types of transportation. Steamboats started traveling the Ohio River in 1811. But they could travel only in deep water. People solved that problem by building canals. A **canal** is a human-made waterway. People could build canals through places with shallow water—or no water at all. By 1825, the Erie Canal connected the Great Lakes to the Hudson River. It was a huge success.

In 1832, Hoosiers began work on the **Wabash and Erie Canal.** Three years later, it connected Fort Wayne and Huntington. Hoosiers began building three more canals. Soon canal boats could travel from the Great Lakes all the way to the Ohio River. But by 1839, the era of canal building ended. It ended because the state ran out of money. It also ended with the coming of the railroads.

REVIEW Would you rather travel on the National Road or on the Wabash and Erie Canal? Explain. **Draw Conclusions**

Early Railroads

Railroads were invented in Great Britain. The first railway in the United States was a horse-drawn line built in Massachusetts in 1827. The next year, work began on a full-scale passenger railroad. The Baltimore and Ohio line reached the Ohio River town of Wheeling, in what is now West Virginia, in 1853.

Hoosiers quickly joined the railroad boom. By the time the Wabash and Erie Canal was finished, Indiana had one thousand miles of track and had plans for over two thousand more.

▶ **People worked on road, canal, and railroad projects throughout Indiana.**

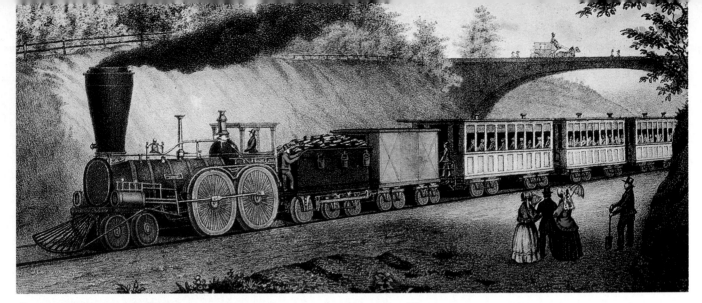

▶ Railroads changed Indiana, helping many towns become big cities.

What made railroads better than canals? Railroads were faster and more dependable. Canals froze in winter and could not be used. Also, canals had to connect to waterways and follow the course of rivers. Trains could take more direct routes.

Indiana's first railroad was the **Madison and Indianapolis Railroad.** It connected the two cities. It also provided a good way to carry freight between the Ohio and Mississippi Rivers and these cities. Soon it became clear that towns on the railroad line would prosper and grow quickly. Workers and businesses flocked to these towns to work for or serve the needs of the railroad.

By 1855, seven railroad lines passed through Indianapolis. Indiana was beginning to earn its motto. It was becoming the "Crossroads of America."

REVIEW Why did towns want to be on railroad lines? Cause and Effect

Working on the Railroad

Canals and railroads changed Indiana in many ways. Farmers could send products to market faster and more cheaply. As a result, they could earn more from their crops. A bushel of corn that sold for ten cents in Indianapolis might sell for fifty cents at Madison. Farmers could send products to where the **demand** —the number of consumers willing and able to buy goods—was greatest. Higher demand meant higher prices.

Indiana needed thousands of workers to dig canals and build railroads. Immigrants came to help. Many came from Ireland. By 1850, Irish people made up 23 percent of Indiana's immigrant population. Germans made up 53 percent of the immigrant population. These newcomers helped give Indiana the sixth largest population in the United States in 1860.

REVIEW How did railroads and canals change Indiana? Compare and Contrast

Map Adventure

Get the Goods to Market

It is September 1859. You need to bring hogs, corn, and beeswax to market from your farm near Lafayette. Where will you ship your products? What method of transportation will you use?

A. You hear that hogs are bringing a good price in Chicago. What method of transportation will you use?

B. You have also heard that beeswax prices are high in New Orleans. How will you get your beeswax there?

C. You want to send your corn to Indianapolis, but you don't want to use the railroad. How will you ship your corn?

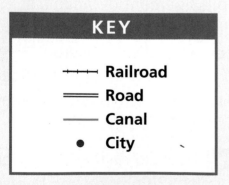

KEY

+—+—+ **Railroad**

===== **Road**

——— **Canal**

● **City**

Money Trouble

The General Assembly passed the **Internal Improvements Act of 1836.** This act called for the state to build three canals and a railroad between Madison and **Lafayette.** It also promised a road from **New Albany** to Vincennes, as well as other projects. The General Assembly borrowed ten million dollars to pay for the act. At the time, Indiana's income was less than seventy-five thousand dollars a year.

Soon the state was unable to repay the money it had borrowed.

This disaster hurt the state's reputation. Work on the canals stopped. Many were left unfinished. In 1851, Indiana adopted a new constitution. The state was no longer allowed to borrow money.

REVIEW Why did the state stop work on the canals? *Cause and Effect*

Summarize the Lesson

- **1811** First steamboat sailed on Ohio River.
- **1834** National Road crossed Indiana.
- **1847** First railroad line in Indiana opened.

▶ Indiana issued its own money in the 1840s.

LESSON 1   REVIEW

Check Facts and Main Ideas

1. ⟳ **Sequence** Copy this chart on a sheet of paper. Arrange these Indiana transportation improvements in the order they took place: steamboats, railroads, canals.

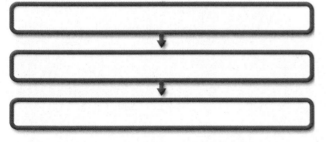

2. What does it mean to "take goods to market"?

3. Where did Indiana find workers for its canals and railroads?

4. Describe the advantages of railroads over canals. What kinds of problems did travel on canals pose?

5. **Critical Thinking:** *Draw Conclusions* Was it a good idea for the new constitution to forbid Indiana from borrowing money? Explain.

Link to ⚭ Mathematics

Are We There Yet?
Read the information and answer the question.

- A keelboat with a large crew could travel as fast as six miles a day upstream.
- By water it is about seven hundred miles from New Orleans to Evansville.

About how many days would it take a keelboat to make the journey? About how many weeks? About how many months?

199

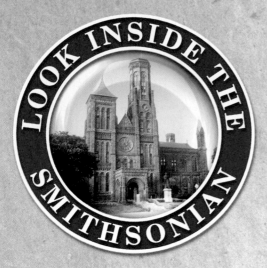

Changes in Transportation

The 1800s brought many changes in the way Americans traveled and transported goods. New roads, railways, and waterways made travel between distant points quicker and easier. Old modes of transportation such as wagons and carriages were adapted for use on these routes. Also, new, steam-powered trains and ships began to change the world of transportation.

The John Bull
This locomotive—the oldest of its kind in working order—was made in England and shipped in pieces to the United States in 1831. When it was reassembled, it was put to work on one of the nation's first railways, the Camden and Amboy Railroad in New Jersey. The locomotive was retired in 1866. In 1981, 115 years after its last run, it ran again. It chugged its way down the track of the old Georgetown Branch line in Washington, D.C.!

Conestoga Wagon
Conestoga wagons hauled wheat, flour, furs, and other goods across southern Pennsylvania and Maryland. Covered wagons similar to the Conestoga carried homesteaders into the farther frontiers of the West.

The Indiana
This steamship carried people and goods on the Great Lakes. Built in 1848, the *Indiana* had a propeller rather than the big paddle-wheel found on most steamships of the time. In 1858, a blade on the *Indiana's* propeller broke, and the ship sank to the bottom of Lake Superior.

This drawing of the *John Bull* is from a letter written by one of its first passengers. Notice the artist has even indicated the car in which he or she rode.

The Pioneer

This locomotive, built in Boston in 1851, is a fine example of a mid-century steam engine. It was damaged in the Civil War when Confederate troops burned the Pennsylvania train yard where it was located.

The Concord Mail Coach

This stagecoach was built in 1851 in Concord, New Hampshire. Stagecoaches such as this one carried passengers in the large main compartment, but if the coach was full, passengers would also ride on the roof! Mail was usually carried in a compartment under the driver's seat. Stagecoaches were in use in the United States well into the early 1900s.

Artifacts are from the ✸ Smithsonian Institution.

Use an Inset Map

What? An **inset map** shows a small area of a larger map in greater detail. The area is outlined on the larger map. Then it is enlarged and reproduced near the larger map. The main map and its inset always have different scales. Remember that **scale** is a unit of measure that is used to represent a real distance on Earth. Because the inset map shows a much smaller area, it uses a different scale. Notice that on the transportation map below, one inch represents 250 miles. On the inset map of Indiana, one inch represents 100 miles.

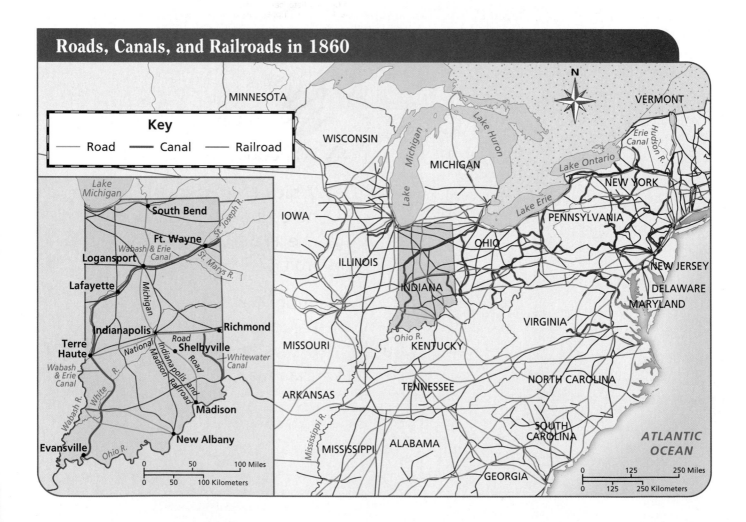

Roads, Canals, and Railroads in 1860

Key
— Road — Canal — Railroad

Why? Maps can give you different kinds of information. The main map gives you information about national transportation routes in the 1850s. The inset map gives you more detailed information about your own state. The amount of detail in a map is related to the amount of area it shows. A map covering a large area, such as the main transportation map, does not show many details. A map of a smaller area, such as the Indiana inset, can give you detailed information about that area.

© Tippecanoe County Historical Association, Lafayette, Indiana.
Gift of Mrs. Cable G. Ball / Tippecanoe County Historical Association

▶ **Building the Wabash and Erie Canal**

How? Look at the main map and the inset map on page 202. Find the scale of the main map. How many miles are represented by one inch? Notice that the map shows many states. Now look at the inset map of Indiana. What is the scale of this map? What information can you find on the inset map that you can't find on the main map?

The kind of map you use depends on the kind of information you need. If you want to find a particular street in Fort Wayne, you may need an inset map of that city. A map of the Midwest will not help you. If you want a map that shows the entire route of a major highway, a less detailed map of a larger area will contain the information you need.

Think and Apply

1. What does an inset map show?

2. Which of the two maps shown here would be best for checking how far Indiana is from New York?

3. Suppose you learned that Parke County has many covered bridges. If you had a state map of Indiana with an inset of Parke County, which map would you use to find the covered bridges?

For more information, go online to the *Atlas* at **www.sfsocialstudies.com**.

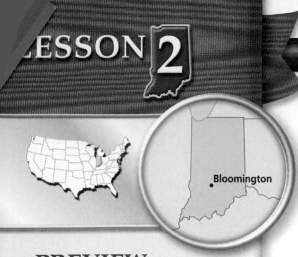
1820	1830	1840	1850	1860

1820
Indiana University opens.

1840s
Caleb Mills campaigns for public education.

1860s
Indiana first has a statewide system of public education.

Bloomington

PREVIEW

Focus on the Main Idea
Hoosiers improved public education and built colleges in the 1800s.

PLACES
Bloomington

PEOPLE
Caleb Mills

VOCABULARY
college
university

TERMS
public education

Learning in Indiana

You Are There

Marion County, Indiana
December 5, 1828

Dear Mother and Father:

I arrived here safely on Friday. My room with the Johnson family is very fine. The Johnson boy, Martin, is an eager student.

The school is a tight log building. It has a good stove and a large woodpile. My young scholars sit on long benches. Twelve children are enrolled for the winter months. Mr. Johnson has kindly given me the use of his Bible. We now have two Bibles and the reader and speller I brought with me. We will make do.

Your loving son,
Oliver

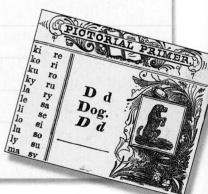

Sequence As you read, look for details of how schools in Indiana changed in the early 1800s and beyond.

Public Schools

The 1816 Constitution promised that the General Assembly would set up

> *"a general system of education…from township schools to a state university, wherein tuition shall be gratis [free], and equally open to all."*

The General Assembly also added a note that it would create this system "as soon as circumstances will permit" [as soon as possible]. However, by the 1840s, Indiana still did not have a system of **public education**—free schooling for all.

Most pioneer children spent little time in school. Abraham Lincoln, for example, went to school for only about one year in all. Parents who were able taught their children to read, write, and do simple arithmetic.

No state or local taxes supported schools. Some towns did start schools, but students had to pay to attend. Many religious groups started private schools. However, by 1840, only about 25 percent of children between ages five and fifteen attended school. As a result, many Hoosiers could not read or write.

In the 1840s, a New England teacher named **Caleb Mills** came to Indiana. He started a campaign for public education. Mills said that Indiana needed schools, teachers, and books. He also said that people should pay taxes to support them. Many Hoosiers agreed. They demanded that the legislature pass laws to pay for schools. They were successful. However, a full public school system was not in place until the late 1860s.

REVIEW How did Indiana's lack of schools affect its residents? **Cause and Effect**

▶ Reunion of students at a log school house in Allen County. The building was taken down in 1900.

College Days

Even before it had a statewide public school system, Indiana had many colleges. A **college** is a school more advanced than a high school. Seven colleges were started in Indiana before the Civil War began in 1861.

The state's first college became Indiana University. A **university** is a school that usually includes two or more colleges. IU, as we call it today, was founded in 1820 in **Bloomington.** It began as a state college that provided religious training. It was set up by the General Assembly.

Although Indiana University was a state college, in its early days it had strong ties to the Presbyterian Church. The other six of the state's first colleges were started by religious groups. In 1827, Hanover College opened. Wabash College welcomed its first students in 1832. Other colleges quickly followed. Franklin College opened in 1834, and Indiana Asbury, later called DePauw, opened in 1837. Eight French priests started Notre Dame in 1842. It was the state's first Catholic college. The Society of Friends, also known as Quakers, started Earlham College in Richmond in 1847.

FACT FILE

Education in Indiana

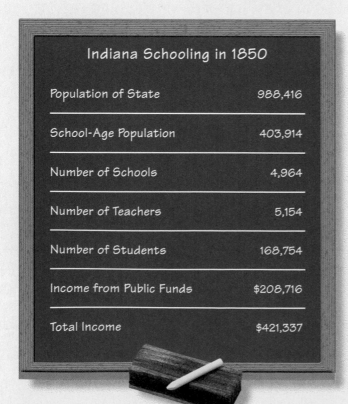

Indiana Schooling in 1850

Population of State	988,416
School-Age Population	403,914
Number of Schools	4,964
Number of Teachers	5,154
Number of Students	168,754
Income from Public Funds	$208,716
Total Income	$421,337

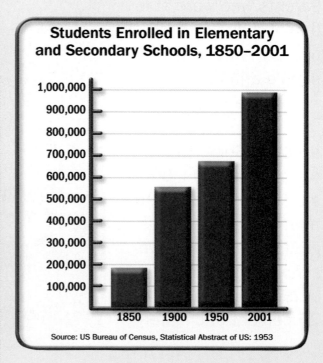

Students Enrolled in Elementary and Secondary Schools, 1850–2001

Source: US Bureau of Census, Statistical Abstract of US: 1953

Among Indiana's first colleges was Wabash, shown here.

Towns fought for colleges just as they fought for railroads. People knew that if a college opened nearby, the town would grow. Its stores and businesses would have more customers.

Many students of Indiana's first colleges became leaders in the state.

Many also worked and campaigned for public schools.

Today, Indiana is home to forty-one four-year colleges and universities. There are also many two-year colleges. Our colleges and universities attract students from around the world. Indiana University is especially famous for its medical, dental, and music schools.

REVIEW What groups started most of the early colleges in Indiana?
Main Idea and Details

Summarize the Lesson

- **1820** Indiana University opened.
- **1840s** Caleb Mills campaigned for public education.
- **1860s** Indiana had a statewide system of public education.

LESSON 2 REVIEW

Check Facts and Main Ideas

1. **Sequence** Draw the chart on a sheet of paper. Find three events in the history of Indiana's schools and colleges. Write one event in each box in the correct sequence.

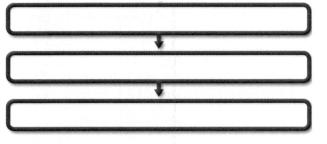

2. Describe what education was like on the Indiana frontier.

3. When did Indiana first have a system of statewide public education?

4. What role did religious groups play in education in Indiana?

5. **Critical Thinking:** *Draw Conclusions* What was one result of the state's failure to set up a public school system?

Link to Art

Paint a Mural Show what a classroom in Indiana might have looked like in the 1860s. You will have to do some research to find details to include. Display your mural for other students in your school.

Seeking Education

Hoosiers debated the need for public education in the 1840s. The debate continues today about what kind of education there should be and about who should pay for it.

The son of a New Hampshire farmer, Caleb Mills attended Dartmouth College in his home state. He became a Presbyterian minister and moved to Crawfordsville, Indiana. There he started a school that later became Wabash College.

The poor system of public education in Indiana shocked Mills. He was surprised that the state had few elementary schools and even fewer high schools.

In 1846, Mills began a campaign for public schools in Indiana. He wrote to state legislators. He spoke to parents. He made people understand that public education was important. Still, some Hoosiers didn't want statewide public education. They believed education was important. But they wanted local schools to be controlled by local people.

Mills was part of a movement in the United States to make the country better—to reform it. Good public education for all children was one of the reform movement's goals.

Caleb Mills

"If the time shall ever come when this mighty fabric shall tatter . . . the cause will be found in the ignorance of the people. If our union is still to continue to cheer the hopes . . . of the oppressed of every nation. . . . EDUCATE ALL THE CHILDREN OF THE LAND."

John B. Dillon, *Indiana, 1836*

Today people hold different views about how to make schools better. Hoosiers want all students to get the best education possible. But there are many different ideas about how to achieve this goal. Should the government help pay for students to attend private schools, as well as public schools? Should students be free to choose the public school of their choice? Should the cities and towns decide how to spend education money?

"I believe in the . . . duty of every government to see that the means of education are provided for all."

Horace Mann, *Massachusetts, 1846*

"One size does not fit all when it comes to educating our children, so local people should control local schools."

George W. Bush, *Philadelphia, 2000*

"School choice . . . encourages students and parents to be more committed to the pursuit of a good education, and encourages schools to be more responsive to the needs of all students."

State Senator Teresa Lubbers, *Indianapolis, 2001*

Horace Mann

Issues and You

List as many reasons as you can think of for going to school. List as many reasons as you can for paying taxes so everyone can go to school. Interview your family and friends. Ask them whether they think public education is important. How does it help each person if everybody in the state is educated? Take notes as you listen to their answers. Plan to report your group's findings to the rest of the class.

1850　1860　1870　1880

1852
First state fair held in Indiana

1869
First Grange begins in Indiana

1874
Purdue University founded

Indianapolis

PREVIEW

Focus on the Main Idea
In 1850, Indiana was an agricultural state with growing cities.

PLACES

Purdue University
West Lafayette
Indianapolis

VOCABULARY

goods
services
industry

TERMS

Grange
state fair
land-grant college
commercial district

Hoosier Life

You Are There
You've forgotten about the buggy ride to the fair grounds. You've forgotten the lunch your mother packed. You can only think about the judges as they take one more look at the melons arranged on the table. The judges have sliced open each melon, studied it, and tasted it. Your melon must be the best. Every day since you planted it, you've checked the melon vine. You've pulled bugs from the plant and watered it carefully. The judges whisper to each other. One places a ribbon on the melon right next to yours. Then a judge puts the "first prize" ribbon on your melon. You've won!

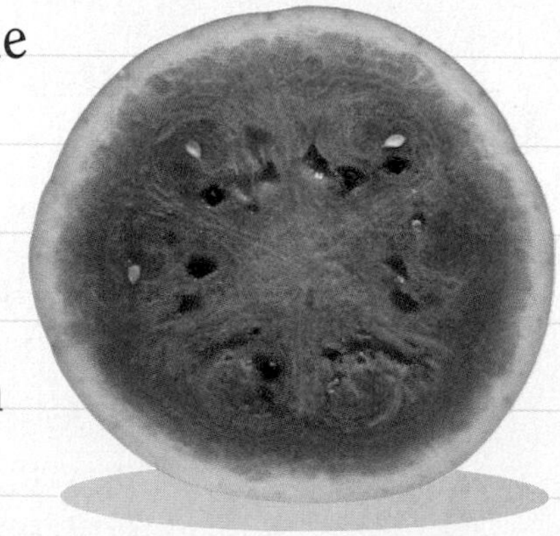

Draw Conclusions As you read, draw conclusions about the changes in Indiana during the mid-1800s.

▶ **A farm in Hamilton County, Indiana, in the late 1800s**

A Farmer's Life

In 1850, most Hoosiers were farmers. Only about five percent of the population lived in towns of more than twenty-five hundred people. Indiana was already one of the top five states for producing corn and hogs.

Farming was lonely work. Families had little chance to visit with other people or to learn about better ways to farm. But farm life began to improve in the mid-1800s. New roads, canals, and railroads helped farmers get their products to market more easily. They helped make life less lonely, as well.

In 1869, a new organization called the **Grange** came to Indiana. The Grange was started to educate farm families. Speakers presented new ideas about farming. Grange meetings were social events as well. In just seven years, Indiana became home to three thousand Grange chapters. Soon the Grange became a strong political force. This organization worked to get lower railroad rates for farmers. Farmers elected Grange members to the General Assembly.

County and state fairs started about this time too. The Indiana **state fair** was held for the first time in 1852. The fair drew exhibits and visitors from all over Indiana. Farmers could study the newest machines at the displays set up by manufacturers. Farm families brought their best livestock and produce for competition. It was a source of pride to win first prize.

Purdue University was founded in **West Lafayette** in 1874. It was a **land-grant college,** a college supported in part by the federal government. The government gave land to the state to start a college strong in agriculture and mechanical arts. State taxes continue to pay for land-grant colleges.

REVIEW What organizations and events improved Hoosier farm life in the mid-1800s? **Summarize**

Towns and Cities

By 1850, towns and cities were becoming more important to Hoosier life. They provided farmers with **goods** — items people buy—and **services** — work that helps others, such as repairing a tool. In 1850, Indiana had over 200 villages, towns, and cities. New Albany was the largest, followed by **Indianapolis**. Each had about 8,000 residents. But by 1860, Indianapolis and its 18,611 people was largest.

Hoosiers built the first large towns on rivers. Later, towns sprang up along railroad lines. Indianapolis became a railroad hub—a place where many railroad lines connect.

Northern Indiana towns started to grow in the 1830s. Fort Wayne had about 300 residents in 1830.

Growing Corn

Then and Now

Indiana farmers grew lots of corn in the mid-1800s, and they still do. But the way we grow corn has changed a great deal.

In the 1800s, farmers saved the best seed from each harvest to use as seed for the next crop. They harvested corn by cutting the plants off near the bottom. Then they gathered the plants, or shocks, into bundles and tied them. The next step was pulling off the ears of corn and gathering them into the barn.

Today's farmers carefully study scientific data about different seeds. Then they buy seed from a seed dealer. Computers help them decide when to plant. Planting and harvesting is done by machine. Most modern farmers use a scientific system of fertilizers and insect controls. A big part of a farmer's time today is spent making business decisions. Farmers need to know how much they have spent on a crop and how much they can sell it for.

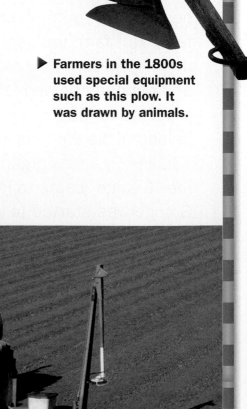

▶ Farmers in the 1800s used special equipment such as this plow. It was drawn by animals.

▶ Modern machinery helps today's farmers produce huge amounts of food.

By 1840, it had five times as many. Some towns in northern Indiana began to attract **industry,** or big business. South Bend and Mishawaka, for example, had mills. They produced goods such as flour, cloth, lumber, and iron.

Most town centers had a courthouse and square. Around the square was the **commercial district** —an area of shops and businesses that served town residents. Streets were made of dirt. No towns had water or sewage systems at this time. There was no garbage collection.

REVIEW What did large Indiana towns have in common? *Summarize*

▶ Indiana towns were important centers of trade for Hoosier farmers.

Summarize the Lesson

— **1852** First state fair held in Indiana

— **1869** First Grange begun in Indiana

— **1874** Purdue University founded

LESSON 3   REVIEW

Check Facts and Main Ideas

1. Draw Conclusions On a sheet of paper, write three facts that support the conclusion.

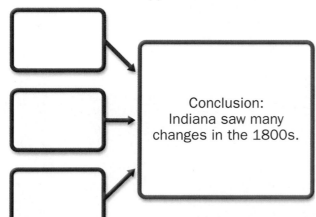

Conclusion: Indiana saw many changes in the 1800s.

2. How did the Grange improve farm life?

3. What was the largest town in Indiana in 1850? In 1860?

4. Describe three ways in which farm life improved in the mid-1800s.

5. Critical Thinking: *Make Predictions* As Indiana towns continued to grow, what problems do you think they faced?

Link to ⚭ Mathematics

How Did They Grow? Choose three Indiana cities or towns and find out about their populations. How many people did they have in 1850? How many in 1860? How many times bigger did they grow during this time?

Indiana and California

The Gold Rush

While Hoosiers were growing corn, a new "crop" was creating excitement out West. A carpenter building a sawmill discovered gold in the American River north of Sacramento, California, on January 24, 1848.

The Gold Rush was on! First reports from the gold fields said miners were earning $30,000 to $50,000 a day. Many young Hoosiers were ready to leave Indiana to find gold in California. Once miners arrived in California, they discovered that gold was not that easy to find and that it took a lot of gold or gold dust just to pay for food and supplies.

◀ Posters like this one advertised for people to go and make their fortunes in the gold fields.

▶ People with goods to sell made a lot of money. Hoosier John Studebaker sold wheelbarrows in California during the Gold Rush. He brought his earnings back to Indiana to help run the family wagon business, which later became the Studebaker Automobile Company.

▲ Gold nuggets were weighed on a scale. The more gold, the more money prospectors earned.

214

▲ Prospectors used pans to scoop sand, rocks, and—they hoped—gold from the river. The gold was then washed out of the sand and rocks in a long trough like the one shown here.

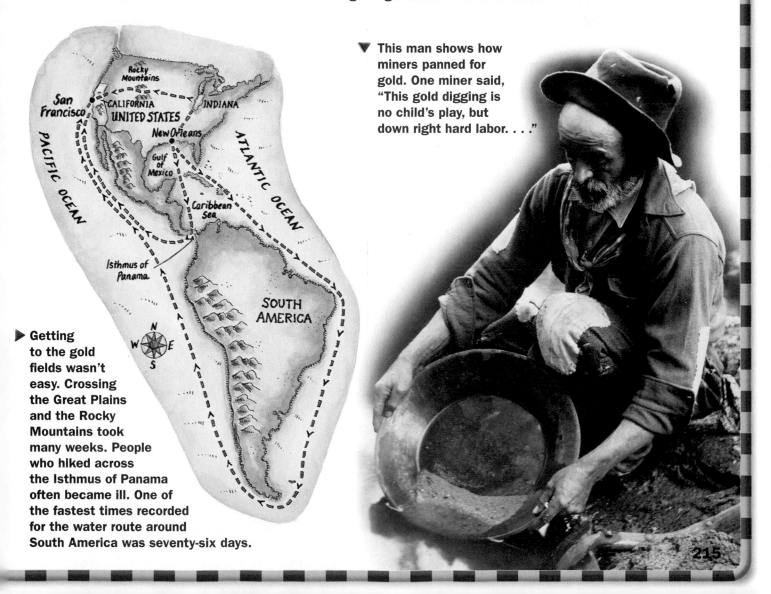

▼ This man shows how miners panned for gold. One miner said, "This gold digging is no child's play, but down right hard labor. . . ."

Rocky Mountains

San Francisco

CALIFORNIA
UNITED STATES

INDIANA

New Orleans

PACIFIC OCEAN

Gulf of Mexico

ATLANTIC OCEAN

Caribbean Sea

Isthmus of Panama

SOUTH AMERICA

N W E S

▶ Getting to the gold fields wasn't easy. Crossing the Great Plains and the Rocky Mountains took many weeks. People who hiked across the Isthmus of Panama often became ill. One of the fastest times recorded for the water route around South America was seventy-six days.

215

Chapter Summary

Sequence

Target Skill

Draw the chart on a sheet of paper. Write one of these events in each box in the correct sequence.

- Indiana builds roads and canals.
- Indiana begins a statewide system of education.
- The first Grange begins in Indiana.

Growth and Change

[ ]
↓
[ ]
↓
[ ]

Vocabulary

Match each word with the correct definition or description.

1. manufacture (p. 195)
2. trade (p. 195)
3. canal (p. 196)
4. demand (p. 197)
5. college (p. 206)
6. university (p. 206)
7. goods (p. 212)
8. services (p. 212)
9. industry (p. 213)

a. a school with two or more colleges

b. a waterway made by humans

c. big business

d. make in a factory

e. exchange of goods and services

f. number of consumers willing to buy goods

g. work that helps others

h. items people buy

i. a school after high school

Terms

Write a sentence explaining why each of the following terms was important in Indiana. You may use two or more in a single sentence.

1. National Road (p. 196)
2. Michigan Road (p. 196)
3. Wabash and Erie Canal (p. 196)
4. Madison and Indianapolis Railroad (p. 197)
5. Internal Improvements Act of 1836 (p. 199)
6. public education (p. 205)
7. Grange (p. 211)
8. state fair (p. 211)
9. commercial district (p. 213)

1850			1860		1870		1880

1847
First railroad line in Indiana opens

1852
First state fair held in Indiana

1853
Wabash and Erie Canal completed

1860s
Indiana first has a statewide system of public education; First Grange begins in Indiana

1874
Purdue University founded

Facts and Main Ideas

1 How did building canals and railroads change the population of Indiana?

2 Why did Hoosiers need better forms of transportation in the early 1800s?

3 Why wasn't the Internal Improvements Act of 1836 carried out?

4 **Time Line** About how many years passed from the time Caleb Mills worked for a statewide system of public education to the time when Indiana actually had such a system?

5 **Main Idea** List three ways in which Indiana changed between 1820 and 1860.

6 **Main Idea** Why did Hoosiers stop building canals in favor of railroads?

7 **Main Idea** How did Caleb Mills influence Indiana's education system?

8 **Critical Thinking:** *Analyze* Where did towns that grew in the mid-1800s tend to be located? Why?

Write About History

1 **Write a paragraph** describing how most Hoosiers earned their living in 1850.

2 **Write a news report** about the General Assembly and its passage of the Internal Improvements Act of 1836.

3 **Write a short skit** about workers on the Wabash and Erie Canal or the Madison and Indianapolis Railroad. Do some research so you can include details about their lives. Think about what they might have said to each other in order to write dialogue for your skit.

Apply Skills

Use an Inset Map

Use the map and inset map on page 202 to answer the questions.

1 You want some detailed information about canals in Indiana. Which map do you use?

2 You want to know where the railroad that goes through Indianapolis ends going east. Which map do you use?

3 What is the scale of the large map? The small map?

Internet Activity

To get help with vocabulary, people, and terms, select the dictionary or encyclopedia from *Social Studies Library* at **www.sfsocialstudies.com**.

UNIT
3

End with a Song

Old Brass Wagon

Play-Party from the United States

Many Hoosier pioneers loved to dance when they got together. Sometimes people played instruments. Sometimes they sang and clapped to make music to dance to.

The famous poet Carl Sandburg included this song in his classic collection of American folk music, *American Songbag,* published in 1927. He noted that it was popular in Indiana, Missouri, and Iowa. This song appears in other song collections, as well.

218

Old Brass Wagon

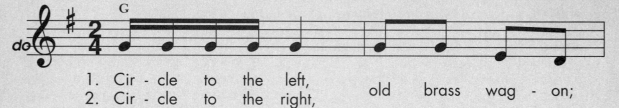

1. Cir - cle   to   the   left,   old   brass   wag - on;
2. Cir - cle   to   the   right,   old   brass   wag - on;

Cir - cle   to   the   left,   old   brass   wag - on;
Cir - cle   to   the   right,   old   brass   wag - on;

Cir - cle   to   the   left,   old   brass   wag - on;
Cir - cle   to   the   right,   old   brass   wag - on;

You're   the   one,   my   dar - ling.

3. Swing, oh, swing, . . .   5. Walk it up and down, . . .

4. Promenade right, . . .   6. Break and swing, . . .

Test Talk

Narrow the answer choices. Rule out answers you know are wrong.

Main Ideas and Vocabulary

TEST PREP

Read the passage below and use it to answer the questions that follow.

After the American Revolution, Virginia held claim to lands west of the Appalachian Mountains. Virginia ceded these claims to the United States government. The Northwest Ordinance set up a government for the Northwest Territory. Land <u>ordinances</u>, or laws, stated how the land was to be divided.

Two great American Indian leaders tried to defend their people's rights to their homelands. After the Battle of Fallen Timbers, Little Turtle signed the Treaty of Greenville. It gave the Americans most of present-day Ohio and part of present-day Indiana. Tecumseh tried to unite American Indian groups into a confederacy to stop white settlement. His forces were defeated at the Battle of Tippecanoe. Tecumseh was killed during the War of 1812 while fighting for Great Britain.

Indiana became a state in 1816. In 1818, American Indians gave up most of central Indiana in the Treaty of St. Mary's. The state capital was moved to Indianapolis. Settlement increased quickly. Many settlers came from the South. Others <u>immigrated</u> from Europe.

Hoosiers needed better means of transportation. In the mid-1800s they built the Michigan Road. They also built the Wabash and Erie Canal. Indiana's first railroad was completed in 1847. The state borrowed money to build roads and canals. It was unable to pay the money back. Building stopped.

Indiana's constitution called for free public education. But the state did not have such a system until the 1860s. However, the state's first seven colleges opened before 1860.

1 The Northwest Ordinance
  A gave Virginia's land to Indiana.
  B gave land to the Miami.
  C set up a government for the Northwest Territory.
  D set up public schools in Indiana.

2 In the passage, the word <u>ordinance</u> means
  A a law.
  B an educational rule.
  C an agricultural plot.
  D a southern division.

3 What does the word <u>immigrate</u> mean?
  A to move from another state to Indiana
  B to move from one's homeland to another country
  C to move inland away from the coastline
  D to move somewhere for a very short time

4 Which is the best description of Indiana history from 1787 to 1850?
  A Defeat of the American Indians, settlement, statehood, growth
  B Frontier life, peace with American Indians, growth of large cities
  C Peace with American Indians, slow growth, frontier settlements
  D Trade with American Indians, statehood, development of education for all

People and Terms

Match each person or term to its definition

1 Chief Little Turtle (p. 159)

2 William Henry Harrison (p. 162)

3 Jonathan Jennings (p. 173)

4 Robert Owen (p. 187)

5 Caleb Mills (p. 205)

6 land-grant college (p. 211)

a. worked for a statewide system of public education

b. first governor of Indiana

c. signed the Treaty of Greenville

d. government funded school

e. destroyed Prophet's Town

f. led New Harmony

Apply Skills

Create an Inset Map

Create a map of Indiana with an inset map of your community. Trace two maps or use two maps as models. Be sure to use scale correctly. Label places on both maps that you have visited or that you would like to visit.

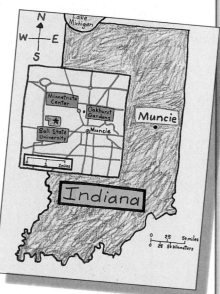

Write and Share

Write a Speech Working with a partner, choose one historical figure you have studied in this unit. Find other students who have chosen the same figure. Work together to write and deliver a speech in which this person describes his or her dreams for Indiana.

Read on Your Own

Look for books like these in the library.

Discovery CHANNEL SCHOOL

UNIT 3 Project

This Just In

Report breaking news in Indiana's history.

1 Choose an important event in Indiana's history.

2 Choose roles to play for a press conference about the event: government officials or experts, news reporters, eyewitnesses, and other participants.

3 Research the event, focusing on one or two important details of the event. Work together to write questions and answers about the event.

4 Create a poster that a TV news station might use to announce breaking news about an event.

5 Hold your press conference as a class activity.

Internet Activity

Discover important events in Indiana's history. Go to **www.sfsocialstudies.com/activities** and select your grade and unit.

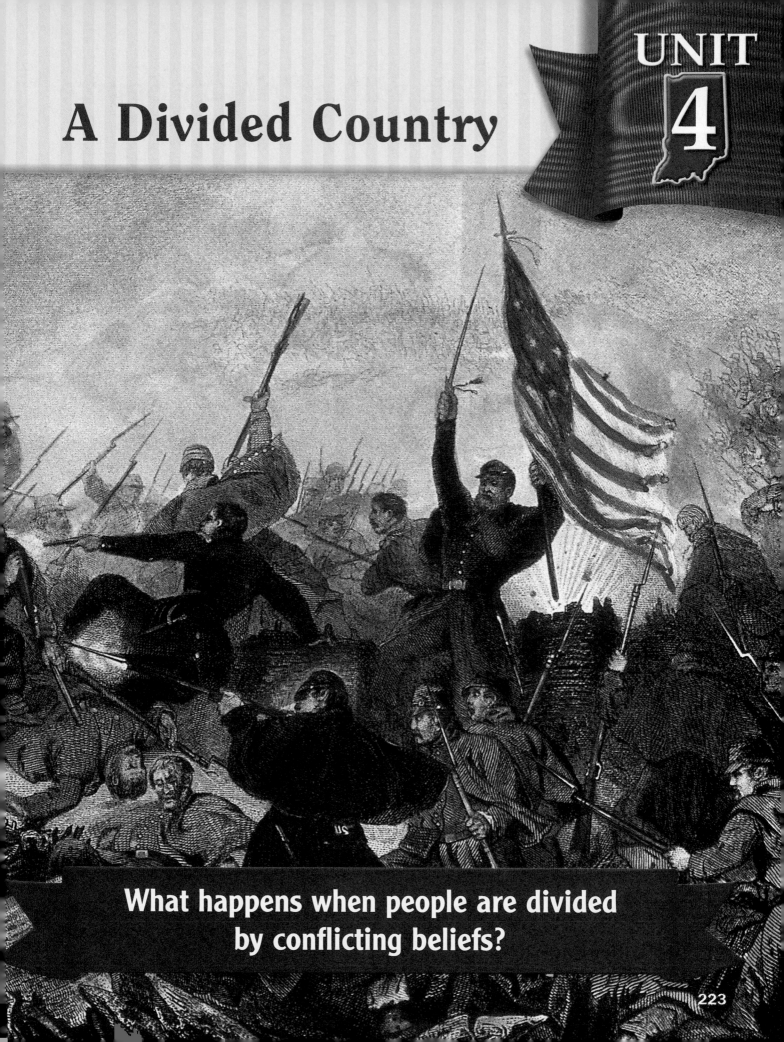

A Divided Country

UNIT
4

What happens when people are divided by conflicting beliefs?

223

UNIT 4

Begin with a Primary Source

1830   1840

1830s
Underground Railroad
begins to reach its peak.

> **"Bear in mind that . . . with you . . . is the question: Shall the Union and shall the liberties of this country be preserved . . . ?**
>
> —President-elect Abraham Lincoln, to a crowd in Indiana, February, 1861

An unknown artist engraved **Capture at Fort Donelson.** It was engraved in 1867.

1850

1850 United States government passes the Fugitive Slave Act.

1852 Harriet Beecher Stowe publishes *Uncle Tom's Cabin.*

1853 John Freeman is falsely arrested under the Fugitive Slave Act.

1860

1860 Abraham Lincoln is elected President.

1861 Confederate States of America forms. Civil War begins.

1863 John Morgan leads a raid into Indiana.

1865 Civil War ends.

Meet the People

Levi Coffin

1798–1877

Birthplace: New Garden (Greensboro), North Carolina

Abolitionist, merchant

- With his wife Katie, was a conductor on the Underground Railroad
- Helped thousands of enslaved people reach the safety of Canada
- Raised money to help newly liberated African Americans

Eliza E. George (Mother George)

1808–1865

Birthplace: Bridport, Vermont

Civil War nurse, war correspondent

- Worked as a nurse on and near the front lines of the war
- Wrote accounts of the war for Fort Wayne newspaper
- Died on duty and buried with military honors

John Freeman

1807–Unknown

Birthplace: Virginia

Businessman

- Wealthy African American in Marion County in 1850
- Falsely arrested under Fugitive Slave Law
- Fled to Canada at the beginning of Civil War

1800	1810	1820	1830	1840	1850

- 1798 • Levi Coffin
- 1807 • John Freeman
- 1808 • Eliza George (Mother George)
- 1822 • Joseph J. Reynolds
- 1823 • Oliver P. Morton
- 1825 • John Hunt Morgan

For more information, go online to *Meet the People* at **www.sfsocialstudies.com**

Joseph J. Reynolds

1822–1899

Birthplace: Flemingsburg, Kentucky

Businessman, Union army officer

- Appointed by Governor Morton to command 10th Indiana Regiment
- Commanded division during Battle of Chickamauga
- Achieved rank of Major General

Oliver P. Morton

1823–1877

Birthplace: Salisbury, Indiana

Politician

- Served as governor of Indiana during Civil War
- Became famous for his fierce commitment to the Union cause and his Hoosier volunteers
- Elected to U.S. Congress after the Civil War

John Hunt Morgan

1825–1864

Birthplace: Huntsville, Alabama

Businessman, Confederate officer

- Brigadier General in the Confederate Army
- Led raiders into Indiana and Ohio
- Killed in action after escaping from a Union prison

| 1860 | 1870 | 1880 | 1890 | 1900 | 1910 |

1877

1865

1899

1877

1864

A Divided Country

Cause and Effect

Cause	Effect
A cause is why something happens. →	An effect is what happens.

- Writers sometimes, but not always, signal cause and effect by using clue words. These include *because, so, since,* and *therefore.*

- A cause can have more than one effect. An effect can have more than one cause. Sometimes an effect can become the cause of another effect.

- Sometimes a cause is not stated in the text. In that case, ask yourself, "Why did this probably happen?" Then back up your answer with information from the text or with facts that you already know.

Read the following paragraph. Causes have been highlighted in **yellow**, and effects have been highlighted in **blue.**

In Chapter 4 you read about the American Revolution. What caused this war? After the French and Indian War, Britain tried to raise money by taxing its American colonists. The colonists protested against the new taxes. So Britain tightened its control over the colonies. Before long, the colonists' protests turned into rebellion.

Causes and Effects of the Civil War

In 1850, the government of the United States passed laws to reduce tensions between the slave-owning states in the South and the free states in the North. One of these laws was the Fugitive Slave Act. This law said that northern citizens had to capture escaped African American slaves and return them to the South. Some people in the North were angry about the cruelty of the law. They decided to work to abolish, or end, slavery. Many helped enslaved people escape to Canada. Relations between slave states and free states worsened.

In 1860, Abraham Lincoln was elected President of the United States. Soon after his election, several southern states seceded, or broke away, from the Union. One of the reasons was that they feared the new President would work to outlaw slavery. A large part of the southern culture and economy depended on slavery. Soon the nation was divided between the free states of the North, which wanted to save the Union, and the slave states of the South, which wanted to preserve a way of life.

Use the reading strategy of understanding cause and effect to answer these questions.

1 Why did the United States government pass the Fugitive Slave Act?

2 What effect did the Fugitive Slave Act have on some people in the North?

3 What caused southern states to break away from the Union?

CHAPTER 8

The Growing Divide

Lesson 1

1850
Washington, D.C.
The United States government passes the Fugitive Slave Act.

1

Lesson 2

1851
Newport
The Underground Railroad is active in Indiana and elsewhere.

2

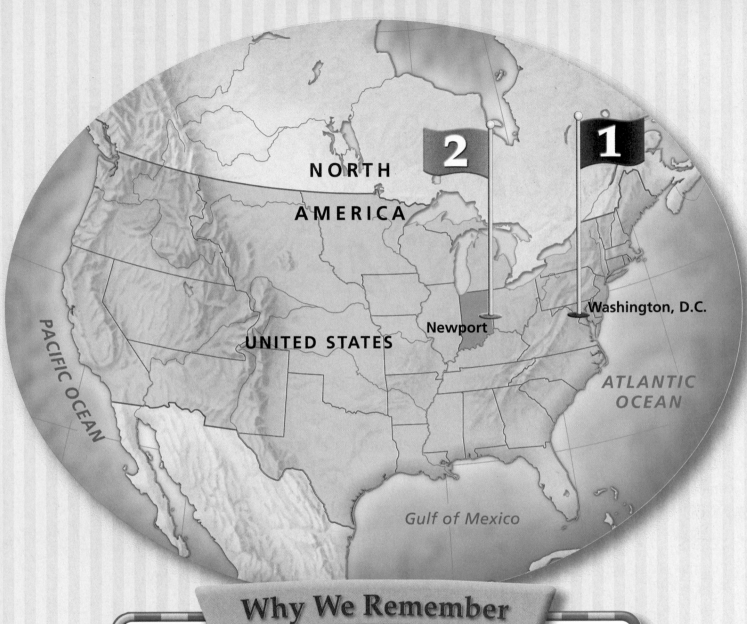

Why We Remember

As citizens of the United States, we often take for granted the right to speak our minds and make choices. From the 1600s to the 1860s, however, hundreds of thousands of African Americans were enslaved in the United States. They were denied the rights guaranteed by the Constitution. You will read about those African Americans who risked everything to gain independence. You will also read about the people of Indiana who worked to end slavery and took great risks to help enslaved people.

1850   1851   1852   1853   1854

1850
Compromise of 1850, which includes the Fugitive Slave Act, is passed.

1851
Indiana passes Article XIII.

1853
John Freeman is accused of being a runaway slave and arrested.

PREVIEW

Focus on the Main Idea
In 1850 the United States government passed the Fugitive Slave Act. This made it harder for runaway African American slaves to find safety, even in Northern free states.

PLACES
Washington, D.C.

PEOPLE
John Freeman

VOCABULARY
enslaved
commissioner

TERMS
Fugitive Slave Act
Article XIII

Indiana: A Free State

You Are There

June 23, 1853
Today we found out that our neighbor, who is a lawyer, is helping John Freeman. Mr. Freeman is the man who was accused of being a runaway slave and arrested a few days ago.

June 25, 1853
Everyone is talking about the case of John Freeman and the Fugitive Slave Act. According to the newspapers, the people of Indianapolis feel that Mr. Freeman's arrest was unjust and unfair. My parents and their friends have written letters to the newspaper saying that the new Fugitive Slave Act is cruel and terrible.

Cause and Effect As you read, look for cause-and-effect relationships between events.

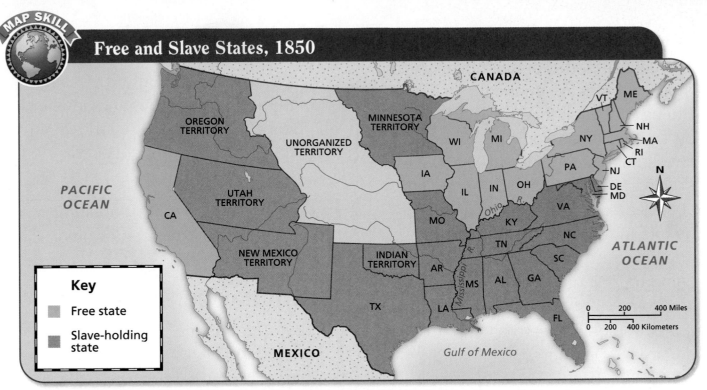

Free and Slave States, 1850

Key
- Free state
- Slave-holding state

► In 1850, large parts of North America called territories had not yet become states.

MAP SKILL Movement *What free states would people pass through to get from Indiana to Canada?*

The Fugitive Slave Act

In the mid-1800s, Indiana was one of fifteen free states. This means that it did not allow slavery. To be **enslaved** means to be owned by another person as a piece of property. Many enslaved African Americans who escaped from the South thought they would be safe in Indiana. Then the United States government in **Washington, D.C.** passed the Compromise of 1850. This compromise included laws meant to ease tensions between North and South. The **Fugitive Slave Act** was one of these laws. In it, the government agreed to help slave owners find slaves who had escaped. It required that citizens of all states help capture escaped slaves. It threatened punishment for people caught helping runaways. African Americans accused of being runaways were not allowed to speak in their own defense or to have a jury trial. Instead, **commissioners** — government officials—made the decisions.

In Indiana and other free states, officials helped slave hunters capture escaped slaves. Sometimes, free African Americans were falsely accused of being runaways. In 1853, **John Freeman** experienced this. You will read more about him on page 235. To avoid the same fate, many free African Americans fled to Canada.

REVIEW Why did many African Americans flee to Canada after 1850?
↻ **Cause and Effect**

Another Bad Law

In 1851, there were just over eleven thousand African Americans in Indiana. During that year, Indiana was at work on a new constitution. One part of that constitution stood out: **Article XIII.** This article said that no African Americans could enter or settle in Indiana. Many people in the state feared that large numbers of runaway slaves would come to Indiana, since it was close to the South.

Many Hoosiers were against this unfair law. One person called it:

> *"an outrage upon all the principles of our boasted institutions. . . ."*

But a large majority of voters approved it. The law was not often enforced, or followed. But its passage showed that there were many Hoosiers who did not want African Americans in their state. The law was declared invalid, or no longer in effect, in 1866.

REVIEW Why did some Hoosiers think that African Americans would come to Indiana? ⟳ **Cause and Effect**

Summarize the Lesson

- **1850** The United States government passed the Fugitive Slave Act.
- **1851** Indiana passed Article XIII, making it illegal for African Americans to enter the state.
- **1853** John Freeman was arrested.

LESSON 1 REVIEW

Check Facts and Main Ideas

1. ⟳ **Cause and Effect** On a sheet of paper, write an effect for each cause shown.

Cause	Effect
Fugitive Slave Act was passed in 1850.	
Accused were not allowed to defend themselves.	
Article XIII was passed in Indiana.	

2. Explain the reasons for the Fugitive Slave Act and Indiana's Article XIII.

3. What was John Freeman accused of?

4. Name two things the Fugitive Slave Act of 1850 made possible.

5. **Critical Thinking:** *Draw Conclusions* How could a free African American arrested under the Fugitive Slave Act, who was not allowed to argue in his or her own defense, avoid being sent to the South and enslaved?

Link to 👁️‍🗨️ Writing

Write an Editorial You are the editor of your student newspaper in 1851. Write an editorial giving your opinion of Indiana's passage of Article XIII.

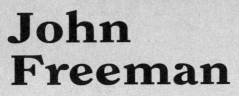

John Freeman

1807–Unknown

In 1850, according to a census, John Freeman was the wealthiest African American in Marion County. He owned a restaurant in Indianapolis and four acres of land, and he had a reputation for being a hard worker. A famous preacher praised Freeman in a newspaper article:

> *"His deportment [behavior] won him general respect and confidence. . . . No man's word was better than Freeman's."*

BIOFACT

In the early 1850s, Freeman grew all the vegetables for his restaurant in his own garden.

In 1853, Freeman was arrested under the Fugitive Slave Act. A Missouri man insisted that Freeman was his runaway slave. Fortunately, Freeman had the support of his community. Lawyers and witnesses came forward to help. Eventually, he was freed. But while he was in jail, the marshal had made him pay his own guard! Freeman was now deeply in debt. He had to sell his restaurant. When the Civil War broke out, John Freeman and his family fled to Canada. He feared for their safety if the South won the war.

Learn from Biographies

What do you think Freeman thought would happen if the South won the war?

For more information, go online to *Meet the People* at **www.sfsocialstudies.com.**

Map and Globe Skills

Use a Road Map

What? A **road map** of a city or town shows its streets and avenues. It also shows important buildings, historic sites, parks, railway lines, and other places of interest.

The map below is of Indianapolis in 1821. Look at the map on the next page to see how much Indianapolis has changed.

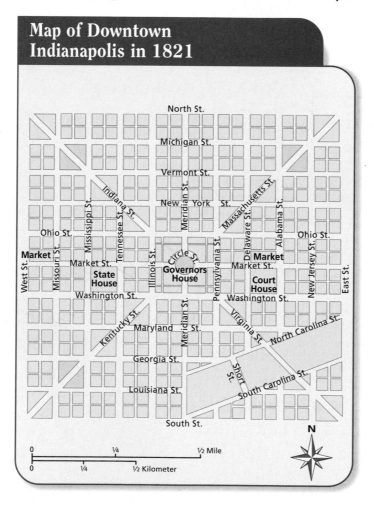

Map of Downtown Indianapolis in 1821

Why? You need to know how to read a road map so that when you travel, you can figure out where you are and how you are getting to the next place.

How? Read the title of the map first. The title will tell you what kind of information you can get from the map. Then look for a **key.** On some maps, the key explains the symbols that are used on the map. Most maps also include a scale. On a map such as the one on this page, a **bar scale** tells you how many miles are represented by each inch on the map. This helps you measure the actual distance between two places. A **compass rose,** included on most maps, tells you the directions: north, south, east, and west.

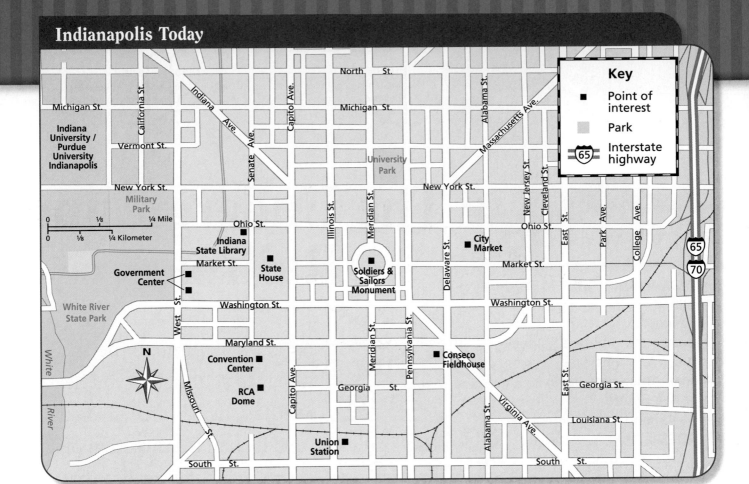

Key

■ Point of interest

Park

🛡65 Interstate highway

When you use a road map, it is important to find where you are. The easiest way to do this is to look at the **intersections** at either end of the block on which you are standing. Intersections are places where roads meet or cross. For example, look on the map above. If you are standing at the intersection of Market Street and Delaware Street, and you want to go to the Soldiers and Sailors Monument, you walk west toward the intersection of Pennsylvania and Market. Once you have found this intersection, you know you are going in the right direction.

For more information, go online to *Atlas* at **www.sfsocialstudies.com**.

Think and Apply

1. You are visiting Indianapolis in 1821. You leave the market on the corner of Market and Alabama. You walk toward the Governor's House. What intersection will you come to next?

2. If you wanted to walk from the market on West St. to the Court House in 1821, what would be the most direct route?

3. If you were at Union Station today, what route would you take to the Soldiers and Sailors Monument?

237

1830   **1840**   **1850**   **1860**

1830s
The term *Underground Railroad* becomes popular.

1850
Fugitive Slave Act is passed.

1852
Harriet Beecher Stowe publishes *Uncle Tom's Cabin.*

The Underground Railroad

PREVIEW

Focus on the Main Idea
Abolitionists in the North opposed slavery. The Underground Railroad helped thousands of enslaved African Americans escape from the South.

PLACES
Newport (Fountain City)

PEOPLE
Harriet Beecher Stowe
Levi and Catharine (Katie) Coffin

VOCABULARY
abolitionist

TERMS
Underground Railroad

You Are There As you walk through the woods to your home, you hear a rustle, then a voice saying, "Ssh!" You stop and look in the direction of the noises. After a moment, you realize that two African American children are staring back at you. The older one is about your age. You guess right away that they must be runaways from a plantation in the South. You know that, by law, you are supposed to report runaways. You also know your parents are against slavery. You wonder what you should do now.

 Cause and Effect As you read, think about the events that are being discussed and why they happened.

Abolitionists Take Action

Many people in Indiana and throughout the North reacted strongly to the Fugitive Slave Act. Some called it the "bloodhound" act. It seemed that African American slaves were being hunted like animals. Many men and women who had not made their opinions about slavery known before 1850 became **abolitionists**—people who worked to end slavery. Members of all religions took up the antislavery cause. In Indiana many abolitionists belonged to the Quaker religion, or Society of Friends. They believed that slavery was wrong.

Abolitionists set up antislavery societies. They taught others about the cruelty of slavery. They published newspapers to help change the opinions of the public and of politicians. They gave speeches and wrote books. **Harriet Beecher Stowe** lived in Cincinnati, Ohio. In 1852, she published *Uncle Tom's Cabin.* It became famous as an antislavery novel. This fiction book tells the story of an enslaved man named Tom—a good man who lives through the cruelties of slavery. Thousands of people who read about Tom's sad life became supporters of the abolitionist cause.

REVIEW What effect did Harriet Beecher Stowe's book have on many people who read it?
🔄 **Cause and Effect**

▶ In this 1844 poster, abolitionists advertise that they can help people escape from slavery.

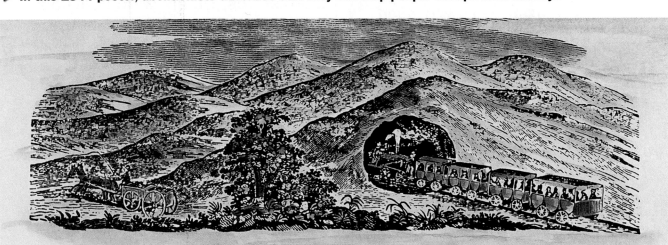

LIBERTY LINE.
NEW ARRANGEMENT---NIGHT AND DAY.

The improved and splendid Locomotives, Clarkson and Lundy, with their trains fitted up in the best style of accommodation for passengers, will run their regular trips during the present season, between the borders of the Patriarchal Dominion and Libertyville, Upper Canada. Gentlemen and Ladies, who may wish to improve their health or circumstances, by a northern tour, are respectfully invited to give us their patronage.

SEATS FREE, *irrespective of color.*

Necessary Clothing furnished gratuitously to such as have *"fallen among thieves."*

"Hide the outcasts—let the oppressed go free."—*Bible.*

☞For seats apply at any of the trap doors, or to the conductor of the train.

J. CROSS, *Proprietor.*

N. B. For the special benefit of Pro-Slavery Police Officers, an extra heavy wagon for Texas, will be furnished, whenever it may be necessary, in which they will be forwarded as dead freight, to the "Valley of Rascals," always at the risk of the owners.

☞Extra Overcoats provided for such of them as are afflicted with protracted *chilly-phobia.*

What Was the Underground Railroad?

In the 1780s, Quakers who believed that slavery was wrong organized a system to help slaves escape. In the 1830s, this system became known as the **Underground Railroad.** The Underground Railroad was not a train track. It was a network of secret routes that ran through all fifteen free states. Many enslaved African Americans crossed the Ohio River and traveled north along the secret routes to reach free states or Canada. The success of the Underground Railroad was one reason that the Fugitive Slave Act was passed.

The term *Underground Railroad* comes from the railway names given to different parts of the network. The routes of the system were called lines. Safe houses and stopping places along the routes were called stations. People who helped the runaways were called conductors. Many conductors were free African Americans. Some had been enslaved themselves. Others were abolitionists and members of religious groups.

"Follow the Drinking Gourd"

*When the sun comes back
and the first quail calls,
Follow the Drinking Gourd.
For the old man is waiting for to
carry you to freedom,
If you follow the Drinking Gourd.*

*The river bank makes a very good
road,
The dead trees show you the way,
Left foot, peg foot, traveling on
Follow the Drinking Gourd.*

*The river ends between two hills,
Follow the Drinking Gourd.
There's another river on the other
side,
Follow the Drinking Gourd.*

*Where the great big river meets
the little river,
Follow the Drinking Gourd.
For the old man is a-waiting for to
carry you to freedom,
If you follow the Drinking Gourd.*

Drinking Gourd = Big Dipper

▶ **Harriet Tubman (c. 1820–1913) was a conductor on the Underground Railroad. She guided nearly three hundred people to freedom. During the Civil War, Tubman served as a cook, nurse, spy, and scout for the Union army.**

Then and Now

The Coffin House

For twenty years, this house, owned by Levi and Katie Coffin, was a station on the Underground Railroad. Today, the Coffins' house is a museum. You can tour the house and think about how runaway slaves must have felt while hiding and listening for every sound and every voice.

▶ The Levi Coffin House (*above right*) was built in 1827. Runaways were hidden in this bedroom (*below*). The beds could be moved in front of the door to hide it.

▶ The house has an indoor well. This allowed the Coffins to hide the large amount of water needed for their guests.

▶ This rag doll reminds visitors that many of the runaways were children.

© Courtesy of the Levi Coffin House Association and Waynet/Levi Coffin House State Historic Site

Activities along the Underground Railroad usually took place at night. Information about routes was passed along through codes in songs like "Swing Low, Sweet Chariot" and "Follow the Drinking Gourd." These songs gave directions and secret messages to help enslaved African Americans find their way north on the Underground Railroad.

Runaway African American slaves usually traveled by themselves or in small groups. They traveled after dark, sometimes walking as many as fifteen to twenty miles a night on back roads and old trails. Since they had no maps, they used the North Star to guide them. This helped them continue walking north. During the day, they hid wherever they could. For many who traveled on the Underground Railroad, the final destination was Canada. Once they reached Canada, the slave hunters could not touch them.

The exact number of enslaved African Americans who escaped using the Underground Railroad is not known. Historians guess that as many as 40,000 to 100,000 people used the system to escape from slavery.

REVIEW What was the Underground Railroad? **Main Idea and Details**

The Underground Railroad in Indiana

Indiana's location between the South and Canada made it an important part of the Underground Railroad. You can see on the map that there were several major routes that passed through Indiana. Along the routes were cities and towns such as Indianapolis, Madison, Richmond, Evansville, and **Newport.**

▶ Levi and Katie Coffin led many slaves to freedom.

Many Quakers settled around Newport, now called Fountain City. **Levi and Catharine (Katie) Coffin,** a Quaker couple, lived in Newport. For twenty years they and other Quakers were conductors on the Underground Railroad. Newport became a central stop for thousands of African Americans. So many passed through Newport that it was known as the Grand Central Station of the Underground Railroad.

Hoosiers who helped enslaved African Americans escape risked being fined or even put in jail. The Fugitive Slave Act made it illegal to help African American slaves escape. Being a conductor on the Underground Railroad was dangerous. But it was a risk many Hoosiers were willing to take.

REVIEW Why do you think conductors on the Underground Railroad risked so much to help slaves escape? **Draw Conclusions**

MAP SKILL

Underground Railroad Routes in Indiana

Lake Michigan

Detroit

Battle Creek

Chicago

MICHIGAN

Lake Erie

South Bend

Plymouth

Auburn

Fort Wayne

N

Rensselaer

Wabash River

Decatur

ILLINOIS

Logansport

Lafayette

Russiaville

Portland

OHIO

Darlington

Winchester

Crawfordsville

Westfield

Bloomingdale

Indianapolis

Fountain City (Newport)

Richmond

White River

Brazil

Terre Haute

Greensburg

Bloomington

Columbus

Cincinnati

Brownstown

Lawrenceburg

Vincennes

E. Fork

Madison

Salem

Wabash River

New Albany

Evansville

Leavenworth

Ohio River

KENTUCKY

Key
← Underground Railroad route
■ Station
★ State capital

| 0 | 50 | 100 Miles |
| 0 | 50 | 100 Kilometers |

▶ There were many Underground Railroad stops in Indiana.

MAP SKILL Use Routes *From Greensburg, travelers on the Underground Railroad had two choices for their next stop. One was the state capital. What was the other?*

Map Adventure

Traveling on the Underground Railroad

You are leading a group of escaping African American slaves to Canada. You have just crossed the Ohio River into Indiana.

1. You know that the next Underground Railroad station is in Greensburg. It is forty-five miles away. You figure that your group can walk only twelve miles a night. How many nights will it take you to reach the station in Greensburg?

2. You and your group are at the Ohio River near the borders of Ohio, Kentucky, and Indiana. To reach Greensburg, you need to travel in which direction?

3. You have just left Russiaville. What is the next station as you travel north?

4. How many rivers must you cross between Indianapolis and Plymouth? Which river or rivers must you cross?

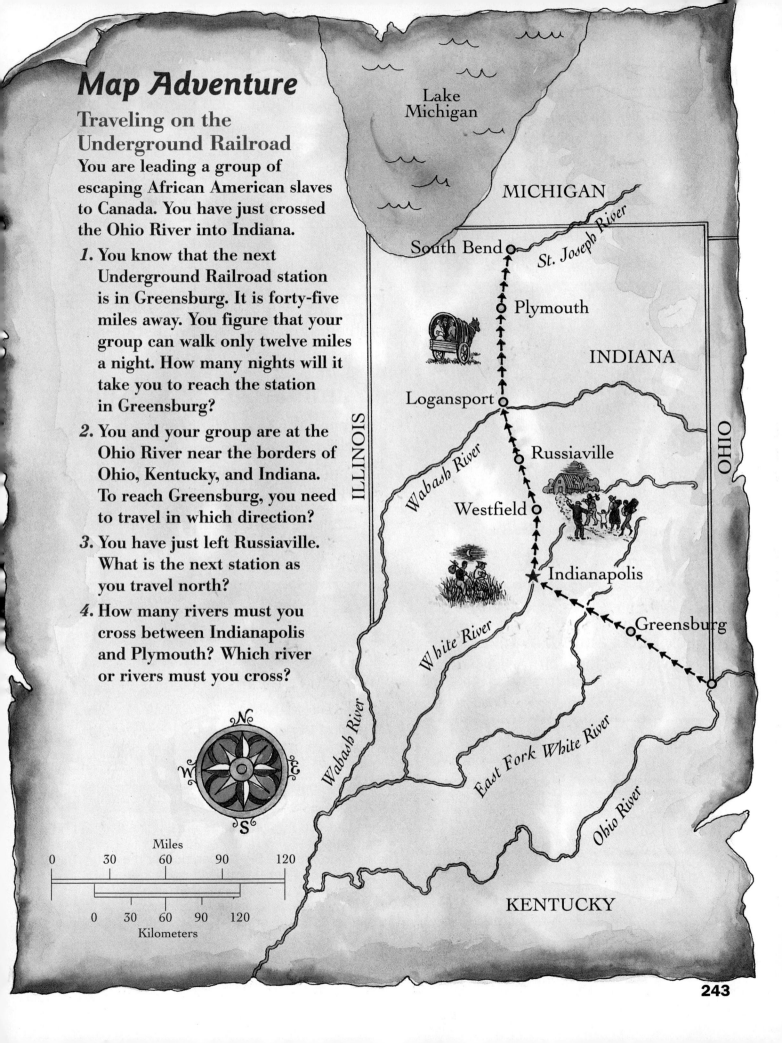

Lake Michigan

MICHIGAN

South Bend

St. Joseph River

Plymouth

INDIANA

Logansport

Russiaville

Wabash River

Westfield

Indianapolis

Greensburg

ILLINOIS

OHIO

White River

Wabash River

East Fork White River

Ohio River

KENTUCKY

N
S
E
W

Miles

0   30   60   90   120

0   30   60   90   120

Kilometers

The North and the South

Attempts to enforce the Fugitive Slave Act made the bad relations between the North and South even worse. After the laws were passed in 1850, the number of abolitionists in the North increased. The Underground Railroad became more successful. Some Southerners grew convinced that the North would eventually try to stop the practice of slavery. Many Northern state governments also passed personal liberty laws. These laws were designed to work against the Fugitive Slave Act. They provided lawyers for accused African Americans. These lawyers worked to get the accused person a trial by jury. Personal liberty laws also divided the North and the South.

▶ **Many Hoosiers took great risks to help slaves escape.**

REVIEW What four things caused problems between Northern states and Southern states? ➲ Cause and Effect

Summarize the Lesson

- **1830s** The term *Underground Railroad* became popular.
- **1850** Fugitive Slave Act was passed.
- **1852** Harriet Beecher Stowe published *Uncle Tom's Cabin.*

LESSON 2 · REVIEW

Check Facts and Main Ideas

1. ➲ **Cause and Effect** On a sheet of paper, write an effect for each cause shown.

Cause	Effect
Fugitive Slave Act	
Publication of *Uncle Tom's Cabin*	
Abolitionists gave speeches and started newspapers.	

2. How did the Underground Railroad work?

3. Why did Indiana play such a big role in the Underground Railroad?

4. What kinds of things did abolitionists do to help enslaved African Americans?

5. **Critical Thinking:** *Make Evaluations* Were the activities of the abolitionists successful? Explain.

Link to 🔗 Science

Research the Big Dipper The drinking gourd mentioned in "The Drinking Gourd" is also known as the Big Dipper, part of the constellation *Ursa Major*. Find out some facts about this constellation. Explain how the people who followed the Underground Railroad used the stars to guide them.

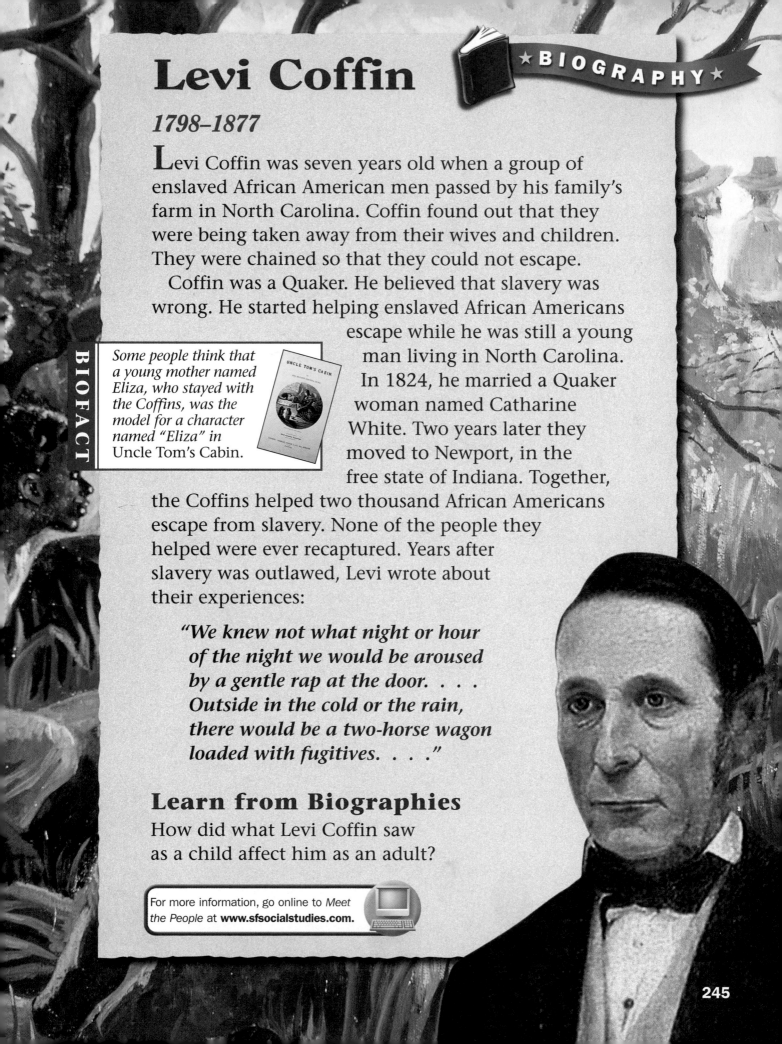

Levi Coffin

1798–1877

Levi Coffin was seven years old when a group of enslaved African American men passed by his family's farm in North Carolina. Coffin found out that they were being taken away from their wives and children. They were chained so that they could not escape.

Coffin was a Quaker. He believed that slavery was wrong. He started helping enslaved African Americans escape while he was still a young man living in North Carolina. In 1824, he married a Quaker woman named Catharine White. Two years later they moved to Newport, in the free state of Indiana. Together, the Coffins helped two thousand African Americans escape from slavery. None of the people they helped were ever recaptured. Years after slavery was outlawed, Levi wrote about their experiences:

BIOFACT

Some people think that a young mother named Eliza, who stayed with the Coffins, was the model for a character named "Eliza" in Uncle Tom's Cabin.

> *"We knew not what night or hour of the night we would be aroused by a gentle rap at the door. . . . Outside in the cold or the rain, there would be a two-horse wagon loaded with fugitives. . . ."*

Learn from Biographies

How did what Levi Coffin saw as a child affect him as an adult?

For more information, go online to *Meet the People* at **www.sfsocialstudies.com**.

1830   1835   1840

1830s
The term *Underground Railroad* became popular.

Chapter Summary

 Cause and Effect

On a sheet of paper, fill in an effect for each cause shown.

Cause	Effect
Abolitionists organized the Underground Railroad in the 1830s.	
Fugitive Slave Act was passed in 1850.	
Abolitionists spoke out against slavery.	

Vocabulary

Match each word with the correct definition or description.

1 enslaved (p. 233)

2 commissioner (p. 233)

3 abolitionist (p. 239)

a. government official

b. owned by another person as property

c. person who wanted to end slavery

People and Terms

Write a sentence explaining why each of the following people and terms was important to Indiana's history in the 1800s.

1 Fugitive Slave Act (p. 233)

2 John Freeman (p. 233)

3 Article XIII (p. 234)

4 Harriet Beecher Stowe (p. 239)

5 Underground Railroad (p. 240)

6 Levi and Catharine Coffin (p. 242)

1850
U.S. passed the Fugitive Slave Act.

1851
Indiana passed Article XIII.

1852
Harriet Beecher Stowe published *Uncle Tom's Cabin.*

1853
John Freeman was arrested.

Facts and Main Ideas

1 Indiana was a "free" state. What does this mean?

2 Why couldn't John Freeman defend himself when he was arrested?

3 How did many Northerners react to the Fugitive Slave Act?

4 **Time Line** How long after the Fugitive Slave Act was passed was John Freeman arrested?

5 **Main Idea** How did the Fugitive Slave Act change the lives of African Americans in Indiana?

6 **Main Idea** Why was the network of safe houses called the Underground Railroad?

7 **Critical Thinking:** *Draw Conclusions* Do you think that the Fugitive Slave Act succeeded in easing tensions between North and South? Explain your answer.

Apply Skills

Use a Road Map

Look at the road map of Indianapolis today on page 237 to answer the questions below.

1 You are giving a group of tourists a walking tour of Indianapolis. They want to visit the City Market first. What street is just south of the City Market?

2 You picked the tour group up on Illinois Street outside Union Station. What route could you take to get to the City Market?

3 Name one street that runs east and west and under an interstate highway.

Write About History

1 **Make a poster** asking your fellow citizens of Indiana in 1850 to speak out against the Fugitive Slave Act.

2 **Write a letter** to a friend in Canada telling about your activities on the Underground Railroad. Explain why you are willing to risk so much to help enslaved African Americans reach freedom.

3 **Write an editorial** for your local newspaper in 1853, explaining why John Freeman should or should not be released from jail.

Internet Activity

To get help with vocabulary, people, and terms, select the dictionary or encyclopedia from *Social Studies Library* at **www.sfsocialstudies.com.**

CHAPTER 9

The Civil War

Lesson 1

1860
Fort Sumter
Abraham Lincoln's election helps trigger the Civil War.

1

Lesson 2

1861
Salem
Hoosier men volunteer in record numbers to defend the Union.

2

Lesson 3

1865
Evansville
The Civil War causes many changes in Indiana.

3

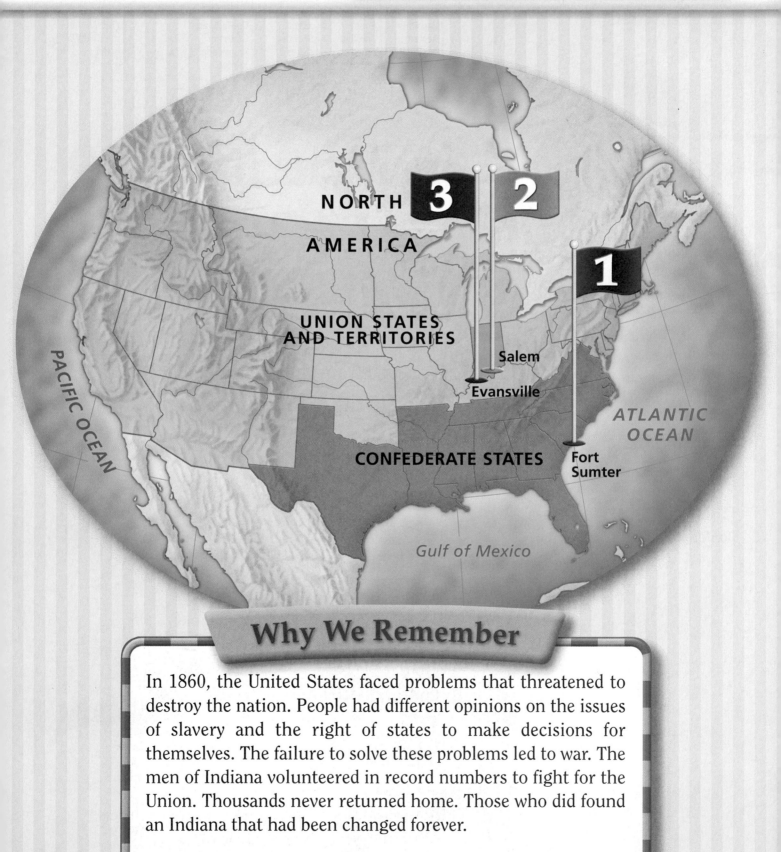

NORTH AMERICA

UNION STATES AND TERRITORIES

CONFEDERATE STATES

PACIFIC OCEAN

ATLANTIC OCEAN

Salem

Evansville

Fort Sumter

Gulf of Mexico

Why We Remember

In 1860, the United States faced problems that threatened to destroy the nation. People had different opinions on the issues of slavery and the right of states to make decisions for themselves. The failure to solve these problems led to war. The men of Indiana volunteered in record numbers to fight for the Union. Thousands never returned home. Those who did found an Indiana that had been changed forever.

November 1860	December 1860	January–February 1861	February 1861	April 1861
Lincoln is elected President.	South Carolina secedes.	Six other states secede.	Confederate States of America is formed.	First shot of the Civil War is fired.

Fort Sumter

PREVIEW

Focus on the Main Idea
Indiana remained loyal to the Union and played an important role in electing Abraham Lincoln as President in 1860.

PLACES
Fort Sumter

PEOPLE
Jefferson Davis

VOCABULARY
secede

TERMS
Confederacy

Indiana in 1860

You Are There

December 27, 1860
Dear Cousin,
Everyone here in Indianapolis is very upset by the news that South Carolina has seceded from the Union. People are shouting in the streets. Mama has been crying all day. She is worried about you and the rest of her family in South Carolina. Papa thinks other states will follow South Carolina and that they will form their own nation. How can that happen? I don't understand, do you?
Love,
Your cousin Pat

CHARLESTON
MERCURY
EXTRA:

Passed unanimously at 1.15 o'clock, P. M., December 20th, 1860.

AN ORDINANCE
To dissolve the Union between the State of South Carolina and other States united with her under the compact entitled " The Constitution of the United States of America."

We, the People of the State of South Carolina, in Convention assembled, do declare and ordain, and it is hereby declared and ordained,

That the Ordinance adopted by us in Convention, on the twenty-third day of May, in the year of our Lord one thousand seven hundred and eighty-eight, whereby the Constitution of the United States of America, was ratified, and also, all Acts and parts of Acts of the General Assembly of this State, ratifying amendments of the said Constitution, are hereby repealed; and that the union now subsisting between South Carolina and other States, under the name of "The United States of America," is hereby dissolved.

THE
UNION
IS
DISSOLVED!

Sequence As you read, note the sequence of events that led up to the Civil War.

Divided Opinions

By 1860, tensions were high between the North and South. Indiana found itself in the middle. Hoosiers were divided over the issue of slavery and divided by loyalty. Hoosiers who lived in the northern regions of Indiana tended to side with other Northern states. They opposed slavery and thought of themselves as Northerners.

However, many Hoosiers in southern Indiana had been born in the South. Many had family there. They thought of themselves as Southerners. They supported slavery in the South.

In November 1860, Republican Abraham Lincoln was elected President. Many white Southerners saw the election of Lincoln, who opposed the spread of slavery into the territories, as a danger to their way of life. They believed in the rights of states.

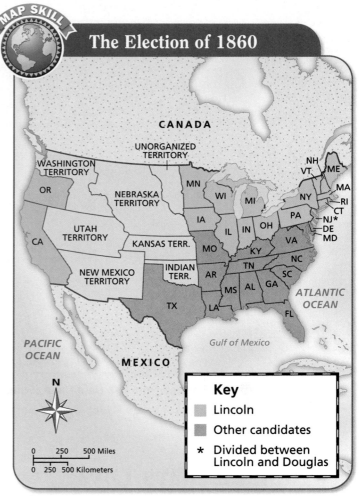

The Election of 1860

▶ States that opposed slavery supported Abraham Lincoln for President in 1860.

MAP SKILL Use a Map Key *One state was divided between Lincoln and his opponent, Stephen Douglas. Where is this state and what is its name?*

They felt that the federal government should not tell them what to do. Some states threatened to **secede**, or leave the Union.

REVIEW Where did Hoosier loyalties lie in 1860?
Summarize

AILY JOURNAL.

WEDNESDAY MORNING, NOVEMBER 7, 1860.

OFFICIAL CITY PAPER.

HE RIGHT TRIUMPHANT!

Good News From All Poin

LINCOLN PRESIDENT OF UNION!

Below we publish the returns State and other States, received other Republicans in this city to the time of going to press. a large gain on the vote for State, a larger gain in Penn a glorious triumph in the Stat

▶ An Indianapolis newspaper announces Lincoln's election.

The Union and the Confederacy

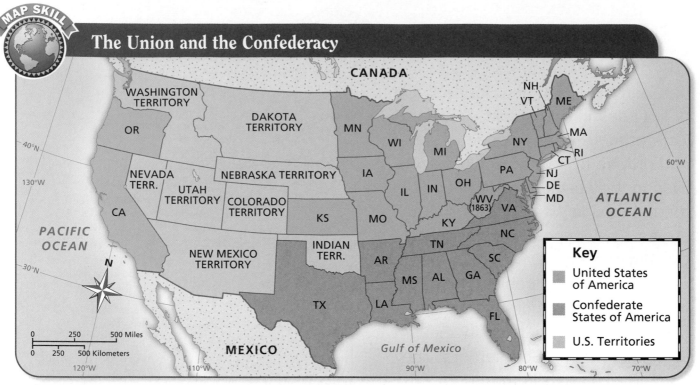

CANADA

WASHINGTON TERRITORY

OR

DAKOTA TERRITORY

MN

WI

MI

NY

NH

VT

ME

MA

RI

CT

NJ

DE

MD

NEVADA TERR.

UTAH TERRITORY

NEBRASKA TERRITORY

IA

PA

40°N

130°W

60°W

CA

COLORADO TERRITORY

KS

IL

IN

OH

WV (1863)

VA

PACIFIC OCEAN

MO

KY

ATLANTIC OCEAN

30°N

NEW MEXICO TERRITORY

INDIAN TERR.

AR

TN

NC

SC

N

MS

AL

GA

TX

LA

FL

0   250   500 Miles
0   250   500 Kilometers

MEXICO

Gulf of Mexico

120°W   110°W   90°W   80°W   70°W

Key

United States of America

Confederate States of America

U.S. Territories

▶ **Southern states seceded from the Union and formed the Confederate States of America.**

MAP SKILL Measure Distance *Which Confederate state is closest to southern Indiana?*

Indiana Stays Loyal

Most Hoosiers—even those in southern Indiana—agreed on one thing. They did not believe it was in Indiana's best interests to leave the Union. Only a few seemed willing to leave. One southern county declared that if the South seceded, the line of separation "must run north of us."

On December 20, 1860, South Carolina became the first state to secede from the United States. Other southern states soon followed. By February 1861, seven states had seceded: South Carolina, Mississippi, Florida, Alabama, Georgia, Louisiana, and Texas. They joined together to form the Confederate States of America, also called the **Confederacy.**

Mississippi's **Jefferson Davis** became the first—and only—President of the Confederacy.

Just days after the seven states formed the Confederacy, Abraham Lincoln visited Indiana. There, he spoke to the crowds, saying:

"It is your business to rise up and preserve the Union and liberty for yourselves, and not for me. . . . [B]ear in mind that with you . . . is the question: Shall the Union and shall the liberties of this country be preserved . . . ?"

Most Hoosiers cheered Lincoln's words. They pledged themselves to the Union cause.

On March 4, 1861, Abraham Lincoln was sworn in as President. On April 12, 1861, the Civil War began when the Confederates fired on **Fort Sumter,** a Union fort in South Carolina. Lincoln called for troops to end the rebellion. Within days, four more states joined the Confederacy—Virginia, Arkansas, Tennessee, and North Carolina. If you look at the map on page 252, you can see that Indiana, like its neighbors, remained loyal to the Union.

REVIEW What event came shortly before South Carolina's secession from the Union?
Sequence

▶ Abraham Lincoln was sworn in as President on March 4, 1861. The Civil War began a few weeks later.

Summarize the Lesson

- **November 1860** Lincoln was elected President.
- **December 1860** South Carolina seceded.
- **January–February 1861** Six other Southern states seceded.
- **February 1861** The Confederate States of America was formed.
- **April 12, 1861** The first shot of the Civil War was fired.

LESSON 1 REVIEW

Check Facts and Main Ideas

1. **Sequence** On a sheet of paper, list events that led up to the Civil War in the order in which they happened.

```
┌─────────────────────────────┐
│                             │
└─────────────────────────────┘
              ↓
┌─────────────────────────────┐
│                             │
└─────────────────────────────┘
              ↓
┌─────────────────────────────┐
│                             │
└─────────────────────────────┘
```

2. How were the views of northern and southern Hoosiers on the issues of slavery and secession the same or different?

3. What political party did Abraham Lincoln represent, and what was his stand on slavery?

4. What were the Confederate States of America? How did Indiana react to the Confederacy's formation?

5. **Critical Thinking:** *Analyze Information* What factors influenced Indiana's decision about which side to support in the war?

Link to ⚭ Mathematics

State Roll Call Before South Carolina seceded, there were thirty-four states, not including territories and West Virginia. Look at the map on page 252 to find out how many states joined the Confederacy. Then find out how many states remained loyal to the Union. What percentage of states remained loyal?

1861	1862	1863	1864	1865

June 3, 1861
Hoosier soldiers first go into battle at Philippi, Virginia.

February 1862
Battle for Fort Donelson

July 8, 1863
Morgan raids southern Indiana.

April 9, 1865
The Civil War ends.

PREVIEW

Focus on the Main Idea
During the Civil War, Hoosiers helped the effort to save the Union.

PLACES
Philippi, Virginia
Salem
Appomattox Court House, Virginia

PEOPLE
Oliver P. Morton
Joseph J. Reynolds
Eliza E. George
John Hunt Morgan
Robert E. Lee
Ulysses S. Grant

VOCABULARY
regiment
front

TERMS
Indiana Legion
Emancipation Proclamation
Twenty-eighth United States Colored Troop

EVENTS
Morgan's Raid

Indiana During the War

You Are There

February, 1862
Dear Family,
My regiment is marching toward its first battle. We are joining other Indiana regiments for an attack. The weather is bitter cold and our supplies are running out. We are still at least a day's march from the action, but we can hear the guns already. Our spirit is still good despite the difficulties of the march. We know that we have been trained by experienced officers.

Your son,
Robert

Main Idea and Details As you read, note details that show how Hoosiers contributed to the war effort.

▶ **Soldiers of the Third Indiana Cavalry**

Preparing Indiana for War

When the Civil War broke out, Oliver P. Morton was Indiana's governor. He was a strong supporter of both the Union and President Lincoln. When others were trying to compromise in order to avoid a war, he said he would fight to save the Union. He offered six thousand soldiers to defend the Union before the war.

As governor, Morton had to choose military officers. Morton wanted experienced officers to lead the inexperienced volunteer soldiers. He appointed Joseph J. Reynolds, a West Point graduate, as commander of the first brigade, or group of soldiers, organized in Indiana. He asked Lew Wallace and Robert Milroy, who had both fought in the Mexican American War, to command Indiana regiments.

Morton also organized the Indiana Legion. This militia's job was to defend the state from internal rebellions and invasions by the enemy. Most of the militia was concentrated in the southern part of the state. This part of Indiana faced the greatest threat of invasion by Confederate soldiers.

REVIEW Why did Governor Morton want experienced officers to lead Indiana soldiers? *Draw Conclusions*

255

Indiana Gives Its All

Within one week of the firing on Fort Sumter, twelve thousand Hoosier men volunteered, or offered themselves, for military duty. Six Indiana regiments were formed. They were commanded by Brigadier General Joseph Reynolds. A **regiment** is a group of about one thousand soldiers.

Some of these volunteers may have been looking for adventure and excitement. Most, however, were inspired by patriotism. By the end of the war, seventy-four percent of Hoosier men of military age had served. Only Delaware sent a higher percentage of its men to the war.

On September 22, 1862, President Lincoln issued a statement. It said that as of January 1, 1863, an **Emancipation Proclamation** would go into effect. This proclamation would

▶ **Many African Americans became Union soldiers.**

free all enslaved people in the rebelling Confederate areas. (To *emancipate* is to set free.) This document also repealed, or withdrew, the ban on African Americans serving in the Union forces. Many had wanted to fight for the Union for a long time.

FACT FILE

Hoosiers in the Civil War

- Number of Hoosiers who fought in the Civil War: **197,141**

- Number of Hoosier regiments formed: **169**

- Number of Hoosiers who joined the Navy or the Marines: **1,000**

- Number of African American Hoosiers who fought in the war: **1,537**

- Number of Hoosier soldiers who died in battle: **7,243**

- Number of Hoosier soldiers who died from disease: **17,785**

- Number of battles in which Hoosier soldiers fought: **308**

▶ **Soldiers and Sailors Monument**

At the beginning of the war they had not been allowed to join the military. Now thousands enlisted. By the end of the war, 180,000 African American men had enlisted. Many of them joined the **Twenty-eighth United States Colored Troop,** which formed in Indiana in November of 1863.

REVIEW What happened after the ban on African Americans in the military was lifted? **Cause and Effect**

Supporting the Troops

When the men of Indiana marched off to war, they left behind their wives, children, and elderly relatives. Many of the women were suddenly faced with unfamiliar, and at times overwhelming, tasks. They had to run both their homes and their farms by themselves. Their efforts to keep the farms going helped supply the Union soldiers with food.

Other women took jobs in the state arsenal—a place where weapons are kept—in Indianapolis. These women worked to supply Indiana soldiers with weapons and ammunition.

Hoosier women turned their work and social clubs into groups that helped the war effort. They sewed clothing and knitted socks and blankets for the soldiers. They rolled bandages for the wounded. Some women may have even sewn the regimental flags that were carried into battle. These groups raised money and collected books, clothing, and food.

Some Hoosier women, such as **Eliza E. George,** left their homes and families to become nurses. Nurses served at military hospitals and at the front. The **front** is where the battles take place. There, they were faced with the task of nursing sick and dying men under terrible conditions.

REVIEW What kinds of things did the women of Indiana do to help the war effort? **Main Idea and Details**

▶ Women working at arsenals helped keep troops supplied.

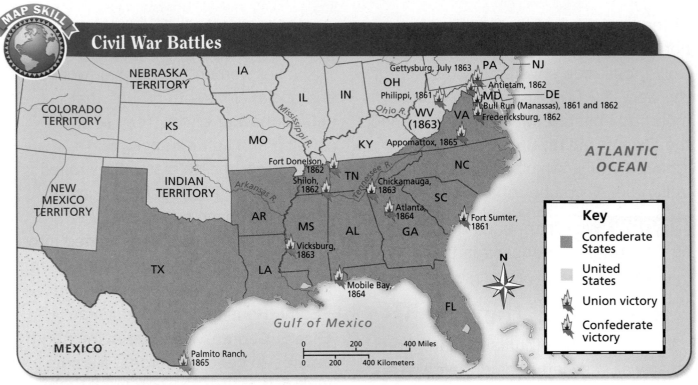

Civil War Battles Map

NEBRASKA TERRITORY

IA

Gettysburg, July 1863 PA — NJ

OH

Philippi, 1861

Antietam, 1862

MD — DE

Bull Run (Manassas), 1861 and 1862

COLORADO TERRITORY

IL

IN

Ohio R.

WV (1863)

VA

Fredericksburg, 1862

KS

MO

KY

Appomattox, 1865

NC

ATLANTIC OCEAN

Mississippi R.

Fort Donelson, 1862

Shiloh, 1862

TN

Chickamauga, 1863

SC

NEW MEXICO TERRITORY

INDIAN TERRITORY

Arkansas R.

Tennessee R.

AR

Atlanta, 1864

Fort Sumter, 1861

MS

AL

GA

TX

Vicksburg, 1863

LA

N

Mobile Bay, 1864

FL

Gulf of Mexico

Key

Confederate States

United States

Union victory

Confederate victory

MEXICO

Palmito Ranch, 1865

0   200   400 Miles
0   200   400 Kilometers

▶ **During the Civil War, Indiana soldiers fought in major battles from Pennsylvania to Texas.**

MAP SKILL Understand Cardinal Directions *What Union victories were won east of Indiana?*

Hoosiers in Battle

On June 3, 1861, the first Hoosier soldiers saw action at **Philippi, Virginia.** Indiana's first men to be killed in battle lost their lives within one week of leaving home. Four years later, Hoosier soldiers were still fighting when the last battle of the Civil War took place at Palmito Ranch in Texas. Some accounts say that the last soldier killed was John J. Williams of the Thirty-fourth Indiana Regiment.

Many Hoosier soldiers got their first taste of battle in February 1862. They fought to capture Fort Donelson in Tennessee.

Soldiers from Indiana fought in some of the worst battles of the war. The Nineteenth Indiana, part of the famous Iron Brigade, is one example. This infantry unit went into the Second Battle of Bull Run in August 1862 with 423 men. Only 164 of these foot soldiers survived. The Nineteenth later fought at the Battle of Gettysburg. During the first day of battle, the regiment lost more than half its men.

REVIEW

Which battle was the first in which Indiana soldiers saw action? Which was the last?

Sequence

Morgan's Raid

On July 8, 1863, **John Hunt Morgan,** a Confederate general, disobeyed orders. He led about two thousand cavalrymen—troops on horseback—across the Ohio River and into southern Indiana. This was called **Morgan's Raid.** He hoped to find horses and supplies there. He may have also hoped to find support for the Confederate cause among southern Hoosiers. If so, he was disappointed.

According to the July 15, 1863, *Indianapolis Daily Sentinel,* Morgan "quickly brushed aside the Indiana militia." As he and his raiders moved from Corydon to Salem to Vernon and Versailles, they stole horses, food, clothing, and money. They burned railway bridges. In **Salem,** Morgan demanded about $1,000 for each mill in town. If he did not get the money,

▶ Morgan's raiders stole supplies and burned buildings.

© Frank Leslie's Illustrated Newspaper, August 8, 1963 / Hamilton Public Library, Special Collections

MAP SKILL

Morgan's Raid

Key
← Morgan's route

Indianapolis

INDIANA

OHIO

Whitewater R.

Harrison

Ohio River

East Fork White River

Muscatatuck R.

Vernon Versailles

Paris Dupont

Lexington

Salem

Palmyra

Corydon Louisville

Brandenburg KENTUCKY

0   15   30 Miles
0   15   30 Kilometers

▶ General Morgan sent small raiding parties out in different directions to attack many different communities.

MAP SKILL Measure Distance *How long was Morgan's main line of march in Indiana?*

he said, he would burn the mills down. The citizens paid.

Sixty-five thousand men banded together and went after Morgan, who was eventually captured. He later escaped and was killed in battle in Tennessee. The *Indianapolis Daily Sentinel* later noted that this one "real taste of war" in Indiana was "interesting and long remembered."

REVIEW Who was John Hunt Morgan, and why did he raid southern Indiana? **Main Idea and Details**

The War Ends

By April 1865, the Confederate army was hopelessly outnumbered by the Union army. On April 9, Confederate General **Robert E. Lee** decided to stop fighting and surrender.

▶ This picture of Grant accepting Lee's surrender shows them at one table. They actually sat at different tables.

Ulysses S. Grant, commander of the Union troops, accepted Lee's surrender at **Appomattox Court House, Virginia.** The war was over. It was time for the soldiers to return home.

REVIEW How long did the Civil War last? **Main Idea and Details**

Summarize the Lesson

— **June 3, 1861** Hoosier soldiers first went into battle at Philippi, Virginia.

— **February 1862** Battle for Fort Donelson

— **August 1862** Second Battle of Bull Run

— **July 8, 1863** Morgan's Raid

— **April 9, 1865** The Civil War ended.

LESSON 2 REVIEW

Check Facts and Main Ideas

1. Main Idea and Details On a sheet of paper, write details that support the main idea shown.

> Many kinds of Hoosiers helped the Union war effort

2. List two actions Governor Oliver P. Morton took to prepare Indiana for the Civil War.

3. What were some of the significant battles in which Hoosier soldiers fought?

4. What event brought the Civil War onto Indiana soil? Explain what happened.

5. **Critical Thinking: *Draw Conclusions*** Some Hoosier soldiers thought the war was going to be a great adventure. What do you think they discovered about war?

Link to ➤ Art

Create a Poster Draw and write a recruitment poster encouraging people to volunteer their services to help win the Civil War.

Eliza E. George

1808–1865

When fifty-four year old Eliza E. George became a nurse for the Union troops during the Civil War, many people thought she was too old. She responded:

"I am old, but my health is good, and I am very desirous [I want] to do something for those who are every day exposing [risking] their lives for our country. If unable to go through as much as some, I will engage [promise] never to be at all troublesome or in the way."

BIOFACT

About two thousand women, from the North and the South, served as nurses during the Civil War.

In 1863, Mrs. George began taking care of soldiers. She lived under the same conditions as the soldiers while she cared for the wounded.

She delivered food, clothing, and hospital supplies to the battlefront. During one battle, an explosion near her killed two of her patients. She saw it as a test of her courage. Her patients called her "Mother George" because of the kind and gentle way she cared for them.

In May 1865, Mrs. George traveled to North Carolina to help care for eleven thousand freed Union prisoners of war. She caught a disease called typhoid fever and died on May 9.

Learn from Biographies

Why do you think Eliza E. George was willing to help wounded soldiers?

 For more information, go online to *Meet the People* at **www.sfsocialstudies.com.**

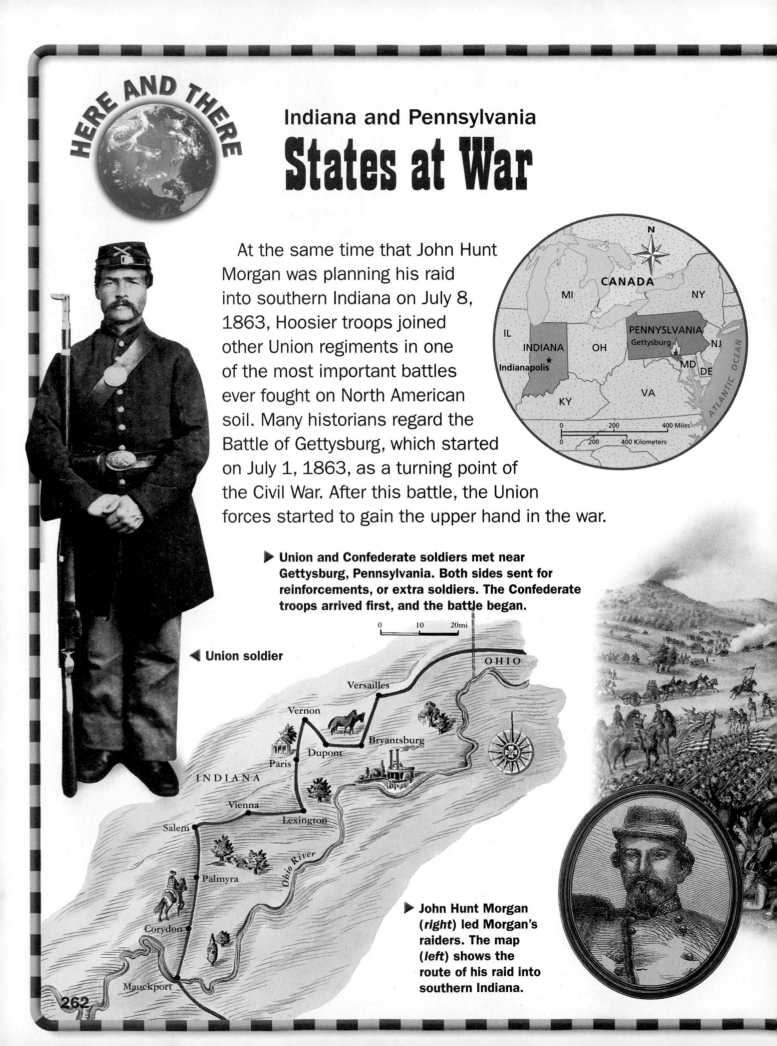

HERE AND THERE

Indiana and Pennsylvania
States at War

At the same time that John Hunt Morgan was planning his raid into southern Indiana on July 8, 1863, Hoosier troops joined other Union regiments in one of the most important battles ever fought on North American soil. Many historians regard the Battle of Gettysburg, which started on July 1, 1863, as a turning point of the Civil War. After this battle, the Union forces started to gain the upper hand in the war.

▶ Union and Confederate soldiers met near Gettysburg, Pennsylvania. Both sides sent for reinforcements, or extra soldiers. The Confederate troops arrived first, and the battle began.

◀ Union soldier

▶ John Hunt Morgan (*right*) led Morgan's raiders. The map (*left*) shows the route of his raid into southern Indiana.

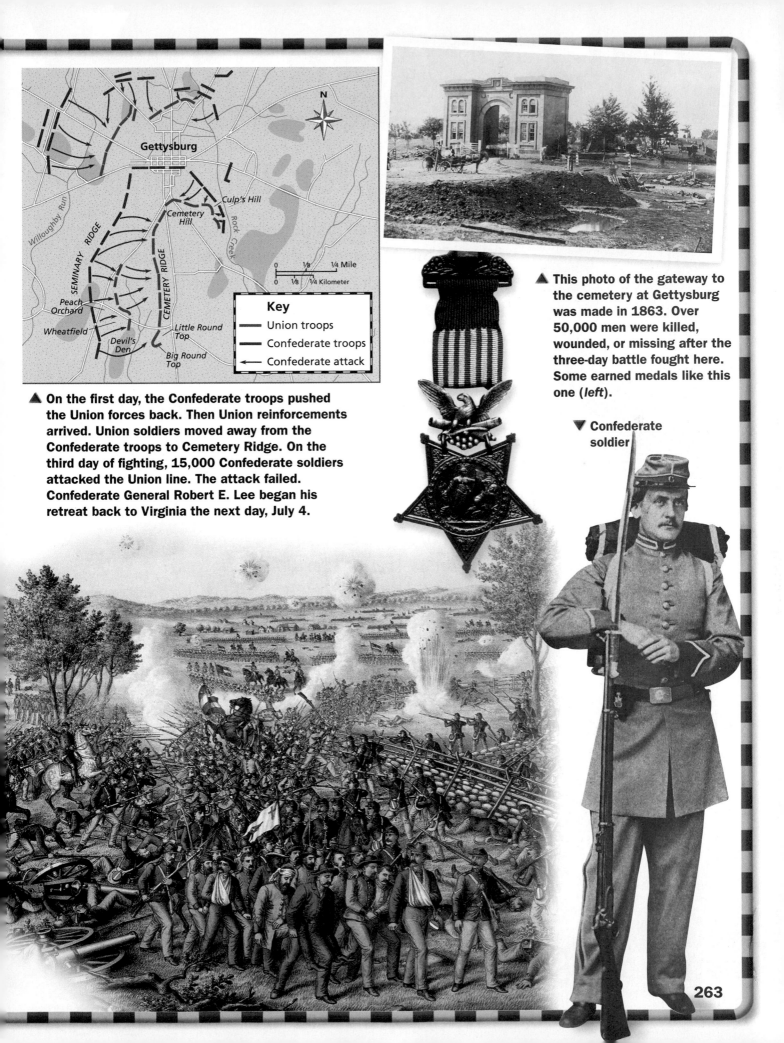

Key
— Union troops
— Confederate troops
← Confederate attack

▲ On the first day, the Confederate troops pushed the Union forces back. Then Union reinforcements arrived. Union soldiers moved away from the Confederate troops to Cemetery Ridge. On the third day of fighting, 15,000 Confederate soldiers attacked the Union line. The attack failed. Confederate General Robert E. Lee began his retreat back to Virginia the next day, July 4.

▲ This photo of the gateway to the cemetery at Gettysburg was made in 1863. Over 50,000 men were killed, wounded, or missing after the three-day battle fought here. Some earned medals like this one (*left*).

▼ Confederate soldier

Fighting for the Union

▶ **Governor Oliver P. Morton**

As governor of Indiana during the Civil War, Oliver P. Morton wanted thousands of Hoosier men to fight for the Union. He took responsibility for the soldiers by giving them weapons, ammunition, and uniforms.

Republican Oliver P. Morton became governor of Indiana when the relationship between the North and the South was at the breaking point. Morton was willing to fight to save the Union.

> *"'May it [the Union] be preserved' is the prayer of every patriotic heart in Indiana, and that it shall be, the determination [goal]."*

Even before the war started, Morton promised six thousand Hoosier soldiers for the Union's defense.

▶ **Civil War soldiers**

BUILDING CITIZENSHIP
Caring
Respect
★ Responsibility
Fairness
Honesty
Courage

▶ Fifty-seventh Indiana Volunteer Infantry

Once the war started, Morton tried to make sure that his soldiers had uniforms and overcoats. He personally inspected training camps and toured battlefields. He earned himself the nickname "the soldiers' friend."

Not everyone approved of Morton's actions. He often did more than he was allowed to, even as governor. When the war started, Morton opened a state arsenal in Indianapolis to make ammunition. Morton's enemies said that Indiana's constitution did not allow him to do this.

Despite the fact that Morton may have misused his power as governor, some historians consider him to have been "the ablest and most energetic of the war governors of the Western States."

Responsibility in Action

Link to Current Events Research the work of a local or state politician. (It can be someone who has been in office within the last ten years.) How has this person shown responsibility to the people of your state or community?

LESSON 3

1860	1865	1870
1860 Evansville becomes the state's second largest city.	**April 9, 1865** The Civil War ends.	**1870s** Indiana goes through many changes.

The Civil War Ends

PREVIEW

Focus on the Main Idea
The Civil War had a great impact on life in Indiana and caused many changes.

PLACES
Evansville

VOCABULARY
reaper
segregate

You Are There
You are so excited! Today your older brother is coming home from the war. He has been gone for almost three and a half years. Things have changed over those years. Your older sister is now a teacher. She took the place of the male teacher who joined the Army.

The biggest changes, however, are on the farm. Last year your father bought one of those amazing machines called a reaper to help with the harvest. What will your brother think of this modern machine?

 Cause and Effect As you read, note cause-and-effect relationships between the war and events in Indiana afterwards.

266

▶ Kindergarten class in the 1870s

Indiana After the War

By the time the war ended in 1865, many soldiers had been killed or had died from disease. Out of every one hundred Hoosiers who went off to fight, only eighty-eight returned.

The people left at home had made changes during the war years as well. Farmers began using new machinery to do the work of the men who had gone to war. They used a machine such as a **reaper,** which cut grain for harvest. They also used threshing machines, which separated grain from the other parts of the plant. These machines helped farmers manage their farms with fewer workers.

The shortage of male workers in Indiana during the war changed the lives of many Hoosier women. Some women went to work in factories, replacing the men who had become soldiers. After the war, some of the women workers continued in the factories. More women were also offered teaching jobs during the war years. After the war, the number of women hired as teachers kept increasing. They worked for less money than men. The people in charge of hiring teachers found that women often taught longer than men. Many men left to find better paying jobs after a year or two. What's more, the people in charge learned that women did just as good a job as men, as the factory owners had learned.

REVIEW Why did many women find work as teachers during and after the Civil War? ⟳ **Cause and Effect**

▶ Women continued working in factories after the war.

A New Indiana

Life in Indiana changed after the Civil War. The population continued to grow, but not as quickly. Farming was still an important business, but modern machines were common in the fertile lands of central and northern Indiana. Old ways of farming held on longer on farms in the hilly, southern areas. In the north, swamplands and forests were drained and cleared to make more farmland. Railroads helped farmers get their goods to market more quickly.

Even though Indiana was still a farming state, more and more people moved to cities and towns. They also left the southern part of the state and moved to the north. In the north, there were factories and mills to work in and rail lines that connected Indiana to other northern states. Older towns along the Ohio River that had served southern markets began to decline. Also, river and canal boats could not compete with the railroads of the north. **Evansville,** however, was one exception. It combined river and rail transportation. It became Indiana's second largest city after 1860.

REVIEW How were farming methods after the Civil War different from those before the war? Compare and Contrast

African American Hoosiers

After the war ended, many African Americans from the South migrated north. They hoped to find work and homes in the new industrial cities of the North. Many African Americans who arrived in Indiana settled in towns along the Ohio River, in Indianapolis, and in cities and towns in northern Indiana.

Many formerly enslaved people moved north, hoping to make a better life for their families. But most of them could not read. They had no money and, in many cases, few job skills that they could use in their new environment.

▶ In 1873, the Studebaker Wagon Works in South Bend was the largest in the world.

© Studebaker National Museum

▶ An Indianapolis family in the late 1800s

Although Hoosier soldiers had fought in the war to help end slavery, African Americans were not always welcomed in Indiana. They faced prejudice and racism. Some white people did not think of African Americans as equals. White people often refused to serve black men and women in restaurants,

hotels, and theaters. In some cases, African American families were forced to move to different communities. Many ended up living in communities in which churches, shops, and schools were segregated. To **segregate** means to separate by race.

REVIEW What caused African Americans to leave the South and move north? ↻ Cause and Effect

Summarize the Lesson

- **Evansville became Indiana's second largest city in the 1860s.**
- **The Civil War ended in 1865.**
- **New machines revolutionized farming methods.**
- **More women worked as teachers, and in factories and mills.**
- **African Americans moved to Indiana to find jobs and homes.**

LESSON 3 REVIEW

Check Facts and Main Ideas

1. ↻ **Cause and Effect** On a sheet of paper, write an effect for each cause shown.

Cause	Effect
A shortage of male workers existed in Indiana during the Civil War.	
Northern Indiana offered industries and rail access.	

2. What two machines did farmers in Indiana begin using in the 1860s?

3. What difficulties did many African Americans face when they moved to Indiana?

4. Compare the development of northern and southern Indiana after the Civil War.

5. **Critical Thinking:** *Make Evaluations* Some people thought that the Civil War was fought to preserve the United States as it had been in the 1850s. How successful was the Civil War in keeping things the same in Indiana?

Link to ⚭ Writing

Write a Letter You have just returned to Indiana after the war. Write a letter to a friend describing the one change at home that you find most dramatic and explain why.

Research and Writing Skills

Use Primary and Secondary Sources

What? A **primary source** is an eyewitness account or observation of an event. Primary sources are created by people who take part in or see an event. Diaries, speeches, letters, drawings, and photographs are all examples of primary sources.

A **secondary source** is an account of an event written by someone who read or heard about it. This person did not take part in or see the event. An encyclopedia article or a history book is an example of a secondary source.

Camp Morton
April the 28/61 [1861]

Dear Father,
It is with pleasure that I have this opportunity to write you a few lines to let you know that I am well and if ever [these] lines reaches you, they may find you the same.

I have enlisted and it may be painful news to you but I am for my country and I thought it would be my duty so to do and I have good times now here in Camp.

. . . I expect to see hard times and some that will not be agreeable to me but still I expect to go through if I live.

If we have to whip every Southern State in the Union and now, father, miles doth separate us from each other, you must not think that I have forgotten you for I have not and I do not want you to worry your self about me for I am in good cause.

I must bring this to a close. Write soon as you get this letter and let me know how you are. So no more at present but ever [I] remain your affectionate son.

WA Hawk

Library of Congress/Laurelton-Westover / Photo Researchers, Inc.

Why? When you read a primary source, you get a firsthand account of the event and the writer's reactions to it. You can also learn about the writer. For example, the letter on page 270 was written by a young Indiana man in an army camp during the Civil War. The letter reveals that the writer just enlisted to fight in the Civil War and that his father may not be happy about it. Primary sources, such as the photo of the young Civil War soldier above, can help make past events seem more real. From a photo you can learn general information about the period of history and personal information about the subject. Secondary sources, such as the encyclopedia entry below, do not usually give such detailed and personal information.

How? You can often identify a primary source by the use of the pronouns *I* and *we*. Phrases such as "I saw," "we heard," and "I felt" can also help identify primary sources such as eyewitness accounts and reactions.

A secondary source may use the pronouns *he*, *she*, and *they*. These pronouns signal that an account is not written by an eyewitness. Secondary sources—such as the encyclopedia entry on the bottom of this page—may summarize historical events or explain their significance.

Think and Apply

Use the letter and the photo to help you answer the following questions.

1 Why did the young man who wrote the letter on page 270 enlist to fight in the war?

2 With a partner, list the different things that you can learn from the photo.

3 The soldier in the photo and the writer of the letter could be about the same age. Both are from Indiana. How does the photo of the young soldier help make the writer of the letter seem more "real"?

FORT SUMTER An island off the coast of Charleston, South Carolina, where a Union fort stood. The first shots of the American Civil War were fired here on April 12, 1861. It is now preserved as a National Monument.

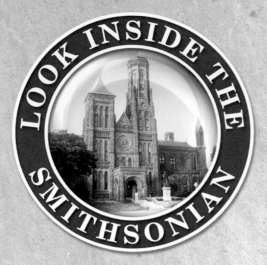

LOOK INSIDE THE SMITHSONIAN

The Civil War

Although very little fighting took place in Indiana, Hoosier soldiers fought in every major battle of the Civil War. Here are some images and artifacts from the Civil War.

Ulysses S. Grant
When the Civil War began, Grant took a post as a brigadier general. By March 1864 Grant was given command of the entire Union army. It was to Grant that Confederate general Robert E. Lee surrendered on April 9, 1865. After the war, Grant was elected President of the United States.

Drummer Boys
Thousands of boys, some of them as young as twelve years old, served on both sides of the conflict. Many young boys served as drummers, beating out military calls for troops to follow.

Union Battle Flags
From top to bottom, these flags include the banner of the Eleventh Regiment, Connecticut Volunteers; the Headquarters Guidon of the Old Vermont Brigade; and the flag of General Sedgewick's 6th Corps Headquarters.

Light Artillery Corporal

Infantry Musician

Union Uniforms
These men wear uniforms of the Union army. One wears the uniform of an infantry musician. The other is a corporal in a light artillery unit.

Bands and Buglers
Both Union and Confederate troops had bands that traveled with regiments and brigades. Cavalry units used buglers rather than drummers to sound battle calls to direct troop movements.

Stars and Stripes Quilt
Mary Rockhold-Teter of Noblesville, Indiana, made this quilt for her son, George. He served in the Union Army. The 34 stars in the center and 34 stars around the border represent the number of states in the Union in 1860.

Artifacts are from the Smithsonian Institution.

1861

November 1860	December 1860	February 1861	April 12, 1861	June 3, 1861
Lincoln was elected President.	South Carolina seceded.	Confederacy was formed.	First shot of the Civil War was fired.	Hoosier soldiers first went into battle.

Chapter Summary

Target Skill

Cause and Effect

On a sheet of paper, fill in a cause or an effect for each statement.

Causes	Effects
Abraham Lincoln was elected President.	Southern states seceded from the Union.
Farmers started using new machines to work.	Men needed for farm work went to fight in the war.
African Americans wanted to find a better life.	African Americans moved north to find work.

Vocabulary

Fill in the blank in each sentence with a word from the list.

secede (p. 251)	front (p. 257)	segregated (p. 269)
regiment (p. 256)	reaper (p. 267)	

1 The farmer bought a _____ to help him harvest his wheat crop.

2 South Carolina was the first state to _____ from the Union.

3 The Indiana _____ proudly carried its flag into battle.

4 African Americans had to wait for the Emancipation Proclamation before they could join the Union army at the _____.

5 Some African Americans lived in _____ communities because of racism.

People and Places

Match each person or place with the correct description.

1 Jefferson Davis (p. 252)

2 Fort Sumter (p. 253)

3 Joseph J. Reynolds (p. 255)

4 Eliza E. George (p. 257)

5 Philippi, Virginia (p. 258)

6 Salem (p. 259)

a. nursed soldiers during the Civil War

b. commanded first six regiments formed in Indiana

c. Civil War began when Confederates fired here

d. location of first fighting by Hoosiers in the Civil War

e. president of the Confederacy

f. town John Hunt Morgan threatened to burn mills

1862	1863	1864	1865

February 1862
Battle for Fort
Donelson is fought.

July 8, 1863
Morgan raided
Indiana.

**April 9,
1865**
The Civil
War ended.

Facts and Main Ideas

1 What issues divided not only the nation in 1860, but also the people of Indiana?

2 Why was Lincoln's election considered a threat to the Southern way of life?

3 How did Governor Morton react to the attempts to avoid war through compromise?

4 **Time Line** How long after the Civil War began did the one Civil War event in Indiana take place?

5 **Main Idea** What side did most Hoosiers support in the Civil War and why?

6 **Main Idea** How did the roles of Hoosier women change during the Civil War?

7 **Main Idea** How did the Civil War affect the lives of the people of Indiana?

8 **Critical Thinking:**
Draw Conclusions
Why do you think many African Americans were eager to join the Union army?

Apply Skills

Use Primary Sources

Read the primary source below. Then answer the questions.

"What to do or where to go, I did not know. People were running here and there, screaming that the town would be shelled. . . . My husband went into the garden and picked a mess of beans . . . for he declared the Rebels should not have one . . .

"We expect to be compelled to leave town tomorrow, as the Rebels say it will most likely be shelled. I cannot sleep."

1 How can you tell that this passage is a primary source?

2 What experience is the writer describing here? To whom do you think the writer is telling this story?

3 What can you find out about the writer from reading this passage?

Write About History

1 Write a **speech** to the Hoosier soldiers under your command in February of 1862, asking them to fight bravely in the upcoming battle for Fort Donelson.

2 Write a **letter to the editor** of your local newspaper in 1863, giving your opinion on the decision to let African Americans fight for the Union.

3 Write a **short story** about an eleven-year-old in 1861, whose father is from Boston and whose mother is from Georgia.

Internet Activity

To get help with vocabulary, people, and terms, select the dictionary or encyclopedia from *Social Studies Library* at **www.sfsocialstudies.com.**

Allen Jay and the Underground Railroad

by Marlene Targ Brill

Eleven-year-old Allen Jay and his family are members of the Society of Friends, or Quakers, who help African American slaves escape the South using the Underground Railroad in the 1840s. One day, Allen realizes that a man's life depends on his actions. . . .

July 1, 1842

As [Allen] crossed the front yard, he saw a horse racing down the road toward the Jay farm. Within seconds the family doctor stopped at the front gate. "Friend Jay! Friend Jay!" the doctor shouted.

Allen's father came out of the barn and walked quickly to the gate. "Thy horse has wings today," said Isaac Jay. "Thee seems in a hurry."

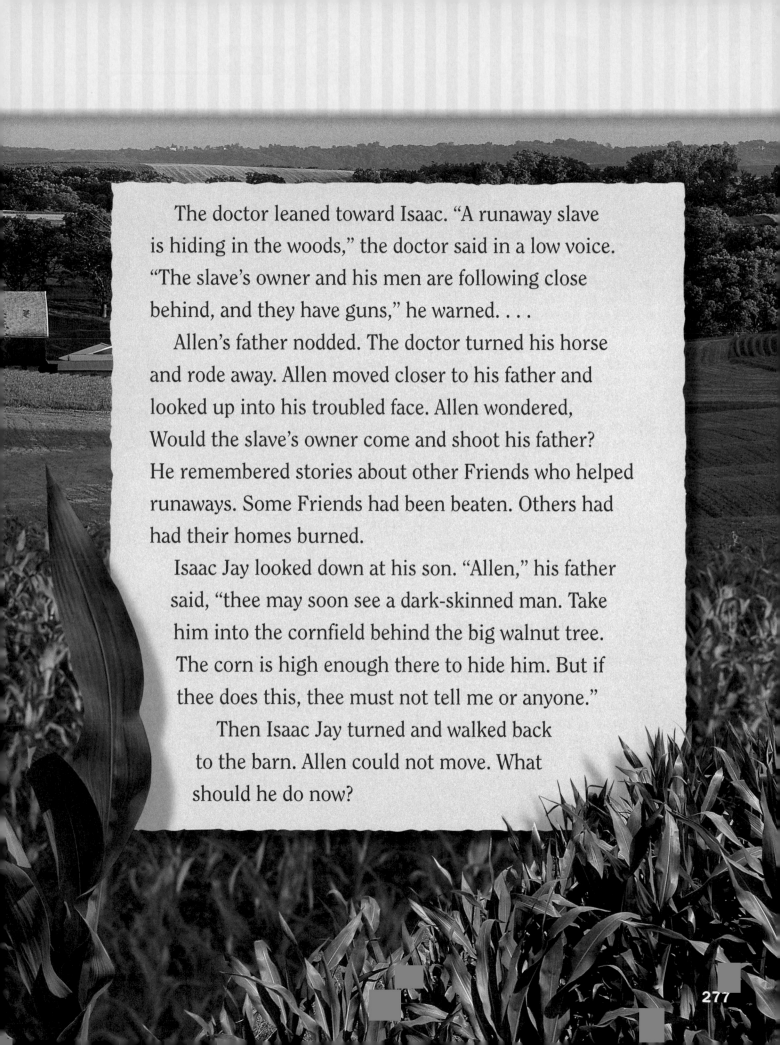

The doctor leaned toward Isaac. "A runaway slave is hiding in the woods," the doctor said in a low voice. "The slave's owner and his men are following close behind, and they have guns," he warned. . . .

Allen's father nodded. The doctor turned his horse and rode away. Allen moved closer to his father and looked up into his troubled face. Allen wondered, Would the slave's owner come and shoot his father? He remembered stories about other Friends who helped runaways. Some Friends had been beaten. Others had had their homes burned.

Isaac Jay looked down at his son. "Allen," his father said, "thee may soon see a dark-skinned man. Take him into the cornfield behind the big walnut tree. The corn is high enough there to hide him. But if thee does this, thee must not tell me or anyone."

Then Isaac Jay turned and walked back to the barn. Allen could not move. What should he do now?

Main Ideas and Vocabulary

TEST PREP

Read the passage below, and use it to answer the questions that follow.

In 1850, the United States government passed the Fugitive Slave Act. This law said that enslaved African Americans who had escaped and were in free states had to be returned to their owners. A year later, Indiana passed a law prohibiting African Americans from entering the state. But these laws did not stop Hoosiers from helping enslaved African Americans. <u>Abolitionists</u> spoke out against slavery. Some, including Quakers in Indiana, risked their own freedom to become conductors on the Underground Railroad. This was a network of secret routes to help enslaved African Americans reach the North and Canada.

In 1860, Abraham Lincoln, an anti-slavery Republican, was elected President. Several Southern states <u>seceded</u> from the Union. War began in 1861. Indiana men volunteered in record numbers to fight to preserve the Union. Many women volunteered as nurses. After four years of fighting, the North won the war, but life in Indiana and elsewhere was never the same.

1 An <u>abolitionist</u> is a person who
   A lives in the South and owns slaves.
   B believes that war is wrong.
   C wants to abolish slavery.
   D is running for public office.

2 In this passage, the Underground Railroad refers to
   A a subway system in Indianapolis.
   B a secret train that carried enslaved people out of the South.
   C an abolitionist newspaper.
   D a network of secret routes leading to the North and Canada.

3 In this passage, <u>seceded</u> means
   A withdrew from the Union.
   B achieved a desired goal.
   C declared war.
   D protested against.

4 According to this passage, what was one reason Indiana men fought in the Civil War?
   A They were forced to fight in the war.
   B They fought to preserve the Union.
   C They wanted adventure.
   D They fought to save Indiana.

People and Terms

Match each person and term to its definition or description.

1 Confederacy (p. 252)

2 Oliver P. Morton (p. 255)

3 Indiana Legion (p. 255)

4 Emancipation Proclamation (p. 256)

5 John Hunt Morgan (p. 259)

6 Ulysses S. Grant (p. 260)

a. group of states that seceded from the Union

b. leader of a Confederate raid on Indiana

c. militia that protected Indiana during the Civil War

d. leader of Union forces

e. governor of Indiana during the Civil War

f. declaration freeing enslaved people in Confederate-held areas

Write and Share

Present a dramatic interpretation of Morgan's Raid. Your teacher will divide you into teams. One team of students should research the details of the event. A second team should write the script for the dramatization. The third team should present the dramatization for another class in the school.

Apply Skills

Create a Time Capsule Use primary sources such as photos, diary and journal entries, and letters to create a scrapbook of one event or period in your life. When you have completed your scrapbook, write a journal entry explaining what you think historians in the future will be able to learn about you and the time you lived in from this scrapbook.

Monday, August 6

Today we visited Lincoln's boyhood home.
Later that day we collected wild flowers.

Wednesday, August 8

We traveled to a farm. Mom bought two apple pies.

Thursday, August 9

Mom and Dad took me to Wyandotte Cave.

Read on Your Own

Look for these books in your library.

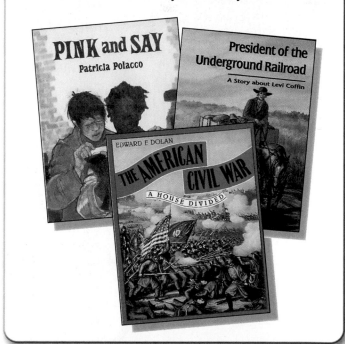

PINK and SAY
Patricia Polacco

President of the Underground Railroad
A Story about Levi Coffin

EDWARD F. DOLAN
THE AMERICAN CIVIL WAR
A HOUSE DIVIDED

UNIT 4 Project

Point of View

People often have different ideas about an issue. Take sides and discuss different points of view.

1 Form a group and choose an issue that was important to the history of Indiana. Write a sentence about your issue.

2 Prepare to debate the issue. Find two sides of the issue and write sentences with facts that support each side. Write several questions and answers about the issue as well.

3 Decide who will argue each side.

4 Debate your issue for the class. You may want to set a time limit for each side's presentation before taking questions.

Internet Activity

Discover more about Indiana on the Internet. Go to **www.sfsocialstudies.com/activities** and select your grade and unit.

Indiana Grows

What benefits and problems might more industry bring to Indiana?

UNIT 5

1880

1900

1880
Twenty percent of Hoosiers live in cities.

1886
First gas wells are drilled in Indiana.

1888
Benjamin Harrison is elected President.

1894
Elwood Haynes drives one of the world's first automobiles.

1907
T.C. Steele moves to Brown County.

1909
U.S. Steel opens its first works in Gary.

1910
Madam C. J. Walker opens business in Indianapolis.

1917
U.S. enters World War I.

"In regard to population, wealth, progress, enterprise, commerce, manufactures, agriculture, intelligence, the State of Indiana . . . is in all senses, a First Rate State."

—a historian writing in 1876, cited in *Indiana, An Interpretation* by John Bartlow Martin

This mural, *Gas City in Boom Days,* by the artist William A. Dolwick depicts Indiana in the late 1800s.

1920

1940

1918
World War I ends.

1919
U.S. Steel strike begins in Gary.

1920
Nineteenth Amendment gives women suffrage.

1929
Great Depression begins.

1941
U.S. enters World War II.

1945
World War II ends.

1949
Indiana schools are desegregated.

Meet the People

Schuyler Colfax

1823–1885

Birthplace: New York City, New York

Politician

- Started important newspaper in St. Joseph, Indiana
- Served in Congress and was Speaker of the House
- Elected Vice-President in 1868

Benjamin Harrison

1833–1901

Birthplace: North Bend, Ohio

Politician

- Set up a law practice in Indianapolis
- Became a general during the Civil War
- Served as President of the United States from 1889 to 1893

James Whitcomb Riley

1849–1916

Birthplace: Greenfield, Indiana

Poet

- Traveled as a sign painter and entertainer
- Contributed poems to *The Indianapolis Journal*
- Published ten volumes of complete works in 1916

Ida Husted Harper

1851–1931

Birthplace: Fairfield, Indiana

Suffragist

- Wrote column called "A Woman's Opinions" for a Terre Haute newspaper
- Wrote official biography of Susan B. Anthony
- Campaigned for passage of the Nineteenth Amendment

1820	1840	1860	1880

1823 • Schuyler Colfax — 1885

1833 • Benjamin Harrison

1849 • James Whitcomb Riley

1851 • Ida Husted Harper

1855 • Eugene V. Debs

1857 • Elwood Haynes

1867 • Madam C. J. Walker

For more information, go online to *Meet the People* at **www.sfsocialstudies.com**.

Eugene V. Debs

1855–1926

Birthplace: Terre Haute, Indiana

Labor organizer, politician

- Became president of the American Railway Union
- Became a Socialist in 1897
- Ran for President of the United States five times

Elwood Haynes

1857–1925

Birthplace: Portland, Indiana

Inventor

- Tested an early automobile on July 4, 1894, near Kokomo, Indiana
- Manufactured automobiles in Kokomo
- Discovered new kinds of metals, including a stainless steel for use in automobiles

Madam C. J. Walker

1867–1919

Birthplace: near Delta, Louisiana

Businesswoman

- Worked first as a washerwoman
- Started a company producing hair products for African American women
- Became very wealthy and gave generously to many causes

Ernie Pyle

1900–1945

Birthplace: near Dana, Indiana

Journalist

- Studied journalism at Indiana University
- Wrote prize-winning columns about World War II
- Killed in World War II

1900   1920   1940   1960

1901

1916

1931

1926

1925

1919

1900 • Ernie Pyle   1945

285

Reading Social Studies

Indiana Grows

Draw Conclusions

Drawing conclusions helps you make judgments or form opinions about what you read. It helps you understand ideas that may not be stated directly.

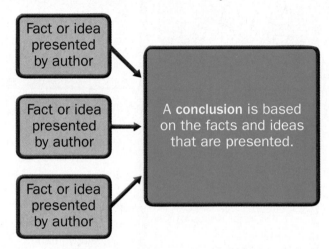

- Read carefully. Ask questions as you read. Before drawing a conclusion, summarize the facts and ideas you have read.

- Think about the facts and ideas as a whole. Draw conclusions after you have read a section, a chapter, or a unit.

Read the following paragraph. Facts are highlighted in yellow. A conclusion that can be drawn from them is highlighted in blue.

After the Civil War, many new industries began in Indiana. These industries needed workers. People moved to Indiana to work in the factories. There were a lot of jobs. But most jobs demanded ten hours of work a day, six days a week. Pay was poor. Some workers made only 10 cents an hour. The lives of factory workers and their families were hard.

The Postwar Era

After the Civil War, Indiana began a period of tremendous development. New industries made Indiana's economy grow. Natural gas was found in the east-central part of the state. Many industries moved to that area. They could use the heat produced by burning natural gas to manufacture their products. When the supply of gas dried up, a new industry—steel—became the most important industry in the state.

Around the same time, Hoosiers gained national attention in politics and in the arts. Both Democrats and Republicans tried to win over the state's voters, so they often chose candidates from Indiana. Benjamin Harrison was elected President in 1888.

Writers such as James Whitcomb Riley, Gene Stratton-Porter, and Booth Tarkington often used Indiana settings for their popular works. When artist Theodore Clement Steele moved to Brown County, other artists followed. They painted Indiana's beautiful landscapes.

At the same time, Indiana had problems. Many workers lived in poverty. Although they worked long hours, their pay was so low that sometimes children had to work to help their families.

Use the reading strategy of drawing conclusions to answer these questions.

1 Which facts and ideas support this statement: "After the Civil War, Indiana entered an era of tremendous development."

2 Which facts and ideas support the conclusion that Indiana had problems during this time period too?

3 Think about your answers to the first two questions. Write a conclusion about whether or not Indiana was a good place to live after the Civil War.

CHAPTER 10

Big Changes

Lesson 1

1880s
Kokomo
Indiana develops industries and finds new resources.

1

Lesson 2

1880
Wabash
Wabash becomes the first city in the world to be lighted by electricity.

2

Lesson 3

1900
Brown County
Many nationally known politicians, artists, and writers bring fame to Indiana.

3

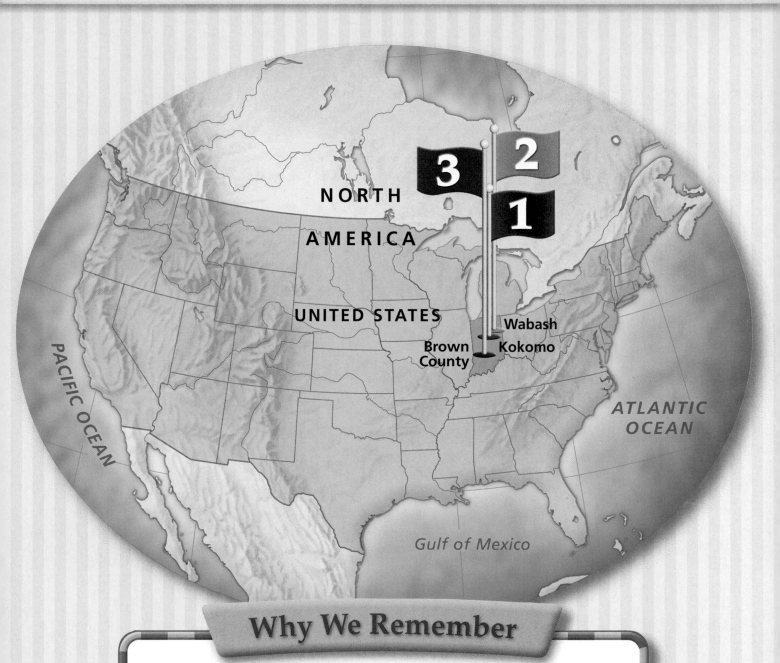

NORTH

AMERICA

UNITED STATES

PACIFIC OCEAN

Wabash

Brown
County

Kokomo

ATLANTIC
OCEAN

Gulf of Mexico

Why We Remember

After the Civil War, Indiana changed in many ways. The state
began to look more like it does today. New industries built
huge factories. Cities grew and were modernized. Immigrants
came to work in Indiana's new industries. Meanwhile, Indiana
politicians took on major roles in the nation. And Hoosier
artists and writers shared Indiana's beauty and spirit with the
rest of the world.

1876
Eli Lilly starts a pharmaceutical company in Indianapolis.

1886
First gas wells are drilled in Indiana.

1888
Ball brothers open a glass company in Muncie.

1894
Elwood Haynes drives one of the first automobiles.

Kokomo

PREVIEW

Focus on the Main Idea
Indiana's economy grew quickly after the Civil War.

PLACES
Kokomo

PEOPLE
Ball brothers
James Oliver
Elwood Haynes
Eli Lilly

VOCABULARY
economy
supply
monopoly
profit
regulate

TERMS
Gas Belt

A Growing Economy

You Are There

It is a beautiful sight. It is also very frightening. You are watching the flame from the gas well at Eaton. The flame is huge! Someone says it can be seen twelve miles away in Muncie. The flame makes a whooshing sound as it devours the gas coming up from deep inside the ground. You can feel its heat from far off. People say that the gas will keep houses warm in the winter. They say that it will light streets and houses. New businesses will move to Indiana to use this fuel. Watching the huge flame, you know that you are watching something that will cause many changes.

Draw Conclusions As you read about the growing economy of Indiana, draw conclusions about the effects of growth on the state.

Fuel Helps Indiana Grow

Indiana's economy was growing, with the help of fuel resources. **Economy** means the business affairs of an area. Hoosier blacksmiths had dug coal for their fires along the Wabash River since pioneer days. As the railroads grew, companies began mining coal to fuel trains as they passed through. Soon trains carried coal from the Terre Haute area to other parts of the country. Coal mining became an important Indiana business.

Natural gas was first discovered in Indiana in the 1860s. In the 1880s, Hoosiers began to burn this natural resource for lighting and to run factories. The first gas wells were drilled in Eaton and Portland in 1886.

When gas was first found, excited drillers lit it and watched it burn. Flames shot into the air. Families came from miles around to see this great wonder—and what they thought was an unlimited supply of gas.

▶ These glass jars were made by Ball Brothers Glass Company around 1900.

Cities such as Muncie, Marion, Alexandria, Anderson, Hartford City, Montpelier, and New Castle used natural gas to attract new businesses. This part of Indiana, now called the **Gas Belt,** boomed. Factories, including canning and glass-making companies, wanted to use the cheap new fuel. The Van Camp Packing Company became one of the country's most successful grocery companies.

Glass had been made in Indiana long before the discovery of natural gas. But the use of this cheap fuel helped glass companies grow. By 1900, more than one hundred factories made glass in Indiana. One was Ball Brothers Glass Company. The **Ball brothers** moved from New York to the Gas Belt town of Muncie and began producing glass in 1888.

REVIEW How did the discovery of natural gas in the state change Indiana? ⟳ **Draw Conclusions**

▶ Gas flames that shot high in the air drew crowds.

▶ Early automobiles, like this one made by Elwood Haynes, looked more like carriages than like the cars we use today.

Growing Industries

After the Civil War, both agriculture and industry grew in Indiana. Farms and industries supplied goods and services to Indiana and the country. A **supply** is what producers are willing and able to sell at various prices. For example, as the number of farms increased, the number of industries supplying things for farms also increased.

Most counties in the state had mills for making flour from grain and sawmills for cutting wood into boards. Meat-packing plants were located along the Wabash, White, and Ohio Rivers. Railroads made it possible to ship products across the country.

Other industries had also begun to grow. **James Oliver** started making plows in South Bend in the 1860s. By the 1880s, his company was the largest maker of plows in the world.

Elwood Haynes began manufacturing automobiles in **Kokomo** in the 1890s. When **Eli Lilly** returned to Indianapolis from the Civil War, he started a company that made medicines. Today, Eli Lilly and Company, Inc., is one of the largest pharmaceutical (far muh SOOT uh kul), or medicinal drug, companies in the world.

From the 1870s on, the Bedford-Bloomington area became home to huge limestone quarries. Another industry was born.

REVIEW Why did Indiana's new industries need the railroads?
◉ **Draw Conclusions**

Moving by Rail

Railroads were first built in Indiana in the 1840s. By 1854, Indiana had about fourteen hundred miles of track, owned by eighteen different companies. After the Civil War, however, most of the small railroad lines were bought out by large national companies. The two largest were the Pennsylvania Railroad and the New York Central. By 1920, these two railroad companies owned more than half of the railroad track in Indiana.

Railroads helped Hoosier farmers ship their products quickly and easily. However, as a few large companies took control, a problem arose.

▶ Farmers load goods onto railroad cars.

Some parts of Indiana had only one railroad line. Those rail companies had a **monopoly,** meaning they had no competition. With no other company to attract customers by offering lower prices, these monopolies could set high prices to ship farmers' crops. This means that prices change as a result of changes in supply and demand. The supply of railroad lines was low, but the demand to use the railroad lines was high. Farmers had little choice but to pay the high rates.

Most railroad owners lived far from Indiana. Hoosiers complained that the owners did not care about them. In 1873, the *Indianapolis Journal* said:

> *"The transportation of our people is at the mercy of men who never see us, who know nothing of us, and who care nothing for us."*

After the Civil War, prices for goods throughout the country fell, so farmers made less profit on their products. **Profit** means the amount someone makes selling a good or service minus the cost of producing the good or service. But freight prices—the cost of shipping products—stayed high. Farmers demanded that officials **regulate,** or control, shipping prices. In the 1890s, farm problems became an important political issue.

REVIEW Why did farmers want the government to regulate the price charged by railroads to ship goods?
⟳ Draw Conclusions

▶ A poster supports the work of farmers.

A Lucky Discovery

Hoosiers thought that their supply of natural gas was unlimited. At the time, gas lights were the main source of indoor lighting. People and businesses often left them burning twenty-four hours a day. Then the gas supply ran out. Indiana's economy might have slowed down.

But Hoosiers got lucky. Just as the natural gas was running out, scientists were finding new ways to refine, or purify, crude oil into useful fuels such as gasoline. Soon Standard Oil of Indiana began refining oil in Whiting. The economy of northwestern Indiana started to grow.

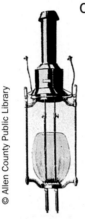

© Allen County Public Library

▶ **Electric lights such as this began replacing gas lighting in the late 1800s.**

By 1919, big business had come to Indiana. The three hundred or so largest companies in the state employed more than 50 percent of the state's workers. They made 70 percent of the state's manufactured products.

REVIEW Why did industries want to be located in Indiana in the late 1800s? ⟲ **Draw Conclusions**

Summarize the Lesson

- **1876** Eli Lilly founded a pharmaceutical company.
- **1886** The first gas wells were drilled.
- **1888** The Ball brothers opened a glass company.
- **1894** Elwood Haynes drove one of the world's first automobiles near Kokomo.

LESSON 1 REVIEW

Check Facts and Main Ideas

1. ⟲ **Draw Conclusions** On a sheet of paper, write three facts from the lesson that support the conclusion shown.

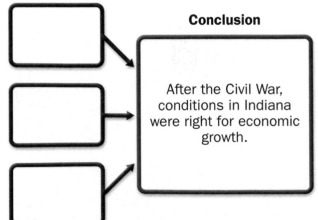

Facts

Conclusion

After the Civil War, conditions in Indiana were right for economic growth.

2. Why did Hoosier farmers want the government to regulate railroads?

3. How did fuel—natural gas, oil, and coal—affect industry in Indiana?

4. Identify at least four of the important new industries in Indiana after the Civil War.

5. **Critical Thinking:** *Make Inferences* How did people help cause Indiana's supply of natural gas to run out so quickly?

Link to ⬭ Science

Where Is Energy? Explain where natural gas, coal, and oil are found in the United States. Do research to learn how these fuels formed inside the Earth. You can present your findings in the form of a poster or drawing, or make an oral presentation to the class.

294

Elwood Haynes

1857–1925

Elwood Haynes loved cars and metals. He was the third person in the world to build a gasoline-powered automobile. He was the second person in the United States to build an automobile that actually worked. On July 4, 1894, Haynes drove his new invention down the Pumpkinville Pike near Kokomo.

Haynes had been a teacher and a high school principal. Then he took a job with the Portland Natural Gas and Oil Company. At the same time, he started making plans for his first automobile.

Haynes started the Haynes-Apperson Automobile Company with two brothers, Elmer and Edgar Apperson. By 1898, the company was turning out about five cars a year. In 1902, the Appersons started their own company and Haynes began the Haynes Company.

Haynes was always experimenting with metals. He was the first person to use aluminum in an automobile engine. He developed several alloys, or combinations of metals, including a form of stainless steel.

Learn from Biographies

What were Elwood Haynes's greatest skills? How did he use them?

For more information, go online to *Meet the People* at **www.sfsocialstudies.com**.

Indiana and the West

Railroads Across the Nation

Railroads not only helped Indiana grow. They helped the country grow as well. President Lincoln signed a bill in 1862 that called for the Union Pacific Railroad to link up with the Central Pacific Railroad between Omaha, Nebraska, and Sacramento, California.

The two railroads met in 1869. They formed the first transcontinental railroad. It stretched across the continent, from the Atlantic to the Pacific. Now people, goods, and mail could move great distances much more easily. Soon the country would be settled from coast to coast.

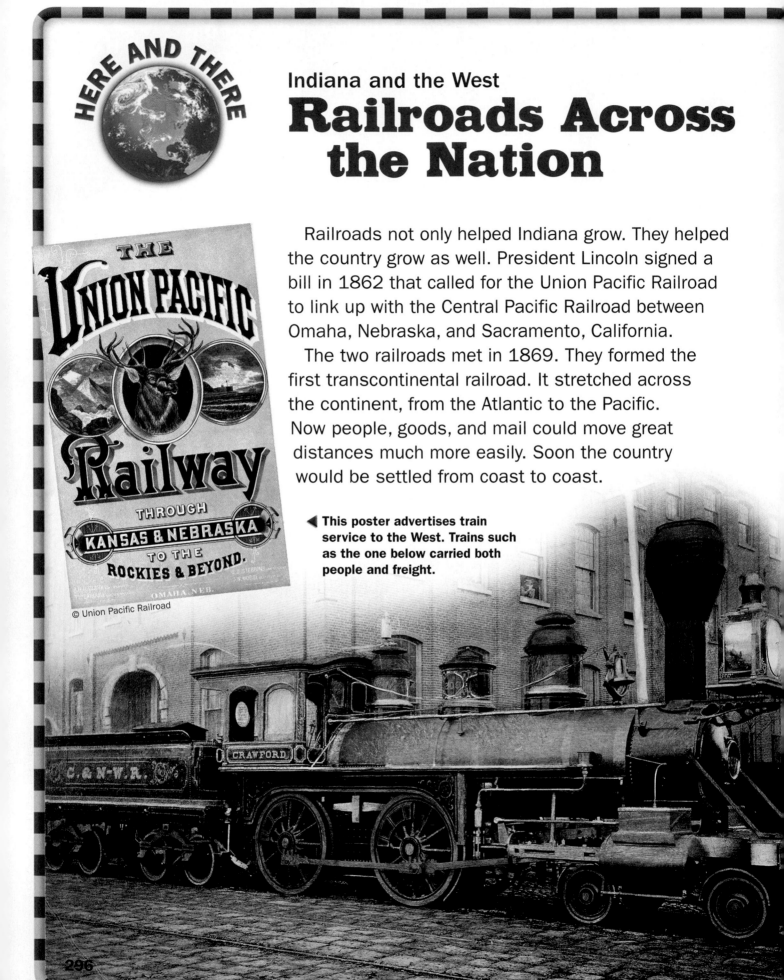

THE UNION PACIFIC Railway THROUGH KANSAS & NEBRASKA TO THE ROCKIES & BEYOND.

OMAHA, NEB.

© Union Pacific Railroad

◀ This poster advertises train service to the West. Trains such as the one below carried both people and freight.

CRAWFORD

C. & N-W. R.

More than ten thousand workers came from China to help build the transcontinental railroad.

© Union Pacific Railroad

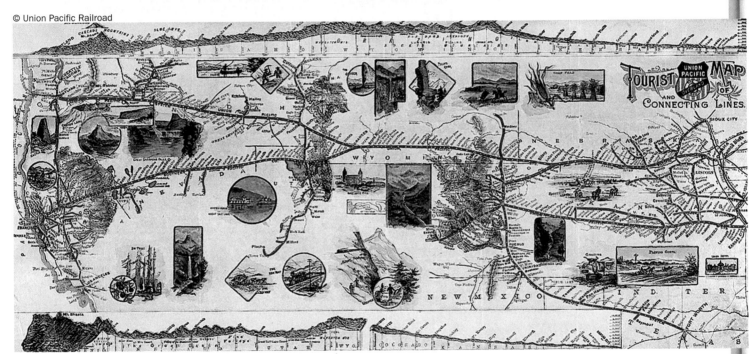

▲ Maps like this one showed tourists where the Union Pacific Railroad could take them.

▶ The Union Pacific and the Central Pacific were joined at Promontory Point, Utah. On May 10, 1869, ceremonial spikes were driven into the track. A telegraph operator sent a single word across the country: "DONE!"

297

Wabash

1850	1865	1880

1850
Only 5 percent of Hoosiers live in cities.

1850s
Cities hire professional firefighters and police.

1880
Twenty percent of Hoosiers now live in cities. Wabash is first city to be lit by electricity.

PREVIEW

Focus on the Main Idea
Certain cities in Indiana grew in the late 1800s.

PLACES
Wabash

VOCABULARY
interurban line
suburb

Growing Cities

You Are There
The sun has just come up, but it's already hot and steamy. Then you remember something exciting as you lie in bed. Your parents are taking you to Robinson Park today!

Robinson Park is the newest and most exciting place in Fort Wayne. It's called an amusement park. There are all sorts of rides and fun games to play. And it's easy to get there. All you have to do is hop on the streetcar and you're across the city in no time.

Mother is packing a picnic lunch for the family. But there will be ice cream for dessert at the park. You can't wait. And you can't imagine how everyone else can still be asleep. This is going to be the best Saturday ever.

Draw Conclusions As you read about Hoosier cities and newcomers to the state, draw conclusions about why cities grew at this time.

Moving to the City

Indiana's new industries needed workers. Most of the new jobs were in cities. In 1850, only 5 percent of Hoosiers were city dwellers. By 1880, about 20 percent of the state's population lived in cities. People left farms to live and find jobs in cities. Many came to Indiana cities from other countries too.

Some cities grew faster than others. The cities in north and central Indiana grew the fastest. This is the part of the state where most of the railroad building took place. Gas Belt cities such as Muncie, Kokomo, and Anderson grew quickly.

Railroads made it possible for workers to get to cities and to jobs. In addition, interurban lines linked cities with surrounding towns. An **interurban line** was an electricity-powered streetcar that ran between cities and towns. These lines made it possible for Hoosiers to work in cities and live in towns around them.

The interurban lines helped the growth of suburbs. A **suburb** is a town near a city. People who live in suburbs

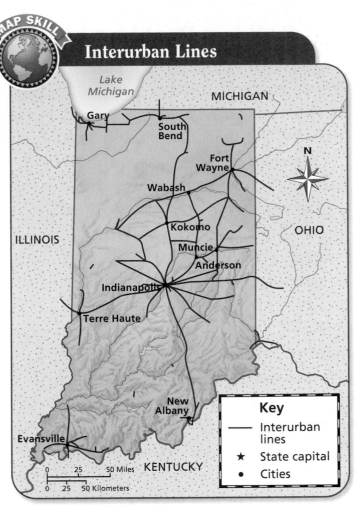

MAP SKILL — Interurban Lines

The cities that grew up in the north and along the Gas Belt were connected to each other by interurban train lines.

MAP SKILL Use a Transportation Map *Which city was connected to the most other cities by interurban lines? Why do you think this was so?*

often work in nearby cities. For example, the streetcars of an interurban line connected the suburb of Lakeside to the city of Fort Wayne.

Streetcar owners also increased their business by building parks and amusement centers. People reached these attractions by streetcar, just as they reached their jobs.

REVIEW In which parts of Indiana did cities grow most quickly between 1850 and 1880? **Summarize**

An early interurban car

299

Solving Problems

As cities grew, so did the problems that went along with more people and more buildings packed into a small area. Problems included fire, crime, the need for a water supply, and the need for safe, clean streets.

Some Hoosiers did not think it was up to city governments to tackle these problems—or to pay for them. They thought that people should solve these problems by themselves. However, cities slowly began to take care of their citizens' needs. City officials realized that the problems were too big, too complicated, and too expensive for most people to solve on their own. Taxes paid by citizens funded these city programs.

One of the first problems to be tackled was fire. Fires spread rapidly in cities made up of closely packed wooden buildings. Early fire companies were made up of volunteers. Later, many cities hired professional firefighters. Indianapolis started its paid fire department in 1860. Cities also built firehouses and bought firefighting equipment.

Around the same time, city governments also started police forces. Police were needed to prevent crime and to keep people safe.

Getting water was another problem that cities faced. At first, people took water from streams, wells, or canals. But as cities grew, this became harder and harder. Sometimes there was not enough water near the city to go around. Besides, it was often too far away to carry home easily.

▶ An early steam-powered fire engine in Richmond

▶ An early fire engine in action

▶ Fort Wayne Fire Department in front of their engine house, 1882

© Indiana State Library

© Allen County Public Library

© Allen County Public Library

▶ **This device cleaned city streets.**

In 1869, Indianapolis hired a company to pump water into the city. That way, people did not have to find water themselves and get it home. Other cities and towns also hired water companies. But the water pumped into the cities was sometimes dirty. It often came from the same streams and rivers where the town's sewer systems drained. At the time, people did not realize how dangerous this could be. For a time many people got sick from drinking dirty water.

Cities also began to pave muddy streets with asphalt or concrete. Asphalt is a product made during the refining of oil. It makes a hard, smooth surface. Cities also hired people to sweep the streets and collect garbage. This greatly improved the health of city dwellers.

People also wanted to be able to enjoy their cities after dark, so cities turned night into day with streetlights. Madison had gas streetlights in 1851. **Wabash** installed four electric lamps in 1880. The *Chicago Tribune* newspaper reported:

"Wabash enjoys the distinction [honor] of being the first city in the world to be lighted by electricity."

People in cities had many other needs. The cities tried to take care of some of them. For example, in 1866, Indianapolis opened its first public hospital—a hospital open to anyone.

REVIEW How did cities try to solve some of their problems? **Summarize**

301

Newcomers to Indiana

When people moved to Indiana's cities, they often chose to live near people like themselves. Wealthy people lived in grand neighborhoods with large houses. Indiana writer Booth Tarkington wrote,

". . . all the women who wore silk or velvet knew all the other women who wore silk or velvet. . . ."

At the same time, poor people lived together in crowded areas with poor housing. This was all they could afford. They had little choice about where they could live.

Most Hoosiers in the mid-1800s were white and had been born in the United States. However, some African Americans and immigrants did live and work in Indiana's cities. In 1851, about 11,000 African Americans lived in the state. After the Civil War, many more moved here from the South. They came for the chance to work in growing industries and make better lives for themselves. By 1880, about 39,000 African Americans lived in Indiana. That number grew to about 57,500 by 1900. Most of these newcomers lived in Indiana's cities. By 1900, almost 16,000 African Americans lived in Indianapolis alone.

African Americans had not always been welcome in Indiana. In 1851, Indiana adopted a constitution banning African Americans from settling in the state. This law was hardly ever enforced. But the same constitution stated that African Americans could not vote. After the Civil War, changes in the United States Constitution guaranteed African American men the right to vote. African Americans were also allowed to settle in Indiana.

Immigrants coming to Indiana generally lived in the state's cities. They often settled in neighborhoods close to other people from their homelands. Many came to find jobs in Indiana's growing industries. By 1850, more than half the foreign-born population was from Germany.

▶ **A street fair in Greenfield, 1899**

© Hinchman Collection / Hancock County Historical Society, Inc.

The second-largest immigrant group was from Ireland. As you read in Chapter 7, many Irish workers came to Indiana to build canals and railroads. Some decided to stay in Indiana.

By 1870, almost 150,000 people born in other countries lived in Indiana. Immigrants were vital to Indiana's growth. However, immigrants never made up even 10 percent of Indiana's population. Even in 1880, 70 percent of all Hoosiers had been born in Indiana.

REVIEW Why did most newcomers to Indiana settle in cities?
🔵 Draw Conclusions

Summarize the Lesson

— **1850** Only 5 percent of Hoosiers lived in cities.

— **1850s** Cities hired professional firefighters and police.

— **1880** Twenty percent of Indiana's population lived in cities.
Wabash was the first city in the world to be lit by electricity.

LESSON 2   REVIEW

Check Facts and Main Ideas

1. 🔵 **Draw Conclusions** On a sheet of paper, write a conclusion that can be drawn from the information given.

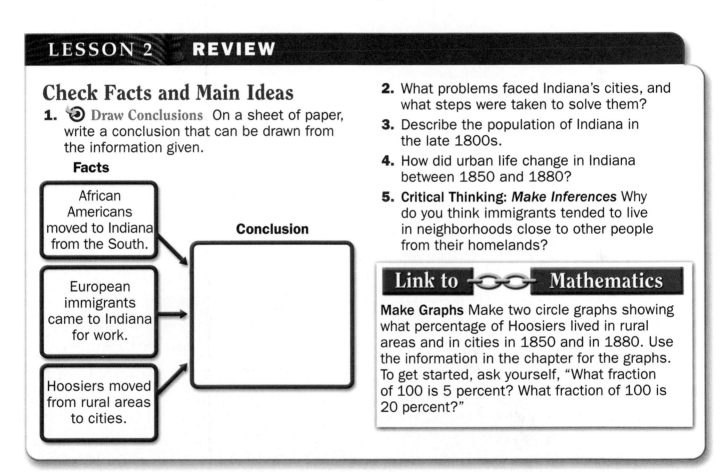

Facts

African Americans moved to Indiana from the South.

European immigrants came to Indiana for work.

Hoosiers moved from rural areas to cities.

Conclusion

2. What problems faced Indiana's cities, and what steps were taken to solve them?

3. Describe the population of Indiana in the late 1800s.

4. How did urban life change in Indiana between 1850 and 1880?

5. **Critical Thinking:** *Make Inferences* Why do you think immigrants tended to live in neighborhoods close to other people from their homelands?

Link to 🔗 Mathematics

Make Graphs Make two circle graphs showing what percentage of Hoosiers lived in rural areas and in cities in 1850 and in 1880. Use the information in the chapter for the graphs. To get started, ask yourself, "What fraction of 100 is 5 percent? What fraction of 100 is 20 percent?"

Use a Cross-Section Diagram

What? A **cross section** is a picture or drawing of an object as if one section of it had been cut away. That's why a cross-section diagram is sometimes called a **cutaway**. It allows you to see inside the object. You can see how it is made and how its parts fit together.

The cross-section diagram on page 305 shows how the inside of some interurban streetcars looked.

© Photograph by Bass Photo Company Collection, Indiana Historical Society, P.130, 67:7 / Indiana Historical Society

▶ **An interurban streetcar terminal (left) and an interurban streetcar (below)**

Why? Cross-section diagrams allow you to see inside an object. They show you how its parts fit together and how it is constructed.

How? Look at the photograph of the interurban streetcar, and then look at the cross-section diagram.

To use a cross-section diagram, you need to understand which part of the object has been cut away. In the diagram of the interurban streetcar, the roof has been removed so you can see down into the car.

Some cross-section diagrams include labels. These labels tell which parts you are seeing as you look at them.

Interurban Streetcar

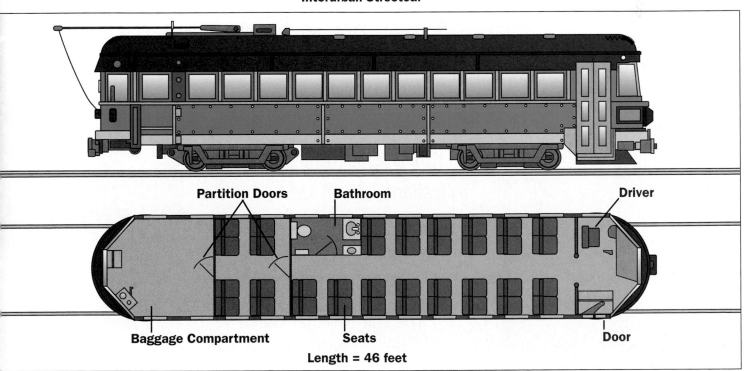

Partition Doors   Bathroom   Driver

Baggage Compartment   Seats   Door

Length = 46 feet

LESSON 3

1860	1870	1880	1890	1900	1910

1868
Schuyler Colfax is elected Vice-President.

1883
James Whitcomb Riley publishes his first book of poetry.

1888
Benjamin Harrison wins his campaign for President.

1907
Theodore Clement Steele moves to Brown County.

Leading Hoosiers

PREVIEW

Focus on the Main Idea
Around 1900, Hoosiers became important in national politics and in the arts.

PLACES
Brown County

PEOPLE
Benjamin Harrison
Schuyler Colfax
James Whitcomb Riley
Booth Tarkington
Gene Stratton-Porter
Theodore Dreiser

VOCABULARY
swing state

TERMS
Australian ballot
Hoosier Group

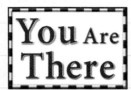 "Hurry up, children! You don't want to miss the ball," your mother shouts.

You and your sister run down the stairs. Both of you are dressed in your best clothes. You are going to see the giant campaign ball rolled into Indianapolis in front of Benjamin Harrison's house. Your father thinks Harrison will be elected President of the United States.

Imagine! You might actually get to see Mr. Harrison come out on the front porch of his house and talk to the people. And to think, all this is happening right here in Indianapolis in 1888.

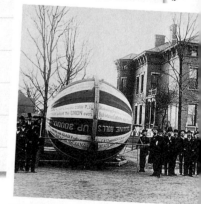

© President Benjamin Harrison Home

 Draw Conclusions As you read about famous Hoosiers of the late 1800s and early 1900s, decide whether those years were really a "golden age" for Indiana.

Hoosier Politics

After the Civil War, Indiana became an important state in national politics. A very high percentage of Hoosiers voted regularly.

Both major political parties—the Republicans and the Democrats—came close to tying in many elections. This made Indiana a **swing state.** This meant that a few votes either way could mean a victory for one party or the other. In order to get every Hoosier vote, both parties often put Hoosiers on the ballot. And both parties worked hard to get Indiana voters' attention. When **Benjamin Harrison** ran for President in 1888, one Democrat noted that

> *"The whole state was a blazing torchlight procession [parade] from one end to the other."*

Harrison was the grandson of President William Henry Harrison. He copied his grandfather's campaign idea—a giant ball that was rolled through the streets of America. People came to see the ball and the parades and picnics that were also a part of Harrison's campaign. He hoped this meant they would vote for him. They did. He won the election.

Sometimes politicians were dishonest. In the election of 1888, parties openly tried to buy votes.

▶ **Benjamin Harrison's inauguration**

This made many people angry. At the time, political parties printed their own ballots. So it was easy for party leaders to see which party's ballot a voter took when he went to vote. In addition, the party ballot almost forced a voter to vote for all the candidates of one party for every office.

In 1889, Indiana changed the ballots. It adopted the **Australian ballot,** or secret ballot. The state—not the political parties—printed the ballot. All candidates were listed on a single ballot. This made it harder for party leaders to see which voters chose their candidate. As a result, it was harder to buy votes.

REVIEW What were some causes of Indiana's importance in national politics? **Cause and Effect**

► **Schuyler Colfax ran for Vice-President in 1868.**

Hoosiers in National Politics

Democrats and Republicans both sought Hoosier votes by putting Indiana residents on the ballot. Hoosier nominees for Vice-President included **Schuyler Colfax** (1868), William H. English (1880), Thomas A. Hendricks (1876 and 1884), and John W. Kern (1908).

Schuyler Colfax was born in New York City, but he moved to Indiana as a boy. He founded an important newspaper, the *St. Joseph Valley Register.* He was its editor for eighteen years. In 1854, Colfax was elected to the United States House of Representatives as a Republican. He served until 1869, including six years as Speaker of the House.

In 1868, the presidential candidate was Ulysses S. Grant, the leader of the Union Army during the Civil War. He chose Colfax as his Vice-President. This was the nation's first election since the end of the Civil War. Grant and Colfax won.

Grant ran again in 1872, but Colfax was not nominated as his Vice-President this time. Colfax had been accused of taking bribes from a large construction company. A bribe is money paid illegally in return for a favor. Colfax's career was ruined.

REVIEW What did Colfax do after his many years as a U.S. Representative? **Sequence**

Hoosier Writers

Hoosier politicians brought national attention to Indiana. Hoosier artists and writers brought the state another kind of attention. Indiana produced so many good writers and artists that this period is sometimes called the state's "Golden Age."

► **A cartoon shows a Hoosier family in which everyone is writing.**

James Whitcomb Riley is probably Indiana's most famous poet. He started publishing his poems in newspapers.

In 1883, he published his first book of poetry, *The Old Swimmin' Hole and 'Leven* [Eleven] *More Poems.* He published fourteen books of poetry in his lifetime.

Other important Hoosier writers of the Golden Age were **Booth Tarkington** and **Gene Stratton-Porter.** Tarkington, a native of Indianapolis, wrote fiction. Some of his books are set in Indianapolis. Most critics think that *The Magnificent Ambersons* and *Alice Adams* are two of Tarkington's best works. Gene Stratton-Porter loved nature and the outdoors. Her most famous book, *A Girl of the Limberlost,* is set in the Limberlost Swamp in Adams County near Porter's home.

Not all Hoosier writers were popular in their home state. **Theodore Dreiser,** who was born in Terre Haute, tried to

▶ **Gene Stratton-Porter**

describe the harsh facts of real life. While Dreiser is recognized today as a great writer, during his lifetime many Hoosiers found his books shocking.

REVIEW How do you think living in Indiana affected the work of Hoosier writers? ⟳ **Draw Conclusions**

Literature and Social Studies

When the Frost is on the Punkin

James Whitcomb Riley first published this poem in the *Indianapolis Journal* on August 5, 1882. Here is one verse from the poem. *Fodder* is dried food, such as cornstalks, for animals. A *shock* is a pile of cornstalks. Like many of Riley's poems, it is written in dialect, meaning it shows local ways of speaking.

They's something kindo' harty-like about the atmusfere [atmosphere]
When the heat of summer's over and the coolin' fall is here—
Of course we miss the flowers, and the blossums on the trees,
And the mumble of the hummin'-birds and buzzin' of the bees;
But the air's so appetizin'; and the landscape through the haze
Of a crisp and sunny morning of the airly autumn days
Is a pictur' that no painter has the colorin' to mock—
When the frost is on the punkin and the fodder's
in the shock.

Hoosier Artists

Indiana has also been home to many painters. The most famous were called the **Hoosier Group.** They painted landscapes, trying to capture Indiana's beauty on canvas. The best-known painter of the Hoosier Group is Theodore Clement Steele. You read earlier about how he and his wife, Selma, moved to **Brown County** in 1907. Other artists followed the Steeles. Soon an "artists' colony" had formed in Brown County.

▶ *Magnolias in Bloom* by Theodore Clement Steele

© T.C. Steele State Historic Site

REVIEW How did Indiana's artists try to capture the state's beauty?
Main Idea and Details

Summarize the Lesson

— **1868** Schuyler Colfax was elected Vice-President.

— **1883** James Whitcomb Riley published his first book of poetry.

— **1888** Benjamin Harrison won his campaign for President.

— **1907** Theodore Clement Steele moved to Brown County.

LESSON 3   REVIEW

Check Facts and Main Ideas

1. Draw Conclusions On a sheet of paper, write the missing conclusion.

Facts

| Voters were almost evenly divided between parties. |

| Both parties often put Hoosiers on the ballot in national elections. |

| Indiana produced many famous writers and artists. |

Conclusion

2. Which Hoosier became Vice-President in 1868? Which Hoosier became President in 1888?

3. What ruined Schuyler Colfax's career?

4. Name two Hoosiers who gained national fame in the arts around 1900. Name two who gained national fame in politics.

5. **Critical Thinking: *Solve Problems*** How did the switch to the Australian ballot help make Indiana elections more honest?

Link to ⚭ Art

Hoosier Artists Look in art books or go online to find examples of paintings by artists of the Hoosier Group. Display them in your classroom, and prepare a short report about the artists.

James Whitcomb Riley *1849–1916*

James Whitcomb Riley wrote hundreds of poems about farm life. But his family members were not farmers. Riley's father was a lawyer and a member of the state legislature.

Riley was working as editor of the *Anderson Dispatch* newspaper when he sent a poem to the *Kokomo Dispatch*. He claimed it was a newly discovered work by the famous writer Edgar Allan Poe. In fact, Riley had written the poem himself. When the truth came out, Riley lost his job. Later he was hired by the *Indianapolis Journal*. He published many poems in that newspaper.

From 1882 to 1903, Riley toured the United States, sometimes with humorist Bill Nye. The two put on shows in which they told funny stories and acted out skits. Riley also read his poetry.

Children especially loved Riley's work. When he died in 1916, he was mourned in Indiana and around the world.

BIOFACT

Riley was so popular in Indiana that in 1916, the state had a special medallion [medal] made in his honor.

Learn from Biographies

Why do you think the *Indianapolis Journal* hired Riley after he was fired from the *Anderson Dispatch?*

For more information, go online to *Meet the People* at **www.sfsocialstudies.com.**

1865	1870	1875	1880

1868
Schuyler Colfax was elected Vice-President.

1876
Eli Lilly founded a pharmaceutical company in Indianapolis.

1880
Wabash was the first city lit with electricity.

Chapter Summary

 Draw Conclusions

On a sheet of paper, write three facts or observations that support the conclusion shown.

© Lester C. Nagley/Indiana State Library / Indiana State Library

Facts or Observations

Conclusion

In the late 1880s, Indiana became nationally well-known in many areas.

Vocabulary

Complete each sentence with the correct word.

economy (p. 291)	monopoly (p. 293)	regulate (p. 293)
suburbs (p. 299)	profit (p. 293)	

1. Better transportation made it possible for workers to live in _____ .

2. Indiana's _____ was growing because of fuel resources.

3. Many farmers wanted the government to _____ the railroads.

4. Railroads could charge high prices because they had a _____ on shipping.

5. Indiana farmers made less _____ after the Civil War because prices fell.

People and Terms

List one important fact about each of the following people or terms.

1. Gas Belt (p. 291)
2. Ball brothers (p. 291)
3. James Oliver (p. 292)
4. Elwood Haynes (p. 292)
5. Eli Lilly (p. 292)
6. Benjamin Harrison (p. 307)
7. Australian ballot (p. 307)
8. Schuyler Colfax (p. 308)
9. James Whitcomb Riley (p. 308)
10. Booth Tarkington (p. 309)
11. Theodore Dreiser (p. 309)
12. Hoosier Group (p. 310)

1885   1890   1895   1900   1905

1883
James Whitcomb Riley published his first book of poetry.

1886
First gas wells were drilled in Indiana.

1888
Benjamin Harrison was elected President.

1894
Elwood Haynes drove one of the first automobiles.

1907
Theodore Clement Steele moved to Brown County.

Facts and Main Ideas

1. How did the growth of railroads affect farmers?

2. Why did the discovery of natural gas bring new industries to Indiana?

3. Why did Indiana's supply of natural gas run out quickly?

4. **Time Line** How many years were there between the election of Schuyler Colfax as Vice-President and the election of Benjamin Harrison as President?

5. **Main Idea** Where did most of Indiana's newcomers come from in the years after the Civil War?

6. **Main Idea** Why was Indiana important in national politics in the late 1800s?

7. **Main Idea** What was Indiana's "Golden Age"? Explain.

8. **Critical Thinking:** *Draw Conclusions* Explain whether you think Indiana's industrial growth would have occurred without natural gas.

Write About History

1. **Write an advertisement** for one of the Indiana industries discussed in this chapter.

2. **Write a journal entry** about a visit to the gas fields near Eaton in 1887. Describe what you see.

3. **Write a two-paragraph essay** explaining why railroads and interurban lines were important to Indiana's people and its economy after the Civil War.

Apply Skills

Use a Cross-Section Diagram

Answer the questions below, which are based on the diagram.

1. What does the diagram show?

2. Why is the cross-section view shown here something you cannot see on a real elevator?

3. What keeps the elevator from falling?

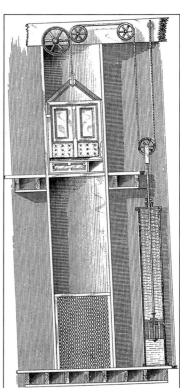

▶ **Passenger elevator from around 1883**

Internet Activity

To get help with vocabulary, people, and terms, select the dictionary or encyclopedia from *Social Studies Library* at **www.sfsocialstudies.com.**

CHAPTER 11

A New Century

Lesson 1

1906
Gary
Big business comes to Indiana.

1

Lesson 2

1920
Indianapolis
Reformers improve the lives of many.

2

Lesson 3

1941
Charlestown
Indiana meets new challenges.

3

Lesson 4

1965
Indiana
Hoosiers work to make life fairer for all.

4

Why We Remember

At the beginning of the 1900s, parts of Indiana seemed to grow practically overnight. The Calumet Region became the area of heavy industry it remains today. The automotive industry also got its start. During the two world wars, Indiana's factories raced to build the equipment soldiers needed. In the latter years of the century, Hoosiers played important roles in the nation's politics and in trying to solve its social problems.

Gary

1890   1900   1910

1894
Elwood Haynes drives his first gasoline-powered automobile near Kokomo.

1902
The Studebaker company makes its first automobile.

1909
U.S. Steel opens its first works in Gary.

PREVIEW

Focus on the Main Idea
The steel and automobile industries grew in Indiana during the early 1900s.

PLACES
Gary

VOCABULARY
steel
steelworks

TERMS
Studebaker Corporation

New Industries

You Are There

You and your friend are in a boat on the Calumet River doing some fishing. It's a beautiful spring day in 1901. Birds are flying over the swamp, swooping down to catch bugs. The swamp grass is swaying in the wind. You lean back and smell the clean, fresh air. You can't wait to bring home all the fish you catch for dinner.

But what is that you see? In the distance, there appears to be some big machinery. They're clearly building something new. It looks like a smokestack. Here in the Calumet? In a swamp? You can't imagine why anyone would want to build a factory here.

Summarize As you read about the growth of the steel industry in Indiana, summarize the details that tell how the northwestern part of the state changed.

The Calumet Region

The northwestern part of Indiana is called the Calumet by geographers. This region gets its name from the Calumet River. French travelers named the river, using an American Indian word for *pipe*. The Calumet River makes the shape of a pipe as it flows into Lake Michigan.

Around 1900, the Calumet was a swampy, marshy place. Fewer than twenty thousand people lived there. Hammond was the largest town. Soon, however, the Calumet became a vast industrial area. Smokestacks and huge piles of coal replaced the swamp grass of this lakeside region.

The area was ideal for industry in many ways. Its sandy, swampy land was inexpensive. Lake Michigan and the other Great Lakes offered one form of transportation. The railroads in and out of Chicago offered another. Workers from Chicago could easily travel to the Calumet for their jobs.

The first large industry to locate in the Calumet was the oil industry. In 1889, Standard Oil built what was then the world's largest refinery at Whiting. Whiting is in the northwestern corner of Indiana.

REVIEW Why was the Calumet good for industry? **Summarize**

▶ **The mills and factories of the Calumet were built quickly in the early 1900s.**

Iron and Steel

The iron and steel industries changed the Calumet greatly. Before iron ore—a mineral found in the earth—can be used, it must be heated to a high temperature to remove waste products. If this process is repeated enough, the iron becomes **steel.** Steel is tough and elastic. That means it can bend without breaking. It is more useful for building than iron, which can be brittle. Steel beams can also hold much more weight than beams made of iron.

In 1844, an enormous area of iron ore called the Mesabi Range was discovered near Lake Superior. Then, in the 1850s, inventors discovered better and faster ways to make steel from iron ore, using coal and limestone.

All the ingredients were now ready for industry in the Calumet: easy access to coal, iron ore, limestone, transportation, and workers. Nearby cities were growing quickly. They wanted steel for building, and they provided workers.

The first steel mill was built by Inland Steel Company in East Chicago, Indiana, in 1901. In 1906, the United States Steel Corporation bought 9,000 acres in Lake County. There it built the largest **steelworks,** or mill, of its time. The works opened in 1909. U.S. Steel built a new city for its workers and named it **Gary,** after Judge Elbert H. Gary, the chairman of the company's board. The company laid out streets and planned for builders to put up houses. By 1910, the city had nearly 17,000 workers, about half of them immigrants. Many came from eastern and southern Europe.

New factories and mills crowded into the Calumet. Soon Gary, East Chicago, and Hammond formed one huge industrial belt.

REVIEW What ingredients made the Calumet Region attractive to steel companies? **Summarize**

MAP SKILL

Mineral Resources

Key
- Coal
- Iron
- Limestone

► The Midwest is a mineral-rich region.

MAP SKILL Interactions *In what part of Indiana might people work as coal miners?*

Map Adventure

You are on a postcard scavenger hunt through Indiana. To win, you must be the first to reach certain places in the state and mail a postcard. Here are the places you must reach.

A. From your home, you must visit the place limestone comes from. In what direction do you travel?

B. Next you need a postcard from an artist's memorial and two postcards that show writers or their homes. Where will you go?

C. You need a postcard showing an event that was important to Indiana transportation. What places might you choose to visit?

D. Your last visit must be to a place that is important for fuel. Where will you head?

E. From your last location, you must meet the other players at Union Depot in Indianapolis. In which direction will you travel?

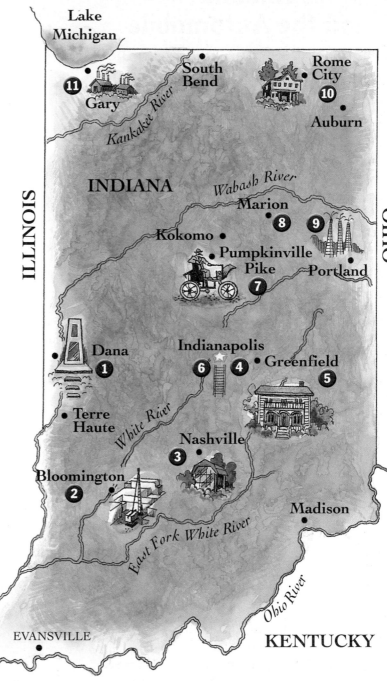

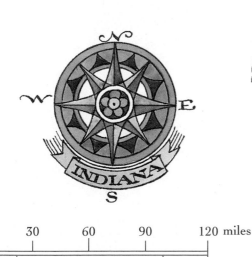

0	30	60	90	120 miles

0	30	60	90	120 kilometers

Places of Interest

1 Ernie Pyle State Memorial

2 Largest limestone quarries

3 Theodore Clement Steele State Memorial

4 Indianapolis Union Depot

5 Birthplace of James Whitcomb Riley

6 Benjamin Harrison's home

7 Pumpkinville Pike

8 One of many early interurban lines 1893–1894 (near Marion)

9 First natural gas well (near Portland)

10 Gene Stratton-Porter State Memorial

11 U.S. Steel Works in Gary

Indiana and the Automobile

Indiana's close connection with the automobile industry began with Elwood Haynes and his trip on the Pumpkinville Pike in 1894. As you have read, Haynes built the world's third gasoline-powered automobile and took it for a test drive near Kokomo.

Haynes started a company to make automobiles in 1895. Soon about two hundred different companies were making automobiles in Indiana.

Automobile manufacturers were drawn to Indiana for some of the same

▶ A 1912 Studebaker like this one cost $750.

reasons that steelworks came to the state. Automobile factories needed good transportation, coal, workers—and the steel made in the northwestern part of the state.

Then and Now

Automotive Industries

The automobile industry has been important to Indiana's economy for over one hundred years. The first cars were made mostly by hand, one at a time. Only a few workers were involved in the process.

▶ An early assembly line

▶ Henry Ford, the founder of Ford Motor Company, pioneered the use of the assembly line to make automobiles. Instead of moving around the car they were building, workers stayed in one place and the cars and the parts came to them on a moving belt.

320

▶ The automotive industry today is highly automated. Computers and machines do much of the work of assembling parts. Robots are used to perform certain tasks.

The automobile company that remained in Indiana the longest was the **Studebaker Corporation.** In 1900, the Studebaker Company of South Bend was the largest maker of wagons in the country. By 1902, the company had made its first electric-powered car. In its first year, the company sold about 23,000 cars. Three years later, it sold about 114,000. In 1904, the company began making gasoline powered cars. By the early 1920s, Studebaker was the nation's fifth largest auto maker. Studebaker closed its last plant in South Bend in 1963.

Although no companies make automobiles in Indiana today, the state is a major producer of automobile parts. Other automobile-related industries are very important to the state's economy as well. Indiana makes more mobile homes, motor homes, travel trailers, and campers than any other state. The state is also number one in the manufacture of truck and bus bodies.

REVIEW Why was the automobile industry attracted to Indiana in the early 1900s? *Cause and Effect*

Summarize the Lesson

— **1894** Elwood Haynes drove his first gasoline-powered automobile near Kokomo.

— **1902** The Studebaker Company made its first automobile.

— **1909** U.S. Steel opened its first works in Gary.

LESSON 1   REVIEW

Check Facts and Main Ideas

1. Summarize On a sheet of paper, write missing facts and observations from the lesson that support the summary.

The Calumet had good transportation. → → The Calumet Region held many attractions for industry.

2. Describe the establishment of Gary.

3. How did the automobile industry become important to the economy of Indiana?

4. Compare Indiana's present-day automotive industry to the industry in the early 1900s.

5. Critical Thinking: *Make Inferences* U.S. Steel opened its Gary works before enough housing had been built for its workers. Why do you think the company might have made that decision?

Link to ∞ Writing

Write an Advertisement Use encyclopedias, history books, or the Internet to research cars made in Indiana before 1920. Write an ad to sell one of them. As you write your ad, think about the reasons people bought cars at that time.

Shaping Metals

The Calumet area of Indiana has many steel mills, but humans were working with cold and hot metals for many years before the mills in Gary were built. When metals are melted, the super-hot, glowing liquid can be formed by different "casting" methods. The simplest one is sand casting. Die casting forces "molten" metal into a mold (die) to make precise metal parts. The ancient "lost wax" process produces hollow castings. Metal can also be squeezed between rollers and pulled through small holes to draw long strands of wire.

The wax patterns are dipped to coat them in clay.

Investment Casting
In this modern form of lost wax casting, workers mold wax patterns and coat them with clay. They heat the coating to melt the wax inside, and pour metal into the clay mold.

ladle

Sand Casting
Castings are made in a foundry. Sand casting, like sand castles, makes use of the way damp sand sticks together and forms shapes. Workers pour hot molten iron or metals into a sand mold. Hot metal does not melt the mold, because sand melts at a much higher temperature. When the metal hardens, the sand mold is simply brushed away.

Molten iron is poured into the mold.

Bronze-Age Pin Mold
This stone mold was used around 1000 BC to cast decorative pins with round heads. The primitive furnace was hot enough to melt bronze.

Mold

Moist sand

Iron box

Wooden pattern

1 Shaping the Sand
A wooden pattern cut to the half-shape of a finished metal casting is pressed into damp sand packed in an iron box. The pattern leaves an exact "footprint." Wood patterns can be used again to make many identical molds and castings.

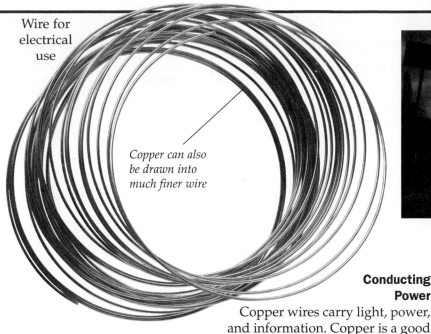

Wire for electrical use

Copper can also be drawn into much finer wire

Hot Rolling

Blacksmiths know that when heated metal glows bright red, it is soft enough to bend, pound, or twist into shape. This hot rolling mill (above) is squeezing steel beams into girders that span wide gaps in the frames of buildings. The beam passes through rollers that gradually squeeze it into shape. Train rails are also made this way.

Conducting Power

Copper wires carry light, power, and information. Copper is a good conductor of electricity, so little energy is lost as power or messages travel over cables. Wire is made by drawing (pulling) metal strips or rods down to size through smaller and smaller holes in a metal form.

Cold-rolled steel

Flexible sheet metal is made by sending cold metal strips of steel or aluminum through sets of heavy rollers. Each roller weighs several tons and squeezes the metal into thin sheets of precise thickness. As strips get thinner, they get longer and travel faster—up to 55 miles per hour.

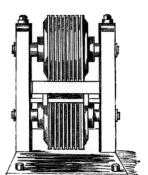

Wiremaking rollers

This 19th-century machine cut sheet iron into strips that were drawn into wire used for carrying telegraph messages or for fencing cattle.

Computer connector housing

Sprue is cut off before use

Diecasting components

Pressure diecasting pumps measure amounts of molten metal into steel molds held shut under great pressure to form precision parts such as these computer connectors.

Channel for molten iron

2 Sand Casting

The patterns are removed, and the mold halves are clamped together. Workers or foundry machines pour metal into an opening called the runner. Extra metal is added to allow for the way metals shrink when cooling.

3 The Finished Product

This sand casting mold made a pair of ornamental iron owls. They are painted with black gloss paint to prevent the iron from rusting.

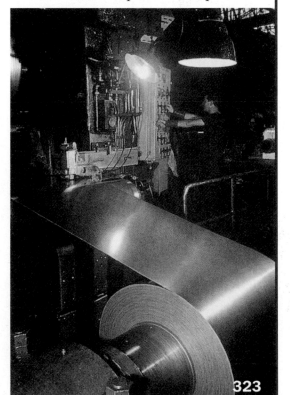

Indianapolis

1895   1905   1915   1925

1897
Eugene V. Debs becomes a leader of the Socialist Party.

1910
Madam C. J. Walker opens her cosmetics business in Indianapolis.

1918
The Ball brothers found a teacher-training college.

1920
The Nineteenth Amendment gives women the right to vote.

PREVIEW

Focus on the Main Idea
In the early 1900s, Hoosiers improved life in Indiana in many ways.

PLACES
Indianapolis

PEOPLE
Ida Husted Harper
Charles Warren Fairbanks
Thomas R. Marshall
Eugene V. Debs
William Wirt
Madam C. J. Walker

VOCABULARY
suffrage
labor union

TERMS
Nineteenth Amendment
socialist

New Leaders

You Are There

September 3, 1920

Dear William,

Mama is so excited! Finally, she'll be able to vote for President in the next election. Do you remember how she used to talk about it? She always thought it was unfair that women couldn't vote. Now they can.

Papa is happy too. He agrees with Mama. But Grandpa said, "What is the world coming to? In my day, women stayed in the kitchen where they belonged. They weren't out voting with the men!" Grandma didn't say anything. But later Mama told me Grandma asked her how to sign up to vote. I wonder if she'll tell Grandpa. I'll let you know when you get home.

Your sister,

Deborah

Draw Conclusions As you read about new leaders in Indiana, draw conclusions about how they served Indiana in the early years of the twentieth century.

Reformers Work for Change

Around 1900, many people wanted to reform, or improve, the way people lived. Many reformers favored women's **suffrage**—the right to vote.

Some reformers in both parties also favored the prohibition, or banning, of the sale of alcoholic beverages. They wanted to stop people from drinking because they thought that alcohol harmed both drinkers and their families. Some reformers also saw the banning of alcohol as a way to control people's behavior.

In 1908, the General Assembly passed a law allowing each county in Indiana to decide whether or not to ban liquor sales. In 1919, the Eighteenth Amendment to the U.S. Constitution made Prohibition the law of the nation.

But the amendment was repealed with the Twenty-first Amendment in 1933. To repeal is to take back or cancel.

The campaign for women's suffrage had started before the Civil War. Women such as Helen M. Gougar, a lawyer who lived in Lafayette, May Wright Sewall of Indianapolis, and **Ida Husted Harper** of Terre Haute worked hard to bring their cause before the public. In 1920, the Indiana legislature ratified the **Nineteenth Amendment** to the Constitution, which guaranteed women the right to vote. Later that year, the amendment became part of the United States Constitution. In 1921, Indiana also made a women's suffrage amendment part of its state constitution.

REVIEW Why was the Nineteenth Amendment to the Constitution important? ⊙ **Draw Conclusions**

▶ **Women campaign for suffrage in Hebron, Indiana**

VOTES FOR WOMEN

© Photograph by Indiana Historical Society, C5368/Indiana Historical Society

Presidential Politics

At the end of the 1800s and in the early 1900s, new Hoosier leaders made headlines. Once again, several Hoosiers became candidates for President and Vice-President. Some of them were reformers.

Charles Warren Fairbanks ran successfully for Vice-President with Theodore Roosevelt, who became President in 1904.

In 1912, **Thomas R. Marshall** was nominated as the Democratic candidate for Vice-President, running with Woodrow Wilson. Wilson and Marshall were elected.

Eugene V. Debs was a crusader for social justice, or a reformer. Later he

▶ **Eugene V. Debs, five-time candidate for President**

helped start a railroad **labor union.** A labor union is an organization of workers united for better wages and working conditions.

In 1897, Debs became a leader of the new Socialist Party. A **socialist** believes that important industries should be controlled by the government, not individuals. Debs ran for President five times as the candidate of the Socialist Party.

REVIEW Identify Charles Warren Fairbanks, Thomas R. Marshall, and Eugene V. Debs. **Summarize**

FACT FILE

Candidates for President and Vice-President from Indiana Since 1868

Republican

Democrat

Socialist

Date	Candidate	Party	Office
1868	*Schuyler Colfax	Republican	Vice-President
1876	Thomas A. Hendricks	Democrat	Vice-President
1880	William H. English	Democrat	Vice-President
1884	**Thomas A. Hendricks**	Democrat	Vice-President
1888	**Benjamin Harrison**	Republican	President
1892	Benjamin Harrison	Republican	President
1900	Eugene V. Debs	Socialist	President
1904	Eugene V. Debs	Socialist	President
1904	**Charles W. Fairbanks**	Republican	Vice-President
1908	Eugene V. Debs	Socialist	President
1908	John W. Kern	Democrat	Vice-President
1912	Eugene V. Debs	Socialist	President
1912	**Thomas R. Marshall**	Democrat	Vice-President
1916	**Thomas R. Marshall**	Democrat	Vice-President
1916	Charles W. Fairbanks	Republican	Vice-President
1920	Eugene V. Debs	Socialist	President
1940	Wendell Willkie	Republican	President
1988	**J. Danforth Quayle**	Republican	Vice-President

*Bold type indicates winners

Making a Better Life

Hoosiers made a better life for themselves by improving education. In 1897, the state passed a law requiring that children from ages eight to fourteen attend school. More Hoosier children began to attend high school as well. By 1920, Indiana had about seventy-nine thousand high school students.

William Wirt, the superintendent of Gary schools, made bold changes in education. The number of students in Gary grew almost every day as new workers came to work in the steel mills and sent their children to school. Wirt doubled the number of students who could attend school by using a platoon system. Students were divided into groups. Instead of using one room, they had lockers for their books and papers. They moved from room to room for classes.

Wirt added many activities to the school day. Students used laboratories for science and gyms for physical education. They learned music and art. Today we take these kinds of activities for granted. But Wirt was among the first to offer them.

Unfortunately, Indiana continued to lag behind in providing education for African American children. Most African American children attended segregated schools. To segregate means to separate by race. Schools for African American children got less money from the government than schools for white children. In 1949, the General Assembly finally ordered that the system of separate schools end in Indiana.

▶ In schools for African American students, books and materials were sometimes not as good as those found in schools for white children.

In the late 1800s, Indiana's state and local governments also began to provide more services for citizens. These included homes for orphans and public hospitals.

Throughout the history of Indiana, private citizens have contributed to the state's improvement. The Ball brothers founded a teacher-training college in Muncie in 1918. **Madam C. J. Walker,** who opened her cosmetics business in **Indianapolis** in 1910, was another good citizen. She helped many of her neighbors and gave money for education, the arts, and other causes.

REVIEW What was the purpose of the platoon system in Gary schools?
Main Idea and Details

Time to Have Fun

Around 1900, many Hoosiers discovered something new: free time. By this time, a lot of people held jobs with set hours. They also lived in cities, where streetlights made more evening activities possible.

After the Civil War, baseball became popular. By the 1870s, many Indiana towns and colleges had baseball clubs. By the 1880s, many Indiana colleges also had football teams. Basketball was invented in 1892. In Indiana, the game was played first in high schools. The most popular outdoor recreation among Hoosiers in the early 1900s was bicycling.

REVIEW Why did Hoosiers have more free time around 1900?
Cause and Effect

▶ **These women were photographed in Crawfordsville.**

Summarize the Lesson

— **1897** Eugene V. Debs became a leader of the Socialist Party.

— **1910** Madam C. J. Walker opened her cosmetics business in Indianapolis.

— **1918** The Ball brothers founded a college to train teachers.

— **1920** The Nineteenth Amendment gave women the right to vote.

LESSON 2   REVIEW

Check Facts and Main Ideas

1. 🔵 **Draw Conclusions** On a sheet of paper, write three facts or observations that support the conclusion shown.

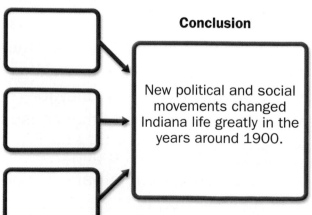

Facts and Observations

Conclusion

New political and social movements changed Indiana life greatly in the years around 1900.

2. Name two Vice Presidents from Indiana in the early 1900s.

3. When and how did women earn the right to vote?

4. How did Hoosiers improve education around 1900? In what ways did they lag behind?

5. **Critical Thinking:** *Express Ideas* Which form of recreation enjoyed by Hoosiers around 1900 do you most enjoy? Why?

Link to 🔗 Writing

Write About Activities William Wirt added many activities to the school day of high school students in Gary. Write a paragraph about the different kinds of activities that make up your school day.

Madam C. J. Walker

1867–1919

Sarah Breedlove worked her way up from doing other people's laundry to running a company that employed thousands of people. She said:

"There is no flower-strewn path to success. And if there is, I have not found it, for if I have accomplished anything in life it is because I have been willing to work hard."

Madam C. J. Walker was the first African American female millionaire in the United States.

Sarah Breedlove was born in Louisiana. In 1906, she married Charles J. Walker.

Madam Walker became a highly successful entrepreneur (ahn truh pruh NOOR).

An entrepreneur is a person who takes a risk to start a business. She developed a line of beauty products especially for African American women.

In 1910, Walker moved her business to Indianapolis. She hired African American women as "Walker Agents" to sell her beauty products.

Walker successfully invested her money. She gave generously to charities and groups, and donated money to the National Association for the Advancement of Colored People (NAACP).

Learn from Biographies

How did Walker improve her life and the lives of others?

For more information, go online to *Meet the People* at **www.sfsocialstudies.com.**

Winning the Vote

Ida Husted Harper worked to win the right to vote for American women. She worked with many other Americans, and together, they succeeded.

▶ **Ida Husted Harper**

Ida Husted Harper was a journalist and a suffragist. A suffragist is a person who works to extend the right to vote to women or other groups.

Harper was born in Fairfield, Indiana, and educated in Muncie. In 1871, she married Thomas Winans Harper and moved to Terre Haute. There she began writing a weekly column for the *Saturday Evening Mail.*

Harper became part of the suffrage movement around 1884. While living in California in the 1890s, Harper worked to pass an amendment to the state's constitution that would allow women to vote.

In 1896, the National American Woman Suffrage Association (NAWSA), headed by Susan B. Anthony, asked Harper to join them. She was to be in charge of relations with newspapers.

In 1897, Anthony asked Harper to help write her biography. Harper also worked with Anthony on a volume of the *History of Woman Suffrage.*

In 1910, Harper became active in NAWSA's National Press Bureau in New York City. Her job was to educate the public about why women wanted the right to vote. She gave lectures and spoke before Congress.

BUILDING CITIZENSHIP
Caring
Respect
Responsibility
Fairness
Honesty
Courage

Harper felt strongly that the right to vote helped women in many ways. In 1902, she said that in the four states where women could vote, women were

> "…better, happier wives, mothers and housekeepers because they are more intelligent and live a broader life."

Harper played an important role in getting the Nineteenth Amendment passed and ratified. However, she is also remembered for an unfair action. In 1918, she discouraged a group of six thousand African American women from joining NAWSA. Harper feared that the membership of African Americans would lead to a loss of support in the South for women's suffrage.

Fairness in Action

Find out what an organization or group is doing today to work for fair treatment of all people.

Use Information Resources

What? **Information resources** include things that are printed, such as books and newspapers. Information resources also include electronic media, such as the Internet, and community resources, such as people and organizations. Newspapers, for example, offer a great deal of information about Indiana's history and current events. Newspapers contain several different kinds of stories.

The **Internet** is a huge network of computers. It contains many **Web sites** (World Wide Web). These may be run by government departments, organizations, universities, businesses, or private citizens.

Why? **Newspapers** present the news of the day. Old newspapers offer a look at daily life in a past time.

The Internet gives you quick access to thousands of sources of information. In fact, major newspapers now publish some of their sections online.

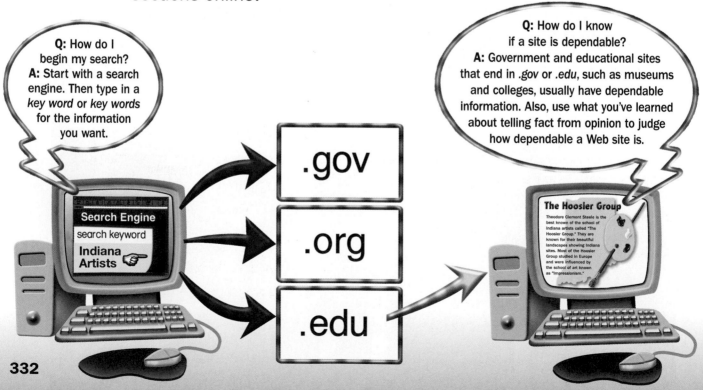

Q: How do I begin my search?
A: Start with a search engine. Then type in a *key word* or *key words* for the information you want.

Q: How do I know if a site is dependable?
A: Government and educational sites that end in *.gov* or *.edu*, such as museums and colleges, usually have dependable information. Also, use what you've learned about telling fact from opinion to judge how dependable a Web site is.

.gov

.org

.edu

How? Newspapers are usually printed in sections.

- News **articles** appear in one section.
- Features on the arts, sports, and other topics may be in separate sections.
- Most newspapers also have an **editorial** section, where people express their opinions.
- Look for a **table of contents** to tell you where to find articles.
- Look at **headlines**—phrases or sentences printed in large type. Headlines often tell you about the subject of an article.

To get started on the Internet, you must **log on.** Then you can look for information in two basic ways.

- Each Internet location has an address, or **URL.** If you know the URL you wish to use, you enter it in the strip at the top of your screen marked *location* or *address.*
- If you're searching for information about a topic, you will need to select a **search engine.** A search engine combs through the Internet looking for pages that contain the topics or words you give it. A teacher or librarian can help you choose a search engine.
- Next type in a **key word** or two. A key word is a word or a phrase related to your topic, such as "Indiana artists."

Then click on "Search." You may have to experiment with different words or phrases. If you need help, click on "Help" or "Search Tips."

- Choose sites from the list the search engine provides that look as if they might have the material you want. Click on one of the sites. The information will appear on your screen.
- If your search brings no results, try another key word, or ask for help from someone with Internet experience.
- Check the information you find on the Internet with another source, such as an encyclopedia.

Think and Apply

1. What is the name of the newspaper shown on page 332?

2. What key words might you type in to find information about writers and artists from Indiana?

3. How would you choose the most reliable sites from a list created by a search engine?

LESSON 3

Charlestown

1915   1925   1935   1945

1917
U.S. enters World War I.

1918
World War I ends.

1919
Steel strike begins in Gary.

1929
Great Depression begins.

1941
U.S. enters World War II.

1945
World War II ends.

PREVIEW

Focus on the Main Idea
Hoosiers rose to the challenges of the 1900s, which included wars and the Great Depression.

PLACES
Charlestown

PEOPLE
Wendell Willkie
Ernie Pyle

VOCABULARY
strike
productivity
unemployment
ration

TERMS
Great Depression
home front

EVENTS
World War I
World War II

New Challenges

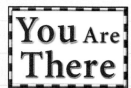 Things are really different now that your family has moved to Indianapolis. Last year at this time, you were on your family's farm. Now you're in a big city. But that's not the biggest change. Your father is in France, fighting in the war. You hope he's all right. And your mother has gone to work in a factory.

Indianapolis is so big. You live in an apartment building, where you've met all sorts of people. Some of them come from as far away as Germany and Ireland. You can't wait for fall to see what it's like to go to school in a big city.

Cause and Effect As you read, note the effects that world events had on Indiana in the early and mid-1900s.

▶ Soldiers train for World War I.

World War I

World War I began in Europe in August 1914. The Allied Powers— Great Britain, France, Russia, and other countries—were fighting the Central Powers of Germany, Austria-Hungary, and other countries.

When the war began, many Americans did not think the United States should fight. In fact, when Woodrow Wilson ran for President, with Hoosier Thomas R. Marshall as his running mate, he wanted to avoid joining the war. Wilson and Marshall won the election. But the United States declared war on Germany in April 1917. Germany had begun sinking American ships.

About ninety thousand young men from Indiana were drafted by the United States. *To draft* means to call into military service for the country. Another forty thousand people volunteered for the military.

Indiana's industries geared up for the war. More people moved from farms to the cities to work in factories. Southerners, including many African Americans, moved to the state's industrial areas. Women took the place of men who had gone to war in some jobs. Families went without meat and bread to save food for soldiers.

German American Hoosiers worked hard to show their neighbors that they supported the United States. They had reason to worry. The United States had passed laws making it a crime to speak against the draft or to encourage disloyalty. Eugene V. Debs was imprisoned for defending free speech and criticizing this law.

The war ended on November 11, 1918. About 3,350 Hoosier servicemen died in World War I.

REVIEW What were some of the effects of World War I on Indiana?
Cause and Effect

Workers and Unions

During the early 1900s, many workers' lives were hard. Most people worked ten hours a day, six days a week. Ironworkers and steelworkers had even longer hours. Wages were low.

Women and children worked too. The work was often dangerous. Workers were frequently injured on the job. Companies were not required to pay an injured worker.

Workers tried to get better pay and better working conditions by joining labor unions. Union members work together to achieve their goals.

Labor unions had an important weapon: the **strike.** During a strike, workers refuse to work until their demands are met.

Indiana has seen many strikes. In 1877, a number of railroads in Indiana tried to cut the wages of their workers. A huge strike followed. Owners used strikebreakers—nonunion workers brought in to take the jobs of strikers—to end the strike.

Still, unions continued to grow. Then in 1919, a large and violent strike began in Gary. The workers wanted an eight-hour workday. U.S. Steel wanted them to work a twelve-hour day. The company brought in large numbers of strikebreakers. Violence broke out when strikers attacked a truckload of strikebreakers. The governor called in the state militia to restore order. Then he called in federal troops. Soon the strike was over. The union had lost. As a result, union membership declined until the 1930s.

REVIEW Why did workers join labor unions? ⟳ **Draw Conclusions**

▶ **An 1892 street car strike**

A Rare old Picture.
The Street Car Strike in 1892.

▶ During the Great Depression, soup kitchens gave hungry people a free meal.

The Great Depression

After World War I, the economy grew. Productivity improved. **Productivity** is the amount of goods and services made during a period of time divided by the amount of resources used. These resources might include people and goods. After World War I, factories could produce the same amount of goods with fewer workers. One reason for this was new factory methods such as Henry Ford's assembly line. Since costs were lower, the owners made more money. But many people and businesses spent too much. They borrowed money they couldn't pay back. In October 1929, these problems created a disaster: The Stock Market crashed, and the **Great Depression** began. The Stock Market is a place where people buy and sell shares in, or part ownership of, businesses. A depression is a time of low production and sales and high **unemployment,** or being out of work.

The Great Depression hit Indiana very hard. Banks closed, and many families lost the savings they had put in these banks. Sales of coal and limestone dropped to almost nothing. Half the people in the southern part of Indiana were without jobs. The steel and automobile industries also suffered. Gary's steel mills were running at only 15 percent of their capacity in 1932.

In 1932, Democrat Franklin Delano Roosevelt (often called FDR) was elected President. He and Congress started programs to get people back to work. FDR was very popular. He was re-elected in 1936 and again in 1940. However, he had his critics. One was **Wendell Willkie,** a New York City lawyer born in Elwood. The Republicans chose Willkie as their candidate for President in 1940. But Willkie was no match for Roosevelt. By 1940, the Depression was easing. And the economy picked up quickly as the nation moved into its next challenge—another world war.

REVIEW Contrast life in Indiana before and after October 1929.
Compare and Contrast

A Second World War

Beginning in the late 1930s, Germany, Italy, and Japan made war on France, Great Britain, the Soviet Union, and other nations. The United States stayed out of the conflict until December 7, 1941, when the Japanese bombed American ships and aircraft at Pearl Harbor, Hawaii. The next day, the United States entered the war.

World War II affected Indiana in many ways. Indiana's steel mills went back into full production. In fact, the steelworks in the Calumet were running twenty-four hours a day, seven days a week. The state's oil refineries made fuel. New factories were built. **Charlestown,** near Louisville, Kentucky, became a boomtown, which means it grew very quickly. Two companies put up plants to make war supplies. Suddenly the population of the town jumped from about 890 to 15,000.

Centers were set up throughout the state for training troops and for testing supplies. One of these large centers, the Crane Ammunition

▶ A ration coupon

Depot in Martin County, covered almost sixty-three thousand acres.

On the **home front,** as the United States was called during the war, Hoosiers worked hard. Women went to work in record numbers. Products in short supply, such as gasoline, sugar, and meat, were rationed. To **ration** means to give only a certain amount to each person. Many products—such as cars—weren't manufactured during the war so that factories could produce things needed for the war. Hoosiers bought war bonds. By buying bonds, they were lending the government money for the war. People also collected metal, paper, and rubber to be made into war supplies.

Once again, Indiana's men and women joined the armed forces. About 338,000 men from the state fought in the war. Of these numbers, about 13,370 were killed in the war. About 118,000 Hoosier women also served in the military.

▶ Hoosiers in Hammond make tanks for the war.

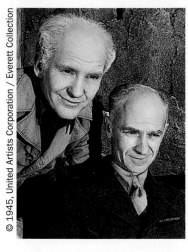

▶ Burgess Meredith (*left*) portrayed Ernie Pyle (*right*) in the 1945 movie *The Story of G.I. Joe.*

One of the most famous Hoosiers in the war was not a soldier. He was a newspaper reporter. Ernie Pyle was born near Dana in 1900. He won several awards for his war reporting. Pyle told stories about ordinary soldiers. For example, he once wrote,

"Our boys couldn't resist the sad . . . little faces of the children, and that was when they started giving away their rations."

Pyle was killed by machine gun fire on an island in the Pacific in 1945. His death came only about a month before the end of the war.

World War II ended in 1945. The United States, Great Britain, France, the Soviet Union, and their allies had won.

REVIEW How did Hoosiers help win World War II? Summarize

Summarize the Lesson

- **1917** The United States entered World War I.
- **1918** World War I ended.
- **1919** A steel strike began in Gary.
- **1929** The Great Depression began.
- **1941** The United States entered World War II.
- **1945** World War II ended.

LESSON 3 REVIEW

Check Facts and Main Ideas

1. **Cause and Effect** On a sheet of paper, write at least one effect for each cause shown.

Cause	Effect
World War I	→
The Great Depression	→
World War II	→

2. How were the people who remained in Indiana affected by World War I?
3. Why did workers join unions?
4. How did the Great Depression and World War II affect Indiana's industries?
5. **Critical Thinking:** *Make Evaluations* Do you think World War I or World War II had the greater effect on Indiana? Explain.

Link to 〜 Art

Design an Ad In your ad, ask Hoosiers to collect rubber, metal, or paper for the war effort during World War II. Try to come up with a catchy slogan to say what you want people to do.

Labor Relations

Ever since the Revolutionary War, Americans have understood that when they worked together, they could get things done. Since the late 1700s, American workers have united for better pay and working conditions. Employers and politicians have not always favored the labor unions that worked for these changes.

As industry grew in the United States, work changed. In small shops and farms, workers knew the business owner. Often the owner and employees worked side by side. However, as factories grew larger, few workers ever met the owners. Employees had to work long hours, often in dirty and unsafe conditions. So workers began forming labor unions to ask for better conditions and higher wages. Unions were illegal at first, and strikers were jailed.

One of the most important strikes in the United States was organized by women who worked in the textile mills in Lawrence, Massachusetts. Labor leader Mary K. O'Sullivan went to Lawrence to see the strike firsthand. A famous song written in 1912, "Bread and Roses," celebrates the women strikers.

Unions were opposed by many business leaders. Among unions' opponents was David M. Parry, a manufacturer. Hoosier Eugene V. Debs was a labor leader before and after he became a Socialist.

▶ **Union members found strength in numbers.**

*As we come marching, marching
in the beauty of the day,
A million darkened kitchens, and
a thousand mill lofts gray
Are touched with all the radiance
that a sudden sun discloses
For the people hear us singing
"Bread and Roses! Bread and Roses!"*

James Oppenheim, 1912

> *"It will be hard to find any fair minded person who went to Lawrence during the strike and examined the conditions there who is not fully in accord [agreement] with the object [goal] of the strikers."*
>
> **Mary K. O'Sullivan,** *recalling the Lawrence strike, 1912*

> *"There is that old battle cry of unionism that labor produces all. If labor had to produce all, mankind would today be next door to starvation...."*
>
> *[The union movement is] a standing mob engaged in acts of open rebellion against the government...."*
>
> **David M. Parry,** *owner of Parry Auto Company and business leader, about 1900*

> *"When you unite and act together, the world is yours."*
>
> *"Stand up and see how long a shadow you cast in the sunlight!"*
>
> **Eugene V. Debs**

Issues and You

Today union membership is legal in the United States, and people from many professions belong to unions. Find out about one of the unions representing people in your community, such as teachers, factory workers, or government employees. What are the advantages of union membership? What are the disadvantages? What has the union done for its members throughout its history?

INDIANA

1950   1960   1970   1980

1949
Indiana ends
segregation in
public schools.

1960s
Indiana
passes
civil rights
laws.

1965
U.S. combat
troops enter
Vietnam War.

1973
U.S. brings
troops
home from
Vietnam.

PREVIEW

Focus on the Main Idea
After World War II, the Civil
Rights Movement and the
Vietnam War caused many
changes in Indiana and the
United States.

PLACES
Indiana
Vietnam

VOCABULARY
discrimination

TERMS
civil rights
Cold War

Social Change in Indiana

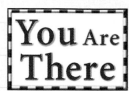

You Are There

Indianapolis, Indiana
September 1949
Dear Billy,

Tomorrow is the first day of school. For the
first time in my life, I will sit in a classroom
with kids of all races. Some of my old friends
will be in my class, but some of the kids will
be from a different part of our town. It will be
nice to meet some new friends.

My parents told me that there might be
reporters at school. They also told me
that I am part of an important change
in the way that the people in Indiana
treat one another.

I'll let you know how it goes.
Your friend,
Mark

Draw Conclusions As you read, look for
information that will help you draw
conclusions about the changes that took
place in Indiana during the 1950s and 1960s.

▶ As a result of the Civil Rights Movement, segregation was not allowed in parks, schools, and other places.

The Civil Rights Movement

A huge social movement gained strength shortly after World War II. The Civil Rights Movement of the 1950s was centered in the South. **Civil rights** are those rights guaranteed to citizens by the United States Constitution. For almost three centuries, however, many of these rights had been denied to African Americans.

Throughout the nation, African Americans faced **discrimination** — that is, they were treated differently because of their race. In the 1950s, a mass movement of both African American and other citizens began. This Civil Rights Movement opposed discrimination and segregation in the United States.

The National Association for the Advancement of Colored People (NAACP) has been working for equality for African Americans since 1909. In 1949, the group won a victory in Indiana when the state finally passed a law ending segregated schools.

By the 1960s, Indiana was leading northern states in civil rights legislation. During the 1960s, Indiana passed laws banning discrimination in jobs and banning segregation in parks and other public places. Hoosiers in general saw how wrong it was to treat African Americans differently because of their race.

REVIEW What are civil rights?
Main Idea and Details

The Postwar World

Hoosiers, like other Americans, felt joy when World War II ended. Even though more than thirteen thousand Hoosiers had died, Indiana itself had not been harmed by the war.

The United States came out of World War II as the most powerful nation on Earth. The Soviet Union was its major rival. Both tried to win allies, often by providing aid to countries in need.

The Soviet Union had a communist government. Communists believe that the state, not individuals, should control the economy. The United States has a capitalist economic system. In a capitalist system, individuals control the industries that make up the country's economy.

The United States is also a democratic republic. In a democracy, all the people have a voice in the government. The Soviet Union was led by a dictator—a leader who held all power over the people.

REVIEW What were the two major world powers after World War II?
Main Idea and Details

The Cold War

This difference in beliefs about government set up a situation that came to be known as the **Cold War.** For the most part, the Cold War was a conflict without fighting. It was a struggle to influence the beliefs of

▶ **Anti-war protesters in Muncie, 1970**

© Ball State University Orient, 1970, Archives and Special Collections, Ball State University Libraries/ Ball State University

people around the world about which form of government was better.

Over the last half of the 1900s, the United States would clash many times with the Soviet Union and other communist nations such as China. Sometimes these clashes led to war. One of these was in **Vietnam** in the 1960s.

In the 1950s, the country had been divided into North Vietnam, which was communist, and South Vietnam. The war began when South Vietnam tried to stop the North Vietnamese communists from taking control of their country.

At first, the United States just advised, or helped, South Vietnam. Then, in 1965, United States Marines entered the fighting. By 1969, more than half a million American troops were in Vietnam. No matter how many troops the United States sent into Vietnam, it was unable to defeat the North Vietnamese communists.

REVIEW What was the Cold War?
Main Idea and Details

Protest and Change

Many brave Americans answered the call to fight in Vietnam. Some gave their lives in the struggle. Meanwhile, some Americans questioned our country's role in the war.

At first, college students held protests against the war. Then the protests began to spread. In 1967 and 1968, huge demonstrations took place in several cities. Many members of Congress opposed the war, including Indiana Senator Birch Bayh.

By 1971, fighting in Vietnam had spread beyond Vietnam's borders. Public opinion in the United States turned against continuing the war. In 1973, the United States decided to bring its troops home.

The protests for peace in Vietnam and for civil rights affected life in Indiana and in the rest of the country. They showed that in the United States, people have the power to bring about important change.

REVIEW Why did Americans increasingly disagree with the war in Vietnam? **Main Idea and Details**

Summarize the Lesson

- **1949** Indiana ended segregation in public schools.
- **1960s** Indiana passed civil rights laws.
- **1965** U.S. Marines entered Vietnam War.
- **1973** U.S. brought troops home from Vietnam.

LESSON 4   REVIEW

Check Facts and Main Ideas

1. ⟲ Draw Conclusions On a sheet of paper, write missing details that support the conclusion shown.

Facts and Observations

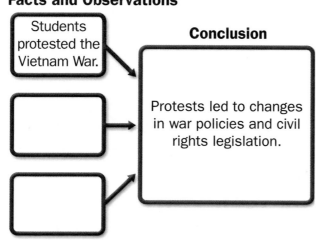

Students protested the Vietnam War.

Conclusion

Protests led to changes in war policies and civil rights legislation.

2. What side did the United States support during the Vietnam War? How did some Americans feel about this support?

3. In what way did schooling in Indiana change after 1949?

4. How did life in Indiana change during and after the Civil Rights Movement?

5. **Critical Thinking:** *Make Evaluations* Do you think that American citizens had a right to protest the Vietnam War? Explain.

Link to 〜 Writing

Write a Speech You have been asked to speak at a civil rights rally in 1964. Write a speech explaining why you think discrimination and segregation should be against the law. Suggest ways to convince others of this point of view.

CHAPTER REVIEW 11

1890	1900	1910	

1894 Elwood Haynes drove one of the first automobiles.

1897 Eugene V. Debs became a Socialist leader.

1902 Studebaker made its first automobile.

1909 U.S. Steel opened in Gary.

1910 Madam C. J. Walker opened business in Indianapolis.

1917 U.S. joined WWI.

1918 WWI ended.

Chapter Summary

 Draw Conclusions

On a sheet of paper, fill in three facts or observations that support the conclusion.

Facts and Observations

Conclusion

Indiana faced many challenges in the 1900s.

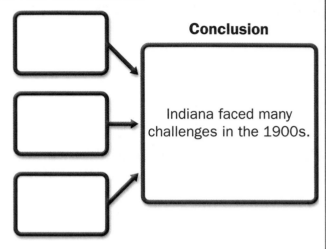

Vocabulary

Use each key term in a sentence that shows what the word means. You may use two or more in a single sentence.

1. steel (p. 318)
2. steelworks (p. 318)
3. suffrage (p. 325)
4. labor union (p. 326)
5. strike (p. 336)
6. unemployment (p. 337)
7. productivity (p. 337)
8. ration (p. 338)
9. discrimination (p. 343)

People and Terms

Write a sentence explaining why each of the following people or terms was important in Indiana's history. You may use two or more in a single sentence.

1. Studebaker Corporation (p. 321)
2. Ida Husted Harper (p. 325)
3. Nineteenth Amendment (p. 325)
4. Charles Warren Fairbanks (p. 326)
5. Thomas R. Marshall (p. 326)
6. William Wirt (p. 327)
7. Wendell Willkie (p. 337)
8. home front (p. 338)
9. Ernie Pyle (p. 339)
10. civil rights (p. 343)

346

1920	1930	1940	1950	1960	1970

1919 Steel strike began in Gary.

1920 Nineteenth Amendment became law.

1929 Great Depression began.

1941 U.S. entered WW II.

1945 WW II ended.

1949 Indiana schools were desegregated.

1965 U.S. Marines entered Vietnam War.

1973 U.S. left Vietnam.

Facts and Main Ideas

1. Why did the Calumet region attract industry?

2. How did the automobile industry become important to Indiana?

3. Why was education in Indiana not truly equal for African Americans until after World War II?

4. **Time Line** How many years passed between the opening of U.S. Steel's Gary works and the steel strike in Gary?

5. **Main Idea** Describe three reforms important to people in Indiana.

6. **Main Idea** How did Hoosiers improve education around 1900?

7. **Main Idea** How did Hoosiers contribute to the war effort during World War I and World War II?

8. **Main Idea** Explain the meaning of *civil rights*.

9. **Critical Thinking:** *Express Ideas* How might you have answered someone who said that protesting against the Vietnam War was unpatriotic?

Write About History

1. **Write a journal entry** as a Hoosier who has just bought his or her first car in 1922. Describe where you will drive and what you want to see.

2. **Write a speech** for a labor organizer to give that encourages workers to join a union, or for a business owner to give that explains why workers should not join a union.

3. **Write a story** set in Indiana during the Great Depression or World War II.

Apply Skills

Use Information Resources

Find a local newspaper from the past week. Use it to answer the questions.

1. Find a news article in the newspaper. What is the headline? Summarize the story that follows it.

2. Find an editorial in the same newspaper. Summarize what it is about.

3. Look through the newspaper. Does it post some or all of its news on a Web site? If so, write down the URL. Then go to the Web site and find the table of contents.

Internet Activity

To get help with vocabulary, people, and terms, select the dictionary or encyclopedia from *Social Studies Library* at **www.sfsocialstudies.com**.

from

A Long Way from Chicago

by Richard Peck

The Wabash Railroad carries Joey from Chicago to visit his Grandma every summer. Times are hard all over the country. It's the Great Depression. There's not a lot to do in small towns except to dream about better times. Here, Joey walks into town and comes face to face with the most beautiful thing he's ever seen.

The town was half-asleep with August and the depression. A checker game was going on in The Coffee Pot Cafe as I went past, but nothing else. A knot of people outside Moore's Store waited for the day-old bread to go half-price. . . .

I crossed the Wabash tracks past the grain elevator on my way to Veech's garage, eating the dust of the trucks hauling in the beans. Veech's garage had been the blacksmith shop, and they still kept the anvil inside. Now it was a one-pump filling station with an outdoor lift. I blundered along toward it. Then the dust cleared, and I saw her.

It was love at first sight, like I'd been waiting for her all my life. She stood on the pavement in front of Veech's, shimmering in her loveliness. And so graceful she might glide past me as if I wasn't there, leaving me in the dust.

She was a showroom-fresh Terraplane 8 from the Hudson Motor Car Company. A four-door sedan, tan, with red striping and another touch of red at the hubcaps. Tears sprang and my eyes stung. I couldn't help it. My hand curled like I had her steering wheel in my grip.

No car company had an agency in Grandma's town, not even Ford. But Veech's would order you a car. Ray'd said nobody had bought one in two years. He ducked out from under an ancient Locomobile up on the lift, working a greasy rag over his big hands. . . .

People around here didn't overreact even when they hadn't seen you for a year. Ray jerked a thumb back at the Locomobile he'd been working under. "Threw a rod."

I nodded like I knew.

But I couldn't take my eyes off the Terraplane.

"Somebody order it?"

Ray rubbed his stubbled chin with the back of his hand in a way I admired. "Who's got seven hundred and ninety-five dollars? This baby's top-of-the-line. Son, it's got a radio."

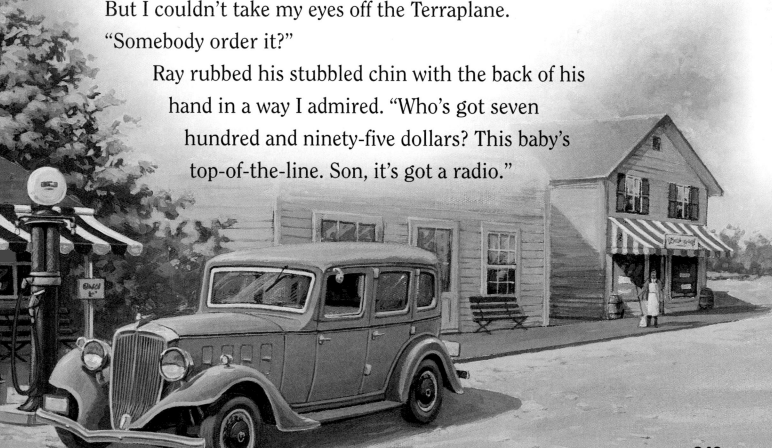

Main Ideas and Vocabulary

TEST PREP

Read the passage below and answer the questions that follow.

After the Civil War, Indiana's economy grew. Natural gas attracted new industry, which created a <u>supply</u> of many goods to be sold. Later, industries such as oil refining and steel making moved to the Calumet region. At the start of the 1900s, the automobile industry became important to the state's economy.

As industries grew, so did cities. Newcomers arrived, including African Americans from the South and European immigrants. Most of these newcomers settled in cities. Hoping to gain better pay and working conditions, many workers joined labor unions.

Cities took on the tasks of fighting fires, crime, and health hazards. Reformers worked to improve life in other ways. Some fought for women's right to vote and won in 1920. Other Hoosiers, such as William Wirt, worked to improve education.

Hoosiers gained national attention in politics and the arts. Indiana was a <u>swing state</u>, so politicians worked hard for the state's votes. Several Hoosiers ran for national office. Writers and artists also brought fame to Indiana.

The 1900s presented many challenges to Indiana and the nation. These included two world wars and the conflict in Vietnam. The Great Depression and the Civil Rights Movement also produced changes in Hoosier society.

1 According to the passage, what effect did the discovery of natural gas have on Indiana?
- **A** More farmers came to Indiana.
- **B** The Calumet region developed.
- **C** Farmers left Indiana for the West.
- **D** New industries came to Indiana.

2 In the passage, <u>supply</u> means
- **A** demand.
- **B** something to be destroyed.
- **C** something to be sold.
- **D** a new economy.

3 In the passage, <u>swing state</u> means
- **A** a state whose voters are almost evenly divided between the two major parties.
- **B** a state that strongly favors Democrats.
- **C** a state that strongly favors Republicans.
- **D** a state whose residents have very little interest in elections.

4 According to the passage, which best summarizes Indiana history since the Civil War?
- **A** Rapid agricultural growth, slow industry growth, little interest in politics
- **B** Reforms in education, new forms of recreation, importance of agriculture
- **C** Industrial and city growth, growth of labor unions, hardships during the two World Wars and the Great Depression
- **D** Industrial growth followed by loss of industry when natural gas ran out, return to agriculture, hardships during the two World Wars and the Great Depression

People and Terms

Match each person or term to its definition.

1 Gene Stratton-Porter (p. 309)

2 Eugene V. Debs (p. 326)

3 socialist (p. 326)

4 Madam C. J. Walker (p. 327)

5 Great Depression (p. 337)

6 Cold War (p. 344)

a. the conflict between the United States and the Soviet Union after World War II

b. cosmetics manufacturer and entrepreneur

c. socialist leader from Indiana

d. Hoosier writer

e. a time when many people were out of work and businesses failed

f. person who believes that major industries should be controlled by government

Write and Share

Present a News Story Choose one of the events or people discussed in this unit. Write a television news story about the event or person for an Indiana television station. Deliver the broadcast to your classmates. You might also videotape the presentation. Ask some of your classmates to participate by taking the roles of interview subjects. Then play the videotape for the entire class.

Read on Your Own

Look for these books in the library.

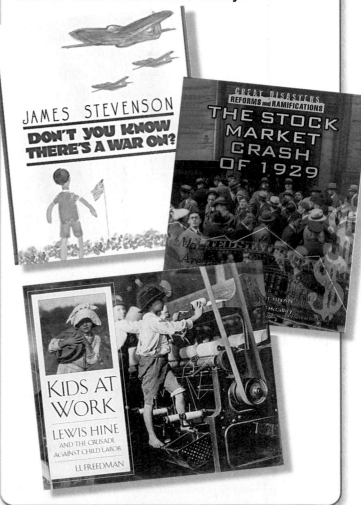

Apply Skills

Create a Cross-Section Diagram

Choose a familiar object, and create a cross-section diagram of it. Pick an object you can examine inside and out. Good examples would be a piece of fruit, a pencil, or a pen. Include a key to explain the different parts. Then use your cross section to help you describe and explain the object to a classmate.

1 = Shell
2 = Nuts

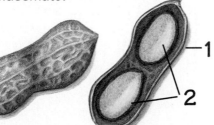

UNIT 5 Project

Ad Sales

Healthy businesses are good for Indiana's economy. Make your own infomercial about a product or a business.

1 Form a group. Choose a product or a business.

2 Research the product or business and write a list of facts about it.

3 Write a script for an infomercial about the product or business. Include the value and cost, as well as the history of the product or business. Give examples of its successes. Tell how it contributes to Indiana's economy.

4 Make an advertisement on a poster or banner to use in your infomercial.

5 Present your infomercial to the class.

Internet Activity

Learn more about the 1900s. Go to **www.sfsocialstudies.com/activities** and select your grade and unit.

Into the Twenty-First Century

**How do you think Indiana will change
in the twenty-first century?**

Begin with a Primary Source

1850

1900

1851
Indiana's current
constitution is
written and
approved.

1911
The first
Indianapolis 500 is held.
Indiana's first statewide
high school boys' basketball
tournament takes place.

1920s
Hoosier
Hysteria
begins.

354

"To know America, you have to take a good, long look at the Wabash River."

—from *The Wabash* by William E. Wilson

Blockbuster by Dale Kennington shows a group of people waiting in a line.

1950

2000

1946
Baby Boom begins.

1967
Richard Hatcher is elected mayor of Gary.

1977
Richard Lugar is elected U.S. Senator.

1995
Myra Selby becomes a justice on Indiana's Supreme Court.

1996
Governor Frank O'Bannon is elected.

Meet the People

Jessamyn West

1902–1984

Birthplace: near North Vernon, Indiana

Writer

- Started writing when ill with tuberculosis
- Wrote *The Friendly Persuasion,* set in southern Indiana in the 1850s
- Helped produce a movie based on her book

Robert Indiana

b. 1928

Birthplace: New Castle, Indiana

Artist, sculptor

- Changed his name from Robert Clark to show his affection for Indiana and to have a less common name.
- Created LOVE sculpture
- Helped design the LOVE stamp

Richard G. Hatcher

b. 1933

Birthplace: Michigan City, Indiana

Politician

- Ran for mayor of Gary with little official support
- One of first African Americans to be elected mayor of a major city
- Served as mayor of Gary from 1968 to 1987

Julia Carson

b. 1938

Birthplace: Louisville, Kentucky

Politician

- First African American woman elected to Indiana's General Assembly
- First woman and first African American elected to U.S. Congress from Indianapolis
- Sponsored bill to enforce minimum wage for domestic workers

1900	1910	1920	1930	1940	1950

1902 • Jessamyn West

b. 1928 • Robert Indiana

b. 1933 • Richard G. Hatcher

b. 1938 • Julia Carson

b. 1941 • Twyla Tharp

For more information, go online to *Meet the People* at **www.sfsocialstudies.com**.

Twyla Tharp

b. 1941
Birthplace: Portland, Indiana
Dancer, choreographer

- Created modern ballets using jazz and popular music
- Created dances for movies
- Served as artistic advisor for American Ballet Theater

Myra Selby

b. 1955
Birthplace: Bay City, Michigan
Lawyer, Indiana Supreme Court Justice

- First woman to serve as a justice on Indiana's Supreme Court
- First African American to serve as a justice on Indiana's Supreme Court
- Served as health care advisor to Governor Evan Bayh

Larry Bird

b. 1956
Birthplace: French Lick, Indiana
Professional basketball player, coach

- Named N.B.A. Most Valuable Player three times as a Boston Celtic
- Helped U.S. team win a gold medal at the 1992 Olympics
- Coached Indiana Pacers for three years

Michael Jackson

b. 1958
Birthplace: Gary, Indiana
Singer

- Known as "King of Pop" in 1980s
- His 1982 album *Thriller* became one of the best selling albums of all time
- Created trademark "Moon Walk" dance step

| 1960 | 1970 | 1980 | 1990 | 2000 | 2010 |

1984

b. 1955 • Myra Selby
b. 1956 • Larry Bird
b. 1958 • Michael Jackson

Into the Twenty-First Century

Summarize

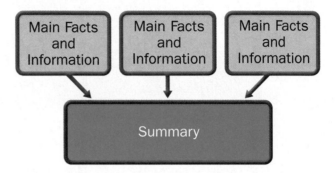

A summary is a short statement that describes a longer piece of text. A good summary presents all the important information briefly and clearly.

- A summary should include only the main facts or information from the text.

- Learning to summarize can help you remember the most important parts of the material you read.

Read the following summary. The **main facts and information** have been highlighted.

In Chapter 11, you learned about the growth of the steel industry in northwestern Indiana around the turn of the twentieth century. **A huge deposit of iron ore was found. Better ways to make steel were developed.** At the same time, cities were growing and demanding **building materials, such as steel. These cities also provided plenty of workers for the new steel industry.**

Who Are Hoosiers Today?

Hoosiers today live in a state that has changed a great deal over the past fifty years. The population has grown. Cities have become bigger and more crowded. Where there once were cornfields, there are now streets with houses and stores. Farms and businesses use all sorts of modern equipment.

Look at a crowd of Hoosiers and you will see faces that represent many more cultures than you would have seen fifty years ago in the state.

At the same time, Hoosiers today understand the importance of holding onto some of the ideas and traditions of the past. Writers look back fondly at the Indiana of a hundred years ago. Major sporting events that began in the early twentieth century still attract thousands of people.

Hoosiers also continue to take the rights and responsibilities of citizenship seriously. They vote in elections, and many work to improve their communities.

Apply it!

Use the reading strategy of summarizing to answer these questions.

1 What are three main ideas contained in the passage above?

2 List details that support the main ideas.

3 Rewrite your main ideas and supporting details to create a short, clear summary of the passage.

CHAPTER 12

Citizenship in Indiana

Lesson 1

Washington, D.C.
Indiana is represented in the national government.

1

Lesson 2

Indianapolis
Hoosiers are serious about their responsibilities as citizens.

2

NORTH

AMERICA

UNITED STATES

PACIFIC OCEAN

2

1

Indianapolis

Washington, D.C.

ATLANTIC OCEAN

Gulf of Mexico

Why We Remember

As a citizen of the United States and of Indiana, you will someday be able to vote for the people you want to serve in government. You will be able to vote for the President of the United States, for your town or city council representative, and for other officeholders. In this chapter, you will learn how the actions of government representatives affect your life. You will also learn that when you vote, you become part of Indiana's proud tradition of political participation.

Washington, D.C.

1850	1900	1950	2000

1851 Indiana's current constitution is approved.

1889 Benjamin Harrison becomes President of the U.S.

1967 Richard G. Hatcher is elected mayor of Gary.

1995 Myra Selby is appointed to Indiana's Supreme Court.

Government in Indiana

PREVIEW

Focus on the Main Idea
Citizens of Indiana are represented in their national, state, and local governments. These governments provide services to citizens.

PLACES
Washington, D.C.
Indianapolis

PEOPLE
Birch Bayh, Jr.
Richard Lugar
Evan Bayh
Frank O'Bannon
Julia Carson
Myra Selby
Richard G. Hatcher

VOCABULARY
democratic republic
representative
senator
sales tax
income tax

TERMS
Supreme Court
General Assembly
Unigov

You Are There

You and your classmates are planning a "Government Day." For one day, you will all take the roles of national or state politicians and run the country and the state. Your class held elections yesterday. You were voted a senator who represents Indiana in Washington, D.C.! You have so many ideas about how to help your home state. You know what your first task is, however. You need to find out how the government works and what your responsibilities as a senator are. You decide to start learning right away.

Summarize As you read, look for details that help summarize how national, state, and local governments work.

Our National Government

In the United States, there are three main levels of government: the national or federal government, state governments, and local governments. Our national government is located in **Washington, D.C.** Even though the United States capital is far away, many of the things that happen there directly affect life in Indiana.

Our national government is a **democratic republic.** The Constitution of the United States, in Article IV, Section 4, guarantees all states a republican form of government. This means that citizens of all states elect people to represent them and to pass laws for them.

The founders of the United States divided the national government into three branches. They felt that these branches would balance each other out. No one group or person would hold all the power.

The executive branch is responsible for carrying out the laws of the country. The chief executive is the President of the United States. Directly below the

▶ President William Henry Harrison

▶ President Benjamin Harrison

President is the Vice-President. So far two Hoosiers have held the office of President. Five Hoosiers have been Vice-Presidents. William Henry Harrison was the governor of the Indiana Territory. He also served the shortest term as United States President. He died just thirty-one days after taking office in 1841. Almost fifty years later, in 1889, his grandson, Benjamin Harrison, became President of the United States. He served one term.

REVIEW What detail explains why our government is considered a democratic republic? ↻ Summarize

▶ United States Capitol, Washington, D.C.

The Legislative and Judicial Branches

The federal government's lawmaking branch is the Congress. It is called the legislative branch, or the legislature. Congress is made up of the Senate and the House of Representatives.

A **representative** is elected by the voters of her or his district and serves a two-year term. They can be elected for more than one term. Each state sends a certain number of representatives to Congress. The number of representatives for each state is based on the state's population. Indiana sends nine representatives to Congress.

Members of the Senate are called senators. Like a representative, a **senator** is elected by the voters of his or her state. Each state is represented by two senators. Senators serve six-year terms. **Birch Bayh, Jr.,** represented Indiana in the Senate from 1963 to 1981. He helped to lower the voting age from twenty-one to eighteen. **Richard Lugar,** former mayor of **Indianapolis,** became a senator in 1977.

The judicial branch interprets the laws, or decides exactly what each law means. It includes the federal court system. The **Supreme Court** is the highest court in the land. There are nine justices who sit on the Supreme

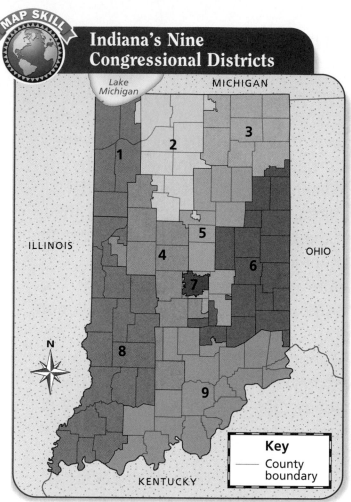

Indiana's Nine Congressional Districts

Lake Michigan

MICHIGAN

ILLINOIS

OHIO

KENTUCKY

N

Key
— County boundary

▶ Indiana is divided into nine congressional districts. The voters of each district elect one representative to send to Washington, D.C.

MAP SKILL Location *How many districts are located on Indiana's eastern border?*

Court. Justices are appointed by the President. Their term is for life. They make rulings on questions about the United States Constitution. In 1910, Willis Van Devanter, a native of Marion, was appointed to the Supreme Court. Sherman Minton, born in Georgetown, was appointed to the Court in 1949.

REVIEW Explain how Indiana is represented in Congress.
↺ **Summarize**

Indiana's Constitution

Our first constitution was written in 1816 when Indiana became a state. It was rewritten in 1851. Although some changes have been made over the years, the Constitution of 1851 remains the basis for our state law and government. It is one of the oldest state constitutions still in effect.

Indiana's constitution guarantees Hoosiers the basic freedoms of religion, speech, assembly, press, and the right to bear arms. An assembly is a gathering of people. It prohibits slavery. It requires the state to provide free public education. Indiana's constitution

▶ **The Indiana state capitol building in Indianapolis.**

divides the state government into three branches. It also forbids the state to borrow money or go into debt. Perhaps most important, the constitution places political power in the hands of Indiana's citizens. We use this power when we vote.

REVIEW Summarize the rights guaranteed by Indiana's constitution.
⟲ Summarize

Literature and Social Studies

Constitution of the State of Indiana

Like the Constitution of the United States, Indiana's constitution opens with a preamble, or introduction. Both have a Bill of Rights as well. Notice that the preamble and Section 1, shown below, establish that political power rests with the people of the state.

. . . .

Preamble
TO THE END, that justice be established, public order maintained, and liberty perpetuated [continued]; WE, the People of the State of Indiana, grateful to ALMIGHTY GOD for the free exercise of the right to choose our own form of government, do ordain this Constitution.

Section 1. Inherent and inalienable rights
Section 1. WE DECLARE, That all people are created equal; that they are endowed by their CREATOR with certain inalienable rights; that among these are life, liberty, and the pursuit of happiness; that all power is inherent in the People; and that all free governments are, and of right ought to be, founded on their authority, and instituted for their peace, safety, and well-being. For the advancement of these ends, the People have, at all times, an indefeasible [not capable of being undone] right to alter and reform their government.

Our State Government

Indiana is guaranteed a republican form of government by the Constitution of the United States. Like the federal government, Indiana's state government is divided into three branches. This system protects against one branch having all the power.

The executive branch is responsible for putting into action any laws or programs passed by the Indiana legislature. The governor is the head of the executive branch. The governor is elected for a four-year term and can serve no more than eight years out of a twelve-year period. Other elected officials of the executive branch include the lieutenant governor, the secretary of state, the attorney general, and the treasurer. The governor must decide who will head most of the state's commissions, departments, and institutions. Not many states give their governors this much power. In 1988, the people of Indiana elected **Evan Bayh** governor. He served two terms. Governor **Frank O'Bannon** succeeded him in 1996. He also served two terms.

The **General Assembly** is Indiana's legislative branch of government. The General Assembly is made up of two houses: the Senate and the House of Representatives. The fifty senators serve four-year terms. The one hundred representatives serve two-year terms.

In 1972, **Julia Carson** was elected as a representative. She became the first African American woman to serve in the Indiana House of Representatives. Four years later, she again made history when she was elected a state senator.

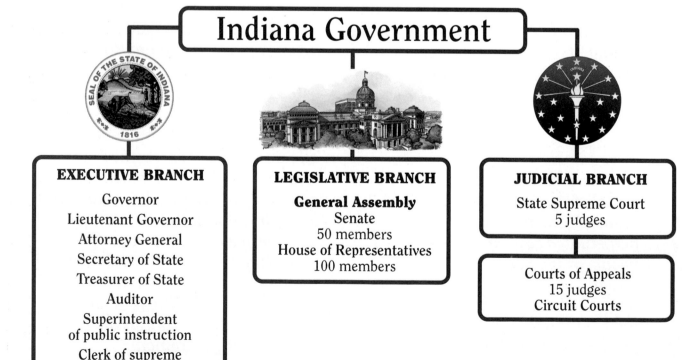

Indiana Government

EXECUTIVE BRANCH

Governor
Lieutenant Governor
Attorney General
Secretary of State
Treasurer of State
Auditor
Superintendent of public instruction
Clerk of supreme and appellate courts

LEGISLATIVE BRANCH

General Assembly
Senate
50 members
House of Representatives
100 members

JUDICIAL BRANCH

State Supreme Court
5 judges

Courts of Appeals
15 judges
Circuit Courts

How a Bill Becomes a Law

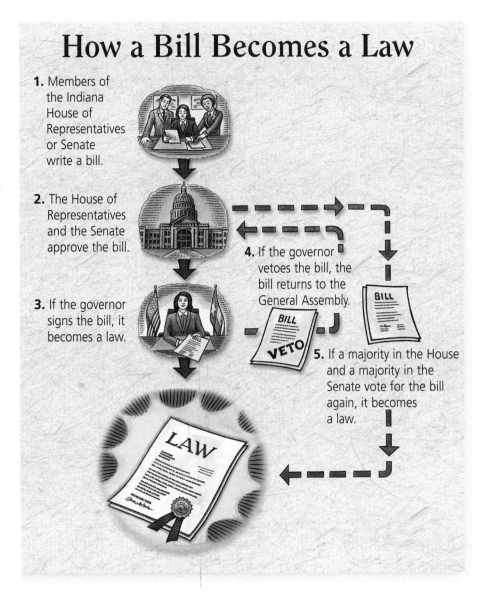

1. Members of the Indiana House of Representatives or Senate write a bill.

2. The House of Representatives and the Senate approve the bill.

3. If the governor signs the bill, it becomes a law.

4. If the governor vetoes the bill, the bill returns to the General Assembly.

BILL

BILL VETO

5. If a majority in the House and a majority in the Senate vote for the bill again, it becomes a law.

LAW

The General Assembly makes laws. The chart above shows how Indiana's laws are made.

Voters elect their senators and representatives within districts. Each district has about the same number of people. Every ten years these districts are adjusted to allow for population changes. This system ensures that all citizens are represented fairly.

Indiana's Supreme Court, the Court of Appeals, and many circuit courts make up the state's judicial branch. Since many laws are very complicated, this branch interprets them, or decides what they mean and whether they have been broken. The governor appoints five judges to sit on the state's Supreme Court. Each new judge first serves a two-year term. At the end of two years, voters decide whether the judge should serve a ten-year term or be replaced. In 1995, **Myra Selby** became the first African American woman to sit on Indiana's Supreme Court. You will read more about Selby on page 370.

The state government has many responsibilities to its citizens. Public education is one of the state's biggest responsibilities—and one of its biggest expenses. The money to pay for education and other programs comes from taxes paid by residents of Indiana. People pay a **sales tax** on some things they buy. People and businesses also pay an **income tax,** which is a tax on the money they earn.

REVIEW Summarize the responsibilities of the three branches of Indiana's state government.

⟲ **Summarize**

Local Government

Indiana's counties, cities, towns, and townships have their own local governments too. The county governments are the largest of these. If you look at the map, you will see that Indiana is divided into ninety-two counties. These counties vary in size. Some have large populations. Others have fewer residents. Most counties are governed by a three-member board of commissioners. Voters elect commissioners to four-year terms.

Residents of Indiana's counties pay taxes. In return, county governments provide services. They maintain and repair roads, run hospitals and libraries, and keep records of births, marriages, and deaths.

Within counties, there are cities, towns, and townships. Indiana has 115 cities, 460 towns, and 1008 townships. Town councils usually govern towns. Residents of townships usually elect trustees to four-year terms. Residents of cities, towns, and townships also pay taxes to these governments. These taxes help pay for services such as police and fire departments. City and town governments also provide water, maintain parks, and run transportation services. Many also collect trash and run recycling programs.

A city is governed by a mayor and a city council. **Richard G. Hatcher** became famous in 1968 when he was

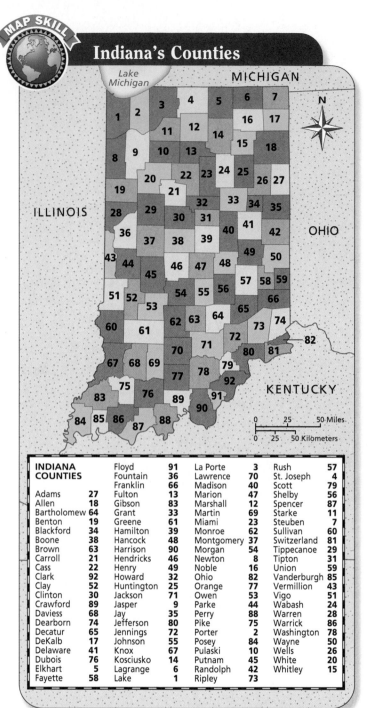

MAP SKILL — Indiana's Counties

INDIANA COUNTIES					
Adams	27	Floyd	91	La Porte	3
Allen	18	Fountain	36	Lawrence	70
Bartholomew	64	Franklin	66	Madison	40
Benton	19	Fulton	13	Marion	47
Blackford	34	Gibson	83	Marshall	12
Boone	38	Grant	33	Martin	69
Brown	63	Greene	61	Miami	23
Carroll	21	Hamilton	39	Monroe	62
Cass	22	Hancock	48	Montgomery	37
Clark	92	Harrison	90	Morgan	54
Clay	52	Hendricks	46	Newton	8
Clinton	30	Henry	49	Noble	16
Crawford	89	Howard	32	Ohio	82
Daviess	68	Huntington	25	Orange	77
Dearborn	74	Jackson	71	Owen	53
Decatur	65	Jasper	9	Parke	44
DeKalb	17	Jay	35	Perry	88
Delaware	41	Jefferson	80	Pike	75
Dubois	76	Jennings	72	Porter	2
Elkhart	5	Johnson	55	Posey	84
Fayette	58	Knox	67	Pulaski	10
		Kosciusko	14	Putnam	45
		Lagrange	6	Randolph	42
		Lake	1	Ripley	73

Rush	57
St. Joseph	4
Scott	79
Shelby	56
Spencer	87
Starke	11
Steuben	7
Sullivan	60
Switzerland	81
Tippecanoe	29
Tipton	31
Union	59
Vanderburgh	85
Vermillion	43
Vigo	51
Wabash	24
Warren	28
Warrick	86
Washington	78
Wayne	50
Wells	26
White	20
Whitley	15

▶ This map shows Indiana's ninety-two counties.

MAP SKILL Use a Map Key *Which county is number 33 on the map?*

elected mayor of Gary. He was one of the first African Americans to win election as mayor of a major city in the United States. He served as Gary's mayor for almost twenty years.

In 1970, Richard Lugar, the mayor of Indianapolis, created a program called **Unigov.** This term stands for "unified government." Under this program the city of Indianapolis and Marion County combined their governments. As a result, there are now six local government agencies instead of sixty. Unigov has a mayor who is elected every four years and can serve an unlimited number of terms. Working with the mayor is a twenty-nine-member council. Council members are also elected every four years.

REVIEW Summarize the responsibilities of local government in Indiana. ↺ **Summarize**

Summarize the Lesson

- **1851** Indiana's current constitution was approved.

- **1889** Benjamin Harrison became President of the United States.

- **1967** Richard G. Hatcher was elected mayor of Gary.

- **1995** Myra Selby became a justice on Indiana's Supreme Court.

▶ **Police and fire departments help our communities.**

LESSON 1 REVIEW

Check Facts and Main Ideas

1. ↺ **Summarize** On a sheet of paper, write the missing details that support the summary.

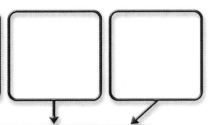

Citizens' taxes pay for services governments provide.

The three levels of government in the United States and Indiana share many characteristics.

2. Why is Indiana's Constitution of 1851 important to your life today?

3. Describe Indiana's government at the state level and at the local level.

4. What are some of the ways the citizens of Indiana benefit from paying state and local taxes?

5. **Critical Thinking:** *Draw Conclusions* The federal government and our state government are both divided into three branches. Why do you think the writers of the federal and state constitutions felt that this was necessary?

Link to ⬤⬤ Mathematics

Throw a Party Your class wants to invite Indiana's U.S. senators and representatives, the governor, state senators, state representatives, and the justices of the state supreme court to a party at your school. If all these people accept the invitation, how many government officials will be at the party?

Myra Selby

born 1955

In 2000, lawyer Myra Selby was named one of Indiana's "Trailblazing Women." As a "trailblazer," Selby opened doors for women and for African Americans. These doors had remained stubbornly closed until the mid-1990s.

Selby's days as a trailblazer started when Governor Evan Bayh appointed her a justice of the Indiana Supreme Court in 1995. She was the first woman to sit on Indiana's Supreme Court. The firsts did not end there, however. She was also the first African American justice on Indiana's Supreme Court. Myra Selby sees these firsts as a step toward equality and fairness. During her time on the bench, Justice Selby spoke out about the role of the judicial branch in working for equality:

"Our nation has long been struggling with racial and gender discrimination. . . . (T)he judiciary, charged as it is with protecting individual rights, has a . . . responsibility to foster and promote equality."

BIOFACT

When Myra Selby became a justice, a women's restroom had to be built. There had never been a need for one in the supreme court before!

Learn from Biographies

What does Myra Selby see as the role of the judicial branch?

For more information, go online to *Meet the People* at **www.sfsocialstudies.com.**

Richard G. Hatcher *born 1933*

In 1967, a young but experienced lawyer and city councilman involved in local politics in Gary decided to run for mayor. He faced serious challenges during his quest. The local Democratic party refused to support his bid for election. He fought an uphill battle to get his name on the ballot in the November elections. Few people thought that Richard G. Hatcher, an African American, could be elected mayor of Gary.

Richard G. Hatcher proved the doubters wrong. Thanks to the support of voters of all races, he won an unexpected victory. He became one of the first elected African American mayors of a major United States city. After the election, Mayor Hatcher faced the challenge of running a city struggling with poverty and unemployment. Richard G. Hatcher worked hard to meet these challenges. His efforts made improvements to Gary. He was reelected four times.

BIOFACT

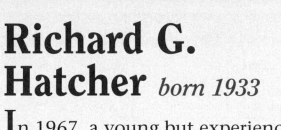

Richard Hatcher was one of two African American Democrats to become mayors of major cities in 1968. Carl B. Stokes (right) *was elected mayor of Cleveland, Ohio.*

Learn from Biographies

What did Richard G. Hatcher do when he was faced with a challenge, such as lack of support by his own political party?

For more information, go online to *Meet the People* at **www.sfsocialstudies.com.**

Indianapolis

1850	1900	1950	2000

1870
Fifteenth
Amendment
passes.

1876
95 percent
of voters in
Indiana vote.

1920
Nineteenth
Amendment
is approved.

1996
49 percent
of voters in
Indiana vote.

PREVIEW

Focus on the Main Idea
Hoosiers have a long tradition of being serious about the rights and responsibilities of citizenship.

PLACES
Indianapolis

PEOPLE
Dr. Mary Thomas

VOCABULARY
amend
civic virtue
civility

TERMS
Fifteenth Amendment

Hoosier Rights and Responsibilities

 June 12

Dear Jess,
Today was my first day working as a campaign volunteer for our state representative. It is very exciting to be part of a reelection campaign. I spent this morning getting flyers ready to mail out. My parents are also volunteering for the representative. I have talked to them about the representative's causes and issues. I have also read articles about her in magazines and newspapers.

Even if my candidate doesn't win, I will have learned a lot about the election process. I never realized how thrilling it is to be involved.

Your friend,
Theresa

 Summarize As you read, summarize the rights and responsibilities of citizens of Indiana.

▶ Citizens exercise their right to vote.

Voters and Voting Rights

Hoosiers have always been active in politics. In the 1876 presidential election, 95 percent of Hoosiers voted—nearly everyone who could vote voted! However, voter participation throughout the United States dropped toward the end of the twentieth century. In the 1996 presidential election, only 49 percent of registered voters in Indiana cast their votes. Those who struggled to gain the right to vote would probably be disappointed by this low turnout.

For almost a hundred years after the signing of the United States Constitution, only white male citizens were allowed to vote. After the Civil War, a group of Indiana Republicans argued that the war had been fought not just to free African American slaves, but to grant them equality. This included the right to vote. In 1870, Indiana agreed to support the **Fifteenth Amendment.** This amendment said that men could not be denied the vote because of their race.

But women had to wait another fifty years until they won voter rights. In 1859, **Dr. Mary Thomas** appeared before the state legislature in **Indianapolis** asking for equal rights for women. She was greeted with laughter and silence, but no positive response. Hoosier women and women across the country did not become discouraged. They tried to gain suffrage for many years—and finally won. In 1920, the Nineteenth Amendment was passed. It granted women the right to vote. One year later Indiana amended its constitution to include this amendment. To **amend** is to formally change.

These historic changes in voter rights show that different groups of people have worked hard so that they could vote. These groups wanted to vote because voting is a way for them to tell the government what they think is important.

REVIEW Compare voter participation in Indiana in 1876 and 1996. **Compare and Contrast**

373

Working for a Better Indiana

Until you are eighteen years old, you cannot vote in state or national elections. But as a citizen of the United States and Indiana, you still have rights and responsibilities. Your responsibilities include showing civic virtues. A **civic virtue** is a personal quality that helps a democracy work. Examples include honesty, respect for the law, and respect for the rights and dignity of all people.

When you support a political candidate whose ideas you believe in, you are also supporting democracy. Volunteering in a campaign is just one way to understand the important role citizens play in running a government.

You can also participate in politics by getting involved in school elections. Doing this can help you learn how to run a campaign. You can write and give speeches for yourself or on behalf of another candidate.

In a school election, just as in a state or national election, you need to be informed. That is, you need to know as much about candidates and issues as possible. Educate yourself on the causes candidates support and on their plans. In this way, you can make an informed vote.

Helping to care for your community is another responsibility that comes with citizenship. You can have a positive effect by helping groups whose causes you believe in. You can also help by identifying problems in your community and by working to find solutions. If you have ever helped with a recycling program or volunteered in a food bank, you have done something for your community.

One way to identify problems and find solutions is to learn about your community and the world around you. Reading is a great way to stay informed. Newspapers, magazines, and books can explain what is happening in the country and the world.

Go to town meetings and school meetings with your parents. Listen to the issues that are being debated and think about them.

▶ **A fourth grader makes a campaign speech at a school assembly.**

► **A girl volunteers her time with a senior.**

Discuss events and issues with your parents, teachers, and friends. Listen to their opinions, and ask questions about things you don't understand.

Notice how people show **civility,** or polite and considerate behavior, toward one another. Remember that it is important to respect people's opinions, even if they are different from yours.

Once you are informed about an issue, you will be able to make an educated decision about what should be done. Then, when it is time for you to vote, you will know how to make a responsible choice.

REVIEW As a young citizen, what rights and responsibilities do you have? **Main Idea and Details**

Summarize the Lesson

- **1870** Fifteenth Amendment was passed.
- **1876** 95 percent of voters in Indiana voted.
- **1920** Nineteenth Amendment was approved.
- **1996** 49 percent of registered voters in Indiana voted.

LESSON 2 REVIEW

Check Facts and Main Ideas

1. ⟳ **Summarize** On a sheet of paper, write a summary of the details shown below.

Citizens should keep themselves informed and vote for candidates who share their views.	African American men got the vote in 1870; women got the vote in 1920.	Citizens have the responsibility to help improve their community and the right to participate in politics.

2. Why did Hoosiers in the late 1800s get a reputation for participating in politics?

3. What rights do the Fifteenth and Nineteenth Amendments guarantee?

4. What is one right that all citizens of Indiana have, and what is one responsibility?

5. **Critical Thinking:** *Make Evaluations* How is voting both a right and a responsibility for citizens of the United States and Indiana?

Link to ⟞⟝ Art

Campaign Poster Work in pairs. Create a campaign poster for your partner, who is running for president of a club. Use pictures or photos of the candidate in action to convince members of the club to vote for your candidate. Display the posters around the room when you have finished.

CITIZEN HEROES

Students Care for Their Community

Every community has problems to solve or situations it could improve. Students at Mount Healthy Elementary School have taken time to look at these issues honestly. And they've found many ways they can help.

Students at Mount Healthy Elementary School near Columbus, Indiana, are always on the lookout for projects. They call it "service learning," or learning by helping others.

Life in the Columbus area is like life in most places. There are people in need—lonely seniors in nursing homes, homeless people in shelters, and people who need help learning to read. The Mount Healthy kids don't shy away from these problems, or make believe they don't exist. They know that problems don't go away just because people want them to.

To find out what their community needs, students read or watch the news. They brainstorm and discuss ideas. They talk to teachers and advisors. They take an honest look at what they can do and what they can't. Then they pick projects that give them the best chance to make a difference.

Each class does at least three service projects a year. Since 1994, more than twenty-seven hundred Mount Healthy students have given more than thirty-six hundred hours of service to nearly fifteen thousand people.

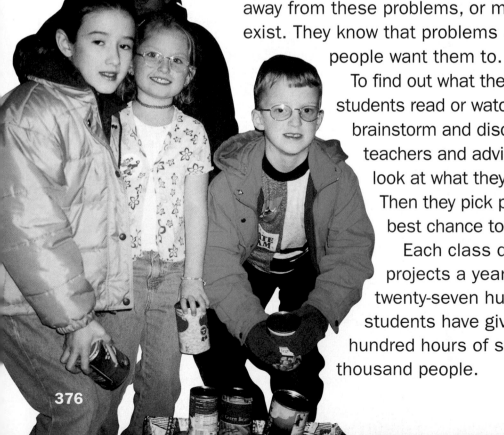

BUILDING
CITIZENSHIP
Caring
Respect
Responsibility
Fairness
★ Honesty
Courage

Derrick really enjoyed collecting winter clothing to give to the Salvation Army. "I don't like the cold. I felt good knowing homeless people would be warm."

Jakeb liked making gift bags to give to seniors at a local nursing home. "My grandma has been a big influence on me. Old folks have great stories."

Kelsey loves finding ways to help. "We heard a news report that the Salvation Army was low on winter clothes. We knew we could collect coats, boots, scarves, and gloves."

Mount Healthy kids have also donated gifts to a homeless shelter. They have planted trees to make a local park more beautiful, bought books for reading programs, and visited nursing homes. And they plan to do much more!

Honesty in Action

Link to Current Events Find out about a person or group working to help the community. How does their work show that taking an honest look at problems and possible solutions is the first step in making a difference?

Chart and Graph Skills

Read a Time Line

What? A time line is a tool we can use to organize events. It is a straight line that is divided into equal time periods. The time line below is divided into periods of ten years. Other time lines may be divided into longer or shorter periods of time.

Why? Time lines help you keep track of when events took place. Time lines can be historical or personal. Looking at a time line is an easy way to remind yourself that, for example, the Nineteenth Amendment was passed after World War I.

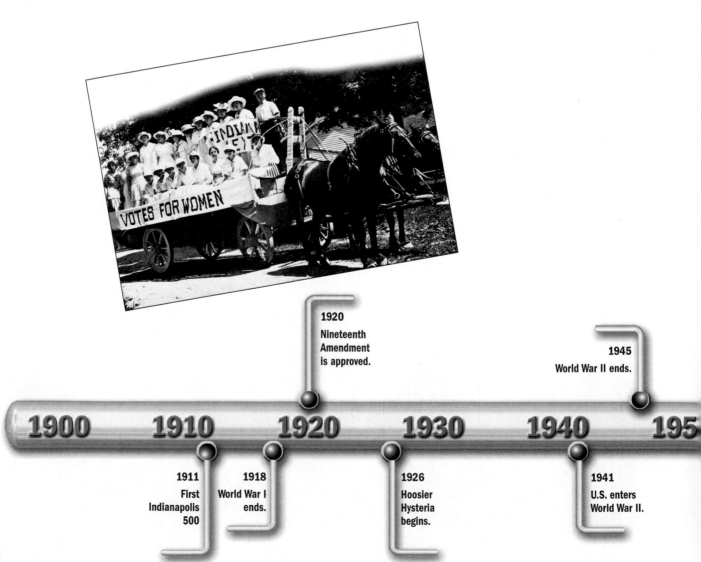

1920
Nineteenth Amendment is approved.

1945
World War II ends.

1900 1910 1920 1930 1940 195

1911
First Indianapolis 500

1918
World War I ends.

1926
Hoosier Hysteria begins.

1941
U.S. enters World War II.

1992
Feb. 10, 1992
Maria is born.

1993

1994

1995

Sept. 6, 1995
Brother Aaron
is born.

1996

1997
Sept. 7, 1996
First day of school

July 4, 1997
Learns to ride bike

1998
Nov. 18, 1997
Loses first tooth

June 6, 1998
First dance recital

1999

2000

2001
Sept. 5, 2001
Starts fourth grade

2002

How? Events on a time line are arranged according to when they happened. Always read a time line from left to right or from top to bottom. The earliest events are placed at the far left or at the top. As events move closer to the present, they move farther right or farther toward the bottom. The event on the far right or the bottom, therefore, is the most recent event on the time line.

Think and Apply

Use the time line at the bottom of pages 378 and 379 to answer the first two questions.

1. What event took place in 1911?

2. What two events happened in the 1920s?

3. On the time line to the left, which event happened in 1995?

1995
Myra Selby becomes
first female Indiana
Supreme Court Justice.

960   **1970**   **1980**   **1990**   **2000**   **2010**

1968
Richard G. Hatcher is
elected mayor of Gary.

1850

1851
Indiana's current constitution was written and approved.

1870

1870
Fifteenth Amendment was passed.

1876
95 percent of voters in Indiana voted.

1890

1889
Hoosier Benjamin Harrison became President.

Chapter Summary

Summarize

On a sheet of paper, write a summary of the details shown here.

The three levels of government are national, state, and local.

Some of the services provided by these governments are police departments, education, libraries, road construction, and fire departments.

Citizens have the right and the responsibility to vote and to work to help their community.

Vocabulary

Match each term with the correct definition or description.

1 democratic republic (p. 363)

2 representative (p. 364)

3 senator (p. 364)

4 civic virtue (p. 374)

5 civility (p. 375)

a. government in which citizens vote for their representatives

b. polite and considerate behavior

c. quality that helps government work

d. a person elected to represent a district

e. member of Congress who represents the state

People and Terms

Match each person or term with the correct description.

1 Richard Lugar (p. 364)

2 Julia Carson (p. 366)

3 Richard G. Hatcher (p. 368)

4 Fifteenth Amendment (p. 373)

5 Dr. Mary Thomas (p. 373)

a. mayor who created Unigov

b. first African American woman elected to the General Assembly

c. gave men of all races voting rights

d. woman who asked Indiana's legislature for female suffrage

e. mayor of Gary from 1968 to 1988

1910	1930	1950	1970	1990

1920
Nineteenth Amendment was approved.

1968
Richard G. Hatcher was elected mayor of Gary.

1995
Myra Selby became a justice on Indiana's Supreme Court.

1996
49 percent of voters in Indiana voted.

Facts and Main Ideas

1 What are the three levels of government in the United States?

2 What are the three branches of both the national and Indiana's state government?

3 What document is the basis for Indiana's state laws and government?

4 **Time Line** How many years passed between the creation of Indiana's current constitution and the passage of the amendment giving women the vote?

5 **Main Idea** Which positions in Indiana's state government are elected offices?

6 **Main Idea** What are two ways in which you can show civic responsibility?

7 **Critical Thinking:** *Make Inferences* The United States Constitution and Indiana's constitution can be changed by adding amendments. How has history shown that making changes to the constitutions is important?

Write About Citizenship

1 **Write a speech** urging your fellow students to vote in a school election. Explain why every one of their votes is important to the outcome of the election.

2 **Write a letter** to the editor of your local newspaper in 1910 giving your view of why women should or should not be given the right to vote. Support your opinions with reasons.

3 **Write a letter** to your state representative describing a problem you have identified in your community. Explain the problem, and suggest ways that the representative might be able to help solve the problem.

Apply Skills

Read a Time Line

Use the time line at the top of pages 380 and 381 to answer the questions.

1 If you wanted to add an event to this time line that occurred in 1956, between which two events would you place it?

2 According to this time line, what event occurred in 1851?

3 If you wanted to add your date of birth to this time line, where would it go?

Internet Activity

To get help with vocabulary, people, and terms, select the dictionary or encyclopedia from *Social Studies Library* at **www.sfsocialstudies.com**.

CHAPTER 13

Living in Indiana

Lesson 1

1946
Fort Wayne
Indiana's urban population grows.

1

Lesson 2

1954
Milan
Hoosier Hysteria reaches its peak.

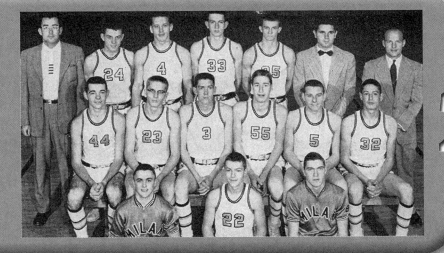

2

Lesson 3

2002
Indiana
Hoosiers continue to influence the arts and media.

3

Locating Time and Place

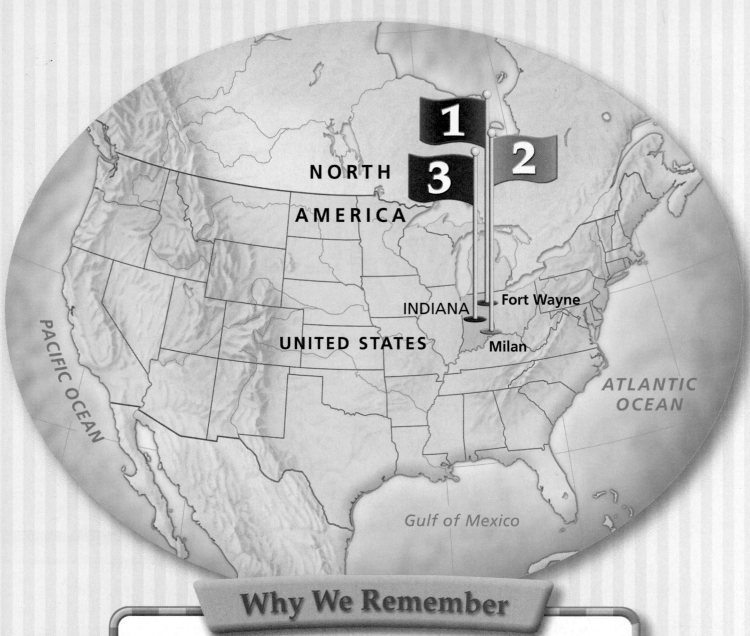

Why We Remember

In this chapter, you will look at your home state of Indiana as it is today. You will see examples of both tradition and change. You will learn how playing sports in school or supporting your local team means that you are helping keep alive the Hoosier spirit. You will learn that when you enjoy works by Indiana's artists and writers, you are participating in your state's literary and artistic traditions. And you will learn how much Indiana has changed over the past several decades.

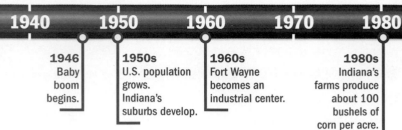

1940   1950   1960   1970   1980

1946
Baby boom begins.

1950s
U.S. population grows. Indiana's suburbs develop.

1960s
Fort Wayne becomes an industrial center.

1980s
Indiana's farms produce about 100 bushels of corn per acre.

Fort Wayne

Changes in Indiana

PREVIEW

Focus on the Main Idea
After World War II, Indiana's population and its urban areas grew. Advances in science and technology changed farm life.

PLACES
Fort Wayne

VOCABULARY
urban
rural
technology

TERMS
baby boom

You Are There

You are traveling through Indiana with your great-grandmother. She hasn't been back to Indiana since the 1930s. She is amazed at the size of cities such as Fort Wayne—and the highways around them. She tells you stories about how things used to be. She remembers when the suburbs of Indianapolis were cornfields. Now there are many houses. Great-Grandma used to love to watch her father plow the soil there with his team of horses. Now all the planting is done with machines! You begin to realize just how much Indiana has changed since your great-grandparents were your age.

Draw Conclusions As you read, draw conclusions about the ways that Indiana has changed since the end of World War II.

Postwar Indiana

The population grew quickly in the years following World War II. So many babies were born that we call the period the **baby boom.** Housing for many of these Hoosiers was built in the new suburbs near cities. Shopping centers, theaters, and restaurants were built there too.

A steady migration of workers from the South also increased Indiana's population. During and after the war, thousands of workers migrated to Indiana's cities from Kentucky, Tennessee, Alabama, Mississippi, and Arkansas to find work in factories.

The population of **urban** areas—those in and around cities—grew more quickly than the population of **rural** areas—those in the countryside. Hoosiers continued to leave their farms to find work and higher wages in the cities. **Fort Wayne** grew in the 1960s when big businesses such as General Electric and International Harvester opened there. Indianapolis, a center of the pharmaceutical and machinery industries, also attracted large numbers of workers.

REVIEW What events caused Indiana's population growth after World War II? **Cause and Effect**

FACT FILE

Indiana's Ten Largest Cities in 2000

City	Population
Indianapolis	791,926
Fort Wayne	205,727
Evansville	121,582
South Bend	107,789
Gary	102,746
Hammond	83,048
Bloomington	69,291
Muncie	67,430
Anderson	59,734
Terre Haute	59,614

▶ The Indianapolis skyline at night

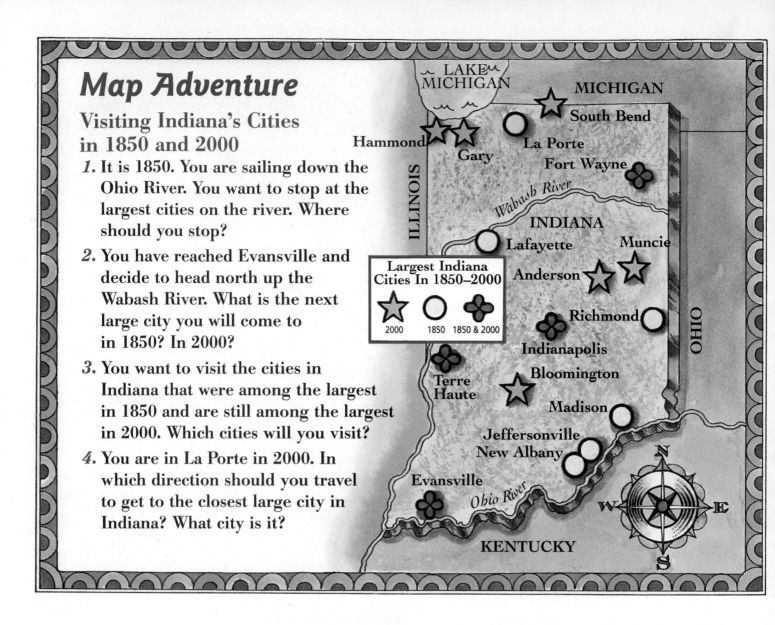

Map Adventure

Visiting Indiana's Cities in 1850 and 2000

1. It is 1850. You are sailing down the Ohio River. You want to stop at the largest cities on the river. Where should you stop?

2. You have reached Evansville and decide to head north up the Wabash River. What is the next large city you will come to in 1850? In 2000?

3. You want to visit the cities in Indiana that were among the largest in 1850 and are still among the largest in 2000. Which cities will you visit?

4. You are in La Porte in 2000. In which direction should you travel to get to the closest large city in Indiana? What city is it?

Largest Indiana Cities In 1850–2000

2000 · 1850 · 1850 & 2000

The People of Indiana

Over the years, immigrants from many cultural groups settled in Indiana. In the 1700s, people from France and Switzerland came here. In the mid-1800s, immigrants from Germany, England, and Ireland arrived looking for work and a better life. Later, workers from Italy, Poland, Czechoslovakia, and Hungary made their way to Indiana. They were attracted by the growth of its industries.

Other Hoosiers can trace their families back to Mexico, Puerto Rico, Cuba, China, India, or Korea. Many African Americans found new homes and jobs in Gary, Indianapolis, and other cities of Indiana after World War II. Today about eight out of every one hundred Hoosiers are African American.

REVIEW To what places can Hoosiers trace their families?

 Summarize

Modern Farming

The twentieth century brought rapid change for farmers in Indiana. **Technology,** or the invention and development of tools, machines, and skills, helped farmers. By the middle of the century, the tractor had replaced the horse in farming. Soon new machines were helping plant, cultivate, and harvest crops.

Farmers began using fertilizers to keep soil healthful and rich and increase plant growth. Chemicals reduce the amount of time and energy that farmers spend weeding crops and protecting them from pests. All this means that more crops are harvested. Between 1910 and 1980, corn production rose from forty bushels per acre to one hundred bushels per acre.

Changes in farming have helped large farms more than smaller ones. Many small farmers had to give up their farms in the second half of the century. In southern Indiana, acres of former farmland have been converted to state and national parks and forests.

REVIEW Compare the effect of technology and other scientific advances on large and small farmers. *Compare and Contrast*

Summarize the Lesson

- **1946** Baby boom began.
- **1950s** Indiana's urban population increased. Suburbs developed.
- **1960s** Fort Wayne became an industrial center.
- **1910–1980s** Technology and scientific advances raised corn production to about one hundred bushels per acre.

LESSON 1 REVIEW

Check Facts and Main Ideas

1. Draw Conclusions On a sheet of paper, write details that support the conclusion shown.

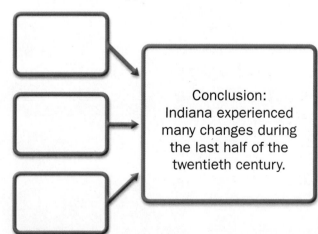

Conclusion: Indiana experienced many changes during the last half of the twentieth century.

2. What happened to Indiana's urban areas after World War II?

3. How did new machines and fertilizers help Indiana's farmers?

4. Name four places that new Hoosiers came from during the twentieth century.

5. Critical Thinking: *Make Evaluations* In your opinion, which change discussed in this lesson was the most important? Explain.

Link to 🔗 Writing

Interview a Baby Boomer Interview a person born during the baby boom about what life was like in fourth grade. Write a report comparing everyday life during the baby boom with everyday life today. Use quotations from your interview.

Indiana and China

Rice in Hunan and Corn in Indiana

At the same time that farmers in Indiana are planting their corn crop in the spring, farmers in Hunan Province, China, are planting their main crop too. But the farmers in China are planting rice, and this is only their first planting. Rice farmers in Hunan plant and harvest their crops twice a year. They plant in April and harvest in July. Then they plant again and harvest in November.

Farmers in both places produce crops that make up a major part of people's diets. Both rice grown in Hunan and corn grown in Indiana help to feed the world.

Some farmers in Hunan use modern machines and fertilizers. Others work with hoes, spades, and ox-drawn plows. In order to plant rice, they must first flood the field and create what is called a paddy. Then they plant the rice in the waterlogged ground. Before the harvest they must drain and dry the paddies.

Indiana farmers plant and harvest a single corn crop each year.

◀ Some farmers in Indiana today use computers to help them chart the weather and prices for their crops. They use modern machines to help them plant and harvest their corn quickly. Fertilizers and pesticides help keep their crops and soil healthy and free of pests.

ATLANTIC OCEAN

LATITUDE

LONGITUDE

ASIA

CHINA
HUNAN

INDIANA

NORTH AMERICA

UNITED STATES

PACIFIC OCEAN

▲ Amish farmers in Indiana use traditional farming methods and tools.

389

1910	1920	1930	1940	1950	1960

1911
The first Indianapolis 500 and first state high school boys' basketball tournament are held.

1920s
Knute Rockne coaches championship football teams. Hoosier Hysteria begins.

1960
Wilma Rudolph wins three Olympic gold medals in track.

PREVIEW

Focus on the Main Idea
Indiana has a long tradition of excellence in sports.

PLACES
Milan

PEOPLE
Knute Rockne
Mark Spitz
Wilma Rudolph
Janet Guthrie
Oscar Robertson
Larry Bird
John Wooden

VOCABULARY
social group

EVENTS
Indianapolis 500
Hoosier Hysteria

Sports in Indiana

You Are There

A hush comes over the crowd as you take your place on the starter's block. Your heart pounds. You crouch down, waiting for the crack of the starter's pistol. Everyone is hoping to see you run the race in record time today.

The pistol sounds and you are off. The crowd jumps to its feet, screaming as you make the first turn. You are far ahead of the pack as you spot the finish line. People are chanting your name, and you know you have won. Then you realize that, in front of your home crowd in Indiana, you have set a new world record!

Compare and Contrast As you read, contrast the various sports events Hoosiers have participated in and supported.

A Rich Sports Tradition

Hoosiers are great fans of both amateur and professional sports. Football competes with basketball in Indiana for being the most watched sport. Hoosiers' love of college and high school football took hold during the 1920s when **Knute Rockne** coached the champion "Fighting Irish" football team at the University of Notre Dame to five undefeated seasons.

Amateur athletes have always been warmly regarded in Indiana. In 1972, swimmer **Mark Spitz** became the first athlete to win seven gold medals at a single Olympic Games. Just months earlier, he had graduated from Indiana University in Bloomington, where he had been captain of the university's swim team. **Wilma Rudolph,** another famous Olympic athlete, found a home in Indiana. In 1960, she became the first American woman runner to win three gold medals at a single Olympic games. Years later, Rudolph moved to Indianapolis where she coached and helped establish sports programs for inner-city students.

Every May, Indiana hosts what many call the "greatest of all automobile races," the **Indianapolis 500.** The race has been a tradition since 1911. In 1977, **Janet Guthrie** became the first woman to race in the "Indy 500."

REVIEW Who are some of the people who have contributed to the tradition of Indiana sports?
Main Idea and Details

▶ *Left to right:* **Mark Spitz, Janet Guthrie** (*on phone*)**, Knute Rockne, and Wilma Rudolph**

391

Sports for Everyone

Like amateur sports, professional sports have found a home in Indiana. In 1984, the Baltimore Colts, a football team, left their home of nearly forty years and moved to Indianapolis. Just weeks after their arrival, they were playing their home games before a full stadium.

The Indiana Pacers, Indiana's professional men's basketball team, have thrilled fans since 1967. In 1999, a second professional basketball team joined the Pacers. This is the women's basketball team called the Indiana Fever.

Indiana also has a rich baseball history. In the 1940s and 1950s, the Indianapolis Clowns were part of the Negro American League. Baseball star Henry "Hank" Aaron began his professional career with this team in 1952.

In the 1940s, women found a place in baseball. During World War II, a women's professional league was started to take the place of the men's teams. The men's teams were unable to play because many players were in the military. Two of the women's teams were the South Bend Blue Sox and the Fort Wayne Daisies.

Throughout Indiana, Hoosiers join social groups. A **social group** is a group of people who share common goals and interests. Some groups run, swim, cross-country ski, and play all types of ball sports together. Of course, Hoosiers join other groups not related to sports. For example, the Mount Healthy students on page 376 are part of a social group. Being part of any social group means that the members of the group are responsible to each other. They listen to each other and join with the group to have fun, develop talents, learn new things, help others, or work toward common goals.

REVIEW What are some reasons why Hoosiers join social groups?
🔊 Summarize

Hoosier Hysteria

Every year, Indiana experiences **Hoosier Hysteria.** This is the nickname given to Indiana's statewide high school basketball tournament. The first was played in 1911, about nineteen years after Reverend Nicholas McKay introduced basketball to Indiana. By the 1920s, crowds of fifteen thousand or more filled the stadium at Butler University in Indianapolis to watch the tournament games. Hoosier Hysteria was born.

▶ The Fort Wayne Daisies, 1949

© Allen Co. - Ft. Wayne Historical Society/Allen County - Fort Wayne Historical Society

Indiana State University fans cheer their team.

At one time, Indiana schools of all sizes competed together. Small schools could end up playing large schools, sometimes with surprising results.

The most famous upset in Indiana history happened in 1954 when **Milan** High School, with just 162 students, beat the much larger Muncie Central High. This "Miracle Milan" team and the game they played later became the subject of the movie *Hoosiers*.

Oscar Robertson, often called the best player in the history of Indiana basketball, played for Crispus Attucks High School in Indianapolis in the 1950s. In 1960, he won a gold medal in basketball at the Olympics.

REVIEW Summarize the history of Hoosier Hysteria.
🔄 **Summarize**

▶ Oscar Robertson

Then and Now

Basketball

Basketball has changed since its birth at the YMCA in Springfield, Massachusetts, in 1891. The first players threw soccer balls into half-bushel peach baskets. Early spectators were allowed to lean over the railings to knock balls away from one basket or the other. This practice ended with the arrival of backboards.

▶ James Naismith (*above*) with the original ball and basket. Indiana Fever (*left*); Larry Bird goes for a rebound (*below*).

College Basketball

Hoosier enthusiasm for basketball extends to college ball as well. Legends **Larry Bird** and **John Wooden** played college basketball in Indiana. Larry Bird played for Indiana State University, then joined the Boston Celtics of the National Basketball Association (NBA). John Wooden started his college career at Purdue University in Lafayette. Wooden later coached his UCLA (University of California at Los Angeles) team to ten national championships during the 1960s and 1970s.

REVIEW What did John Wooden do before coaching at UCLA? **Sequence**

Summarize the Lesson

1911 First annual Indianapolis 500 was held.

Indiana held its first statewide high school boys' basketball tournament, nicknamed Hoosier Hysteria.

1920s Knute Rockne coached a championship football team at the University of Notre Dame.

1960 Wilma Rudolph won three Olympic gold medals.

© The Indianapolis Star, Matt Detrich

▶ Hoosier greats Larry Bird, Oscar Robertson, and John Wooden met at center court at an Indiana Pacers game on November 6, 1999.

LESSON 2 ▶ REVIEW

Check Facts and Main Ideas

1. **Compare and Contrast** On a sheet of paper, use a Venn diagram to compare and contrast Hoosiers' involvement in football and basketball.

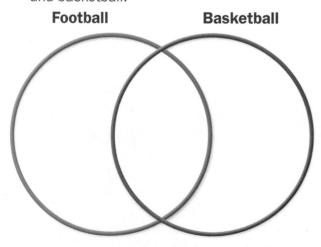

Football   Basketball

2. Why do so many Hoosiers participate in social groups, including sports teams?

3. What is Hoosier Hysteria?

4. Name two outstanding athletes from Indiana who were discussed in this lesson.

5. **Critical Thinking:** *Make Evaluations* In the past, small schools could end up playing large schools in the state basketball tournament. Was this a good way to organize the tournament? Explain your answer.

Link to ⟨—⟩ Writing

Write an Essay Think about a social group to which you belong. Remember that a social group can be related to something besides sports. Write an essay about why you like being a member of the group. Explain the ways in which you show responsibility to your group.

Larry Bird

born 1956

Larry Bird was born in the small southern Indiana town of French Lick. He started playing basketball in fourth grade. He made the high school team as a sophomore. During the next three years, basketball became the focus of Bird's life. His coach at the time remembers:

> *"Most kids are afraid to fail but Larry wasn't. Most kids keep practicing what they're good at but Larry practiced on his weaknesses. He spent one whole summer doing things left-handed. He was obsessed."*

BIOFACT

Both Larry Bird and fellow Hoosier Oscar Robertson led U. S. Olympic basketball teams to gold medals as co-captains. Bird did it in 1992 and Robertson, in 1960.

By the time Bird was a senior in high school, huge crowds would gather to watch his team play. Bird made a name for himself when he played for Indiana State. After college, he went on to play for the Boston Celtics. He won the Most Valuable Player Award three years in a row and led the team to three championships. In 1992, after 897 games, Larry Bird announced his retirement due to back problems. Later he returned home to coach the Indiana Pacers. He was elected to the Basketball Hall of Fame in 1998.

Learn from Biographies

According to Larry Bird's former coach, what qualities, other than talent, helped Bird become successful?

For more information, go online to *Meet the People* at **www.sfsocialstudies.com.**

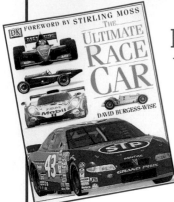

Indianapolis 500

The Indianapolis or "Indy" 500 was first run in 1911. The race attracts huge crowds every Memorial Day holiday weekend. However, by the end of World War II, its future was in doubt. Abandoned and choked with weeds, the brick-surfaced racetrack seemed beyond repair. Local entrepreneur Tony Hulman rebuilt the crumbling Indianapolis track and began a golden era for all American racers.

One-seat wonder
Ray Harroun won the first Indianapolis 500 in 1911 in this 7.8 liter six-cylinder Marmon Wasp, the world's first single-seater racing car. The car's average speed was almost 75 miles per hour.

Long lineage
In the 1950s, cars such as this one were popular with drivers. This Belond Equa-Flow Exhaust Special Kurtis Kraft car was driven by Johnnie Parsons at Indianapolis in 1954.

Thirst costs first

Swedish driver Kenny Brack's V8 Dallara-Aurora was leading on the 87th lap of the 1998 Indy 500 when it began to run low on fuel. The resulting refueling stop dropped Brack down to sixth position.

Ansted Rotary Special

Lindsey Hopkins Special

John Zink Special

Front row of the 1956 grid

The John Zink Special, built by A.J. Watson and driven by Pat Flaherty, won the 1956 Indy 500.

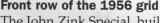

Lola found wanting

These three Lola T9 3/00 cars were strong contenders in the 1993 Indy 500. Mario Andretti, in the center, led for 72 laps out of 200, but Emerson Fittipaldi won in a Penske-Chevrolet. Andretti came in fifth.

Out of contention

Billy Boat started in pole position in the Conseco/A. J. Foyt in the 1998 Indy 500. He led for the first dozen laps, but he lost that position when his car's transmission jammed.

Glittering prize

The Indianapolis 500 is run every Memorial Day weekend for this trophy and a million-dollar-plus prize. The trophy bears the name and face of each Indy 500 winner.

Map and Globe Skills

Use a Time Zone Map

What? A **time zone** is a region in which people use the same time. A **time zone map** shows different time zones from one region to the next. The world is divided into twenty-four time zones. The map on this page shows the time zones in the United States. Indiana is officially in the Eastern Time Zone. A few areas of Indiana, though, use Central Time, like our neighbors to the west.

Why? Suppose you work for a company in Fort Wayne. You want to call a company in Chicago, Illinois, to order some supplies.

Hawaii-Aleutian

Alaska

Pacific

Mountain

Central

Eastern

Time Zones of North America

▶ The girl on the left is eating breakfast in Hawaii. Where could the boy on the right be eating lunch? Check your time zone map.

The time in Fort Wayne is 9 A.M. What time is it in Chicago? You can use a time zone map to find out. Since Chicago is in the Central Time Zone and Fort Wayne is in the Eastern Time Zone, it will be one hour earlier in Chicago. If the office in Chicago does not open until 9 A.M., Chicago time, then you will need to wait until 10 A.M. to call from Fort Wayne.

You can use a time zone map when you travel. Will your trip take you to a city in a different time zone? What time will it be when you arrive?

Television programs are also affected by time zones. A program that is shown at 9 P.M. in your town could be showing at 8 P.M. in another town.

How? To read and understand a time zone map, follow these steps.

- Notice that each time zone on the map is shown in a different color. You can see that some states are in more than one time zone. Find Evansville. In what time zone is it?
- Next, look at the clock face above each time zone. What times do they show? When it's 10 A.M. in Chicago, what time is it in Indianapolis?
- Compare the times on all the clock faces shown on the map on page 398. Begin at the Eastern Time Zone. What do you notice as you move from east to west across the map? What is the time difference between Boston, Massachusetts, and Portland, Oregon?

Think and Apply

❶ It is 10 A.M. in Indianapolis, where you live. You want to phone your cousin in San Francisco. What time is it there?

❷ You live in Indianapolis. You are going to Washington, D.C. What is the time difference between Indianapolis and Washington, D.C.?

❸ If you drove from Pennsylvania to Oregon, how many time zones would you pass through? By how many hours would the time be different?

For more information, go online to the *Atlas* at **www.sfsocialstudies.com**.

1925	1950	1975	2000

1922
Kurt Vonnegut, Jr.,
is born in
Indianapolis.

1950s
Wes Montgomery
becomes a famous
jazz musician.

1986
The movie
Hoosiers is
released.

1991
Phyllis
Reynolds
Naylor's award-
winning *Shiloh*
is published.

PREVIEW

Focus on the Main Idea
Indiana continues to produce
well-known artists.

PLACE
Indiana

PEOPLE
Kurt Vonnegut, Jr.
Jessamyn West
Phyllis Reynolds Naylor
Kay Chorao
Robert Indiana
Cole Porter
Hoagy Carmichael
Wes Montgomery
Michael Jackson
John Mellencamp
Twyla Tharp
James Dean
Jane Pauley
David Letterman

The Arts

You Are There
You eagerly climb onto the
bus. Today your class is
visiting the Indianapolis
Museum of Art. You've never been in the
museum before, and you are excited about
seeing the paintings and sculptures your
teacher has described. It seems like no time
at all before you notice your friends excitedly
pointing out the window at something. It is
the LOVE sculpture in
front of the museum. To
see the sculpture this
close is amazing. You
can't wait to start your
museum tour!

Indianapolis Museum of Art, Gift of the Friends of
the IMA in memory of Henry F. DeBoest.

Summarize As you read, pay attention to
details that summarize Indiana's many
contributions to the arts.

▶ A scene from the movie *Friendly Persuasion* starring actors Gary Cooper and Dorothy McGuire.

Indiana's Writers and Artists

Indiana has produced many famous writers and artists during its history. Over the past fifty years, Hoosiers such as Kurt Vonnegut, Jr., Jessamyn West, and Phyllis Reynolds Naylor have carried on this tradition. These writers often bring something of Indiana into their works.

Kurt Vonnegut was born in 1922 in Indianapolis. He has written several best-selling novels, including *Slaughterhouse Five.* Jessamyn West was born in Indiana in 1902. Her most famous book, *The Friendly Persuasion,* was set in nineteenth-century Indiana.

Many award-winning writers of children's books also come from Indiana. Phyllis Reynolds Naylor of Anderson has won awards for her novel *Shiloh,* published in 1991. *Cathedral Mouse* by Kay Chorao of Elkhart was voted one of the year's ten best children's books of 1988.

Robert Indiana was born Robert Clark in 1928 in New Castle. He decided to change his name to Robert Indiana in order to be "the *most* American painter." He designed the LOVE sculpture that stands at the entrance to the Indianapolis Museum of Art. This sculpture was the model for the United States Post Office's LOVE stamp.

REVIEW What details support the main idea that Indiana continues to produce great writers and artists? **Main Idea and Details**

Music, Dance, Movies, and Television

Many musicians have called Indiana home. **Cole Porter,** born in Peru in 1891, wrote some of America's most well-known songs, such as "Night and Day." **Hoagy Carmichael** was born in Bloomington in 1899. His most famous song is "Stardust."

During the 1950s, a guitarist from Indianapolis named **Wes Montgomery** began making a name in the jazz world. His sound inspired generations of musicians.

More recently, Indiana has been the birthplace of musicians such as the singing Jackson family from Gary. **Michael Jackson** and his brothers sang together as the Jackson Five. In the 1980s, Michael became hugely successful on his own, with hits such as "Thriller." His sister Janet also became famous for songs from her album *Rhythm Nation*.

Singer-songwriter **John Mellencamp**'s Hoosier roots show up often in his songs of small town life. Portland's **Twyla Tharp,** a dancer and choreographer, is known for her creative and often humorous approach to dance. She has created ballets, such as *Push Comes to Shove,* and dance pieces for movies.

Many actors, such as **James Dean,** Steve McQueen, Vivica A. Fox, and Greg Kinnear, were born in Indiana. Dean is remembered for his intense roles as a troubled young man. Indiana has also been the setting for several Hollywood movies. *Breaking Away* was a 1979 movie about four young men from Bloomington. The 1986 movie *Hoosiers* tells the story of the historic "Miracle Milan" team of 1954.

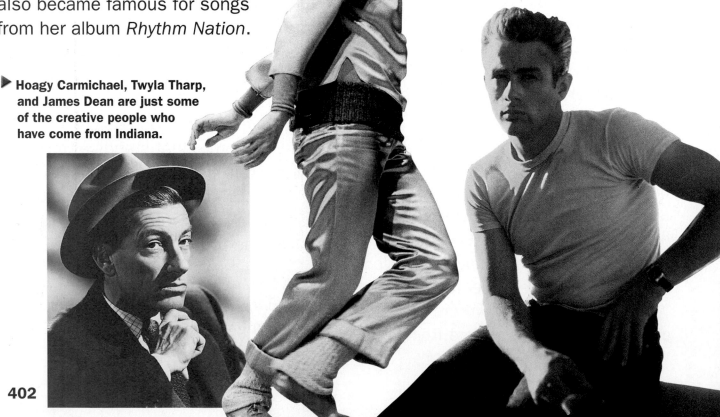

▶ Hoagy Carmichael, Twyla Tharp, and James Dean are just some of the creative people who have come from Indiana.

Watch television and you will probably see a Hoosier on the screen sooner or later. If you like to watch news programs, you might see Indianapolis native **Jane Pauley.** She is a television journalist.

▶ Television personalities David Letterman and Jane Pauley

David Letterman is also an Indianapolis native. He hosts a late-night talk show that is famous for its "Top Ten" lists. He often asks his mom, Dorothy, an Indiana resident, to report and comment for his program.

REVIEW Draw a conclusion about Indiana and the arts. **Draw Conclusions**

Summarize the Lesson

- **1922** Kurt Vonnegut, Jr., was born in Indianapolis.
- **1950s** Wes Montgomery became a famous jazz musician.
- **1986** The movie *Hoosiers* was released.
- **1991** Phyllis Reynolds Naylor's award-winning novel *Shiloh* was published.

LESSON 3 **REVIEW**

Check Facts and Main Ideas

1. 🔁 **Summarize** On a sheet of paper, write details that support the summary below.

Indiana has been the home of many famous writers, artists, and performers.

2. How have modern writers from Indiana kept alive the tradition of Hoosier writers?

3. Name a famous work of art by sculptor Robert Indiana.

4. Name one writer, one musician, and one actor who have helped continue Indiana's tradition of excellence in the arts and literature.

5. **Critical Thinking:** *Draw Conclusions* Writers Kurt Vonnegut, Jr., and Jessamyn West and musician John Mellencamp all bring elements of their Indiana roots into their works. Why do you think they choose to do this?

Link to 🔗 **Music**

Compose a Song Write lyrics that express your feelings about Indiana or describe life in Indiana. Set your lyrics to music. Hold an "Indiana Music Festival" in your class and take turns performing your songs.

1910	1920	1930	1940
1911 The first Indianapolis 500 and first state high school basketball tournament were held.	**1920s** Notre Dame had champion football teams. Hoosier Hysteria began.	**1922** Kurt Vonnegut, Jr., was born in Indianapolis.	**1946** Baby boom began.

Chapter Summary

 **Summarize**

On a sheet of paper, write details from this chapter that support the summary below.

Indiana has experienced many changes over the past fifty years.

Vocabulary and Terms

Fill in the blank in each sentence with the correct word from the list below.

baby boom (p. 385)   **urban** (p. 385)
rural (p. 385)   **social group** (p. 392)
technology (p. 387)

1. After World War II, many people left their farms and moved to Indiana's _____ areas.

2. The population in the United States increased in the 1950s partly because of a _____.

3. In Indiana, there are many farms located in its _____ areas.

4. A group of people who share common goals and interests can be called a _____.

5. The invention of tools, machines, and skills, or _____, has helped many people.

People and Events

Match each person or event with the correct description.

1. **Indianapolis 500** (p. 391)
2. **Mark Spitz** (p. 391)
3. **Hoosier Hysteria** (p. 392)
4. **Oscar Robertson** (p. 393)
5. **Robert Indiana** (p. 401)
6. **Jessamyn West** (p. 401)
7. **Hoagy Carmichael** (p. 402)
8. **David Letterman** (p. 403)

a. nickname for high-school basketball tournament

b. wrote about life in nineteenth-century Indiana

c. played basketball at Crispus Attucks High School

d. created the LOVE sculpture

e. Olympic swimmer

f. talk show host

g. annual car race

h. Hoosier songwriter

1950s
Population increased. Wes Montgomery became famous.

1960s
Fort Wayne became an industrial center.

1980
Indiana's farms produced about 100 bushels of corn per acre.

1986
Movie *Hoosiers* was released.

1991
Phyllis Naylor's novel *Shiloh* was published.

Facts and Main Ideas

1 Why were so many small farms unable to keep up with technological changes in the twentieth century?

2 From where did many African American Hoosiers move in the twentieth century?

3 What led to the development of Fort Wayne as an industrial center in the 1960s?

4 **Time Line** In which decade did Fort Wayne become an industrial center?

5 **Main Idea** In what two ways did the population of Indiana change after World War II?

6 **Main Idea** What do Mark Spitz, Oscar Robertson, and Larry Bird have in common?

7 **Main Idea** Explain this statement: *Indiana has a long tradition of excellence in the arts.*

8 **Critical Thinking:** *Make Evaluations* One goal of technology and science is to make farm life easier and more efficient. Do you agree with this statement? Explain.

Write About Citizenship

1 **Write a speech** to give to your teammates during halftime at the finals of the statewide basketball tournament. Your team is behind by four points, and you want them to remember how other underdogs have come from behind to win games.

2 **Write an editorial** encouraging Indiana's state government to adopt "Indiana Authors' Day." Include in your editorial specific writers you think should be honored and tell why.

3 **Write a short story** from the viewpoint of a girl who lives on a small farm. What problems does her family face, and what is going to happen to them?

Apply Skills

Use a Time Zone Map

Refer to the time zone map on page 398 to answer the questions below.

1 You live in Indianapolis. You want to have a three-way chat online with your friend in New York City and your friend in Seattle. If it is 11 A.M. in Indianapolis, what time is it in New York? What time is it in Seattle?

2 You are visiting Denver. You tell your mother you will call her at noon tomorrow, Denver time. What time will it be in Evansville?

3 You just landed in Honolulu, Hawaii. Your watch is still set for Indianapolis time. If it is 2 P.M. in Hawaii, what time does your watch say it is?

Internet Activity

To get help with vocabulary, people, and terms, select the dictionary or encyclopedia from *Social Studies Library* at **www.sfsocialstudies.com.**

End with a Song

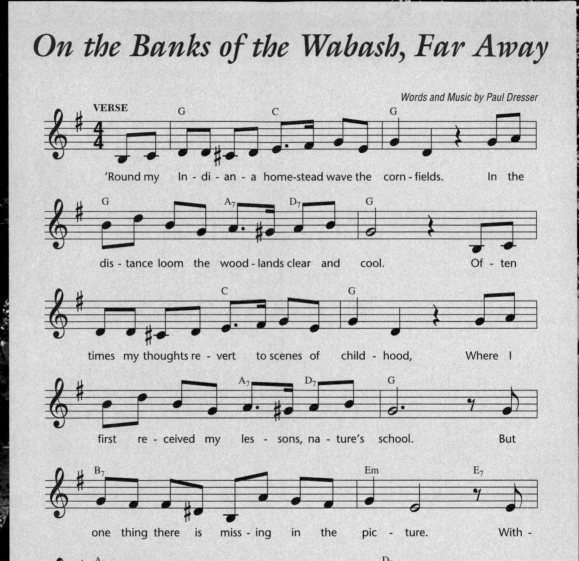

On the Banks of the Wabash, Far Away

Words and Music by Paul Dresser

VERSE

'Round my In - di - an - a home-stead wave the corn - fields. In the

dis - tance loom the wood - lands clear and cool. Of - ten

times my thoughts re - vert to scenes of child - hood, Where I

first re - ceived my les - sons, na - ture's school. But

one thing there is miss - ing in the pic - ture. With -

out her face it seems so in - com - plete. I

Paul Dresser published this song in 1897. Hoosiers loved it so much that they made it the state song in 1913.

Main Ideas and Vocabulary

TEST PREP

Read the passage below and use it to answer the questions that follow.

Throughout the 1900s, Indiana has experienced many changes. Groups of people have gained the right to vote. This has led Indiana to <u>amend</u> its constitution. Indiana is a place where citizens understand the rights and responsibilities of citizenship. Hoosiers receive services from their government. In return, the citizens pay <u>income tax</u> on their earnings and other taxes to help pay for these services. They also help the government run smoothly by electing the people who best represent their interests. They elect members of the legislative branch to Congress in Washington, D.C. They also elect state and local representatives. Many citizens volunteer their time to help in their communities.

Some changes in the past years include larger urban areas and new suburbs. Rural areas are now less populated. People who stayed on the farms have changed the way they work their land. Farm machines have taken the place of people and work animals. At the same time, Hoosiers have kept alive the valued Indiana traditions of sports enthusiasm and excellence in the arts.

1 According to this passage, how do citizens help their government run smoothly?
  A by voting
  B by paying taxes
  C by understanding their responsibilities as citizens
  D all of the above

2 In this passage, the term <u>amend</u> means to
  A seriously consider amending.
  B formally make amends.
  C formally change something.
  D seriously say you are sorry.

3 In this passage, <u>income tax</u> means
  A a tax paid on what you spend.
  B a tax paid on what you earn.
  C a tax paid on the value of your home.
  D a tax on water.

4 One big change in Indiana life over the past fifty years was
  A the birth of suburbs.
  B the increased use of farm machinery.
  C the growth of urban areas.
  D all of the above.

People and Terms

Match each person or term to its description or definition.

① **Supreme Court** (p. 364)

② **General Assembly** (p. 366)

③ **Unigov** (p. 369)

④ **Knute Rockne** (p. 391)

⑤ **Kurt Vonnegut, Jr.** (p. 401)

a. highest court in the United States

b. Indiana's legislature

c. writer from Indiana

d. coach of the "Fighting Irish" in the 1920s

e. a program of unified government

Apply Skills

Plan Your Calls

You and a friend are taking a train across the country. You will stop in Indianapolis, Davenport, Denver, and San Francisco. You have to phone your mother every day at 1 P.M. *her time.* She lives in New York City. At what time do you need to phone her from each city? Use the time zone map on page 398 to create a schedule of phone calls.

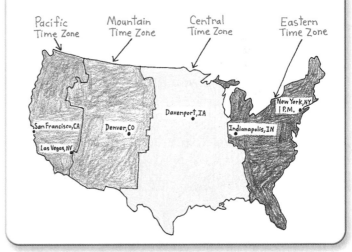

Read on Your Own

Look for these books in your library.

Write and Share

Present a Skit Work in a small group to write a skit about the changes an Indiana farming family experiences after World War II. First do background research for the project. Outline the important facts and clearly show the changes the family undergoes. Then write the script for the skit. Present the skit to the class.

Great State

Create a booklet that shows what's great about Indiana today—and what will be great in the future.

1 Form a group. Choose a current event in Indiana.

2 Write a paragraph about the event. Predict what will happen in the future and write several sentences.

3 Draw or find pictures that illustrate the event today and what might occur in the future.

4 Put your group's paragraphs and pictures together into a booklet. Share it with the class.

Internet Activity

Learn more about Indiana. Go to **www.sfsocialstudies.com/activities** and select your grade and unit.

Table of Contents

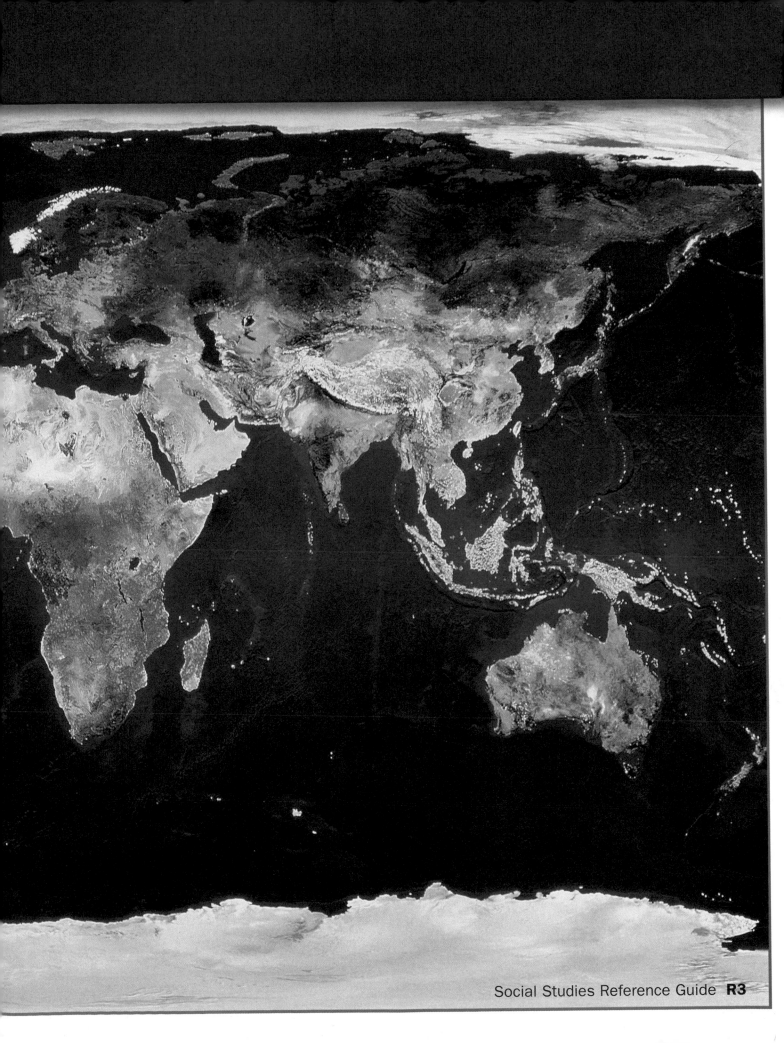

ARCTIC OCEAN

GREENLAND (DENMARK)

Arctic Circle

ALASKA (U.S.)

CANADA

NORTH AMERICA

UNITED STATES

BERMUDA (U.K.)

ATLANTIC OCEAN

See inset below

MIDWAY ISLANDS (U.S.)

Tropic of Cancer

HAWAII (U.S.)

MEXICO

PACIFIC OCEAN

VENEZUELA

GUYANA

SURINAME

FRENCH GUIANA (FRANCE)

COLOMBIA

GALÁPAGOS ISLANDS (ECUADOR)

ECUADOR

SOUTH AMERICA

Equator

SAMOA

AMERICAN SAMOA (U.S.)

FRENCH POLYNESIA (FRANCE)

PERU

BRAZIL

TONGA

BOLIVIA

Tropic of Capricorn

PARAGUAY

URUGUAY

CHILE

ARGENTINA

FALKLAND ISLANDS (U.K.)

SOUTH GEORGIA (U.K.)

Antarctic Circle

Central America and the West Indies

Gulf of Mexico

BAHAMAS

Tropic of Cancer

TURKS AND CAICOS IS. (U.K.)

ATLANTIC OCEAN

CUBA

CAYMAN ISLANDS (U.K.)

JAMAICA

HAITI

DOMINICAN REPUBLIC

VIRGIN ISLANDS (U.K.)

ST. KITTS AND NEVIS

ANTIGUA AND BARBUDA

PUERTO RICO (U.S.)

VIRGIN ISLANDS (U.S.)

GUADELOUPE (FRANCE)

BELIZE

DOMINICA

GUATEMALA

HONDURAS

MARTINIQUE (FRANCE)

ST. LUCIA

EL SALVADOR

N

Caribbean Sea

ST. VINCENT AND THE GRENADINES

BARBADOS

PACIFIC OCEAN

NICARAGUA

NETHERLANDS ANTILLES (NETHERLANDS)

GRENADA

ARUBA (NETHERLANDS)

TRINIDAD AND TOBAGO

0 250 500 Miles

COSTA RICA

0 250 500 Kilometers

PANAMA

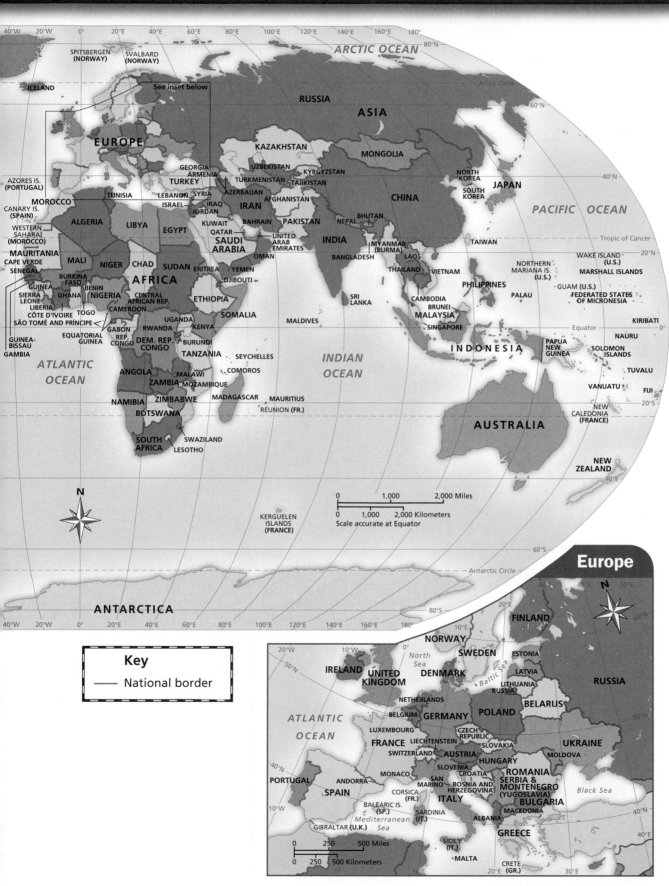

40°W 20°W 0° 20°E 40°E 60°E 80°E 100°E 120°E 140°E 160°E 180°

ARCTIC OCEAN 80°N

SPITSBERGEN (NORWAY)
SVALBARD (NORWAY)
ICELAND

RUSSIA
ASIA
60°N

EUROPE

KAZAKHSTAN
MONGOLIA

AZORES IS. (PORTUGAL)
GEORGIA
ARMENIA
TURKEY
UZBEKISTAN
KYRGYZSTAN
40°N

TUNISIA
LEBANON
SYRIA
ISRAEL
JORDAN
AZERBAIJAN
TURKMENISTAN
TAJIKISTAN

NORTH KOREA
JAPAN
SOUTH KOREA

PACIFIC OCEAN

MOROCCO
CANARY IS. (SPAIN)
IRAQ
IRAN
AFGHANISTAN
CHINA

ALGERIA
LIBYA
EGYPT
KUWAIT
BAHRAIN
PAKISTAN
NEPAL
BHUTAN

WESTERN SAHARA (MOROCCO)
QATAR
UNITED ARAB EMIRATES
SAUDI ARABIA
INDIA
MYANMAR (BURMA)
TAIWAN
Tropic of Cancer 20°N

MAURITANIA
OMAN
BANGLADESH
LAOS
WAKE ISLAND (U.S.)

CAPE VERDE
MALI
NIGER
CHAD
SUDAN
ERITREA
YEMEN
THAILAND
VIETNAM
NORTHERN MARIANA IS. (U.S.)
MARSHALL ISLANDS

SENEGAL
AFRICA
DJIBOUTI

BURKINA FASO
GUINEA
BENIN
NIGERIA
CENTRAL AFRICAN REP.
ETHIOPIA
SRI LANKA
CAMBODIA
PHILIPPINES
GUAM (U.S.)

SIERRA LEONE
GHANA
CAMEROON
BRUNEI
PALAU
FEDERATED STATES OF MICRONESIA

LIBERIA
CÔTE D'IVOIRE
TOGO
MALAYSIA
KIRIBATI

SÃO TOMÉ AND PRÍNCIPE
EQUATORIAL GUINEA
GABON
REP. CONGO
UGANDA
RWANDA
KENYA
DEM. REP. CONGO
BURUNDI
SINGAPORE
Equator 0°
NAURU

GUINEA-BISSAU
TANZANIA
SEYCHELLES
INDONESIA
PAPUA NEW GUINEA
SOLOMON ISLANDS

GAMBIA
MALDIVES

ATLANTIC OCEAN
ANGOLA
MALAWI
COMOROS
INDIAN OCEAN
TUVALU

ZAMBIA
MOZAMBIQUE
VANUATU
FIJI

NAMIBIA
ZIMBABWE
MADAGASCAR
MAURITIUS
20°S

BOTSWANA
RÉUNION (FR.)
NEW CALEDONIA (FRANCE)

SOUTH AFRICA
SWAZILAND
LESOTHO
AUSTRALIA

N

NEW ZEALAND
40°S

KERGUELEN ISLANDS (FRANCE)

0   1,000   2,000 Miles
0   1,000   2,000 Kilometers
Scale accurate at Equator

60°S

Antarctic Circle
80°S

ANTARCTICA

40°W 20°W 0° 20°E 40°E 60°E 80°E 100°E 120°E 140°E 160°E 180°

Europe

N

FINLAND

NORWAY
SWEDEN
ESTONIA

IRELAND
UNITED KINGDOM
North Sea
DENMARK
Baltic Sea
LATVIA
RUSSIA

LITHUANIA
RUSSIA

NETHERLANDS
BELARUS

ATLANTIC OCEAN
BELGIUM
GERMANY
POLAND

LUXEMBOURG
CZECH REPUBLIC
UKRAINE

FRANCE
LIECHTENSTEIN
SLOVAKIA
MOLDOVA

SWITZERLAND
AUSTRIA
HUNGARY

SLOVENIA
ROMANIA

PORTUGAL
ANDORRA
MONACO
CROATIA
SERBIA & MONTENEGRO (YUGOSLAVIA)
Black Sea

SPAIN
SAN MARINO
BOSNIA AND HERZEGOVINA
BULGARIA

CORSICA (FR.)
ITALY
MACEDONIA

BALEARIC IS. (SP.)
SARDINIA (IT.)
ALBANIA

GIBRALTAR (U.K.)
Mediterranean Sea
SICILY (IT.)
GREECE

0   250   500 Miles
0   250   500 Kilometers

MALTA

CRETE (GR.)

Key
— National border

Atlas
Map of the World: Physical

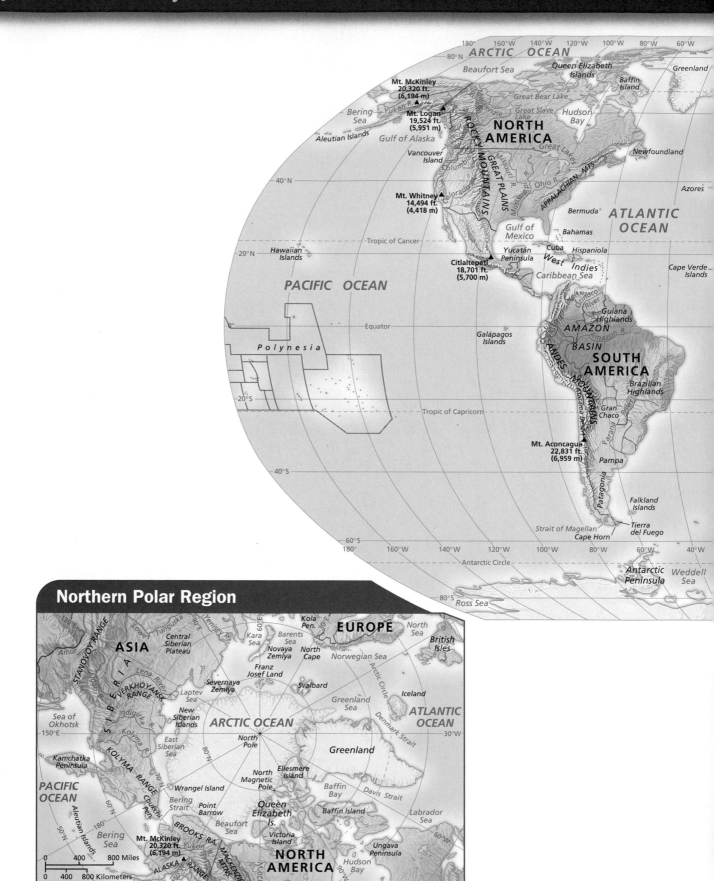

ARCTIC OCEAN

Beaufort Sea
Queen Elizabeth Islands
Greenland
Baffin Island

Mt. McKinley
20,320 ft.
(6,194 m)
Bering Sea
Yukon R.
Mt. Logan
19,524 ft.
(5,951 m)
Great Bear Lake
Great Slave Lake
Hudson Bay

NORTH AMERICA
ROCKY MOUNTAINS
Gulf of Alaska
Aleutian Islands
Vancouver Island
Columbia R.
Great Lakes
Newfoundland
Missouri R.
GREAT PLAINS
Ohio R.
APPALACHIAN MTS.
Azores

Mt. Whitney
14,494 ft.
(4,418 m)
Colorado R.
Bermuda
ATLANTIC OCEAN

Tropic of Cancer
Gulf of Mexico
Bahamas

Hawaiian Islands
Yucatán Peninsula
Cuba
Hispaniola
West Indies
Cape Verde Islands

Citlaltepetl
18,701 ft.
(5,700 m)
Caribbean Sea

PACIFIC OCEAN

Galápagos Islands
Orinoco River
Guiana Highlands
AMAZON BASIN
Amazon R.

Equator

Polynesia
ANDES MOUNTAINS
SOUTH AMERICA
Brazilian Highlands

Tropic of Capricorn
Atacama Desert
Gran Chaco
Paraná

Mt. Aconcagua
22,831 ft.
(6,959 m)
Pampa

Patagonia
Falkland Islands

Strait of Magellan
Tierra del Fuego
Cape Horn

Antarctic Circle
Antarctic Peninsula
Weddell Sea
Ross Sea

Northern Polar Region

STANOVOY RANGE
Amur
Lower Tunguska
Yenisey R.
Kola Pen.
Barents Sea
North Sea
EUROPE
British Isles

ASIA
Central Siberian Plateau
Kara Sea
Novaya Zemlya
North Cape
Norwegian Sea

SIBERIA
VERKHOYANSK RANGE
Lena River
Franz Josef Land
Svalbard
Arctic Circle
Iceland

Severnaya Zemlya
Indigirka R.
Laptev Sea
Greenland Sea
ATLANTIC OCEAN

Sea of Okhotsk
150°E
Kolyma R.
New Siberian Islands
East Siberian Sea
ARCTIC OCEAN
North Pole
Denmark Strait
30°W

KOLYMA RANGE
Kamchatka Peninsula
Wrangel Island
North Magnetic Pole
Ellesmere Island
Greenland

Chukchi Pen.
Bering Strait
Point Barrow
Baffin Bay
Davis Strait

PACIFIC OCEAN
Aleutian Islands
Bering Sea
Queen Elizabeth Is.
Baffin Island
Labrador Sea

BROOKS RA.
Beaufort Sea
Victoria Island
Ungava Peninsula

Mt. McKinley
20,320 ft.
(6,194 m)
ALASKA RANGE
Yukon R.
MACKENZIE MTS.
NORTH AMERICA
Hudson Bay

0   400   800 Miles
0   400   800 Kilometers

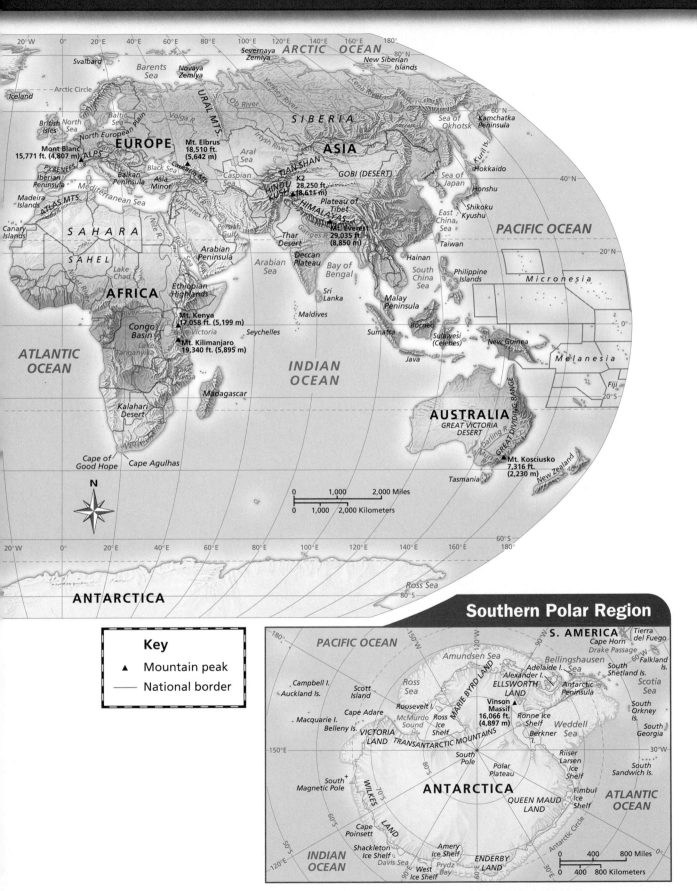

20°W 0° 20°E 40°E 60°E 80°E 100°E 120°E 140°E 160°E 180°

ARCTIC OCEAN 80°N

Svalbard
Severnaya Zemlya
New Siberian Islands

Barents Sea
Novaya Zemlya

Iceland
Arctic Circle

British Isles
North Sea
Baltic Sea
North European Plain
URAL MTS.
Ob River
Yenisey River
Lena River
SIBERIA
60°N
Sea of Okhotsk
Kamchatka Peninsula

EUROPE
Mont Blanc 15,771 ft. (4,807 m)
ALPS
PYRENEES
Iberian Peninsula
Volga R.
Irtysh River

Mt. Elbrus 18,510 ft. (5,642 m)
Aral Sea
ASIA
TIAN SHAN
Kuril Is.
Hokkaido
40°N

Balkan Peninsula
Black Sea
Asia Minor
Caspian Sea
Caucasus Mts.
HINDU KUSH
K2 28,250 ft. (8,611 m)
GOBI (DESERT)
Sea of Japan
Honshu
Shikoku
Kyushu

Madeira Islands
ATLAS MTS.
Mediterranean Sea
Euphrates R.
Persian Gulf
HIMALAYAS
Plateau of Tibet
East China Sea
Taiwan

Canary Islands
SAHARA
Nile R.
Red Sea
Arabian Peninsula
Thar Desert
Mt. Everest 29,035 ft. (8,850 m)
Ganges R.
Deccan Plateau
Hainan
20°N

SAHEL
Lake Chad
Arabian Sea
Bay of Bengal
South China Sea
Philippine Islands
Micronesia

AFRICA
Ethiopian Highlands
Sri Lanka
Maldives
Malay Peninsula

Congo Basin
Mt. Kenya 17,058 ft. (5,199 m)
Lake Victoria
Mt. Kilimanjaro 19,340 ft. (5,895 m)
Seychelles
Sumatra
Borneo
Sulawesi (Celebes)
New Guinea

ATLANTIC OCEAN
Lake Tanganyika
Lake Nyasa
INDIAN OCEAN
Java
Melanesia
Fiji
20°S

Kalahari Desert
Madagascar
AUSTRALIA
GREAT VICTORIA DESERT
GREAT DIVIDING RANGE
Darling R.
Murray R.

Cape of Good Hope
Cape Agulhas
Mt. Kosciusko 7,316 ft. (2,230 m)
New Zealand

Tasmania

N

0   1,000   2,000 Miles
0   1,000   2,000 Kilometers

20°W 0° 20°E 40°E 60°E 80°E 100°E 120°E 140°E 160°E 180° 60°S

ANTARCTICA
Ross Sea 80°S

Key
▲ Mountain peak
— National border

Southern Polar Region

180°
PACIFIC OCEAN
150°W
120°W
90°W
S. AMERICA
Tierra del Fuego
Cape Horn
Drake Passage

Amundsen Sea
Bellingshausen Sea
Adelaide I.
Alexander I.
Antarctic Peninsula
South Shetland Is.
Falkland Is.
Scotia Sea
60°W

Campbell I.
Auckland Is.
Scott Island
Ross Sea
ELLSWORTH LAND
MARIE BYRD LAND
Roosevelt I.
Vinson Massif 16,066 ft. (4,897 m)
Ronne Ice Shelf
Berkner I.
Weddell Sea
South Orkney Is.
South Georgia
30°W

Cape Adare
McMurdo Sound
Ross Ice Shelf
VICTORIA LAND
TRANSANTARCTIC MOUNTAINS
South Pole
Polar Plateau
Riiser Larsen Ice Shelf
South Sandwich Is.

Macquarie I.
Belleny Is.

150°E
South Magnetic Pole
WILKES LAND
ANTARCTICA
QUEEN MAUD LAND
Fimbul Ice Shelf
ATLANTIC OCEAN
30°W

120°E
Cape Poinsett
Shackleton Ice Shelf
Davis Sea
West Ice Shelf
Amery Ice Shelf
Prydz Bay
ENDERBY LAND
Antarctic Circle

INDIAN OCEAN

0   400   800 Miles
0   400   800 Kilometers

Atlas
Map of the Western Hemisphere: Political

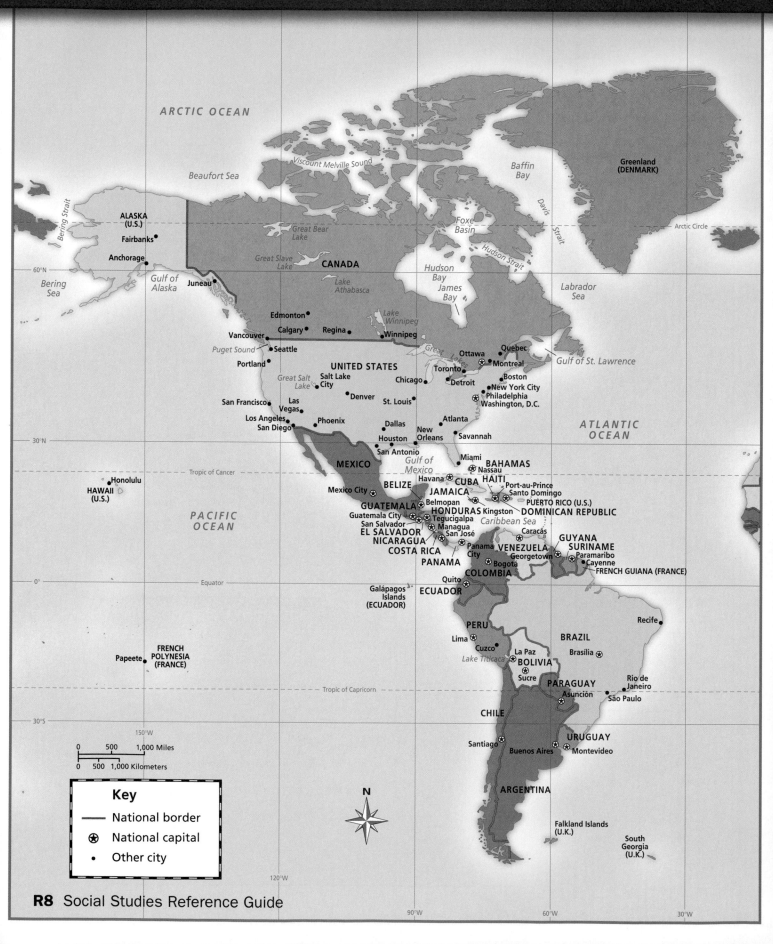

ARCTIC OCEAN

Beaufort Sea

Viscount Melville Sound

Baffin Bay

Greenland (DENMARK)

Bering Strait

ALASKA (U.S.)

Fairbanks

Anchorage

Great Bear Lake

Foxe Basin

Arctic Circle

60°N

Bering Sea

Gulf of Alaska

Juneau

Great Slave Lake

CANADA

Hudson Bay

James Bay

Davis Strait

Hudson Strait

Labrador Sea

Edmonton

Calgary

Regina

Winnipeg

Lake Winnipeg

Lake Athabasca

Vancouver

Puget Sound

Seattle

Portland

Great Salt Lake

Salt Lake City

UNITED STATES

Great Lakes

Ottawa

Toronto

Detroit

Chicago

Quebec

Montreal

Boston

New York City

Philadelphia

Washington, D.C.

Gulf of St. Lawrence

Denver

St. Louis

San Francisco

Las Vegas

Los Angeles

San Diego

Phoenix

Dallas

Houston

New Orleans

Atlanta

Savannah

ATLANTIC OCEAN

30°N

San Antonio

MEXICO

Gulf of Mexico

Miami

BAHAMAS

Nassau

Tropic of Cancer

HAWAII (U.S.)

Honolulu

Havana

CUBA

HAITI

Port-au-Prince

PUERTO RICO (U.S.)

PACIFIC OCEAN

Mexico City

BELIZE

JAMAICA

Santo Domingo

DOMINICAN REPUBLIC

GUATEMALA

Belmopan

Kingston

Guatemala City

HONDURAS

Tegucigalpa

San Salvador

Managua

EL SALVADOR

San José

NICARAGUA

Caribbean Sea

Caracas

GUYANA

SURINAME

COSTA RICA

PANAMA

Panama City

VENEZUELA

Georgetown

Paramaribo

Cayenne

FRENCH GUIANA (FRANCE)

Bogotá

COLOMBIA

Quito

0°

Equator

ECUADOR

Galápagos Islands (ECUADOR)

Recife

PERU

BRAZIL

FRENCH POLYNESIA (FRANCE)

Papeete

Lima

Cuzco

La Paz

Brasília

Lake Titicaca

BOLIVIA

Sucre

Tropic of Capricorn

PARAGUAY

Rio de Janeiro

Asunción

São Paulo

30°S

CHILE

150°W

URUGUAY

Santiago

Buenos Aires

Montevideo

0 500 1,000 Miles

0 500 1,000 Kilometers

Key

— National border

⊛ National capital

• Other city

ARGENTINA

Falkland Islands (U.K.)

South Georgia (U.K.)

N

120°W

90°W

60°W

30°W

ARCTIC OCEAN

North Magnetic Pole

Queen Elizabeth Islands

Ellesmere Island

Melville Island

Viscount Melville Sound

Devon Island

Banks Island

Baffin Bay

Greenland

Point Barrow

Beaufort Sea

Victoria Island

Baffin Island

Brooks Range

Yukon River

Foxe Basin

Davis Strait

Arctic Circle

Mt. McKinley 20,320 ft. (6,194 m)

Bering Strait

Alaska Range

Yukon Plateau

Mackenzie Mts

Mackenzie River

Great Bear Lake

Hudson Strait

Cape Farewell

Bering Sea

60°N

Gulf of Alaska

Mt. Logan 19,524 ft. (5,951 m)

Liard R.

Great Slave Lake

Peace River

Saskatchewan River

Lake Athabasca

Hudson Bay

James Bay

Labrador

Labrador Sea

Kodiak Island

Alaska Peninsula

Aleutian Islands

Queen Charlotte Islands

Coast Mountains

ROCKY

Athabasca R.

CANADIAN

Lake Winnipeg

SHIELD

GREAT

St. Lawrence R.

Newfoundland

Gulf of St. Lawrence

Vancouver Island

Puget Sound

Cascade Range

Coast Ranges

MOUNTAINS

PLAINS

NORTH AMERICA

Black Hills

Missouri R.

Great Lakes

Mississippi R.

Ohio R.

APPALACHIAN MTS.

Nova Scotia

Bay of Fundy

Cape Cod

Long Island

Snake R.

Great Salt Lake

GREAT BASIN

Sierra Nevada

Platte R.

INTERIOR PLAINS

Arkansas R.

Ozark Plateau

Mt. Whitney 14,495 ft. (4,418 m)

Colorado R.

Cape Hatteras

ATLANTIC OCEAN

Death Valley (lowest point in N.A.) -282 ft. (-86 m)

Sonoran Desert

Sierra Madre Occidental

Sierra Madre Oriental

Rio Grande

COASTAL PLAIN

30°N

Baja California

Gulf of Mexico

Bahamas

Hawaiian Islands

Tropic of Cancer

Yucatán Peninsula

Cuba

Greater Antilles

Hispaniola

Puerto Rico

Lesser Antilles

Citlaltépetl 18,701 ft. (5,700 m)

Caribbean Sea

PACIFIC OCEAN

Lake Nicaragua

Isthmus of Panama

Lake Maracaibo

Orinoco R.

Llanos

Guiana Highlands

Line Islands

Equator

0°

Galápagos Islands

Chimborazo 20,561 ft. (6,267 m)

Río Negro

Amazon R.

Cape São Roque

Marquesas Islands

AMAZON BASIN

Tapajós R.

Xingu R.

Tocantins R.

São Francisco R.

Huascarán 22,205 ft. (6,768 m)

ANDES

Mato Grosso Plateau

Paraguay R.

Brazilian Highlands

Cook Islands

Tuamotu Archipelago

Society Islands

Lake Titicaca

Altiplano

SOUTH AMERICA

Tropic of Capricorn

MOUNTAINS

Gran Chaco

Paraná R.

Iguazú Falls

30°S

Mt. Aconcagua 22,831 ft. (6,959 m)

Atacama Desert

Uruguay R.

Pampa

0 500 1,000 Miles

0 500 1,000 Kilometers

Valdés Peninsula (lowest point in S.A.) -131 ft. (-40 m)

N

Patagonia

Strait of Magellan

Tierra del Fuego

Falkland Islands

South Georgia

Cape Horn

Key

▲ Mountain peak

▼ Below sea level

— National border

150°W

120°W

90°W

60°W

30°W

RUSSIA

ARCTIC OCEAN

60°N

AK

Arctic Circle

160°E

40°N

180°

PACIFIC OCEAN

WA

OR

ID

NV

UT

CA

AZ

0   250   500 Miles

0   250   500 Kilometers

Key
★ National capital
— National border

20°N

HI

160°W

Tropic of Cancer

140°W

120°W

Greenland
(DENMARK)

CANADA

MT ND MN WI ME
SD VT
VY NE IA MI NY NH MA CT RI
CO KS IL IN OH PA NJ
MO WV DE MD DC
KY VA
NM OK AR TN NC
MS AL GA SC
TX LA
FL
ATLANTIC
OCEAN
Gulf of Mexico
N
MEXICO BAHAMAS
CUBA
HAITI DOM. REP.
JAMAICA

100°W 80°W

State or area	Abbreviation
Alabama	AL
Alaska	AK
Arizona	AZ
Arkansas	AR
California	CA
Colorado	CO
Connecticut	CT
Delaware	DE
District of Columbia	DC
Florida	FL
Georgia	GA
Hawaii	HI
Idaho	ID
Illinois	IL
Indiana	IN
Iowa	IA
Kansas	KS
Kentucky	KY
Louisiana	LA
Maine	ME
Maryland	MD
Massachusetts	MA
Michigan	MI
Minnesota	MN
Mississippi	MS
Missouri	MO
Montana	MT
Nebraska	NE
Nevada	NV
New Hampshire	NH
New Jersey	NJ
New Mexico	NM
New York	NY
North Carolina	NC
North Dakota	ND
Ohio	OH
Oklahoma	OK
Oregon	OR
Pennsylvania	PA
Rhode Island	RI
South Carolina	SC
South Dakota	SD
Tennessee	TN
Texas	TX
Utah	UT
Vermont	VT
Virginia	VA
Washington	WA
West Virginia	WV
Wisconsin	WI
Wyoming	WY

Atlas
Map of the United States: Political

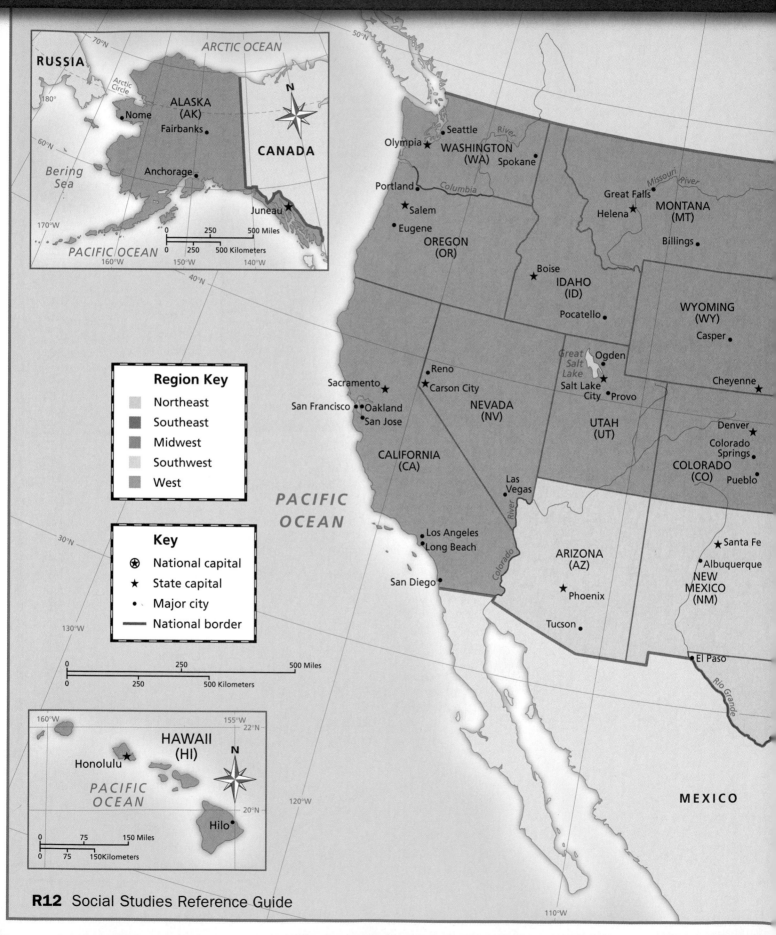

RUSSIA

ARCTIC OCEAN

70°N

180°

Arctic Circle

ALASKA (AK)

• Nome

Fairbanks •

CANADA

N

Anchorage •

60°N

Bering Sea

Juneau ★

170°W

PACIFIC OCEAN

0   250   500 Miles

0   250   500 Kilometers

160°W   150°W   140°W

40°N

50°N

River

• Seattle

Olympia ★   WASHINGTON (WA)

Spokane •

Portland •   Columbia

★ Salem

• Eugene

OREGON (OR)

Great Falls •

Missouri River

MONTANA (MT)

Helena ★

Billings •

Boise ★   IDAHO (ID)

Pocatello •

WYOMING (WY)

Casper •

Great Salt Lake

Ogden •

Reno •

Sacramento ★   ★ Carson City

Salt Lake City   • Provo

Cheyenne ★

San Francisco • • Oakland

• San Jose

NEVADA (NV)

UTAH (UT)

Denver ★

Colorado Springs •

CALIFORNIA (CA)

COLORADO (CO)   Pueblo •

Region Key

Northeast

Southeast

Midwest

Southwest

West

Las Vegas •

Colorado River

Los Angeles •
Long Beach •

Santa Fe ★

Key

⊛ National capital

★ State capital

• Major city

— National border

PACIFIC OCEAN

San Diego •

ARIZONA (AZ)

• Albuquerque

NEW MEXICO (NM)

★ Phoenix

30°N

Tucson •

El Paso •

Rio Grande

130°W

250   500 Miles
0

0   250   500 Kilometers

160°W

155°W

22°N

HAWAII (HI)

N

Honolulu ★

PACIFIC OCEAN

120°W

20°N

Hilo •

0   75   150 Miles

0   75   150 Kilometers

MEXICO

110°W

CANADA

NORTH DAKOTA
(ND)
Grand
Forks
Bismarck
Fargo

SOUTH DAKOTA
(SD)
Pierre
Sioux
Falls

NEBRASKA
(NE)
Omaha
Lincoln

Kansas
City
Topeka
KANSAS
(KS)
Wichita

Tulsa
Oklahoma
City
OKLAHOMA
(OK)
Fort
Smith

Fort
Worth   Dallas

TEXAS
(TX)
Austin

San
Antonio   Houston

Laredo
Corpus
Christi

Duluth

MINNESOTA
(MN)
Minneapolis   St. Paul
Missouri
River

Green
Bay
WISCONSIN
(WI)
Madison
Milwaukee
Rockford
Chicago

IOWA
(IA)
Cedar
Rapids
Davenport
Des
Moines
Peoria
Springfield
ILLINOIS
(IL)
St.
Louis
Jefferson
City
Kansas
City
MISSOURI
(MO)
Evansville

ARKANSAS
(AR)
Little
Rock
Memphis

Shreveport
Jackson
LOUISIANA
(LA)
MISSISSIPPI
(MS)
Baton Rouge
New Orleans
Biloxi

Lake Superior

Lake Michigan

MICHIGAN
(MI)
Lansing
Grand
Rapids
Detroit
Gary
Fort
Wayne
INDIANA
(IN)
Indianapolis
Cincinnati
Ohio
River

KENTUCKY
(KY)
Louisville
Frankfort

Columbus
OHIO
(OH)
Toledo
Cleveland
Wheeling
Pittsburgh

Lake Huron

Lake Erie

Lake Ontario

Buffalo

NEW YORK
(NY)
Albany
Hartford

Newark
New York
Trenton
Harrisburg
PENNSYLVANIA
(PA)
Philadelphia
Baltimore
Dover
Annapolis
Washington, D.C.

NEW HAMPSHIRE (NH)
VERMONT (VT)
Burlington
Montpelier
Concord

MAINE
(ME)
Augusta
Portland

MASSACHUSETTS
(MA)
Boston
Providence
RHODE ISLAND
(RI)
CONNECTICUT
(CT)
NEW JERSEY (NJ)
DELAWARE (DE)
MARYLAND (MD)

WEST
VIRGINIA
(WV)
Charleston
VIRGINIA
(VA)
Richmond
Norfolk

TENNESSEE
(TN)
Nashville
Knoxville

Raleigh
NORTH CAROLINA
(NC)
Charlotte

Birmingham
ALABAMA
(AL)
Montgomery
GEORGIA
(GA)
Atlanta
Columbus

Columbia
SOUTH
CAROLINA
(SC)
Charleston
Savannah

Mobile
Tallahassee
Jacksonville

FLORIDA
(FL)
Tampa
Miami

Gulf of Mexico

ATLANTIC
OCEAN

BAHAMAS

N

50°N
40°N
70°W
30°N
80°W
100°W
90°W

R13

Atlas
Map of the United States: Physical

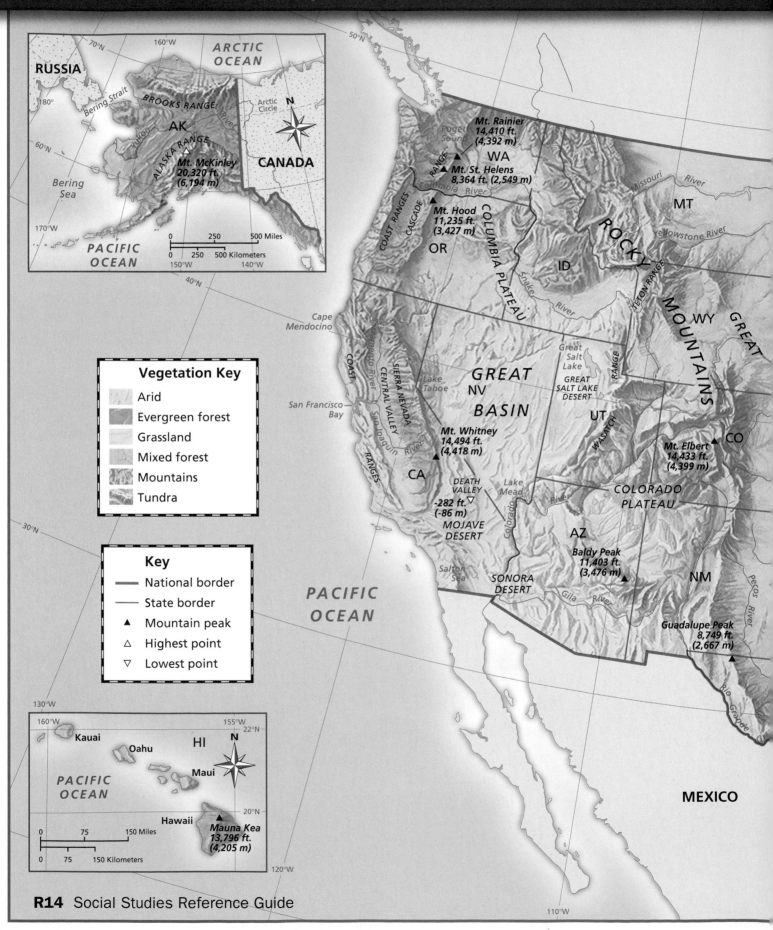

ARCTIC OCEAN

RUSSIA

70°N
160°W

180°

Bering Strait

BROOKS RANGE

AK

ALASKA RANGE

Yukon River

Mt. McKinley
20,320 ft.
(6,194 m)

Bering Sea

60°N

170°W

PACIFIC OCEAN

Arctic Circle

N

CANADA

0   250   500 Miles
0   250   500 Kilometers

150°W   140°W

40°N

Vegetation Key
- Arid
- Evergreen forest
- Grassland
- Mixed forest
- Mountains
- Tundra

30°N

Key
- National border
- State border
- ▲ Mountain peak
- △ Highest point
- ▽ Lowest point

130°W

160°W   155°W

Kauai

Oahu

HI   N

22°N

Maui

PACIFIC OCEAN

Hawaii

Mauna Kea
13,796 ft.
(4,205 m)

20°N

0   75   150 Miles
0   75   150 Kilometers

120°W

50°N

Mt. Rainier
14,410 ft.
(4,392 m)

WA

CASCADE RANGE

Puget Sound

Mt. St. Helens
8,364 ft. (2,549 m)

COAST RANGES

Mt. Hood
11,235 ft.
(3,427 m)

OR

Columbia River

COLUMBIA PLATEAU

Snake River

ID

MT

Missouri River

Yellowstone River

ROCKY MOUNTAINS

TETON RANGE

WY

GREAT

RANGE

Great Salt Lake

GREAT SALT LAKE DESERT

Cape Mendocino

COAST RANGES

Sacramento River

SIERRA NEVADA

CENTRAL VALLEY

San Joaquin River

Lake Tahoe

GREAT

NV

BASIN

UT

WASATCH

Mt. Elbert
14,433 ft.
(4,399 m)

CO

San Francisco Bay

Mt. Whitney
14,494 ft.
(4,418 m)

CA

DEATH VALLEY

-282 ft. ▽
(-86 m)

MOJAVE DESERT

Lake Mead

Colorado River

COLORADO PLATEAU

AZ

Baldy Peak
11,403 ft.
(3,476 m)

NM

Salton Sea

SONORA DESERT

Gila River

Guadalupe Peak
8,749 ft.
(2,667 m)

Pecos River

PACIFIC OCEAN

Rio Grande

MEXICO

110°W

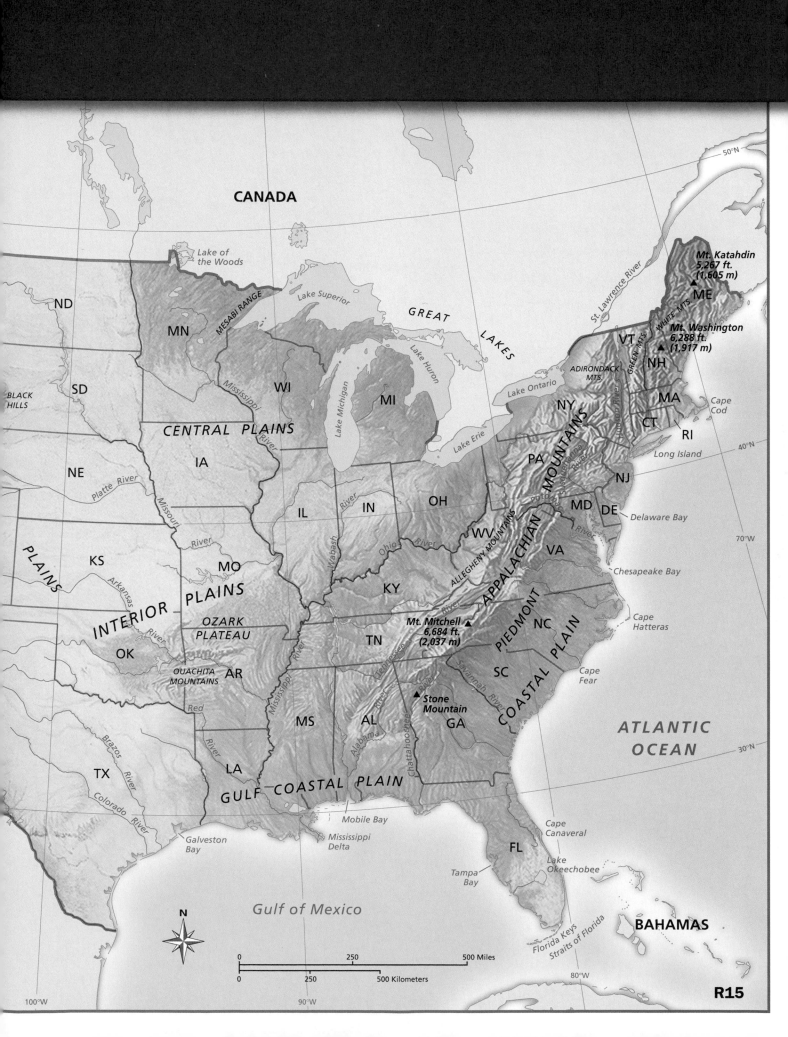

CANADA

Lake of
the Woods

ND

MN

MESABI RANGE

Lake Superior

GREAT

LAKES

St. Lawrence River

50°N

Mt. Katahdin
5,267 ft.
(1,605 m)

ME

Mt. Washington
6,288 ft.
(1,917 m)

BLACK
HILLS

SD

WI

Lake Michigan

Lake Huron

MI

VT

GREEN MTS.

WHITE MTS.

NH

CENTRAL PLAINS

Mississippi River

ADIRONDACK
MTS.

Lake Ontario

NY

Hudson River

MA

Cape
Cod

NE

IA

Platte River

IL

Wabash River

IN

OH

Lake Erie

PA

CT

RI

40°N

Long Island

Missouri River

Susquehanna River

NJ

70°W

KS

Arkansas River

MO

PLAINS

KY

Ohio River

WV

APPALACHIAN MOUNTAINS

ALLEGHENY MOUNTAINS

Potomac River

MD

DE

Delaware Bay

VA

Chesapeake Bay

INTERIOR PLAINS

OZARK
PLATEAU

Mt. Mitchell
6,684 ft.
(2,037 m)

TN

Tennessee River

PIEDMONT

NC

COASTAL PLAIN

Cape
Hatteras

OK

OUACHITA
MOUNTAINS

AR

Mississippi River

SC

Savannah River

Cape
Fear

Red River

Stone
Mountain

GA

TX

Brazos River

MS

AL

Alabama River

Chattahoochee River

LA

Colorado River

GULF COASTAL PLAIN

30°N

Galveston
Bay

Mobile Bay

Mississippi
Delta

Cape
Canaveral

FL

Lake
Okeechobee

ATLANTIC
OCEAN

Tampa
Bay

Gulf of Mexico

BAHAMAS

N

Florida Keys

Straits of Florida

100°W

90°W

80°W

0   250   500 Miles

0   250   500 Kilometers

R15

Geography Terms

basin bowl-shaped area of land surrounded by higher land

bay narrower part of an ocean or lake that cuts into land

canal narrow waterway dug across land mainly for ship travel

canyon steep, narrow valley with high sides

cliff steep wall of rock or earth, sometimes called a bluff

coast land at the edge of a large body of water such as an ocean

coastal plain area of flat land along an ocean or sea

delta triangle-shaped area of land at the mouth of a river

desert very dry, barren land without trees

fall line area along which rivers form waterfalls or rapids as the rivers drop to lower land

forest large area of land where many trees grow

glacier giant sheet of ice that moves very slowly across land

gulf body of water, smaller than a bay, with land around part of it

harbor sheltered body of water where ships safely tie up to land

hill rounded land higher than the land around it

island land with water all around it

lake large body of water with land all or nearly all around it

mesa flat-topped hill, with steep sides

mountain a very tall hill; highest land on Earth

mountain range long row of mountains

mouth place where a river empties into another body of water

ocean any of the four largest bodies of water on Earth

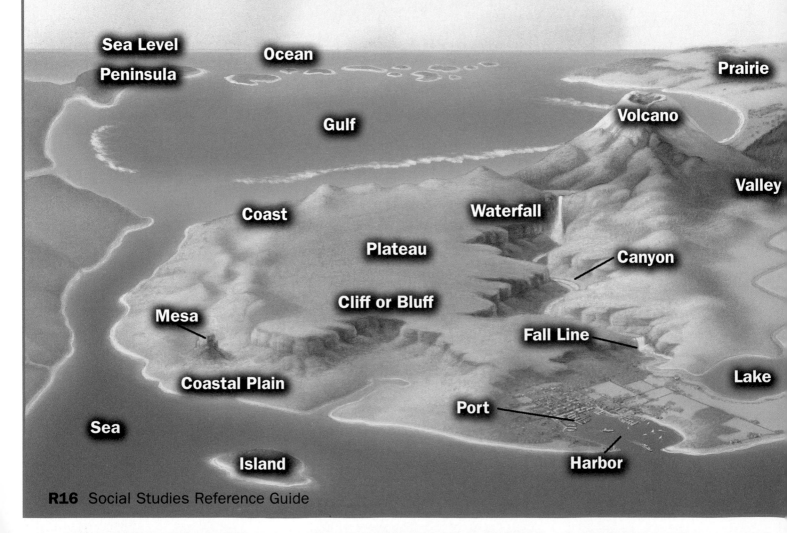

peak pointed top of a mountain

peninsula land with water on three sides

plain very large area of flat land

plateau high, wide area of flat land, with steep sides

port place, usually in a harbor, where ships safely load and unload goods and people

prairie large area of flat land, with few or no trees, similar to a plain

river large stream of water leading to a lake, other river, or ocean

riverbank land at a river's edge

sea large body of water somewhat smaller than an ocean

sea level an ocean's surface, compared to which land can be measured either above or below

slope side of a mountain or hill

source place where a river begins

swamp very shallow water covering low land filled with trees and other plants

tributary stream or river that runs into a larger river

valley low land between mountains or hills

volcano mountain with an opening at the top, formed by violent bursts of steam and hot rock

waterfall steep falling of water from a higher to a lower place

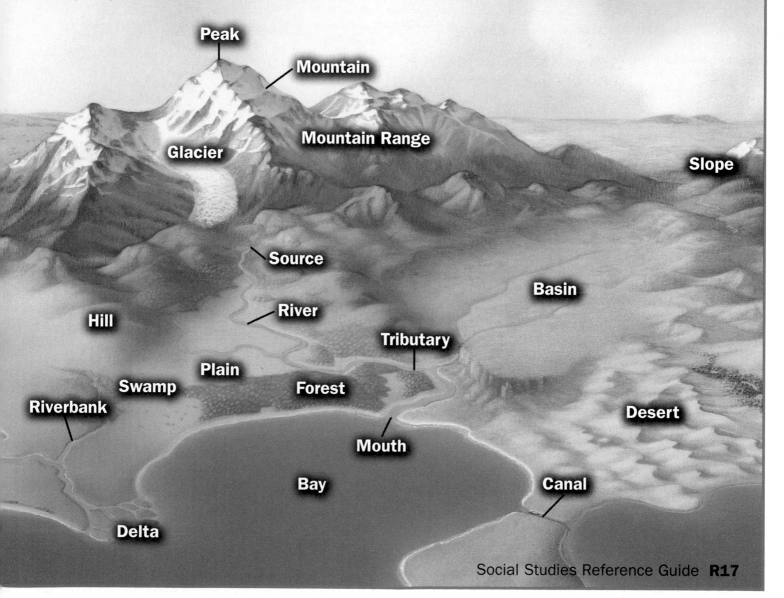

Facts About Our Fifty States

	AL Alabama	**AK** Alaska	**AZ** Arizona	**AR** Arkansas	**CA** California	**CO** Colorado
Capital	Montgomery	Juneau	Phoenix	Little Rock	Sacramento	Denver
Date and order of statehood	1819 (22)	1959 (49)	1912 (48)	1836 (25)	1850 (31)	1876 (38)
Nickname	Heart of Dixie	The Last Frontier	Grand Canyon State	Land of Opportunity	Golden State	Centennial State
Population	4,447,100	626,932	5,130,632	2,673,400	33,871,648	4,301,261
Square miles and rank in area	50,750 (28)	570,374 (1)	114,000 (6)	52,075 (27)	155,973 (3)	103,730 (8)
Region	Southeast	North	Southwest	Southeast	West	West

	IN Indiana	**IA** Iowa	**KS** Kansas	**KY** Kentucky	**LA** Louisiana	**ME** Maine
Capital	Indianapolis	Des Moines	Topeka	Frankfort	Baton Rouge	Augusta
Date and order of statehood	1816 (19)	1846 (29)	1861 (34)	1792 (15)	1812 (18)	1820 (23)
Nickname	Hoosier State	Hawkeye State	Sunflower State	Bluegrass State	Pelican State	Pine Tree State
Population	6,080,485	2,926,324	2,688,418	4,041,769	4,468,976	1,274,923
Square miles and rank in area	35,870 (38)	55,875 (23)	81,823 (13)	39,732 (36)	43,566 (33)	30,865 (39)
Region	Midwest	Midwest	Midwest	Southeast	Southeast	Northeast

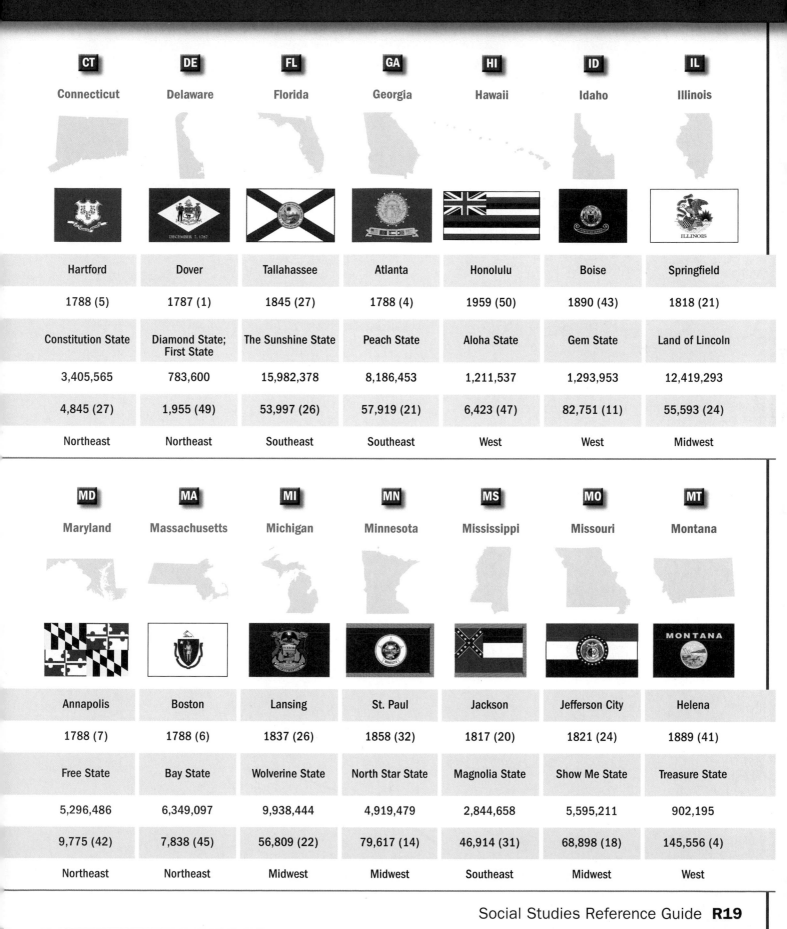

	CT	DE	FL	GA	HI	ID	IL
	Connecticut	Delaware	Florida	Georgia	Hawaii	Idaho	Illinois
Capital	Hartford	Dover	Tallahassee	Atlanta	Honolulu	Boise	Springfield
Statehood	1788 (5)	1787 (1)	1845 (27)	1788 (4)	1959 (50)	1890 (43)	1818 (21)
Nickname	Constitution State	Diamond State; First State	The Sunshine State	Peach State	Aloha State	Gem State	Land of Lincoln
Population	3,405,565	783,600	15,982,378	8,186,453	1,211,537	1,293,953	12,419,293
Area	4,845 (27)	1,955 (49)	53,997 (26)	57,919 (21)	6,423 (47)	82,751 (11)	55,593 (24)
Region	Northeast	Northeast	Southeast	Southeast	West	West	Midwest

	MD	MA	MI	MN	MS	MO	MT
	Maryland	Massachusetts	Michigan	Minnesota	Mississippi	Missouri	Montana
Capital	Annapolis	Boston	Lansing	St. Paul	Jackson	Jefferson City	Helena
Statehood	1788 (7)	1788 (6)	1837 (26)	1858 (32)	1817 (20)	1821 (24)	1889 (41)
Nickname	Free State	Bay State	Wolverine State	North Star State	Magnolia State	Show Me State	Treasure State
Population	5,296,486	6,349,097	9,938,444	4,919,479	2,844,658	5,595,211	902,195
Area	9,775 (42)	7,838 (45)	56,809 (22)	79,617 (14)	46,914 (31)	68,898 (18)	145,556 (4)
Region	Northeast	Northeast	Midwest	Midwest	Southeast	Midwest	West

Facts About Our Fifty States

	NE Nebraska	NV Nevada	NH New Hampshire	NJ New Jersey	NM New Mexico	NY New York
Capital	Lincoln	Carson City	Concord	Trenton	Santa Fe	Albany
Date and order of statehood	1867 (37)	1864 (36)	1788 (9)	1787 (3)	1912 (47)	1788 (11)
Nickname	Cornhusker State	Silver State	Granite State	Garden State	Land of Enchantment	Empire State
Population	1,711,263	1,998,257	1,235,786	8,414,350	1,819,046	18,976,457
Square miles and rank in area	76,644 (15)	109,806 (7)	8,969 (44)	7,419 (46)	121,365 (5)	47,224 (30)
Region	Midwest	West	Northeast	Northeast	Southwest	Northeast

	SC South Carolina	SD South Dakota	TN Tennessee	TX Texas	UT Utah	VT Vermont
Capital	Columbia	Pierre	Nashville	Austin	Salt Lake City	Montpelier
Date and order of statehood	1788 (8)	1889 (40)	1796 (16)	1845 (28)	1896 (45)	1791 (14)
Nickname	Palmetto State	Mount Rushmore State	Volunteer State	Lone Star State	Beehive State	Green Mountain State
Population	4,012,012	754,844	5,689,283	20,851,820	2,233,169	608,827
Square miles and rank in area	30,111 (40)	75,898 (16)	41,220 (34)	261,914 (2)	82,168 (12)	9,249 (43)
Region	Southeast	Midwest	Southeast	Southwest	West	Northeast

NC	ND	OH	OK	OR	PA	RI
North Carolina	North Dakota	Ohio	Oklahoma	Oregon	Pennsylvania	Rhode Island
Raleigh	Bismarck	Columbus	Oklahoma City	Salem	Harrisburg	Providence
1789 (12)	1889 (39)	1803 (17)	1907 (46)	1859 (33)	1787 (2)	1790 (13)
Tar Heel State	Sioux State	Buckeye State	Sooner State	Beaver State	Keystone State	Ocean State
8,049,313	642,200	11,353,140	3,450,654	3,421,399	12,281,054	1,048,319
48,718 (29)	68,994 (17)	40,953 (35)	68,679 (19)	96,003 (10)	44,820 (32)	1,045 (50)
Southeast	Midwest	Midwest	Southwest	West	Northeast	Northeast

VA	WA	WV	WI	WY
Virginia	Washington	West Virginia	Wisconsin	Wyoming
Richmond	Olympia	Charleston	Madison	Cheyenne
1788 (10)	1889 (42)	1863 (35)	1848 (30)	1890 (44)
Old Dominion	Evergreen State	Mountain State	Badger State	Equality State
7,078,515	5,894,121	1,808,344	5,363,675	479,602
39,598 (37)	66,582 (20)	24,087 (41)	54,314 (25)	97,105 (9)
Southeast	West	Southeast	Midwest	West

Atlas
Indiana Physical

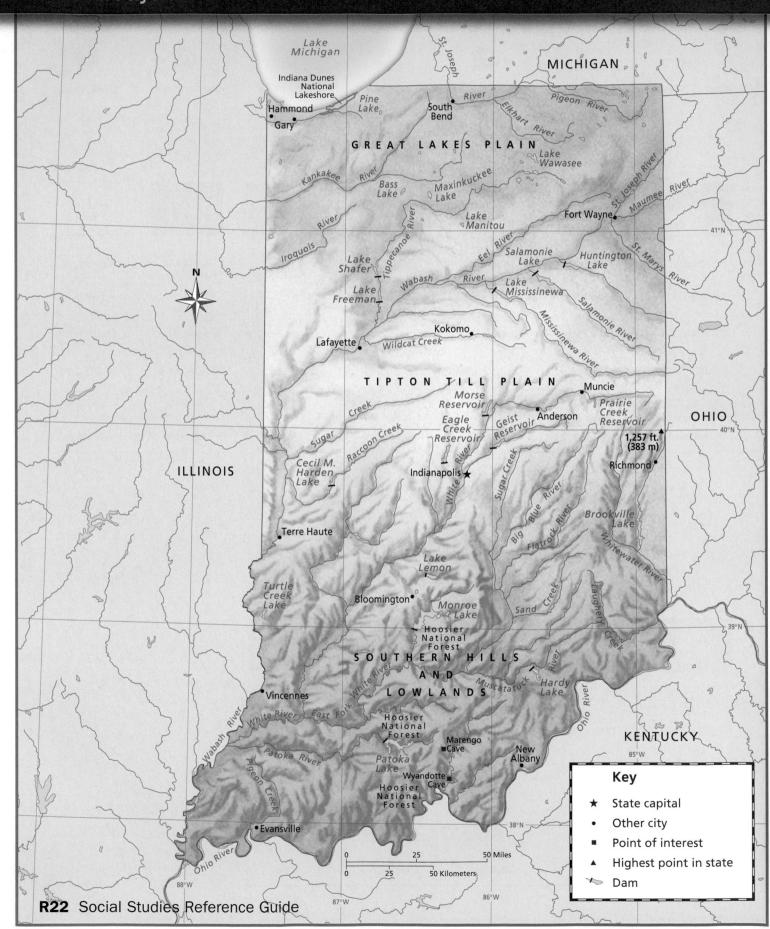

Lake Michigan

MICHIGAN

Indiana Dunes National Lakeshore

Pine Lake

Hammond

Gary

St. Joseph River

South Bend

Pigeon River

Elkhart River

GREAT LAKES PLAIN

Lake Wawasee

Kankakee River

Bass Lake

Maxinkuckee Lake

Lake Manitou

Fort Wayne

St. Joseph River

Maumee River

Iroquois River

Lake Shafer

Tippecanoe River

Eel River

Salamonie Lake

Huntington Lake

St. Marys River

41°N

N

Lake Freeman

Wabash River

Lake Mississinewa

Salamonie River

Lafayette

Kokomo

Wildcat Creek

Mississinewa River

TIPTON TILL PLAIN

Muncie

Morse Reservoir

Prairie Creek Reservoir

OHIO

Creek

Eagle Creek Reservoir

Geist Reservoir

Anderson

40°N

Sugar

Raccoon Creek

1,257 ft. (383 m)

Cecil M. Harden Lake

ILLINOIS

White River

Indianapolis ★

Richmond

Sugar Creek

Big Blue River

Brookville Lake

Terre Haute

Flatrock River

Whitewater River

Lake Lemon

Turtle Creek Lake

Bloomington

Monroe Lake

Sand Creek

Laughery Creek

Hoosier National Forest

SOUTHERN HILLS

River

39°N

White River

AND

Muscatatuck

Hardy Lake

Vincennes

East Fork White River

LOWLANDS

Ohio River

KENTUCKY

Wabash River

White River

Hoosier National Forest

Marengo Cave

New Albany

85°W

Patoka River

Patoka Lake

Wyandotte Cave

Pigeon Creek

Hoosier National Forest

38°N

Evansville

Ohio River

88°W

87°W

86°W

0   25   50 Miles

0   25   50 Kilometers

Key
★ State capital
● Other city
■ Point of interest
▲ Highest point in state
🝖 Dam

Indiana Road Map

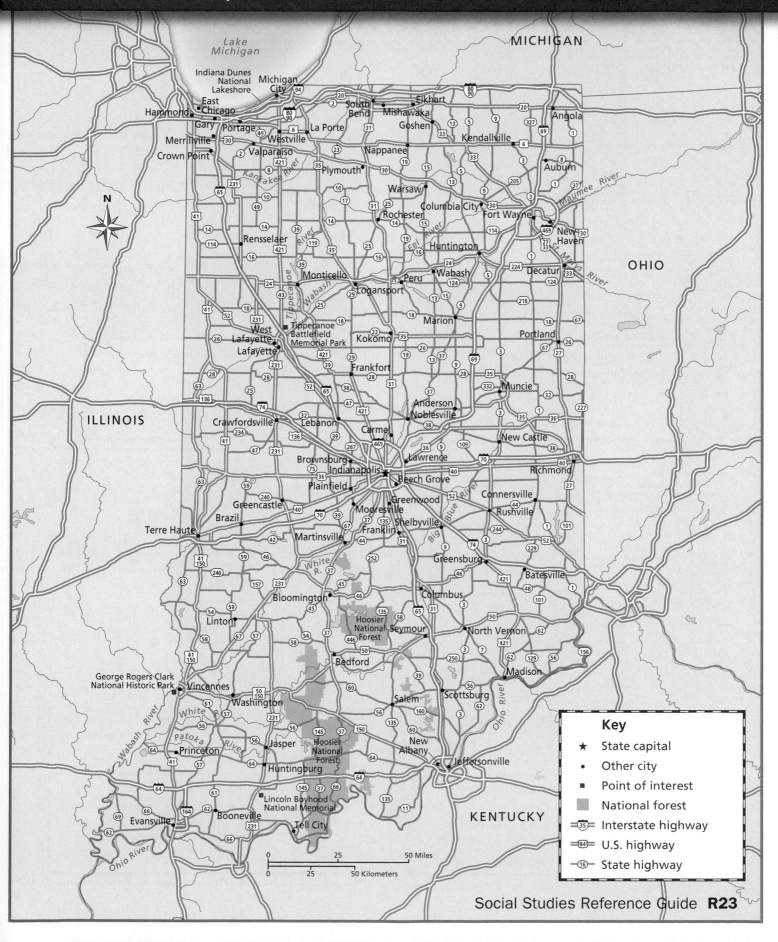

MICHIGAN

Lake Michigan

Indiana Dunes National Lakeshore
Michigan City
East Chicago
Hammond
Gary Portage
Merrillville Westville
Crown Point
Valparaiso

OHIO

South Bend
Mishawaka
Goshen
Elkhart
Angola
Kendallville
Auburn
New Haven
Fort Wayne
Columbia City
Warsaw
Rochester
Huntington
Peru
Wabash
Marion
Decatur
Portland
Muncie
Nappanee
Plymouth
La Porte
Rensselaer
Monticello
Logansport
Kokomo
West Lafayette
Lafayette
Frankfort
Anderson
Noblesville
New Castle
Tippecanoe Battlefield Memorial Park
Crawfordsville
Lebanon
Carmel
Lawrence
Richmond
Brownsburg
Indianapolis
Beech Grove
Plainfield
Greenwood
Connersville
Greencastle
Mooresville
Shelbyville
Rushville
Brazil
Franklin
Greensburg
Batesville
Terre Haute
Martinsville
ILLINOIS
Bloomington
Columbus
Linton
Hoosier National Forest
Seymour
North Vernon
Bedford
Madison
George Rogers Clark National Historic Park
Vincennes
Salem
Scottsburg
Washington
Jasper
Hoosier National Forest
New Albany
Princeton
Huntingburg
Jeffersonville
Lincoln Boyhood National Memorial
Booneville
Tell City
Evansville
Ohio River
KENTUCKY

Key
★ State capital
• Other city
■ Point of interest
▦ National forest
〓35 Interstate highway
〓84 U.S. highway
—16 State highway

0   25   50 Miles
0   25   50 Kilometers

Atlas
Indiana Temperature, Precipitation, and Population

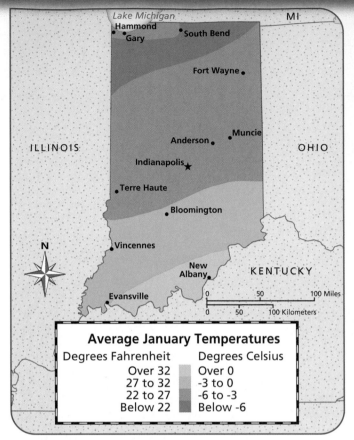

Average January Temperatures

Degrees Fahrenheit	Degrees Celsius
Over 32	Over 0
27 to 32	-3 to 0
22 to 27	-6 to -3
Below 22	Below -6

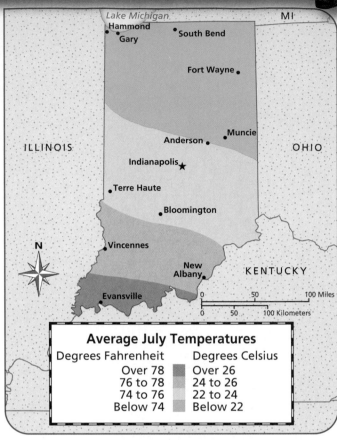

Average July Temperatures

Degrees Fahrenheit	Degrees Celsius
Over 78	Over 26
76 to 78	24 to 26
74 to 76	22 to 24
Below 74	Below 22

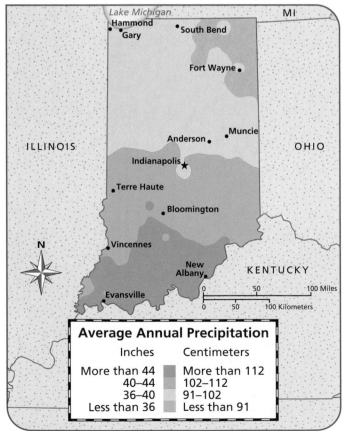

Average Annual Precipitation

Inches	Centimeters
More than 44	More than 112
40–44	102–112
36–40	91–102
Less than 36	Less than 91

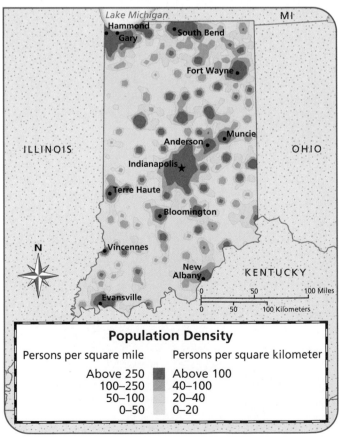

Population Density

Persons per square mile	Persons per square kilometer
Above 250	Above 100
100–250	40–100
50–100	20–40
0–50	0–20

Indiana Symbols

State Bird

Cardinal
Adopted in 1933

State Tree

Tulip Tree
Adopted in 1931

State Stone

Limestone
Adopted in 1971

State Flower

Peony
Adopted in 1957

State Flag

Adopted in 1917

State Seal

Adopted in 1963

State River

The Wabash River
Adopted in 1996

Indiana Time Line

About 1,000 years ago
Mississippian mound builders settle in Indiana.

1680
New groups of American Indians move into Indiana.

1800
The Indiana Territory is established.

1794
Anthony Wayne defeats the Miami at Fallen Timbers.

1779
George Rogers Clark captures Fort Sackville for the Americans.

1680	1700	1720	1740	1760	1780	1800

About 13,000 years ago
The first people arrive in Indiana.

1679
La Salle explores Indiana.

1763
Pontiac captures Fort Miami and Fort Ouiatenon.

1787
The Northwest Ordinance is passed.

1811
William Henry Harrison defeats the Shawnee in Battle of Tippecanoe.

1853
John Freeman is falsely arrested under the Fugitive Slave Act.

1836
The General Assembly passes the Internal Improvements Act.

1863
John Hunt Morgan leads Confederate raiders into Indiana.

1911
The first statewide high school boys' basketball tournament is held.

1968
Richard G. Hatcher is elected mayor of Gary.

1816
Indiana becomes the nineteenth state.

1941–1945
More than 300,000 Hoosiers serve in World War II.

1909
U.S. Steel opens its first works in Gary.

1995
Myra Selby becomes a justice on Indiana's Supreme Court.

1820	1840	1860	1880	1900	1920	1940	1960	1980	2000

1861
Governor Morton raises troops to fight for the Union in the Civil War.

1919
Steel strike begins in Gary.

1949
The General Assembly ends school segregation in Indiana.

1984
The first CD in the United States is made in Terre Haute.

1851
Indiana's present constitution is written and approved.

1886
The first gas wells are drilled in Indiana.

1910
Madam C. J. Walker opens her cosmetics business in Indianapolis.

1825
Robert Owen buys New Harmony.

2001
Helio Casteneves wins the Indianapolis 500 on its 90th anniversary.

Indiana Governors

Territorial Governors

William Henry Harrison
1800–1812

John Gibson
1800–1801, 1812–1813

Thomas Posey
1813–1816

Governors of the State of Indiana

Jonathan Jennings
1816–1822

Ratliff Boon
1822

William Hendricks
1822–1825

James Brown Ray
1825–1831

Noah Noble
1831–1837

David Wallace
1837–1840

Samuel Bigger
1840–1843

James Whitcomb (D)
1843–1848

Paris Chipman Dunning (D)
1848–1849

Joseph Albert Wright (D)
1849–1857

Ashbel Parsons Willard (D)
1857–1860

Abram Adams Hammond (D)
1860–1861

Henry Smith Lane (R)
January 14–16, 1861

Oliver Perry Morton (R)
1861–1867

Conrad Baker (R)
1867–1873

Thomas Andrews Hendricks (D)
1873–1877

James Douglas Williams (D)
1877–1880

Isaac Pusey Gray (D)
1880–1881

Albert Gallatin Porter (R)
1881–1885

Isaac Pusey Gray (D)
1885–1889

Alvin Peterson Hovey (R)
1889–1891

Ira Joy Chase (R)
1891–1893

Claude Matthews (D)
1893–1897

James Atwell Mount (R)
1897–1901

Winfield Taylor Durbin (R)
1901–1905

James Frank Hanly (R)
1905–1909

Thomas Riley Marshall (D)
1909–1913

Samuel Moffett Ralston (D)
1913–1917

James Putnam Goodrich (R)
1917–1921

Warren Terry McCray (R)
1921–1924

Emmett Forrest Branch (R)
1924–1925

Edward L. Jackson (R)
1925–1929

Harry Guyer Leslie (R)
1929–1933

Paul Vories McNutt (D)
1933–1937

Maurice Clifford Townsend (D)
1937–1941

Henry Frederick Schricker (D)
1941–1945

Ralph F. Gates (R)
1945–1949

Henry Frederick Schricker (D)
1949–1953

George N. Craig (R)
1953–1957

Harold W. Handley (R)
1957–1961

Matthew E. Welsh (D)
1961–1965

Roger D. Branigin (D)
1965–1969

Edgar D. Whitcomb (R)
1969–1973

Otis R. Bowen (R)
1973–1981

Robert D. Orr (R)
1981–1989

Evan Bayh (D)
1989–1997

Frank O'Bannon (D)
1997–present

(D) Democrat   **(R)** Republican

Gazetteer

This Gazetteer is a geographic dictionary that will help you locate and pronounce places in this book. It also gives latitude and longitude for many places. The page numbers tell you where each place appears on a map (m.) or in the text (t.).

Angel Mounds (ān′jəl moundz) remains near Evansville of a settlement of Mississippian people. Angel Mounds was built between 1100 and 1300, but it was abandoned by 1450; 38°N, 87°W. (m. 87, t. 88)

Appomattox Court House (ap′ə mat′əks kôrt hous) small town in northern Virginia on the Appomattox River. Site of Robert E. Lee's surrender in 1865; 37°N, 79°W. (m. 258, t. 260)

Bering Land Bridge (bir′ing land brij) a strip of land that allowed prehistoric peoples to migrate from Asia to North America. The land was exposed when the Ice Age froze oceans and sea levels dropped. (m. 81, t. 83)

Bering Strait (bir′ing strāt) a narrow body of water between Siberia and Alaska that separates the continents of Asia and North America. (m. 81, t. 83)

Bloomington (blü′ming tən) manufacturing, limestone, and university city in the Southern Hills and Lowlands region. Home of Indiana University; 39°N, 86°W. (m. 13, t. 49)

Brown County (broun koun′tē) southern Indiana county of farms, hills and covered bridges. In the 1890s its landscape attracted many artists. (m. 289, t. 310)

Cahokia (kə hō′kē ə) British fort on the Mississippi River in southwestern Illinois. Captured without a fight in 1778 by Col. George Rogers Clark; 38°N, 90°W. (m. 126, t. 126)

Calumet (kal′yə met) the densely populated Indiana shore of Lake Michigan. The region contains steel mills, pipelines, refineries, and shipping ports, as well as the Indiana Dunes. (m. 61, t. 61)

Chain O'Lakes State Park (chān ō lāks stāt pärk) area with eight small kettle lakes connected by small streams; 42°N, 86°W. (m. 31, t. 17)

Charlestown (chärlz′toun) southeastern Indiana community near Louisville, Kentucky, that became a boom town in World War II; 38°N, 86°W. (m. 315, t. 338)

Clarksville (klärks′vil) town on the Ohio founded in 1784 by soldiers who served with George Rogers Clark and received land there as a reward; 38°N, 86°W. (m. 151, t. 153)

Concord (kong′kərd) Massachusetts town west of Boston where British soldiers and American colonists fought in April 1775; 42°N, 71°W. (t. 124)

Corydon (kôr′ē dən) town that was Indiana's territorial capital from 1810 to 1816, and its first state capital from 1816 to 1822; 38°N, 86°W (m. 171, t. 173)

Evansville (ev′ənz vil) important business hub on the Ohio River in southwestern Indiana; 38°N, 88°W. (m. 13, t. 49)

Pronunciation Key

a in hat	ō in open	sh in she
ā in age	ȯ in saw	th in thin
ä in far	ô in order	ŦH in then
â in care	oi in oil	zh in measure
e in let	ou in out	ə = a in about
ē in equal	u in cup	ə = e in taken
ė in term	u̇ in put	ə = i in pencil
i in it	ü in rule	ə = o in lemon
ī in ice	ch in child	ə = u in circus
o in hot	ng in long	

Gazetteer

F

Fort Detroit (fôrt di troit′) fort on the Detroit River. Built by the French in 1701, it guarded the way from Lake Erie to the western Great Lakes. The British used it during the Revolution and the War of 1812 as a base for raids on the Ohio River Valley; 42°N, 83°W. (m. 125, t. 120)

Fort Miami (fôrt mī am′ē) French trading outpost built in 1750 near the Miami town of Kekionga, near present-day Fort Wayne; 41°N, 85°W. (m. 112, t. 112)

Fort Ouiatenon (fôrt wē′ ä tə non) French fur trading fort built in 1717 near present-day Lafayette in the Wea tribal homelands; 40°N, 86°W. (m. 112, t. 112)

Fort Sackville (fôrt sak′vil) British army outpost built in 1777 near Vincennes. George Rogers Clark's men captured the fort in 1779; 39°N, 87°W. (m. 125, t. 126)

Fort Sumter (fôrt sum′tər) an island fort in the harbor of Charleston, South Carolina. The shelling of the fort in 1861 marked the start of the Civil War; 32°N, 79°W. (m. 249, t. 253)

Fort Vincennes (fôrt vin senz′) French fur-trading fort built in 1732 on the lower Wabash River; 39°N, 87°W. (m. 112, t. 112)

Fort Wayne (fôrt wān) northeastern Indiana city located where the Maumee, St. Marys, and St. Joseph Rivers meet. Started as a French and later British colonial trading post. Named for General Anthony Wayne; 41°N, 85°W. (m. 13, t. 62)

Fountain City (foun′tən sit′ē) Indiana town later renamed Newport. Major stop for the Underground Railroad; 40°N, 87 W. (m. 242, t. 242)

G

Gary (gâr′ē) industrial city on Lake Michigan, founded in 1905; 42°N, 87°W. (m. 13, t. 62)

Gas Belt (gas belt) underground deposits of natural gas in central Indiana that were very productive in the 1880s. (t. 291)

Great Lakes Plain (grāt lāks plān) shoreline plain spanning northern Indiana. This region includes the Lake Michigan shoreline and hundreds of other glacial lakes and ponds. (m. 15, t. 15)

H

Hoosier National Forest (hü′zhər nash′ə nəl fôr′ist) protected woodland area in Orange County. (t. 40)

I

Indiana (in′dē an′ə) Midwestern state bordered by Ohio, Kentucky, Illinois, Lake Michigan, and Michigan. (m. 13, t. 11)

Indiana Dunes National Lakeshore (in′dē an′ə dünz nash′ə nəl lāk′shôr) recreation area created in 1966 to preserve the Lake Michigan shore; 42°N, 87°W. (t. 31)

Indiana Dunes State Park (in′dē an′ə dünz stāt pärk) area created in 1925 to preserve part of the Lake Michigan dunes; 42°N, 87°W. (m. 31, t. 31)

Indiana Territory (in′dē an′ə ter′ə tôr′ē) territory formed in 1800 when Congress divided Ohio from the rest of the Northwest Territory. William Henry Harrison was named governor, with his capital at Vincennes. (m. 173, t. 162)

Indianapolis (in′dē ə nap′ə lis) Indiana's capital and a hub for business, culture, and transportation; 40°N, 86°W. (m. 13, t. 54)

J

Jamestown (jāmz′toun) the first permanent English settlement in North America, built in 1607 on Virginia's James River; 37°N, 77°W. (t. 117)

Jug Rock (jug rok) a 60-foot-tall sandstone pillar that is a famous natural landmark in Martin County; 38°N, 86°W. (t. 50)

K

Kaskaskia (kas kas′kē ə) British fort on the Mississippi River in southwestern Illinois, captured by George Rogers Clark in 1778; 37°N, 89°W. (m. 126, t. 126)

Kekionga (kə kē ōn′gə) Miami Indian village and trading center on the Maumee River, at the site of today's Fort Wayne; 41°N, 85°W. (m. 118, t. 98)

Kokomo (kō′kō mō) central city north of Indianapolis. Site of Elwood Haynes's first automobile factory; 40°N, 86°W. (m. 53, t. 292)

Lafayette (lä′fē et′) city on the Wabash River that grew up around the French Fort Ouiatenon. Founded in 1825, it was an important stop on the Wabash and Erie Canal; 40°N, 87°W. (m. 13, t. 199)

Lake Michigan (lāk mish′ə gən) one of the Great Lakes. It provides a waterway for Indiana shippers through Canada to the Atlantic Ocean. (m. 13, t. 13)

Lake Wawasee (lāk wä wä′sē) largest of the glacial lakes in northern Indiana; 41°N, 86°W. (m. 15, t. 16)

Lexington (lek′sing tən) Massachusetts town west of Boston where the first shots of the Revolutionary War were fired in April 1775; 42°N, 71°W. (t. 124)

Madison (mad′ə sən) town on the Ohio River that became an important trading hub. It was the southern end of the Madison and Indianapolis Railroad, and the Michigan Road; 38°N, 85°W. (m. 13, t. 196)

McCormick's Creek State Park (mə kôr′miks krēk stāt pärk) park near Indianapolis created by conservationist Richard Lieber in 1916. (m. 31, t. 31)

Miamitown (mī am′ē toun) Miami Indian village on the Maumee River, near present-day Fort Wayne. Little Turtle defeated Gen. Harmer's troops there in 1790; 41°N, 85°W. (t. 159)

Milan (mi lan′) tiny rural town whose high school basketball team won the 1954 state basketball tournament; 39°N, 85°W. (m. 383, t. 393)

Mounds State Park (mounz stāt pärk) area west of Muncie that preserves ten ancient mounds; 40°N, 86°W. (m. 31, t. 87)

Muncie (mun′sē) Tipton Till Plain city on the White River. Muncie became an industrial center in the 1880s; 40°N, 85°W. (m. 13, t. 55)

New Albany (nü ȯl′bə nē) town southwest of Madison on the Ohio River that was an early trading and transportation center; 38°N, 86°W. (m. 13, t. 199)

New France (nü frans) early French settlements in North America on the St. Lawrence River in present-day Canada. (m. 105, t. 107)

New Harmony (nü här′mə nē) utopian town founded as Harmonie in 1814 by George Rapp. Robert Owen bought and renamed the town in 1825. 38°N, 88°W. (m. 171, t. 187)

Newport (nü′pôrt) originally called Fountain City, it served as a major stop for the Underground Railroad; 40°N, 87°W. (m. 231, t. 242)

Northwest Territory (nôrth′west′ ter′ə tôr′ē) land stretching north from the Ohio River to Canada, and west from Pennsylvania to the Mississippi River. Ohio, Michigan, Indiana, Illinois, and parts of Wisconsin and Minnesota were created from this territory. (m. 154, t. 155)

Philippi (fil lip′ī) West Virginia town where Indiana troops saw their first action of the Civil War in 1861; 39°N, 80°W. (m. 258, t. 258)

Pickawillany (pi kə wil′ə nē) Miami Indian fur trading village near present-day Piqua, Ohio. Settled in 1747 by Chief La Demoiselle to begin trade with the British; 40°N, 84°W. (m. 118, t. 118)

Pronunciation Key

a in hat	ō in open	sh in she
ā in age	ȯ in saw	th in thin
ä in far	ô in order	ᴛʜ in then
â in care	oi in oil	zh in measure
e in let	ou in out	ə = a in about
ē in equal	u in cup	ə = e in taken
ė in term	ù in put	ə = i in pencil
i in it	ü in rule	ə = o in lemon
ī in ice	ch in child	ə = u in circus
o in hot	ng in long	

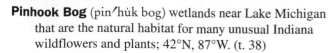

Gazetteer

Pinhook Bog (pin′hŭk bog) wetlands near Lake Michigan that are the natural habitat for many unusual Indiana wildflowers and plants; 42°N, 87°W. (t. 38)

Prophet's Town (prof′its toun) village of Tenskwatawa, near present-day Lafayette. Burned by Governor Harrison's forces after the Battle of Tippecanoe in 1811; 40°N, 87°W. (t. 162)

Purdue University (pėr dü′ yü′nə vėr′sə tē) land grant college founded in 1874 in West Lafayette; 40°N, 87°W. (t. 211)

Roanoke Island (rō′ə nōk ī′lənd) a North Carolina island located between Pamlico Sound and Albemarle Sound. Site of first English colony. (t. 117)

St. Mary's (sānt mâr′ēz) western Ohio town on the St. Mary's River. Site of the 1818 signing of the New Purchase; 40°N, 84°W. (t. 177)

Salem (sā′ləm) town north of Corydon. In 1863, Confederate Gen. John Hunt Morgan threatened to burn Salem's mills if he was not paid $1,000 for each building; 39°N, 86°W. (m. 249, t. 259)

South Bend (south bend) city on the St. Joseph River that is home to the University of Notre Dame; 41°N, 86°W. (m. 13, t. 62)

Southern Hills and Lowlands (suᴛʜ′ərn hilz and lō′ləndz) area of hills, knobs, and farms along Indiana's Ohio River border. (m. 15, t. 15)

Tipton Till Plain (tip′tən til plān) area of rolling land across central Indiana. Rich soil left by retreating glaciers makes this region the state's best farmland. (m. 15, t. 15)

Turkey Run State Park (tėr′kē run stāt pärk) woodlands northeast of Terre Haute created by the efforts of Hoosier conservationists Juliet Strauss and Richard Lieber; 40°N, 87°W. (m. 31, t. 31)

Vevay (və vā′) Switzerland County town founded by Swiss immigrants who planted vineyards there; 39°N, 85°W. (t. 178)

Vietnam (vē et′näm′) Southeast Asian nation that was the site of a war between the United States and local communist forces. (t. 344)

Vincennes (vin senz′) historic city on the Wabash River that grew up around a colonial French fort. Capital of the Indiana Territory from 1800 to 1810; 39°N, 87°W. (m. 13, t. 126)

Wabash (wȯ′bash) town northeast of Kokomo that was the first city in the world to be lighted by electricity when it installed four streetlights in 1880; 41°N, 86°W. (m. 289, t. 301)

Wabash Lowland (wȯ′bash lō′lənd) an area of rich, fertile farmland called "the Pocket" that borders the Wabash River in southwest Indiana. (t. 48)

Washington, D.C. (wäsh′ing tən dē sē) capital of the United States, located on the Potomac River between Maryland and Virginia; 39°N, 77°W. (m. 231, t. 233)

West Lafayette (west lä′fē et′) Wabash River town that is the home of Purdue University; 40°N, 87°W. (t. 211)

Wyandotte Cave (wī′ən dot kāv) underground network containing 25 miles of passages in five levels. Prehistoric people may have lived there; 38°N, 86°W. (m. 14, t. 48)

Biographical Dictionary

This Biographical Dictionary tells you about the people in this book and how to pronounce their names. The page number tells where the person first appears in the text.

Ball Brothers (bȯl) Founders of a company that made glass jars for home food canning. They moved their factory to Muncie in 1887. (p. 291)

Bayh, Birch, Jr. (bī) (1928–) U.S. Senator for Indiana from 1963 until 1981. He ran unsuccessfully in 1976 for the Democratic presidential nomination. (p. 364)

Bayh, Evan (bī) (1955–) Political leader who has served as Indiana's secretary of state, governor, and U.S. senator. Son of Birch Bayh, Jr. (p. 366)

Bird, Larry (bėrd) (1956–) Basketball star with Indiana State University and the Boston Celtics, and former coach of the Indiana Pacers. (p. 394)

Blue Jacket (blü′jak ət) (1700s) Shawnee chief who led the fight against Gen. Anthony Wayne at the Battle of Fallen Timbers in 1794. (p. 160)

Carmichael, Hoagy (kär′mi kəl) (1899-1981) Pianist, singer, and songwriter who composed many popular songs of the 1930s and 1940s. (p. 402)

Carson, Julia (kär′sən) (1939–) First female African American elected to Congress from Indiana. She also served as Indiana's first female African American state senator. (p. 366)

Chapman, John (chap′mən) (1774–1845) Called "Johnny Appleseed," this Massachusetts native traveled through Indiana and the Ohio Valley planting seedlings to help settlers start apple orchards. (p. 27)

Chorao, Kay (shu rō) (1936–) Award-winning Indiana author and illustrator of children's books. (p. 401)

Clark, George Rogers (klärk) (1752–1818) Military leader during the Revolution. In 1778, Clark's troops captured British forts in the Northwest Territory. His victories helped the U.S. claim the region. (p. 126)

Coffin, Levi (kȯ′fən) (1798–1877) Along with his wife Catharine, served as "conductor" on Indiana's Underground Railroad. The Coffins helped more than 2,000 people escape to freedom. (p. 242)

Colfax, Schuyler (kol′fax) (1823–1885) Hoosier newspaper publisher and political leader who served as Ulysses S. Grant's vice president. (p. 308)

Davis, Jefferson (dā′vis) (1808–1889) First and only President of the Confederate States of America. (p. 252)

Dean, James (dēn) (1931–1955) Movie actor who portrayed restless teenagers. He starred in only three movies before dying in a car crash. (p. 402)

Debs, Eugene V. (debs) (1855–1926) Labor union organizer who started the Socialist Party of America in 1898. (p. 326)

Dreiser, Theodore (drī′zər) (1871–1945) Journalist and author who wrote about the struggles of immigrants and poor people trying to succeed in American business and culture. (p. 309)

Dresser, Paul (dres′ər) (1859–1906) Composer who became America's favorite songwriter in the 1890s. In 1897 he published "On the Banks of the Wabash, Far Away." (p. 16)

Fairbanks, Charles Warren (fâr′bangks) (1852–1918) Hoosier politician who served as Theodore Roosevelt's vice president from 1905 to 1909. Born in a log cabin, he became a lawyer and a powerful U.S. Senator. (p. 326)

Freeman, John (frē′mən) (1813-?) African American businessman in Indianapolis. He was wrongly arrested in 1853 as a fugitive slave. He was soon released, but he was so worried about his safety that he moved to Canada. (p. 233)

Pronunciation Key

a in hat	ō in open	sh in she
ā in age	ȯ in saw	th in thin
ä in far	ô in order	ᴛʜ in then
â in care	oi in oil	zh in measure
e in let	ou in out	ə = a in about
ē in equal	u in cup	ə = e in taken
ė in term	u̇ in put	ə = i in pencil
i in it	ü in rule	ə = o in lemon
ī in ice	ch in child	ə = u in circus
o in hot	ng in long	

Biographical Dictionary

George, Eliza E. (jôrj) (1808–1865) Civil War nurse who cared for wounded Union soldiers. She died from a fever she caught while nursing prisoners in North Carolina. (p. 257)

Grant, Ulysses S. (grant) (1822–1885) Commander of the Union armies that defeated the Confederates in the Civil War. He served as the 18th U.S. President from 1869 to 1877. (p. 260)

Grissom, Virgil "Gus" (gris′əm) (1926–1967) Second U.S. astronaut sent into space in 1961, and the first man ever to return to space in 1965. Grissom and two other astronauts died in 1967 when fire swept through their capsule on the launch pad. (p. 10)

Guthrie, Janet (guth′rē) (1938–) First woman to race in the Indianapolis 500. She drove in three Indy 500s from 1977 to 1979. (p. 391)

Hamilton, Henry (ham′əl tən) (1734?–1796) British colonial governor who paid American Indians to raid Northwest Territory settlers during the Revolution. In 1779, Hamilton surrendered Fort Vincennes to Col. George Rogers Clark. (p. 125)

Harper, Ida Husted (här′pər) (1851–1931) Indiana journalist and women's suffrage supporter. Her work helped win American women the right to vote. (p. 325)

Harrison, Benjamin (har′ə sən) (1833–1901) 23rd U.S. President, from 1889 to 1893. Grandson of William Henry Harrison, he outlawed unfair business practices and defended immigrants' rights. (p. 307)

Harrison, William Henry (har′ə sən) (1773–1841) Indiana Territory governor who defeated the Shawnee in 1811 at the Battle of Tippecanoe. In 1813 he defeated British and Indian forces at the Battle of the Thames in Canada. Elected 9th U.S. president in 1840. (p. 162)

Hatcher, Richard G. (hach′ər) (1933–) One of the first African Americans elected mayor of a major U.S. city. He served as mayor of Gary from 1968 to 1987. (p. 368)

Haynes, Elwood (hānz) (1857–1925) Indiana inventor who built and tested one of America's first automobiles near Kokomo in 1894. Haynes Automobile Company produced autos from 1898 to 1925. (p. 292)

Hennepin, Father Louis (hen′ə pin) (1626–1701?) European missionary who traveled with La Salle across the Great Lakes into present-day Illinois. He later explored the upper

Indiana, Robert (in′dē an′ə) (1928–) Indiana-born artist. His colorful work in the 1950s and 1960s was inspired by traffic signs, amusement machines, and advertising names. (p. 401)

Jackson, Michael (jak′sən) (1958–) Singer, songwriter, and dancer raised in Gary. (p. 402)

Jennings, Jonathan (jen′ingz) (1784–1834) Lawyer who helped make Indiana a state. He was the state's first governor from 1816 to 1822 and a congressman from 1822 to 1830. He also negotiated land purchases from American Indians. (p. 173)

Jolliet, Louis (jō′lī et) (1645–1700?) Explorer and mapmaker. In 1673, he traveled down the Mississippi with Father Marquette. (p. 110)

La Demoiselle, Chief (lä də mwä zel′) (?–1752) Miami leader who left the French near Fort Wayne to trade with the British in Ohio. In 1752, the French burned his new village. (p. 118)

La Salle, René-Robert Cavalier, Sieur de (lä säl) (1643–1687) French explorer who discovered and claimed territories in the Ohio, Illinois, and Mississippi River valleys for France. (p. 110)

Lee, Robert E. (lē) (1807–1870) Confederate general who commanded the Army of Northern Virginia. He defeated stronger Union armies, but finally surrendered at Appomattox Court House. (p. 260)

Letterman, David (let′ər mən) (1947–) Television comedian and talk-show host. (p. 403)

Lieber, Richard (lē′bər) (1869–1944) First director of Indiana's State Department of Conservation, from 1919 to 1933. Born in Germany, Lieber created state parks at McCormick's Creek, Turkey Run, and Indiana Dunes. (p. 31)

Lilly, Eli (lil′ē) (1838–1889) Druggist and Civil War colonel who founded Eli Lilly and Company in 1876. He wanted to make medicines based on scientific formulas that would replace dangerous potions. (p. 292)

Lincoln, Abraham (ling′kən) (1809–1865) 16th U.S. President who preserved the Union during the Civil War. He was assassinated in 1865. (p. 178)

Little Turtle (lit′l tėr′tl) (1752–1812) Miami chief who fought against Northwest Territory settlers. After losing the Battle of Fallen Timbers, Little Turtle signed a 1795 treaty giving Indian lands in Ohio, Illinois, Indiana, and Michigan to the United States. (p. 159)

Lugar, Richard (lü′gər) (1932–) Indiana U.S. Senator, first elected in 1976. As mayor of Indianapolis from 1968 to 1975, Lugar merged city and county governments in a plan called Unigov. (p. 364)

Marquette, Father Jacques (mär ket′) (1637–1675) French missionary to the Indians in Canada, the Great Lakes, and the Midwest. In 1673, he and Louis Jolliet traveled down the Mississippi River. (p. 110)

Marshall, Thomas R. (mär′shəl) (1854–1925) Lawyer and governor who served as Woodrow Wilson's vice president from 1913 to 1921. He supported the League of Nations but opposed women's suffrage. (p. 326)

Mellencamp, John (mel′ən kamp) (1951–) Singer and songwriter whose songs tell about small-town life and rural values. In 1985, he staged the first Farm Aid concert. (p. 402)

Menominee (mə nom′ə nē) (1800s) Potawatomi leader. He told President Andrew Jackson that he never signed an 1836 treaty giving up his tribal homelands. In 1838, his tribe was forced to march the Trail of Death to Kansas. (p. 186)

Mills, Caleb (milz) (1806–1879) Called "father of Indiana's public schools," Mills moved to Indiana in 1833 and began calling for state-supported public schools. (p. 205)

Montgomery, Wes (mont gum′ər ē) (1923–1968) Jazz guitarist and composer. One of America's most creative jazz musicians in the 1950s and 1960s. (p. 402)

Morgan, John Hunt (môr′gən) (1825–1864) Confederate cavalry leader who led a raid through southern Indiana and Ohio in 1863. Captured in Ohio, he later escaped to rejoin Southern forces. (p. 259)

Morton, Oliver P. (môr′tən) (1823–1877) Indiana governor during the Civil War. He rallied Hoosiers to support the Union war effort. (p. 255)

Naylor, Phyllis Reynolds (nā′lər) (1933–) Award-winning Hoosier author of children's books that examine emotional problems that young people face. (p. 401)

O'Bannon, Frank (ō bân′ən) (1930–) the 47th governor of Indiana, elected in 1996 and again in 2000. (p. 366)

Oliver, James (ol′iv ər) (1823–1908) Farm equipment manufacturer. From 1855 until the 1980s, his South Bend company produced millions of plows, planters, cultivators, harvesters, and tractors. (p. 292)

Owen, Robert (ō′ən) (1771–1858) British textile mill owner who became a utopian and preached socialism, communal living, and cooperative labor. He gathered a utopian group at New Harmony, Indiana. (p. 187)

Pauley, Jane (pȯl′ē) (1950–) TV personality and talk-show host, born in Indianapolis. (p. 403)

Pontiac (pon′tē ak) (1720–1769) Ottawa chief who tried to drive the British out of the Great Lakes region. (p. 120)

Porter, Cole (pôr′tər) (1891–1964) American composer and songwriter who created memorable songs for films, musicals, and popular performers. (p. 402)

Porter, Gene Stratton- (pôr′tər) (1863–1924) Popular Indiana nature writer, and one of America's best nature photographers. Her home "The Cabin in the Wildflower Woods" is now a state historic site. (p. 309)

Pyle, Ernie (pīl) (1900–1945) Popular journalist and a war correspondent in World War II. He was killed in the battle to capture Okinawa in 1945. (p. 339)

Rapp, George (rap) (1757–1847) German immigrant who led utopians called Rappites, or Harmonists. In 1814, they settled Harmonie in southern Indiana. In 1825, they sold the town to Robert Owen, who renamed it New Harmony. (p. 187)

Reynolds, Joseph J. (ren′əldz) (1822–1899) Union general from Indiana who commanded Indiana troops in Civil War battles in West Virginia, Tennessee, Georgia, Alabama, and Arkansas. (p. 255)

Riley, James Whitcomb (rīl′ē) (1849–1916) Popular poet of the late 1800s. He praised the Hoosier landscape and people in poems written in natural words and speaking voices. (p. 308)

Pronunciation Key

a in hat	o in open	sh in she
ā in age	ȯ in saw	th in thin
ä in far	ô in order	ᴛʜ in then
â in care	oi in oil	zh in measure
e in let	ou in out	ə = a in about
ē in equal	u in cup	ə = e in taken
ė in term	ů in put	ə = i in pencil
i in it	ü in rule	ə = o in lemon
ī in ice	ch in child	ə = u in circus
o in hot	ng in long	

Biographical Dictionary

Robertson, Oscar (rob′ərt sən) (1938–) Hoosier who became one of the top players in college and professional basketball. He is in the Basketball Hall of Fame. (p. 393)

Rockne, Knute (rok′nē) (1888–1931) Coach who built the University of Notre Dame's football teams into national college champions from 1919 to 1930. (p. 391)

Rudolph, Wilma (rü′dôlf) (1940–1994) Sprinter who became the first American woman to win three gold medals at a single Olympic Games in Rome, Italy, in 1960. (p. 391)

Selby, Myra (sel′bē) (1955–) first woman and first African American lawyer ever appointed to the Indiana Supreme Court. (p. 367)

Sheehan, Elizabeth "Bess" (shē′ən) (?-1968) Environmentalist who organized a movement to save the Indiana Dunes from destruction. Small donations, including schoolchildren's pennies, helped open Indiana Dunes State Park in 1925. (p. 31)

Spitz, Mark (spits) (1950–) Indiana University graduate and swimmer. In 1972 he became the first athlete to win seven gold medals in a single Olympic Games. (p. 391)

Steele, Theodore Clement (stēl) (1847–1926) Indiana landscape painter. After studying art in Europe, he bought a Brown County farm in 1907. His farm became a famous artists' colony. (p. 48)

Stevens, Curtis (stē′vənz) (1968–) Geographer who studied how Indiana's African American population became settled along old Underground Railroad routes. (p. 62)

Stowe, Harriet Beecher (stō) (1811–1896) Writer and abolitionist who wrote the anti-slavery novel *Uncle Tom's Cabin*. (p. 239)

Strauss, Juliet (strous) (1863–1918) Writer who led the fight to save an Indiana forest called Turkey Run. (p. 31)

Studebaker Brothers (stü′də bā′kər) Blacksmiths who became the world's largest maker of horse-drawn wagons. Their company later became a major American automobile maker from 1902 to 1963. (p. 62)

Tarkington, Booth (tär′king tən) (1869–1946) Indiana writer of novels and dramas set in the American Midwest. He was one of America's most popular writers in the early twentieth century. (p. 309)

Tecumseh (tə kum′sə) (1768–1813) Shawnee leader who organized American Indian groups against Northwest Territory settlers. He was killed at the Battle of the Thames in 1813. (p. 162)

Tenskwatawa (tensk wä tou′wä) (1775–1837) Tecumseh's brother, called "The Prophet." He taught people to give up white customs and goods and to drive out settlers. His forces were defeated at the Battle of Tippecanoe in 1811. (p. 162)

Tharp, Twyla (tharp) (1941–) Dancer and choreographer whose works express a bold, modern sense of movement. (p. 402)

Thomas, Mary (tom′əs) (1816–1888) Pioneering doctor who focused on women's healthcare and rights. In 1859 she presented the Indiana legislature with a petition asking for women's suffrage. (p. 373)

Tipton, John (tip′tun) (1786–1839) Militia general who fought under William Henry Harrison at the Battle of Tippecanoe. He later became an Indiana political leader (p. 163)

Vonnegut, Kurt, Jr. (vȯn′ə gət) (1922–) Indiana author whose dark, humorous tales show the complexity of twentieth-century life. (p. 401)

Walker, Sarah Breedlove (wȯ′kər) (1867–1919) Indianapolis businessperson who became wealthy selling hair products. She used her money to support education, cultural revival, and justice for African Americans. (p. 327)

Wayne, Anthony (wān) (1745–1796) Revolutionary War general and military commander who defeated Little Turtle at the Battle of Fallen Timbers in 1794. (p. 160)

West, Jessamyn (west) (1902–1984) Writer of stories and novels about her Indiana farm childhood and her pioneer Quaker ancestors. (p. 401)

Willkie, Wendell (wil′kē) (1892–1944) Hoosier who ran for U.S. President in 1940 against Franklin D. Roosevelt. (p. 337)

Wirt, William (wėrt) (1874–1938) Indiana educator who created the "Gary plan." It split school days between classroom study and recreation or job training activities. (p. 327)

Wooden, John (wu̇d′n) (1910–) A star basketball player at Purdue University and a hall-of-fame coach who guided UCLA to ten national championships. (p. 394)

Glossary

This glossary will help you understand and pronounce the terms and vocabulary words in this book. The page number tells you where the word first appears.

★ A ★

abolitionist (ab′ə lish′ə nist) a person who worked to end slavery (p. 239)

adapt (ə dapt′) to change or adjust ways of life to fit different conditions (p. 85)

ally (al′ī) a partner or supporter who pledges friendship and help (p. 119)

amend (ə mend′) to change laws, rules, or governing plans (p. 373)

archaeologist (är′kē ol′ə jist) scientist who studies civilizations of the past (p. 84)

articles (är′tə kəlz) stories in a newspaper or magazine (p. 333)

Article XIII (är′tə kəl thèr′tēn′) 1851 Indiana law that forbade African Americans from entering the state. Lawmakers wanted to keep out fugitive slaves and to stop the Underground Railroad. (p. 234)

artifact (är′tə fakt) a tool, weapon, or other object made by humans (p. 84)

Australian ballot (o′strā′lyən bal′ət) secret voting ballot adopted by Indiana in 1889 to make sure state elections were honest and fair (p. 307)

★ B ★

baby boom (bā′bē büm) fast population growth in the years after World War II (p. 385)

band (band) a small group of people who join together to live or work (p. 94)

bar graph (bär graf) a diagram that shows quantities by using vertical rectangles or strips of different lengths or heights. A bar graph often compares things by showing their sizes and numbers. (p. 156)

★ C ★

canal (kə nal′) a human-made waterway dug to carry small boats or ships (p. 196)

cede (sēd) to hand over or give up (p. 153)

civic virtue (siv′ik vèr′chü) a positive action or quality that shows a person's respect for the duties, rights, and privileges of citizenship (p. 374)

civility (sə vil′ə tē) polite, considerate behavior towards others (p. 375)

civil rights (siv′əl rīts) the basic rights guaranteed by law to all citizens (p. 343)

clan (klan) a group of related people or families that descend from a common ancestor. (p. 94)

climate (klī′mit) the type of weather an area has over a long period of time (p. 37)

Cold War (kōld wôr) the struggle for world leadership between communist and democratic nations from 1945 to 1989 (p. 344)

college (kol′ij) a school of higher learning or special training that gives degrees beyond high school diplomas (p. 206)

colonist (kol′ə nist) a person who settles a colony in a new land or territory (p. 95)

colony (kol′ə nē) a settlement of people in a new land or territory who remain loyal to their home nation (p. 108)

commercial district (kə mèr′shəl dis′trikt) an area where shops and businesses are located (p. 213)

commissioner (kə mish′ə nər) a member of a commission, or a government official (p. 233)

confederacy (kən fed′ər ə sē) a group of countries, states, or people united in a common cause (p. 94)

Pronunciation Key

a in hat	ō in open	sh in she
ā in age	ȯ in saw	th in thin
ä in far	ô in order	ᴛʜ in then
â in care	oi in oil	zh in measure
e in let	ou in out	ə = a in about
ē in equal	u in cup	ə = e in taken
ė in term	u̇ in put	ə = i in pencil
i in it	ü in rule	ə = o in lemon
ī in ice	ch in child	ə = u in circus
o in hot	ng in long	

Glossary

conservation (kon′sər vā′shən) carefully using, protecting, and preserving a natural resource or treasured possession (p. 29)

constitutional convention (kon′stə tü′shə nəl kən ven′shən) a meeting or assembly called together to create principles or laws that govern a nation, state, or social group (p. 173)

continent (kon′tə nənt) one of the seven great land masses on Earth (p. 12)

cross section (krȯs sek′shən) a picture or drawing of an object that shows one section cut away from the object (p. 304)

cultural group (kul′chər əl grüp) a group of people connected by a common language, religion, and culture (p. 88)

culture (kul′chər) the ways of living, social customs, and arts of a nation, a people, or a community (p. 88)

cutaway (kut′ə wā′) a diagram that allows you to see inside an object, to show how it is made and how parts fit together (p. 304)

Declaration of Independence (dek′lə rā′shən ov in′dē pen′dəns) a document officially declaring that the American colonies were breaking away from Great Britain to form a new nation (p. 124)

degree (di grē′) a unit of measure for temperature (p. 134)

demand (de mand′) the number of consumers willing and able to buy a product or service (p. 197)

democratic republic (dem′ə krat′ik ri pub′lik) a country where people elect representatives to pass laws and make governing decisions for them (p. 363)

desert (di zėrt′) to abandon one's military post, or to leave a home or settlement empty (p. 127)

discrimination (dis krim′ə nā′shən) the unfair treatment of people because of their race, gender, or beliefs (p. 343)

economy (i kon′ə mē) the business affairs of a country or region (p. 291)

editorial (ed′ə tôr′ē əl) an article in a newspaper or magazine in which a person expresses his or her opinion (p. 333)

elevation (el′ə vā′shən) the height of land above sea level (p. 20)

elevation map (el′ə vā′shən map) a map that shows the contours of the earth's surface, including the heights of hills and mountains (p. 20)

Emancipation Proclamation (i man′sə pā′shən prok′lə mā′shən) a declaration that granted freedom to slaves held in the Confederate states in 1863 (p. 256)

Enabling Act (en ā′bəl ing akt) act passed by Congress in 1816 giving the people of the Indiana Territory the right to write a constitution and become a state (p. 173)

enforce (en fôrs′) to make sure that people obey a law or regulation (p. 185)

enslaved (en slāv′d) held captive by another person and forced to work for that person (p. 233)

equator (i kwā′tər) imaginary line drawn around the middle of the Earth, halfway between the North and South Poles; it divides the globe into the Northern and Southern Hemispheres. (p. 11)

erosion (i rō′zhən) the slow wearing away of soil and stone by wind or water (p. 28)

executive branch (eg zek′ yə tiv branch) the branch of government in charge of carrying out laws (p. 174)

fact (fakt) something that can be proven to be true (p. 90)

Fifteenth Amendment (fif′tēnth′ ə mend′mənt) amendment to the U.S. Constitution that gave all male U.S. citizens the right to vote (p. 373)

front (frunt) where battles take place (p. 257)

fugitive slave (fyü′jə tiv slāv) a person who had fled from slavery (p. 185)

Fugitive Slave Act (fyü′jə tiv slāv akt) 1850 law requiring that all runaway slaves (even those in free states) be captured and returned to their owners. Anyone who helped runaway slaves broke this law. (p. 233)

General Assembly (jen′ər əl ə sem′blē) Indiana's state legislature (p. 366)

generalization (jen′ar ə lə zā′shən) a broad statement or rule which may prove to be true (p. 64)

glacier (glā′shər) a huge mass of ice and packed snow that moves very slowly across a land surface (p.15)

goods (gůdz) items that are for sale (p.212)

government (gov′ərn mənt) an organized system of leaders, delegates, or assemblies that controls a community or country (p.88)

Grange (grānj) a national organization founded in 1867 to improve the economic, political, and social position of American farmers (p. 211)

Great Depression (grāt di presh′ən) worldwide slowdown in business activity during the 1930s that left many people jobless, homeless, and hungry (p. 337)

habitat (hab′ə tat) natural home of a particular animal, insect, or plant (p. 40)

headlines (hed′līnz′) sentences or phrases printed in large type at the beginning of a newspaper article, to tell readers what the story's about (p. 333)

hemisphere (hem′ə sfir) halves of the globe, usually divided by the prime meridian or by the equator (p. 11)

home front (hōm frunt) citizens at home working to support a war effort (p. 338)

Hoosier Group (hü′zhər grüp) artists such as T. C. Steele, Otto Stark, and William Forsyth, who chose to live and paint in Indiana in the 1890s (p. 310)

hub (hub) a center of activity, or a crossroads for transportation routes (p. 49)

immigrate (im′ə grāt) to settle in a new or different country (p. 178)

income tax (in′kum′ taks) a tax placed on the money a person or a business earns (p. 367)

Indiana Legion (in′dē an′ə lē′jən) state militia during the Civil War. It was called into service by Governor Morton to defend Indiana against Confederate attacks. (p. 255)

industry (in′də strē) groups of businesses that produce or manufacture related goods or services or the organized work needed to design and produce things. (p. 213)

information resources (in′fər mā′shən ri sôrs′əs) books, newspapers, magazines, Web sites, and other sources for facts and information (p. 332)

inset map (in′set′ map) a small map within a larger map that shows a specific area in greater detail (p. 202)

Internal Improvements Act of 1836 (in tèr′nl im prüv′mənts akt) a law that allowed Indiana to borrow money for canals, railroads, and road improvements (p. 199)

Internet (in′tər net′) a worldwide network that links personal, government, cultural, and business computers (p. 332)

interurban line (in′tər èr′bən līn) streetcars or trolleys that carried people between communities in the late 1800s (p. 299)

Iroquois Confederacy (ir′ə kwoi kən fed′ər ə sē) united groups of American Indians in New York and Pennsylvania. They pushed other tribes west into the Ohio Valley and Indiana (p. 94)

judicial branch (jü dish′əl branch) the branch of government that interprets and enforces laws of the land (p. 174)

key word (kē′wèrd) words or phrases you enter into a search engine to locate certain Web sites (p. 333)

knob (nob) a rounded, cone-shaped hill or mountain (p. 48)

labor union (lā′bər yü′nyən) workers organized to protect their interests by dealing as a group with employers (p. 326)

Pronunciation Key

a in hat	ō in open	sh in she
ā in age	ȯ in saw	th in thin
ä in far	ô in order	ᴛʜ in then
â in care	oi in oil	zh in measure
e in let	ou in out	ə = a in about
ē in equal	u in cup	ə = e in taken
ė in term	ů in put	ə = i in pencil
i in it	ü in rule	ə = o in lemon
ī in ice	ch in child	ə = u in circus
o in hot	ng in long	

Glossary

landform (land′fôrm′) hills, plains, mountains, or other physical features of Earth's surface (p. 15)

land-grant colleges (land grant kol′ij/əs) state agricultural and technical schools created by the Land-Grant College Act of 1862. Congress gave each state 30,000 acres of land for each congressional representative. States sold this land to raise the money to start these colleges. (p. 211)

landmark (land′märk′) a landform or object that can easily be seen, identified, and used as a guide by travelers and navigators (p. 50)

latitude (lat′ə tüd) a grid of horizontal lines on maps that represents distance north or south of the equator (p. 134)

legislative branch (lej′ə slā′tiv branch) the branch of government that makes laws (p. 174)

line graphs (līn grafs) diagrams that compare information and show how it has changed over time (p. 156)

log on (log on) to make an Internet connection (p. 333)

longhouse (lông′hous′) a large rectangular dwelling used by the Iroquois and other North American Indian groups (p. 98)

longitude (lon′jə tüd) a grid of vertical lines on maps and globes that represents distance east or west of the prime meridian (p. 134)

Madison and Indianapolis Railroad (mad′ə sən and in′dē ə nap′ə lis rāl′rōd′) Indiana's first railroad line, started in 1836 (p. 197)

manufacture (man′yə fak′chər) to make products by hand or by machines (p. 195)

market (mär′kit) a place where buyers and sellers exchange goods and services (p. 55)

meridian (mə rid′ē ən) a line of longitude (p. 134)

Michigan Road (mish′ə gən rōd) an early nineteenth century road running from the Ohio River to Lake Michigan (p. 196)

migrate (mī′grāt) to move from one region to settle in another (p. 83)

monopoly (mə nop′ə lē) complete control over the manufacturing, trading, and pricing of a product or service; a company that has a monopoly has no competitors. (p. 293)

moraine (mə rān′) a mass of dirt and rocks, scraped up by a glacier, that remains after the glacier melts or retreats (p. 56)

mound (mound) a pile of earth, sand, and stone shaped to form a small hill; some American Indians in the Midwest and South built mounds as temples, tombs, or forts. (p. 87)

National Road (nash′ə nəl rōd) an early route that carried settlers west from Maryland to the Mississippi River (p. 196)

natural resource (nach′ər əl ri sôrs′) a material found in nature that people use (p. 25)

neutral (nü′trəl) not taking sides in a quarrel or a war (p. 165)

New Purchase (nü pėr′chəs) land in central Indiana given up by American Indians in the 1818 Treaty of St. Mary's (p. 177)

newspapers (nüz′pā′pərz) daily or weekly publications printed on folding sheets of paper. They contain stories, articles, and other useful information (p. 332)

Nineteenth Amendment (nīn′tēnth′ ə mend′mənt) the amendment to the U.S. Constitution, ratified in 1920, that gave women the right to vote (p. 325)

Northwest Ordinance of 1787 (nôrth′west′ ôrd′n əns) law directing how the Northwest Territory would be divided into states. It outlawed slavery in the region and gave religious freedom and civil rights to settlers. (p. 155)

notes (nōts) words or phrases written down as a way to help you remember important ideas (p. 188)

opinion (ə pin′yən) a belief that is not based on proof (p. 90)

ordinance (ôrd′n əns) a rule or law made by an authority (p. 154)

outlines (out′līnz) written plans that list and map out ideas and important points (p. 188)

parallel (par′ə lel) a line of latitude (p. 134)

pipeline (pīp′līn) a long system of pipes that carry oil or other products across great distances (p. 61)

pollute (pə lüt′) to harm Earth's land, air, or water by making it dirty (p. 28)

precipitation (pri sip′ə tā′shən) water that falls as rain, ice, hail, sleet, or snow (p. 37)

prehistoric (prē′hi stôr′ik) of a time before history was written or recorded (p. 84)

primary sources (prī′mer′ē sôrs′əs) information that comes from an eyewitness account or observation (p. 270)

prime meridian (prīm mə rid′ē ən) a line on maps running between the North and South Poles, marked zero degrees longitude, that divides east and west (p. 11)

proclamation (prok′lə mā′shən) an official public announcement made in a speech or document (p. 120)

productivity (prō′duk tiv′ə tē) the level of efficiency in the production of goods and services (p. 337)

profit (prof′it) revenues from selling a good or service, minus the costs of producing the good or service (p. 293)

public education (pub′lik ej′ə kā′shən) schooling paid for by state and local taxes (p. 205)

R

ration (rash′ən) to limit the available portions of food, fuel, or other substances that may be in short supply (p. 338)

reaper (rē′pər) a person or machine that cuts and harvests grain or crops (p. 267)

rebellion (ri bel′yən) an uprising or fight against a ruling government (p. 120)

regiment (rej′ə mənt) a military unit containing two or more battalions and about 1,000 soldiers (p. 256)

regulate (reg′yə lāt) to control by using rules, laws, principles, or standards (p. 293)

repeal (ri pēl′) to withdraw or cancel a law or a tax (p. 123)

representative (rep′ri zen′tə tiv) person chosen or elected to speak for others in an assembly or legislative body (p. 364)

road map (rōd map) a travel map showing streets and roads, distances between locations, landmarks, and other details (p. 236)

rural (rur′əl) located in or belonging to the countryside (p. 385)

S

sachem (sā′chəm) an American Indian leader (p. 98)

sales tax (sālz taks) money people pay to a government based on certain things they buy (p. 367)

scale (skāl) a unit of measure used to represent a real distance on Earth (p. 202)

search engine (sèrch en′jən) a software program that looks through the Internet for Web sites that contain topics or words you want to find (p. 333)

secede (si sēd′) to formally leave an organization or group (p. 251)

secondary sources (sek′ən der′ē sôrs′əs) accounts of an event written or told by people who were not there (p. 270)

segregate (seg′rə gā′t) to separate different races, classes, or ethnic groups, particularly in public schools, restaurants, and other facilities (p. 269)

senator (sen′ə tər) an elected representative in the upper body of the legislative branch of government; a member of a state or the U.S. Senate. (p. 364)

services (sèr′vis ez) useful work that is done for others (p. 212)

shale (shāl) a type of rock formed in thin layers from hard mud or clay at the bottom of ancient seas. Shale is very brittle and can easily be split into flat slabs. (p. 50)

silt (silt) very fine dirt particles carried in moving water which becomes fertile soil when left behind. (p. 48)

social group (sō′shəl grüp) people who share common goals and interests, often as organized groups that work or play together (p. 392)

socialist (sō′shə list) a person who believes that wealth should be owned by the community and shared equally among its members (p. 326)

state fair (stāt fâr) a yearly event where farmers and manufacturers can show their best livestock, produce, and products. Indiana's first state fair was held in 1852. (p. 211)

steel (stēl) a very strong but flexible metal formed by combining iron and carbon (p. 318)

steelworks (stēl wèrks) a mill for forging steel (p. 318)

Pronunciation Key

a in hat	ō in open	sh in she
ā in age	ȯ in saw	th in thin
ä in far	ô in order	ᴛʜ in then
â in care	oi in oil	zh in measure
e in let	ou in out	ə = a in about
ē in equal	u in cup	ə = e in taken
ė in term	u̇ in put	ə = i in pencil
i in it	ü in rule	ə = o in lemon
ī in ice	ch in child	ə = u in circus
o in hot	ng in long	

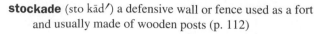
stockade (sto kād′) a defensive wall or fence used as a fort and usually made of wooden posts (p. 112)

strike (strīk) an organized refusal to stop work until certain demands are met (p. 336)

Studebaker Corporation (stüd′ə bā kər kôr′pə rā′shən) America's largest maker of horse-drawn wagons, started in 1852 in South Bend. It later became a major automobile maker. (p. 321)

suburb (sub′ėrb) a community on the outskirts of or nearby a city (p. 299)

suffrage (suf′rij) the right to vote (p. 325)

supply (sə plī′) what producers are willing and able to sell at various prices (p. 292)

Supreme Court (sə prēm′ kôrt) the highest authority in the judicial branch of government (p. 364)

surrender (sə ren′dər) to give up to another, such as to an opponent in a battle (p. 127)

swing state (swing stāt) in a national election, a state whose votes can win the election for either candidate (p. 307)

table of contents (tā′bəl ov kon′tents) an outline at the beginning of a book or magazine that lists the chapters, stories, or other information inside (p. 333)

technology (tek nol′ə jē) any tool, device, machine, or method based on scientific knowledge that controls objects or harnesses forces (p. 387)

temperate (tem′pər it) a climate in which the seasons are not too hot or cold (p. 37)

time line (tīm līn) a chart divided into equal units of time that shows a sequence of events (p. 378)

time zone (tīm zōn) one of the 24 regions into which Earth is divided for measuring standard time (p. 398)

time zone map (tīm zōn map) a map showing the boundaries between time zones (p. 398)

township (toun′ship) a surveyed part of a county with governmental powers; in Indiana, townships are divided into 36 one-mile squares containing 640 acres of land (p. 154)

trade (trād) the voluntary exchange of goods or services (p. 195)

Trail of Death (trāl ov deth) the forced march of the Potawatomi people from their northern Indiana homes west into Kansas in 1838 (p. 186)

Treaty of St. Mary's (trē′tē ov sānt mâr′ēz) the 1818 treaty in which American Indians gave up lands in central Indiana; also called the New Purchase (p. 177)

Twenty-eighth United States Colored Troop (twen′tē āth′yü nī′tid stāts kul′ərd trüp) Indiana's only African American regiment in the Civil War, formed in 1863 (p. 257)

Underground Railroad (un′dər ground′rāl′rōd) planned escape routes and hiding places to help people escape slavery and reach freedom in Canada (p. 240)

unemployment (un′em ploi′ment) being out of work or without a paid job (p. 337)

Unigov (yü′nə guv) a plan created in 1970 that combines the city of Indianapolis and Marion County under a "unified government" with a mayor and a Unigov council (p. 369)

university (yü′nə vėr′sə tē) a school of higher learning that contains several colleges and grants degrees in many different subjects (p. 206)

urban (ėr′bən) located in or belonging to a city (p. 385)

URL (yü ar əl) an Internet address (p. 333)

utopia (yü tō′pē ə) an ideal place to live and work, or the vision of a perfect society where everyone is happy (p. 187)

voyageur (vwä yä zhėr′) a French Canadian who traveled far into North America to trade for furs with American Indians (p. 108)

Wabash and Erie Canal (wȯ′bash and ir′ē kə nal′) 468-mile-long waterway begun at Fort Wayne in 1832. By 1853, it was America's longest canal system, linking Lake Erie with the Ohio River. (p. 196)

war hawk (wôr hȯk) settlers who wanted the U.S. to drive the British and their allies out of the Northwest Territory; their demands helped trigger the War of 1812 (p. 164)

waterway (wȯ′tər wā′) a lake, river, canal, or any body of water that provides a route for transportation (p. 16)

Web site (web sīt) Internet pages connected by the World Wide Web (p. 332)

wigwam (wig′wäm) a hut made of bark, mats, or animal skins laid over a dome-shaped frame of bent poles (p. 97)

Index

Titles appear in *italics*. Bold page numbers indicate vocabulary definitions. An *m* before a page number indicates a map. The terms *See* and *See also* direct the reader to alternative entries.

Aaron, Hank, 392

Abolitionist, 239

Adams, John, 124

Adapt, 85

African Americans in Indiana, 185, 233, 234, 302, 386

  after the Civil War, 268–269

Alcohol reform, 325

Allen Jay and the Underground Railroad **(literature),** 276–277

Ally, 119

A Long Way from Chicago **(story),** 348–349

Amend, 373

American Indians, 83

  and the American Revolution, 125

  artifacts, 100–101

  and the early Europeans, 108, 109

  "fact file," 96

  and the French, 114

  Indiana groups, 93, *m*93

  and Indiana's growth, 186

  and land ownership, 158–166, 177

  life of, 97

  migration into Indiana, *m*94

  Mississippians, 88–89

  Woodland Indians, 86–87

American Indian treaties, *m*163

American Revolution, 122–133

  Indiana and Virginia in, 130–131

American River, 214

Amish people, 178

Anderson, Mary Catherine, 177

Angel Mounds, 88

Animals, 40

Anti-war protest, 345

Appomattox Court House, 260, *m*258

Archaeologist, 84

Article XIII, 234

Articles, 333

Artifact, 84

  American Indian artifacts, 100–101

Artists, 310, 401

Australian ballot, 307

Automobile industry, 54, 320–321

Baby boom, 385

Ball brothers, 291, 327

  glassmaking, 55

Baltimore Colts, 392

Bands, 94

Baseball, 328, 392

Battle of Bull Run, 258, *m*258

Battle of Fallen Timbers, 161

Battle of Gettysburg, 258, *m*258, 262–263, *m*263

Battle of the Thames, 165

Battle of Tippecanoe, 163

Bayh, Evan, 366

Bayh, Birch, J., 345, 364

Bering Land Bridge, *m*81, 83

Bering Strait, *m*81, 83

Bird, Larry, 357, 394, 395

Bloomington, *m*13, 49, 206

Blue Jacket (Shawnee leader), 160

Boats, 195

Boston Tea Party, 124

Boulder clay, 23

Branches of government, 363, 366

  and Indiana's first constitution, 174

Breaking Away **(movie),** 402

Bribe, 308

Britain

  and American Revolution, 123, 125, 130–131

  and War of 1812, 164–165

Brown County, 310

Bugles of the Civil War, 273

Business, 294

Cahokia, *m*126, 126

California, 214

Calumet, 61

Calumet Region, 317

Canals, 16, **196**

Carmichael, Hoagy, 402

Carson, Julia, 356, 366

Cause and effect, 228–229

Cavelier, René-Robert, 110, 115

Cede, 153

Cemetery Ridge, 263

Central Pacific Railroad, 296–297

Chain O' Lakes State Park, 17, *m*31

Chapman, John, 4, 27

Charlestown, 338

Chief La Demoiselle, 118

Chief Little Turtle (Michikinqua), 146, 159, 160

Chief Pontiac, 120

Children's Museum, 54

Chinese railroad workers, 297

Chorao, Kay, 401

Cities and towns, *m*15, 49, 54, 62, 212, 299. *See also* names of cities

  growth of, 268

  problems in, 300–301

Index

Fort Detroit, 120, *m125*

Fort Donelson (Tennessee), 258, *m258*

Fort Miami, 112, *m112*

Fort Ouiatenon, 112, *m112*

Fort Sackville, *m125*, 126, 130

Forts of the French, 112

Fort Sumter, *m249*, 253

Fort Vincennes, 112, *m112*

Fort Wayne, 62, 161, 385

Fountain City, *m242*, 242

Fox, Vivica, 402

Franklin College, 206

Freedoms of the constitution, 365

Freeman, John, 226, 232, 233, 235

French and Indian War, 119

French in North America, 108

French people, 105–114

French trade routes, *m118*

Front, 257

Frontier conflicts, 159

Fugitive Slave Act, 233, 239, 242

Fugitive slaves, 185

Furniture manufacturing, 49

Fur trade, 108

Fur trading, 112, 114

Gary, *m13*, 62, 318

Gary, Judge Elbert H., 318

Gas Belt, 25, 291
  city growth, 299

General Assembly, 366

General Electric Company, 385

Geography, 8–41

George, Eliza E., 226, 257, 261

German people, 178, 197, 302
  and World War I, 335

Gettysburg, *m263*

Glaciation, 22–23

Glacier grater, 23

Glaciers, 15, 22–23

Glass making, 55, 291

"Golden Age," 308

Gold nuggets, 214

The Gold Rush, 214–215

Goods, 195, **212**

Gougar, Helen M., 325

Government, 88
  growth in cities, 300
  national, 363

Grange, 211

Grant, Ulysses S., 260, 272, 308

Graphs, line and bar, 156–157

Great Depression, 337

Great Lakes Plain, *m15*, 15, 60–63, 78

Grissom, Virgil I. (Gus), 5, 10, 11, 19

Growth, 385

Guthrie, Janet, 391

Habitat, 40

Hamilton, Henry, 77, 125, 126–127

Hanover College, 206

Harmer, General Josiah, 159

Harmonie, 187

Harper, Ida Husted, 284, 325, 330–331

Harrison, Benjamin, 284, 307, 363

Harrison, William Henry, 162, 363

Hatcher, Richard G., 62, 356, 368, 371

Haynes, Elwood, 285, 292, 295, 320

Headlines, 333

Hemispheres, 11

Hennepin, Father Louis, 76, 111

Highest point, 53

Home front, 338

Hoosier Group, 310

Hoosier Hysteria, 392

Hoosier National Forest, 40

Hoosiers, 184–187

"Hoosiers: Indiana's Greatest Resource," 30

Hoosiers (movie), 402

Hub, 49

Hulman, Tony, 396

Hunan Province, China, 388–389, *m389*

Hunters and gatherers, 85

Iberian Peninsula, 58, *m58*

Ice Age, 15, 79, 83

Illinois border, 17

Illinois Territory, 173

Immigrant groups, 386

Immigrants, 178

Immigrate, 178

Income tax, 367

Indiana, 11, *m13*
  after statehood, 171
  after War of 1812, 166
  after World War II, 344
  and the American Revolution, 125
  and the arts, 401
  and California in the Gold Rush, 214–215
  and change, 384
  changes in, 149
  and China, 388–389
  and the Civil War, 254–261
  and Pennsylvania in the Civil War, 262–263
  and transcontinental railroad, 296–297
  and Virginia in the American Revolution, 130–131
  and the West, 296–297
  first hospital, 301
  "Golden Age," 308
  location, *m9*
  location on the Earth, 11, *m12*
  lowest point, 48
  population growth, 179
  rainfall, *m37*

Index

Index

Index

Credits

Text

Excerpts from *Allan Jay and the Underground Railroad* by Marlene Targ Brill. Copyright © 1993 by Marlene Targ Brill. Reprinted by permission of Carolrhoda Books, Inc. pp. 240, 276–279

Excerpts from "Journal of the Proceedings of George R. Clark" by Major Joseph Bowman. Reprinted by permission of Indiana Historical Bureau. pp. 127, 133

From *A Long Way from Chicago* by Richard Peck, copyright © 1998 by Richard Peck. Used by permission of Dial Books for Young Readers, an imprint of Penguin Putnam Books for Young Readers, a division of Penguin Putnam Inc. pp. 348–349

From *Toliver's Secret* by Esther Wood Brady, copyright © 1976 by Esther Wood Brady. Used by permission of Crown Children's Books, a division of Random House, Inc. pp. 138–139

Excerpts from *Johnny Appleseed: A Tall Tale Retold and Illustrated* by Steven Kellogg. Copyright © 1988 by Steven Kellogg. Reprinted by permission. pp. 68–69

Dorling Kindersley (DK) is an international publishing company specializing in the creation of high quality reference content for books, CD-ROMs, online and video. The hallmark of DK content is its unique combination of educational value and strong visual style. This combination allows DK to deliver appealing, accessible and engaging educational content that delights children, parents and teachers around the world. Scott Foresman is delighted to have been able to use selected extracts of DK content within this Social Studies program.

22–23 from Eyewitness: Earth by Suzanna Van Rose. Copyright © 1994 by Dorling Kindersley Limited.; 322–323 from Eyewitness: Technology by Roger Bridgman. Copyright © 1995 by Dorling Kindersley Limited.; 396–397 from The Ultimate Race Car by David Burgess-Wise. Copyright © 1999 by Dorling Kindersley Limited.

Maps

MapQuest.com, Inc.

Illustrations

4, 68 Stephen Johnson; 5, 115, 227, 341 Robert Gunn; 14, 262 Rodica Prato; 27, 28, 56, 305 Greg Harris; 38, 262 Rodica Prato; 64, 243, 319 Hal Just; 71, 188, 189, 191, 221, 279, 362, 409 Daniel DelValle; 77 Tamara Guion; 77 Stephen Snider; 80 Cliff Spohn; 85 Neal Armstrong; 138, 282 Guy Porfirio; 198 Gary Antonelli; 208 Frank Riccio; 218 Beata Szpura; 226, 261 Dan Brown; 227, 235 Manuel Garcia; 293 Larry Schwinger; 324 Paul Perreault; 349 Wendy Smith-Griswold; 367 Kevin Sprouls; 386 Hal Just

Photographs

Every effort has been made to secure permission and provide appropriate credit for photographic material. The publisher deeply regrets any omission and pledges to correct errors called to their attention in subsequent editions.

Unless otherwise acknowledged, all photographs are the property of Scott Foresman, a division of Pearson Education.

Cover: Superstock; **Endsheets:** Left Page, (TL) © David Davis/Picturequest, (Bkgd) © Siede Preis/PhotoDisc, (CR) © Larry Lefever/Grant Heilman Photography, (B) © Steve Raymer/Corbis; Right page, (RC) Superstock, (TL) © Richard Cummins/Viesti Collection, Inc., (TR) © Bob Rowan/Corbis, (BR) © Tom Tietz/Getty Images; **Front Matter:** iii Indianapolis Museum of Art, John Herron Fund; iv Courtesy Indiana Historical Bureau; v The Granger Collection, New York; vii North Wind Picture Archives; ix Dale Kennington/SuperStock; x (B) © Gary W. Carter/Corbis, (TL) Earth Imaging/Getty Images; xi © Joseph Sohm; Visions of America/Corbis; xii Bruce S. Cushing/Visuals Unlimited; xiii © Photo Dyenamics; H4 (TL) Chris Sheridan, (TC) © Jeff Cadge/Getty Images, (TR) David Young-Wolff/PhotoEdit, (BL) Jeff Greenberg/Index Stock Imagery, (BC) Jeff Greenberg/Unicorn Stock Photos, (BR) © Peter Cade/Getty Images; H5 (R) © Stephen Wilkes/Getty Images, (L) Bill Aron/PhotoEdit; H6 Hoosier National Forest, USDA, Forest Service; H7 (L) Hoosier National Forest, USDA, Forest Service, (R) Tom Till Photography, Inc.; H8 (T) Earth Imaging/Getty Images; H17 (B) © David Young-Wolff/Getty Images; **Unit 1:** 1, 2, 3 Indianapolis Museum of Art, John Herron Fund; 4 (CL) Hohenberger mss./The Lilly Library, Indiana University, Bloomington, Indiana, (CR) Martin Collection, Indiana Historical Society, 18990, (R) Bass Photo Co Collection/Indiana Historical Society; 5 (L) Bass Photo Company Collection, Indiana Historical Society, (CR) Photri, Inc., W.E. Waters Middle School, (R) Sylvia Mayayo/Courtesy Curtiss P. Stevens; 7 Indianapolis Museum of Art, John Herron Fund; 8 (T) Cary Benbow, © David Muench Photography, Inc, (B) © David Muench/Corbis; 10 Bavaria/Viesti Collection, Inc.; 11 Photri, Inc.; 13 © Joseph Sohm; Visions of America/Corbis; 15 © Hans Strands/Getty Images; 16 SuperStock; 17 (R) Joe Viesti/Viesti Collection, Inc., (L) Dean A. Orewiler/Kendallville Publishing Co.; 18 Courtesy of Ports of Indiana; 19 (Bkgd), (R) Photri, Inc., (L) Courtesy Wilma Grissom Beavers/Wilma Grissom Beavers; 20, 21 Michael Hubrich/Photo Researchers, Inc.; 22 (B) Bryan and Cherry Alexander Photography, (T) NASA/Science Source/Photo Researchers, Inc.; 23 (TL), (C) © Dorling Kindersley, (BL) Colin Keates/Natural History Museum/© Dorling Kindersley, (BR) Clive Streeter/© Dorling Kindersley; 24 Arthur Gurmankin/Mary Morina/Unicorn Stock Photos; 25 Adam Jones/Photo Researchers, Inc.; 26 D.O.E./Science Source/Photo Researchers, Inc.; 27 Richard Cummins/Viesti Collection, Inc.; 28 Richard Baker/Unicorn Stock Photos; 29 David Muench Photography, Inc; 30 The Granger Collection, New York; 32 Tom McCarthy/Unicorn Stock Photos; 33 (TL), (TCL) Martha McBride/Unicorn Stock Photos, (Bkgd) Clint Farlinger/Visuals Unlimited, (BCL) Mark Romesser/Unicorn Stock Photos, (BL) SuperStock, (R) Courtesy, The Lilly Library, Indiana University, Bloomington, Indiana; 34 (B) James P. Rowan Stock Photography, (T) Bass Photo Co Collection/Indiana Historical Society; 35 Joe Viesti/Viesti Collection, Inc.; 36 Daniel Bailey/Index Stock Imagery; 38 © David Muench Photography, Inc, (R) © Frank Lane Picture Agency/Corbis, (L) Visuals Unlimited; 39 (R) Inga Spence/Visuals Unlimited, (L) Photo Dyenamics; 40 Ted Ross/Unicorn Stock Photos; 41 Lynn Stone/Animals Animals/Earth Scenes; 44 (C) Steve Strickland/Visuals Unlimited, (T) Robert Frerck/Odyssey Productions, (B) David Muench Photography, Inc; 46 Jeff Greenberg/Unicorn Stock Photos; 47 Robert Frerck/Odyssey Productions; 48 John Sheckler; 49 Photographic Services/Indiana University; 50 Samuel Frushour/Indiana Geological Survey, Indiana University; 51 Indiana Department of Natural Resources/T.C. Steele State Historic Site; 52 Martha McBride/Unicorn Stock Photos; 53 © Andy Sacks/Getty Images; 54 Robert Laberge/Allsport; 55 (T) Andre Jenny/Unicorn Stock Photos, (TR) Minnetrista Cultural Center & Oakhurst Gardens; 57 Courtesy of Indiana Geological Survey, Indiana University; 58 (TL) SuperStock, (BC) E.H. Robl Photography, (BL) Aneal Vohra/Unicorn Stock Photos; 59 (TL) Robert Frerck/Getty Images, (B) Walter Bibikow/Viesti Collection, Inc., (TR) Beryl Goldberg; 61 LaPorte County Historical Society Museum; 62 Bettmann/Corbis; 63 David Muench Photography, Inc; **Unit 2:** 73, 74, 75 Courtesy Indiana Historical Bureau; 76 (L) Minnesota Historical Society/Corbis, (CL) Stock Montage Inc.; 76 (CR) The Granger Collection, New York; 77 The Granger Collection, New York; 79 The Granger Collection, New York; 82 Lubbock Lake Landmark, Museum of Texas Tech University; 86 (T) Dale Pickett/Adventure Studios, (BL), (BR) Glenn A. Black Laboratory of Archaeology; 87 A. Goodall/Glenn A. Black Laboratory of Archaeology; 88 (T), (B) James P. Rowan Stock Photography; 90 (R) © Terry Donnelly, (L) James P. Rowan Stock Photography; 91 Cathy Melloan/PhotoEdit; 92 Detroit Institute of Arts; 93 (L), (C) Marilyn "Angel" Wynn/Nativestock, (R) The Detroit Institute of Arts, USA/Founders Society Purchase/Bridgeman Art Library International Ltd.; 95 National Museum of American Art, Washington DC/Art Resource, NY; 96 (R) Jim Rementer/Delaware Tribe of Indians (C) Marilyn "Angel" Wynn/Nativestock, (L) Reinhard Brucker/Westwind Enterprises; 97 Marilyn "Angel" Wynn/Nativestock; 100, 101 Smithsonian Institution; 102 James P. Rowan Stock Photography; 103 Mary Evans Picture Library; 104 The Granger Collection, New York; 106 Phil Martin Photography; 107 Giraudon/Art Resource, NY; 108 © Robert Holmes/Corbis; 109 Mary Evans Picture Library; 111 (L) Hulton Archive/Getty Images, (R) Culver Pictures Inc.; 112 James P. Rowan Stock Photography; 115 (Bkgd) David David Gallery, Philadelphia/SuperStock; 117 The Granger Collection, New York; 119 Hulton Archive/Getty Images; 121 (R), (Bkgd) The Granger Collection, New York, (L) Reinhard Brucker/Westwind Enterprises; 122 Gary W. Carter/Visuals Unlimited; 124 The Granger Collection, New York; 125 Indiana State Library; 126 Culver Pictures Inc.; 128 Stock Montage Inc.; 129 (Bkgd) Martha McBride/Unicorn Stock Photos; 130 (B) Chateau de Versailles, France/Lauros-Giraudon/Bridgeman Art Library International Ltd., (T) Courtesy Indiana Historical Bureau; 131 (L) Dick Poe/Visuals Unlimited, (R) Charles Phelps Cushing/H. Armstrong Roberts, (C) The Granger Collection, New York; 132 The Granger Collection, New York; 133 Habitat for Humanity in the Roanoke Valley, Inc.; 136 Hulton Archive/Getty Images; 141 Bachmann/Photri, Inc.; **Unit 3:** 143, 144, 145 The Granger Collection, New York; 146 (L) Stock Montage Inc., (CR) The Granger Collection, New York, (CL) North Wind Picture Archives, (R) The Granger Collection, New York; 147 (L) Courtesy of the Tippecanoe County Historical Association, Lafayette, Indiana, (CR) Indiana Picture Collection/Indiana State Library, (R) US Naval Academy, Annapolis/Jack Novak/SuperStock, (CL) North Wind Picture Archives; 149 Indiana State Library; 150 (T) The Filson Historical Society, Louisville KY, (B) Hulton Archive/Getty Images; 152 Brown Brothers; 153 The Granger Collection, New York; 154 © Richard Hamilton Smith/Corbis; 155 The Granger Collection, New York; 156 Hancock County Historical Society, Inc.; 158 North Wind Picture Archives; 159 Central Photo Archive/Brooklyn Museum; 160 The Granger Collection, New York; 161 (B) Hulton Archive/Getty Images, (T) The Granger Collection, New York; 162 (B) Patrick Gulley/Photo Dyenamics, (TR), (TL) The Granger Collection, New York; 164 The Granger Collection, New York; 165 Bettmann/Corbis; 166 Corbis; 167 (R) Hulton Archive/Getty Images, (Bkgd) The Granger Collection, New York, (L) The Royal Ontario Museum; 168 North Wind Picture Archives; 170 (B) Joslyn Art Museum, Omaha, Nebraska. Gift of Enron Art Foundation, (C) Indiana State Library, (T) Indiana Picture Collection/Indiana State Library; 172 Indiana Picture Collection/Indiana State Library; 174 Indiana State Library; 175 (Bkgd) Gift of Mrs. Cable G. Ball/Courtesy of the Tippecanoe County Historical Association, Lafayette, Indiana, (L) © Gary W. Carter/Corbis, (R) Courtesy of the Tippecanoe County Historical Association, Lafayette, Indiana; 176 Indiana State Library; 178 Hulton Archive/Getty Images; 179 Courtesy Frances Eagleston/Hancock County Historical Society, Inc.; 180 Courtesy The Lilly Library, Indiana University, Bloomington, Indiana; 181 (Bkgd) © Morton Beebe/Corbis, (R) Hulton Archive/Getty Images, (L) SuperStock; 182 (T) North Wind Picture Archives, (B) © Morton Beebe/Corbis; 183 © Chip Henderson/Getty Images; 185 The Granger Collection, New York; 186 Courtesy of the Tippecanoe County Historical Association, Lafayette, Indiana; 190 Bettmann/Corbis; 192 (C) Delia Born, Courtesy Allen County Public Library, (B) North Wind Picture Archives, (T) The Granger Collection, New York; 195 The Granger Collection, New York; 196 Bettmann/Corbis; 197 The Granger Collection, New York; 199 The Granger Collection, New York; 200, 201 Smithsonian Institution; 203 Gift of Mrs. Cable G. Ball/Courtesy of the Tippecanoe County Historical Association, Lafayette, Indiana; 204 The Granger Collection, New York; 205 Allen Co.-Ft. Wayne Historical Society; 206 Lawrence Manning/Corbis; 207 Ramsay Archival Center/Wabash College; 208 Indiana Picture Collection/Indiana State Library; 209 The Granger Collection, New York; 210 © Davies & Starr/Getty Images; 211 Courtesy Conner Prairie Rural History Project Archive; 212 (B) © Richard Hamilton Smith/Corbis, (T) Courtesy Conner Prairie Rural History Project Archive; 213 North Wind Picture Archives; 214 (BR) © Mary Mishler/Getty Images, (TR), (TL) Bettmann/Corbis, (BL), (BC) Culver Pictures Inc.; 215 (T) The Granger Collection, New York, (B) SuperStock; 216 North Wind Picture Archives; 220 The Granger Collection, New York;

Credits